Sanctifying the World

*The Augustinian Life and Mind
of Christopher Dawson*

Bradley J. Birzer

CHRISTENDOM PRESS
Front Royal, Virginia

Printed in the U. S. A.

All inquiries should be addressed to:
Christendom Press, Front Royal, VA 22630
http://christendompress.com

Cover photo courtesy of Edward King and *Jubilee*.

Bill Powell crafted this book at Wineskin Media.
http://wineskinmedia.com

This edition has been typeset with TEX.

Library of Congress Cataloguing-in-Publication Data:

Birzer, Bradley J., 1967–

Sanctifying the world : the Augustinian life and mind of Christopher Dawson / Bradley J. Birzer.—Front Royal, VA: Christendom Press, 2007.

p. ; cm.

ISBN-13: 978-0-931888-86-1
ISBN-10: 0-931888-86-7
Includes bibliographical references.

1. Dawson, Christopher, 1889-1970. 2. Historians—Great Britain—Biography. 3. Civilization, Christian. 4. Civilization, Western. 5. Europe—Politics and government—20th century. I. Title.

CB18.D38 B57 2007
907.202—dc22   CIP

To

W. Winston Elliott III

*A man of deep loyalties
and an exemplar of fortitude.*

Foreword

I FIRST MET BRADLEY J. BIRZER AROUND FIVE YEARS AGO WHEN WE WERE ALmost neighbours in Michigan. I, newly arrived in the United States from England, was teaching literature at Ave Maria College in Ypsilanti; he was teaching history at Hillsdale College. I liked him instantly, recognizing in him a kindred spirit who shared my passion for Tolkien, Lewis and Chesterton. I was honoured when he asked me to write an introduction to his book, *J. R. R. Tolkien's Sanctifying Myth*, which I still consider to be one of the finest introductions to the Christian presence in Middle-earth.

I first met Christopher Dawson a few years earlier during my research for *Literary Converts*. I had heard of him prior to my research for this particular book, but had never actually met him. When I did meet him it was not in the flesh, because he had been dead for almost thirty years, but *in the spirit of the truth* that he served and elucidated. As in my meeting with Professor Birzer, I again recognized a kindred spirit. It was not merely that Dawson was one of the *illustrissimi* of literary converts of whom I was writing; nor that he was one of the most important Catholic historians of the past two centuries, holding a seat of honour in the company of Lingard, Acton, Belloc and, more recently, Eamon Duffy. It was also because he had *seen* history as few other historians had seen it. It was as though he had got beyond the nitty-gritty and the nuts-and-bolts and, to switch metaphors, had soared on eagle's wings to a height where the whole panoramic past came into breathtaking perspective. Christopher Dawson was to history what E. F. Schumacher, another convert, was to economics. Just as Schumacher had seen beyond the mechanistic and materialistic understanding of economics, arriving at a meta-economics that transcended and transfigured conventional economic assumptions, so Dawson had seen beyond the mechanistic and materialistic understanding of history, arriving at a meta-history that transcended and transfigured conventional historical assumptions.

My first meeting with Dawson and my first meeting with Schumacher were true epiphanies. In both cases I was shown reality, as if for the first time, and, in so doing, enjoyed that wonderful experience of standing on one's head, an experience that Chesterton refers to as the only way of seeing things as they really are. It is the disconcerting disorientation that precedes reorientation.

One stands on one's head and one realizes that, in fact, one is now the right way up for the first time, and, surprise of all disconcerting surprises, that, until then, one had always been looking at reality upside down. This whole paradox was put more eloquently by Evelyn Waugh when he wrote that "conversion is like stepping across the chimney piece out of a Looking-Glass world, where everything is an absurd caricature, into the real world God made; and then begins the delicious process of exploring it limitlessly". Waugh was referring to his own conversion to the Catholic Church but the experience is as true of these lesser conversions: the conversion to a true perspective of history or economics.

It is, therefore, as much of an honour to have been asked to introduce this book by Professor Birzer as it had been to introduce the other. I feel as though I am being asked to introduce two good friends to those who are destined to enjoy their company as much as I have over the past several years. The fact that one of the friends is alive and the other dead is neither here nor there; nor is it strictly true. Dawson is very much alive, as alive as Professor Birzer and more alive than many of the materialistic somnambulists walking around today. He is alive in the sense that his labours continue to bear fruit, and continue to open the eyes of the blind. He is also alive in that more important sense that lies beyond the grave.

There seems little else to say that will not be said better by Messrs Birzer and Dawson in the pages that follow. I shall finish, however, with one final observation: A true historian makes the past present by the light of the eternal omnipresent. According to this criterion, Christopher Dawson is a true historian *par excellence* and Bradley J. Birzer is his worthy disciple. As such, this book is written by one true historian about another. What more could a true student of history desire?

JOSEPH PEARCE

Preface

"WHATEVER ELSE IS OBSCURE, IT IS CERTAIN THAT GOD IS THE GOVERNOR OF the universe and behind the apparent disorder and confusion of history there is the creative action of divine law," Christopher Dawson wrote in 1959 from his new home in Boston, Massachusetts. Though he remained in academic obscurity for much of his life, at the age of 69 he received a job offer from Harvard University to become the first Chauncey Stillman Chair in Catholic Studies. "Man is a free agent and is continually attempting to shape the world and the course of history to his own designs and interests," he continued. But no matter how much man exercises his free will and attempts to determine his destiny, God remains sovereign. For, "behind the weak power and the blind science of man, there is the overruling purpose of God which uses man and his kingdoms and empires for ends of which he knows nothing and which are often the opposite of those which man desires and seeks to attain."[1] The purposes of man and of God, at least in modernity, had come dramatically into conflict. Man's vision of man—a mass of matter to be manipulated and used in some obscene Picassoesque fashion as any ideologue might desire—was not God's vision of man. God, unlike the fascists and the communists of the twentieth century, saw man as good but fallen, made in His Image, each one unique in time and space.

Dawson saw himself as no exception. Whatever his own will for himself, God had a higher purpose for him. When Harvard asked him to come and teach, Dawson uncharacteristically jumped at the chance. As a man of letters called by God, Dawson believed it his job to play the Jeremiah, prophesying lament and doom as the world followed down the paths of the various ideologues. But he also played the role of the saint, using his considerable intellectual gifts to demonstrate the necessity of virtue and the light of the Logos to the modern world through his writing, his teaching, and his public speaking.

This book, *Sanctifying the World: The Augustinian Life and Mind of Christopher Dawson*, attempts to get into the mind of Dawson and explore his signif-

---

[1] Christopher Dawson, *The Movement of World Revolution* (New York: Sheed and Ward, 1959), 101.

icance to western civilization and to the history of the Church, especially in
the twentieth century. This book also seeks to view the world—and the first
significant vehicle of Christendom, the West—as Dawson did. It considers the
meaning of the West, as well as its many internal and external threats. "Hellenism gradually expanded during the Hellenistic and Roman periods, until
it embroiled the whole of the ancient world, so too Western culture has expanded during the last 500 years to embrace the whole of the modern world,"
Dawson wrote in 1952. "And as the unity of the ancient world was finally broken in two by the sin of Islam, so the modern world is being broken by in two
by the sin of communism."[2] While Dawson was certainly a relevant thinker
during the Manichean struggle of the Cold War, he is, perhaps, even more
relevant in a post-Cold War, post-9/11 world. The present interest in defining and assessing western civilization may help explain the current revival of
Dawson within Catholic and traditionalist circles. Strangely, though, very little has been written on Dawson. At the moment, there is only one biography, *A
Historian and His World*, written by his daughter, and two books dealing with
his intellectual contributions, *Eternity in Time*, edited by Stratford Caldecott
and John Morrill, and *The Dynamic of Christian Character*, edited by Peter
Cataldo. Adam Schwartz's *Third Spring* from Catholic University Press brilliantly compares the thought of G. K. Chesterton, Dawson, Graham Greene,
and David Jones. Despite this lack of secondary sources, Dawson is being discussed in many places at the beginning of the twenty-first century: in college
and university courses; in books assessing the various failings and achievements of the twentieth century; in books dealing with historiography (Dawson was one of the first "world historians"); in Tolkien and Inklings circles;
and, especially, in traditionalist and Roman Catholic circles and periodicals.
Indeed, it is hard to turn around without someone mentioning Dawson. The
time for his intellectual revival is upon us, to be sure. After all, even if one
radically disagrees with Dawson's specific solutions and views, his questions
and analysis remain insightful, intriguing, and, often, timeless.

Admittedly, Dawson disliked such books as this one claims to be. "The
historian who concentrates his attention on concrete individual personalities
and events that are the raw material of history," he wrote in 1933, "tends
to lose sight of the deeper spiritual forces that make history intelligible to
us."[3] For in the best histories, he argued, the historian places the individual within a larger mythological understanding of story and history, what he
called a "metahistory." If anything, though, I have failed in the opposite direction, giving too much attention to the perceived movements of the Holy

---

[2]Dawson to Mulloy, 5 March 1952, in Box 1, Folder 1, in Christopher Dawson Collection,
University of Notre Dame, Indiana (hereafter ND/CDAW).

[3]Christopher Dawson, "Introduction," to David Mathew, *The Celtic Peoples and Renaissance
Europe: A Study of the Celtic and Spanish Influences on Elizabethan History* (London and New
York: Sheed and Ward, 1933), xiv.

Spirit and relying too much on Dawson's own interpretation of things. In the attempt to view the world as Dawson did—as much as is possible for someone who lived in the world only during Dawson's last three years and who comes from a different cultural and ethnic background, Kansas (and of very German ancestry) as opposed to Wales (and of Welsh and English ancestry)—I have drawn upon Dawson's works, his unpublished letters, the published and un-published letters of those friends and adversaries around him, contemporary news stories about him, and interviews with and about him. Each of these sources, first and foremost, reveal Dawson to be a man of the mind, a person who put ideas and intellectual and spiritual interpretations above all things. Indeed, he was a man of letters in a democratic and ideological era that had forgotten or shunned the natural aristocracy and the liberal arts. The sources also reveal that Dawson lacked much in the way of social skills and suffered from long incapacitating bouts of depression. But what awkwardness he may have suffered in the presence of others was made up for in his intense and anxious intellect. It was his assistant in the Sword of the Spirit movement of the 1940s, Barbara Ward, who summed him up best. He was, she confided to her reading audience, "a man of angelic intelligence and very human person-ality."[4]

This book, then, seeks to explore not only Dawson's mind and thoughts, but also his mission, which he considered God-given and driven by the Holy Spirit. It is an intellectual and spiritual biography of sorts, though the two interludes offer an in-depth look at his Augustinian understanding of history and his definition of western civilization, respectively. In each part of the book, I have done my best to use Dawson's words and thoughts and to follow his life's work of restoring Christendom. I have also attempted to show the importance of the imagination to Dawson's thinking as well as to his defini-tion of the human person. He feared that almost every aspect of modernity attempted to mechanize the human person, making him less than God in-tended him to be. The imagination—what Plato called "divine madness," a mind beside itself—allowed one to order his soul properly, Dawson believed.

Though I first came to Dawson indirectly as an undergraduate through the teaching of several of my professors at the University of Notre Dame—especially through his influence on Father Marvin O'Connell, one of the great-est orators I have ever been privileged to hear and study under—I came to him directly several years ago in Houston, Texas, that most modern, cemented, and air-conditioned of American metropolises. It was in the last years of the twentieth century, and Gleaves Whitney, having completed his dissertation at the University of Michigan on Dawson and several other Christian Humanists, gave a typically moving talk at the Center for the American Idea on the mean-

---

[4]Anne Freemantle, "Christopher Dawson Comes to Harvard," *Catholic Digest*, vol. 23 (1959), 51.

ing of Dawson and his relevance to the modern world. Gleaves tied Dawson's work to that of J. R. R. Tolkien, C. S. Lewis, Romano Guardini, Jacques Maritain, and John Paul II. In response, I devoured Dawson's *Religion and the Rise of Western Culture* over a Thanksgiving break, and followed it quickly with Dawson's most insightful book, *The Judgment of the Nations*. This was not the jargonish, politicized, and overly professionalized academic history I was taught in graduate school; it was metahistory, something profoundly deep, catholic, poetic, and significant. And, better still, it took seriously the importance of the Creator, the profound implications of the Incarnation, and the movement of the Holy Spirit in history. It showed that the communists were as bad as the Nazis (finally!), and it demonstrated that no manmade plan, system, or ideology can reshape the world. Only prayer, grace, and the submission to God's will could do this, Dawson argued. In words that can only come across as trite on the printed page, Dawson resonated with me. I quickly devoured everything I could get my hands on written by or about Dawson from bookstores, libraries, and archives. While I do not agree with all of the venerable scholar's views, much of what he wrote has vast and important implications for the world and the Church.

At the time that I was encountering Dawson deeply, I was also busily writing on Tolkien as a Christian Humanist and attempting to explore Tolkien's use of myth and his attacks on modernity. I was certainly struck by how similar Tolkien's words were to Dawson's. Dawson was born three years before Tolkien, and the two men attended the same Roman Catholic parish, St. Aloysius, during the 1930s and 1940s. The two men also shared the same physician in Oxford and had at least three mutual close friends. Tolkien cites Dawson's work in his famous academic work "On Fairy Stories" at two critical moments in the address, first delivered at the University of St. Andrews on March 8, 1939.[5] Each man embraced the notion of imagination and creativity as the breath of the Holy Spirit and the light of the Logos. The evidence for a personal relationship between them is mixed. Despite all of the mutual friends they had as well as each being a member of the same parish, Father Peter Milward, the famous Jesuit scholar of Shakespeare and a student of C. S. Lewis, writes:

> I knew both Tolkien and Dawson when I was at Oxford in the early 1950s, but Dawson lived on Boar's Hill without any professional connection with the university. It seems likely that they appreciated each other's work, but I do not know if they ever met each other. Dawson was perhaps too shy to make Tolkien's acquaintance, and they moved in different circles from each other.[6]

---

[5] J. R. R. Tolkien, "On Fairy Stories," in *The Monsters and the Critics and Other Essays*, Christopher Tolkien, ed. (London: George Allen and Unwin, 1983), 109–161.

[6] Peter Milward, S.J., Tokyo, Japan, to present author, Hillsdale, MI, August 20, 2003.

John Ryan, one of Tolkien's last undergraduate students, remembers Hugo Dyson, a member of the Inklings, telling him that Tolkien and Dawson were friends.[7] Regardless, they were two devout English Roman Catholics and intellectuals of the same generation. They had the same fears, the same hopes, the same love of myth, and the same hatred of ideologies. In short, each was a Roman Catholic, an Augustinian, and a Stoic who wanted the twentieth century to repent from its ideological sins and embrace some form of Christendom. In his vision of Christendom, Dawson offered a far more ecumenical and pro-Protestant version than did Tolkien. Each ultimately believed creativity and imagination to be the greatest gifts God had bequeathed to the human person.

Tolkien was not the only one similar to Dawson in his thought and faith. Dawson, instead, was one of many men and women of the twentieth century who attempted to confront the monstrosities of the ideologues with a return to some form of Christendom. Their number includes: Jacques Maritain (French), Romano Guardini (Italian/German), Eric Voegelin (Austrian/American), Étienne Gilson (French), Aleksandr Solzhenitsyn (Russian), C. S. Lewis (Northern Irish), E. I. Watkin (English), Barbara Ward Lady Jackson (English), Josef Pieper (German), Roy Campbell (South African of Scottish descent), Hans Urs von Balthasar (Swiss), Wilhelm Roepke (Swiss), Aurel Thomas Kolnai (Hungarian), T. S. Eliot (American/English), and Nicholas Berdyaev (Russian), to name just a few. Among Americans, certainly Flannery O'Connor, Allen Tate, Thomas Merton, Walker Percy, Peter Kreeft, Edward E. Ericson, Jr., and Vigen Guroian would qualify. Among Western Europeans, there are Pope Benedict XVI, Stratford Caldecott, and Joseph Pearce. And preeminent among Eastern Europeans are Karol Wojtyla, who became Pope John Paul II in 1978, Thomas Molnar, and John Lukas. Some of these men have been studied well. Strangely, however, many have not been studied or acknowledged as important at all, either to Catholicism or to twentieth-century philosophy and history.

Certainly, these men have many labels. Gleaves Whitney has labeled the preceding group "Christian Humanists"; C. S. Lewis called himself and his friends "Old Western Men," men who accepted the best of the western tradition but objected stringently to the modern West; historian Adam Schwartz writes of the movement as a "Third Spring"; and Joseph Pearce has placed them collectively at the forefront of the Catholic Literary Revival, calling them a "network of minds" who acted in "an adventure story in which belief and unbelief clash in creative collision."[8] While the members of this group rarely

---

[7] John S. Ryan, Armidale, New South Wales, Australia, to present author, Hillsdale, MI, October 12, 2003.

[8] See Gleaves Whitney, "'Sowing Seeds in the Wasteland': The Perennial Task of Christian Humanists," public lecture, given 1997; C. S. Lewis, "De Descriptione Temporum," *Essays in Criticism*, vol. 6 (1956); Adam Schwartz, Front Royal, VA, to author, Hillsdale, MI, February 2004;

worked together and infrequently, if ever, acknowledged a kinship with the other members of the group, there were at least three things upon which these diverse intellectuals agreed. Each of the figures above saw a continuity in the classical and Christian traditions; each believed that only through Christianity could one begin to understand the human person and find a true anthropology; and each advocated a return to the liberal arts in education.

As will be seen throughout this book, though, these figures were somewhat divided between the neo-Thomists and Augustinians. Whether this difference was real or contrived remains an open question, though I believe the division existed and has been ignored or glossed over by most Catholic scholars. The greatest difference seems to have stemmed from a very different understanding of the role of imagination in the economy of grace. The neo-Thomists tended to reject the importance of imagination as deceptive and unreal, while the Augustinians embraced it as the *via media* between intellect and passion.

The most important American Christian Humanist was Russell Amos Augustine Kirk, the founder of the modern intellectual conservative movement. Indeed, it was Kirk who best summarized and synthesized the works of the European Christian Humanists for an American audience. And though Kirk never identified himself in his works as a Christian Humanist, he was one *par excellence*. Not only was Kirk close friends with Roy Campbell, Eliot, and Roepke, but he also drew on Voegelin and Dawson numerous times in his own historical and philosophical works.[9] Prior to his death in 1994, Kirk had even planned to serve as editor for Dawson's collected works. Through his published works and public lectures, Kirk introduced at least three generations of American students to Christopher Dawson and the English and European Christian Humanists.

In the spring semester of 2003, Dr. Mark Kalthoff, my department chair and a serious Christian Humanist himself, allowed me to teach a senior seminar in the history department entitled "The Historical Visions of Christopher Dawson and Eric Voegelin." Though only two names appeared in the course title, my class also considered the thought of J. R. R. Tolkien, Russell Kirk, Romano Guardini, C. S. Lewis, Aidan Nichols, Joseph Pearce, Hans Urs von Balthasar, and John Paul II. My college, Hillsdale, typically has very good students, and the students in this seminar were the best of the best at the college. We had one incredible romp through twentieth-century Christian thought. Almost evenly divided between Calvinists, evangelicals, and Roman Catholics (not atypical for Hillsdale), the seminar engaged in some of the

---

and Joseph Pearce, *Literary Converts: Spiritual Inspiration in an Age of Unbelief* (San Francisco, CA: Ignatius, 2000), xii.

[9]On Kirk's various friendships and ties, see especially his autobiography, *The Sword of Imagination: Memoirs of a Half-Century of Literary Conflict* (Grand Rapids, MI: William B. Eerdmans, 1995), and his *Confessions of a Bohemian Tory: Episodes and Reflections of a Vagrant Career* (New York: Fleet Publishing Corp., 1963).

best discussions I have ever had, and I was extremely proud of every student for entering into the debates with a virtuous temperance, faith, passion, and intellect. I very much would like to thank each one of them for sharpening my thoughts on Dawson, the Church, and God. To Philip Nielsen, one of the students of the Dawson class, I especially owe a profound thanks for the innumerable conversations on Dawson, Tolkien, von Balthasar, and the role of imagination, beauty, and creativity in the life of a Christian. I would also like to single out Michael Francisco, Keith Miller, David Talcott, and Dusty Wendland for their friendship and contributions. I taught the course a second time in Spring 2005. In that class, I would like to thank Kelly Flake, Laurel Schamp, Stephen and Matt Gaetano, Erica and T. J. Nielsen, Hans Zeiger, Chris Walker, Allison Platter, Megan Lacey, and Alycia Polce.

As always, I owe a huge thanks to Winston Elliott, Barbara Elliott, and John Rocha of the Center for the American Idea in Houston, who continue to provide friendship and support. Winston also proofed the entire book. One may find my due thanks to Winston on the dedication page. Affiliated with the Center, Fathers Donald Nesti and Michael Barrett provide invaluable religious guidance and unadulterated friendship. Father Brian Stanley, a Kirkian in his own right, continues to provide prayers, guidance, and friendship. Fathers Eric Weber and Tom Butler continue to inspire me as well. My very close friend and expert in historiography, Paul Moreno, offered help in a number of areas. A native New Yorker, Paul has a razor-sharp eye and wit. He read and dissected each of the following chapters, and I thank him for the many suggestions and criticisms he offered. Many of those suggestions were offered over a good pint and Paul's specialty, the Moreno martini. We each thank G. K. Chesterton for his inspiration on how to live the good life. Laurel Schamp, a student and friend, skilled in editing far beyond her years, copy-edited the manuscript for me. Joseph Pearce and his family never cease to amaze me in their dedication to intellect, faith, and a love of just plain normal life. Joseph's book, *Literary Converts*, helped put the subject of Dawson into perspective as one of the grand Christian Humanists. Adam Schwartz, a comrade in arms, also lent his rather brilliant insights on Christian humanism. Ann Kenne at the Dawson Collection at the University of St. Thomas, St. Paul, Minnesota, Ed King of The Christopher Dawson Centre of Christian Culture in Kanata, Ontario, and Sharon Sumpter and Kevin Cawley at the University of Notre Dame Archives each provided me with invaluable information and advice. Kevin even helped me with typos and factual errors. He's also just a fine and interesting person. Ed, especially, has been a constant inspiration, a wonderful resource, and a good friend. Hillsdale College History Department Chair and Dean of Faculty Mark Kalthoff, former Division Dean Tom Conner, and Provost Bob Blackstock provided financial support and time to research and write this book. Mark, an excellent friend, has also sharpened my ideas in almost every possible venue. I would also like to thank many other colleagues at Hillsdale College, all of whom have helped shape my own thoughts regarding Christian humanism in one way or another: Stephen Smith, Harold Siegel, Richard Gamble, Michael Jordan, John Willson, Mark Steckbeck, Andrew Cuneo, Dan Sundahl, and Don Turner. I would also very much like to thank President Larry Arnn for his continued friendship and extremely able leadership and vision. Many of the ideas presented in this book were also first discussed in Bloomington, Indiana, in the mid-1990s with Fran Flavin, Kevin McCormick, Bernard Sheehan, and James LaGrand. These three very Irish men and one Dutch Calvinist often ganged up on me (the lone Kansas-Bavarian), and I very much miss our discussions. Long before my time in Bloomington, and since, James Otteson, perhaps the finest exponent of classical liberalism in the world today, has challenged a number of my ideas, but always in a spirit of friendship. The friendship began in the autumn of 1986 in the North Quad dining hall at the University of Notre Dame, and it has remained a blessed constant in my life. Annette Kirk gave me her recollections of Dawson from the late 1950s and discussed with me her late husband's intellectual and spiritual relationship to St. Augustine and Dawson. She has also graciously allowed me to give several talks on Christian humanism at the Kirk Center for Cultural Renewal in Mecosta, Michigan. William Fahey, my editor, has consistently demonstrated enthusiasm for this project, and I thank him profoundly for his friendship and his faith (at many levels). His intellectually astute wife, Amy, has kept me on the straight and narrow as she has painstakingly checked every aspect of this book. And, of course, a huge thanks to Bill Powell for a beautiful layout and his many excellent suggestions. If errors still remain after the diligence of each, I alone am to blame. Casey and Kelly Heying always keep me entertained during my many research trips to Notre Dame, and I thank them for their very family-friendly entrepreneurial success, BuyMeToys. Various members of my family—Rita Birzer, Kevin Birzer, Todd Birzer, and Ken McDonald—have each offered their thoughts as well. Finally, I would like to thank my beautiful and sagacious wife, Dedra, and my four children—Nathaniel Wendelin, Gretchen Marie, Maria Grace, and Harold Kenneth—for giving up a considerable amount of Lego time to allow me to write this book. I usually wrote until pestered long enough to come play. Playtime ensued, and then, after the children were safely asleep, I wrote again. What more could a father ask for?

BRADLEY J. BIRZER
Hillsdale College, Michigan
Easter Monday, 2007

Contents

Introduction

Christopher Dawson and the
Twentieth-Century Catholic Literary Revival

THOUGH PRECIOUS FEW REMEMBER HIM NOW, CHRISTOPHER DAWSON STOOD at the very center of the Catholic literary and intellectual revival throughout the four decades preceding Vatican II. "For Dawson is more like a movement than a man," his publisher and friend, Frank Sheed, wrote of him in 1938. "His influence with the non-Catholic world is of a kind that no modern Catholic has yet had, both for the great number of fields in which it is felt and for the intellectual quality of those who feel it."[1] During the Great Depression of the 1930s, Catholic promoters such as Francis X. Talbot listed Dawson as a select member of *America*'s "Permanent Gallery of Living Catholic Authors." Additionally, prominent American Catholic colleges began teaching courses on the thought of Christopher Dawson and other figures of the Catholic Literary Revival as early as the mid-1930s.[2] Dawson's influence "can be seen on almost every major lay Catholic movement in the American Church between 1930 and 1955," historian Arnold Sparr has written.[3] In 1933, the American Catholic journal *Commonweal* stated that "the writings of Christopher Dawson demand the thoughtful attention of all educated men."[4] Six years later, the Jesuit journal, the *Month*, claimed that to "commend Mr. Dawson's work is unnecessary; nothing that he writes could be unimportant."[5] In 1949, Waldemar Gurian, a refugee from the Nazis and a professor at the University of Notre Dame, wrote that Dawson's "very ability to make brilliant understatements and to display without pride, as something self-evident, his extraordi-

---

[1] Frank Sheed, "Christopher Dawson," *Sign*, vol. 17 (June 1938), 661.

[2] Arnold Sparr, *To Promote, Defend, and Redeem: The Catholic Literary Revival and the Cultural Transformation of American Catholicism, 1920–1960* (New York: Greenwood Press, 1990), 24, 103.

[3] Ibid., 110.

[4] T. Lawrason Riggs, "A Voice of Power," *Commonweal*, vol. 18 (August 4, 1933), 330.

[5] Thomas Corbishley, "Our Present Discontents," *The Month*, vol. 173 (1939), 440.

nary broad knowledge make his synthesis particularly impressive."[6] In 1950, the English Dominican journal, *Blackfriars*, claimed "that Mr. Dawson is an educator; perhaps the greatest that Heaven has sent us English Catholics since Newman."[7] Four years later, Frederick Wilhelmsen, himself soon to become a major player in post-war American Catholicism, concluded that Dawson was "the foremost medievalist in the English speaking world." Further, "this union of genius and Catholic scholarship has put us all in his debt."[8]

It would be difficult to find a more prominent Roman Catholic scholar not only in the English-speaking world, but throughout the Catholic world and beyond during the forty years preceding Vatican II.[9] As Maisie Ward, the famous biographer and co-founder of the Sheed and Ward publishing house, admitted to Dawson in 1961, "You were, as I said on Sunday, truly the spearhead of our publishing venture."[10] Ward put it into greater context in her autobiography, *Unfinished Business*. "Looking back at the beginnings of such intellectual life as I have had, I feel indebted to three men of genius: Browning, Newman, and Chesterton," she admitted. "But in my middle age, while we owed much as publishers to many men and women, foreign and English, the most powerful influence on the thinking of both myself and my husband was certainly Christopher Dawson."[11] Even among the clergy, none held the reputation that Dawson did by the 1950s. Again, as Ward noted rather bluntly in a letter to Dawson, "There is no question in my mind that no priest exists at the moment whose name carries anything like the weight in or outside the church that yours does."[12] This is an impressive claim, especially when one recalls the intellect and influence of a Martin D'Arcy, a John Courtney Murray, or a Fulton Sheen, all eminent priests.

It was in the decade prior to Vatican II that Dawson was at his most influential. Throughout the 1950s, invitations for Dawson to speak, write papers, and present his ideas in almost any form arrived from various countries, political institutions, colleges, and religious groups. As the Iron Bloc divided East from West, the citizens of the western world grew intensely interested in the significance of the West and the deeper meanings of western civilization.

---

[6]Waldemar Gurian, "Dawson's Leitmotif," *Commonweal*, vol. 50 (June 3, 1949), 102.

[7]Kenelm Foster, "Mr. Dawson and Christendom," *Blackfriars*, vol. 31 (1950), 423.

[8]Frederick D. Wilhelmsen, "Seeking for the Source of a Long-Lost Unity," *Commonweal*, vol. 60 (June 18, 1954), 274.

[9]Jacques Maritain and Etienne Gilson are obvious exceptions. See Aidan Nichols, O.P., "Christopher Dawson," in *Catholic Thought since the Enlightenment: A Survey* (Pretoria: University of South Africa Press, 1998), 127–29.

[10]Maisie Ward, New York, to Dawson, Harvard, 1961, in the Christopher H. Dawson Collection, Box 11, Folder 25, "Frank Sheed 1960," Department of Special Collections, University of St. Thomas, St. Paul, MN (hereafter UST/CDC).

[11]Maisie Ward, *Unfinished Business* (New York: Sheed and Ward, 1964), 117.

[12]Maisie Sheed, London, to Dawson, October 1953, Box 11, Folder 18, "Frank Sheed 1953," in UST/CDC.

In the non-academic world, the United Nations and NATO sought Dawson's advice.[13]

In the spring of 1959, Henry Luce, publisher of *Time, Life,* and *Fortune,* who had appreciated Dawson's work since World War II, used the editorial column of the 16 March issue of *Life* magazine to promote Dawson's work and theories. The son of Presbyterian missionaries to China, Luce desired something more than the then-common materialist explanations of history. Unlike the Marxists and their materialist views or the then-eminent position of the American Historical Association President Walter Prescott Webb, who had developed all of his views from his life in Texas, Dawson offered the world a broad vision. The editorial admitted that most readers would find Dawson's take to be "unfashionable." Despite this, "such a theory is at least as scholarly as those merely 'ideological' (i.e., political or economic) interpretations which straitjacket many a man's view of world events." Thus, *Life* concluded, one should not readily dismiss Dawson, for his ideas "may well be true."[14] Additionally, Luce ordered a copy of Dawson's then latest book, *The Movement of World Revolution,* for each of his nineteen editors at *Time.*[15] The English Roman Catholic Christopher Dawson, not the Marxists or the Texans, would shape *Time* and *Life* editorial policy in the late 1950s.

American colleges and religious institutions especially sought his influence, advice, and prestige, whether as a guest lecturer, a visiting professor, or a full-time faculty member. During the 1950s, lecture invitations arrived from St. Paul's University Chapel of the University of Wisconsin; from the University of Washington; from the University of Loyola-Chicago; from Mercyhurst College of Erie, Pennsylvania; from the University of Portland; from Mount St. Scholastica of Atchison, Kansas; from Marymount College of Salina, Kansas; from the Archdiocese of Boston; from the University of San Francisco; from the University of Illinois Newman Club; from the Newman Club of Ohio State University; from Pennsylvania State University; from Manhattanville College of the Sacred Heart in New York; from St. John's University in New York; from Bellarmine College in Louisville, Kentucky; and from the Paulists of Boston.[16] Gonzaga University in Spokane, Washington, asked him to lead an eight-week seminar for historians and various scholars from all over North America, training them in the meaning of western civilization. St. Benedict's College of Atchison, Kansas, offered Dawson a one-semester

---

[13]See the various correspondence in Box 14, Folder 3, General Correspondence, 1950–1959, in UST/CDC.

[14] Editorial, "Welcome, Son, Who Are You?" *Life*, March 16, 1959, 32.

[15]Sheed, New York, to Dawson, Harvard, March 16, 1959, in Box 11, Folder 24, "Frank Sheed 1959," in UST/CDC.

[16]See the various correspondence in Box 14, Folder 3, General Correspondence, 1950–1959, in UST/CDC.

position to teach a course on the meaning of the liberal arts.[17] The Association of American Colleges requested something similar, hoping that Dawson might speak on "strengthening the intellectual, the religious and the cultural aspects of liberal education in the United States."[18] However tempting he might have found these offers, Dawson refused to accept any permanent or semi-permanent position at an American university until a letter arrived in early 1958 from Harvard University. Chauncey Stillman, a Harvard graduate and convert to Catholicism, provided funds for an endowed chair in Catholic Studies. Dawson accepted the position and held the chair from 1958 until poor health forced him to resign in 1962.

Dawson also significantly influenced an impressive number of poets, scholars, and public intellectuals throughout his lifetime, many of whom are remembered and who have remained influential long after Christopher Dawson had been forgotten. In his own writings and life, Dawson never failed to use his pen as a mighty sword. Yet he did so in a manner that was so intellectually respectable that even his academic detractors appreciated him, at least to the relative degree of taking him seriously. Indeed, political views aside, scholars and public intellectuals from many parts of the political spectrum respected Dawson. Lewis Mumford, one of the most prominent public intellectuals on the left, for example, wrote Dawson in 1924, at the beginning of the conservative Englishman's career, confessing, "I follow your writings with so much pleasure and profit that I cannot forbear to write you at last and make my acknowledgements."[19] On the other side of the spectrum, neo-Thomist historian and philosopher Etienne Gilson also acknowledged his profound admiration for Dawson in a 1950 letter to Frank Sheed. Gilson especially appreciated Dawson's *Making of Europe* and *Religion and the Rise of Western Culture*.[20] The latter "provided me with what I had needed during forty years without being able to find it anywhere: an intelligent and reliable background for a history of mediaeval philosophy," Gilson admitted. "Had I been fortunate in having such a book before writing my [*Spirit of the Middle Ages,*] my own work would have been other and better than it is."[21] Further, Gilson assured Sheed, he would be using the book as the background to his new series of lectures at the Collège de France.[22]

---

[17]Father Tim Fray, O.S.B., St. Benedict's College, Atchison, KS, to Dawson, Devon, England, April 15, 1958, in Box 14, Folder 3, General Correspondence, 1950–1959, in UST/CDC.

[18]Norwood Baker, Association of American Colleges, New York, to Dawson, Devon, February 3, 1958, in Box 14, Folder 3, General Correspondence, 1950–1959, in UST/CDC.

[19]Lewis Mumford, New York, to Dawson, May 8, 1924, in Box 15, Folder 58, "Mumford, Lewis," in UST/CDC.

[20]Sheed to Dawson, 1936, in Box 11 (Sheed and Ward Papers), Folder 2, "Frank Sheed, 1936," in UST/CDC.

[21]Etienne Gilson to Frank Sheed, August 22, 1950, in Box 11, Folder 16, "Frank Sheed 1950," in UST/CDC.

[22]Ibid.

Other impressive twentieth-century thinkers, such as Dom Bede Griffiths, Thomas Merton, David Jones, and Allen Tate, also acknowledged an immense debt to Dawson. "In the wider sphere of the relation of Christian thought and culture to other forms of culture and civilisation," Griffiths wrote in his auto-biographical reflections, *The Golden String*, "my guide was Christopher Dawson."[23] Griffiths, famous and controversial in his own right, was a close friend of C. S. Lewis and a convert to Catholicism. Most Catholics best remember him for his attempt to synthesize Hinduism and Catholicism. American Trappist Monk and author Thomas Merton claimed to have found his purpose in life while reading Dawson's 1952 book, *Understanding Europe*. "Whether or not [Dawson] came too late, who can say? In any case I have a clear obligation to participate, as long as I can, and to the extent of my abilities, in every effort to help a spiritual and cultural renewal of our time. This is the task that has been given me, and hitherto I have not been clear about it, in all its aspects and dimensions."[24] Given Merton's own brilliance and dedication to the Church—despite lingering controversies over his motives and his relationships with those outside of his order—this cannot be considered faint praise.

David Jones, a close friend of Dawson's and one who shared his Welsh ancestry, wrote his famous epic poem, *Anathemata*, using Dawson's theories and works as a background and inspiration. Christina Scott, one of Dawson's daughters, described Jones as "a very good friend" and "an awfully nice man" in an interview with Joseph Pearce. "My father and he had a lot in common: the Welsh side, the mystical side of religion and history."[25] Jones devoured everything Dawson wrote, and it shows in his poetic works.[26]

Allen Tate, an American southerner, famous literary critic, and a convert to Roman Catholicism in 1950, first met Dawson in 1953. The two talked immediately following a lecture Dawson had given on the study of Christian Culture at Oriel College, Oxford. Taken with the meeting, Tate afterward cited Dawson frequently in his essays.[27] Tate came away from reading Dawson's

---

[23] Dom Bede Griffiths, *The Golden String* (London: Harvill Press, 1954), 150.

[24] Thomas Merton, journal entry for August 22, 1961, *Turning toward the World: The Pivotal Years*, Victor A. Kramer, ed. (San Francisco, CA: Harper, 1995), 155. See also *Conjectures of a Guilty Bystander* (New York: Image, 1966), 55, 194–95; and *The Intimate Merton: His Life from His Journals*, Patrick Hart and Jonathan Montaldo, eds. (San Francisco, CA: Harper, 1999), 190.

[25] Pearce, *Literary Converts*, 208. See also David Jones, "Round About a Burning Tree," *Tablet* (January 5, 1957), 10.

[26] Thomas Dilworth, *The Shape and Meaning in the Poetry of David Jones* (Toronto: University of Toronto Press, 1988), 6; and Adam Schwartz, *The Third Spring: G. K. Chesterton, Graham Greene, Christopher Dawson, and David Jones* (Washington, D.C.: Catholic University of America Press, 2005), 286–88. See also Guy Davenport, "In Love with All Things Made," *New York Times Book Review*, October 17, 1982, 9.

[27] On Dawson's influence on Tate, see Ross Labrie, *The Catholic Imagination in American Literature* (Columbia, MO: University of Missouri Press, 1997), 10, 51; Robert S. Dupree, *Allen Tate and the Augustinian Imagination: A Study of the Poetry* (Baton Rouge: Louisiana State University

works fully convinced of the sheer corruption of morality and the spiritual life, which Tate believed to have been caused by twentieth-century materialism's erosion of traditional community. Following Dawson's lead, Tate argued that the West traditionally possessed a spiritual and material unity—"a peculiar balance of Greek culture and Christian other-worldliness, both imposed by Rome upon the northern barbarians." But by the mid-twentieth century, the Southern Agrarian lamented, western "civilization is just about gone."[28]

Perhaps first and foremost in terms of Dawson's significant influence was that on poet, playwright, and social critic T. S. Eliot. Eliot first contacted Dawson, through Dawson's publishers, Sheed and Ward, in the summer of 1929. He expressed his fondness for Dawson's works, his desire to have Dawson contribute to his journal, the *Criterion*, and his wish that the two could meet.[29] Eliot specifically hoped that Dawson would consider writing a piece on the "views of a practising Catholic layman about marriage reform, birth control, the relations of the sexes in general in the modern world."[30] Dawson agreed, and he wrote one of his most perceptive articles, also published in booklet form, "Christianity and Sex."[31] In the article, described more fully in later chapters, Dawson argued that the ideological attack on the family—the true central institution in society—would inevitably lead to the increase of the power of the state, a theme that Dawson would take up in his five books written from 1931 to 1942.

As Eliot's best biographer, Russell Kirk, wrote, "Of social thinkers in his own time, none influenced Eliot more than Dawson."[32] For three decades, Eliot was quite taken with Dawson's views, and it would be difficult if not impossible to find a scholar who influenced Eliot more. In the early 1930s, Eliot told an American audience that Dawson was the foremost thinker of his generation in England.[33] He explicitly acknowledged his debt to Dawson in the introductions to his two most politically and culturally oriented books, *The Idea of a Christian Society* and *Notes Towards the Definition of Culture*.[34] One can also find Dawson's influence in two of Eliot's most important writings of

---

Press, 1983), 130. On the two meeting in 1953, see Dawson to Mulloy, January 6, 1953, in Box 1, Folder 16, ND/CDAW.

[28]Allen Tate, *Essays of Four Decades* (Wilmington, DE: ISI Books, 1999), 538.

[29]T. S. Eliot, London, to Dawson, through Sheed and Ward, London, August 16, 1929, in Box 14, Folder 120, UST/CDC.

[30]T. S. Eliot, London, to Dawson, December 10, 1929, in Box 14, Folder 120, UST/CDC.

[31]Christopher Dawson, *Christianity and Sex* (London: Faber and Faber, 1930).

[32]Russell Kirk, *Eliot and His Age; T. S. Eliot's Moral Imagination in the Twentieth Century* (Peru, IL: Sherwood Sugden, 1988), 300. See also Bernard Wall, "Giant Individualists and Orthodoxy," *Twentieth Century*, vol. 155 (January 1954), 59.

[33]Christina Scott, *A Historian and His World: A Life of Christopher Dawson* (New Brunswick, NJ: Transaction, 1992), 210.

[34]The two have been republished together as T. S. Eliot, *Christianity and Culture* (San Diego: Harvest, 1976).

the moral imagination, *Murder in the Cathedral* and *The Four Quartets*.[35] Eliot continued to acknowledge a debt to Dawson after World War II. In a speech to the London Conservative Union in 1955, Eliot told his fellow conservatives that they should understand conservatism as Dawson does, not as political, but as ante-political and anti-ideological. Only then, Eliot argued, could English conservatives truly and effectively shape society.[36] Dawson wrote of Eliot fondly in his personal correspondence, though the two never became close friends socially, as "they were both very reserved."[37] Much of their influence on one another came from a group of Christian academics and scholars who met on a fairly regular basis over a ten-year period beginning in 1938. Called the Moot, it included those whom Eliot considered "the Christian elite," such as Dawson, Reinhold Neibuhr, Paul Tillich, and Arnold Toynbee.[38]

Dawson played a serious role in C. S. Lewis's work as well. Lewis seems not to have admitted this outright, but Dawson assumed—probably correctly—that Lewis had taken much of the argument in his *Abolition of Man* from Dawson's own 1929 work, *Progress and Religion*.[39] Though Dawson may have influenced Lewis intellectually, the two had next to nothing in common in terms of personality, at least at the beginning of their relationship. Humphrey Havard, the physician affectionately known to Lewis and the other Inklings as the "Useless Quack," brought Lewis and Dawson together one evening during the second world war, and the results were less than satisfying for either one of them. Dawson asked Havard to meet Lewis, and Havard took him to Lewis's offices at Magdalen College. Havard remembered Dawson, in contrast to Lewis, as a "physically frail, shy, disappointed man" whose intellectual style "was tortuous, full of qualifications and abstractions." C. S. Lewis "did his best to draw Dawson out; but he shrank from our vigorous humour and casual manners."[40] Strangely, this first meeting did not put an end to their relationship, and a friendship of sorts, or at least an alliance based on mutual respect, developed. When Dawson took over the editorship of the most important English Catholic intellectual journal, the *Dublin Review*, in 1940, he made a list of roughly twenty persons he wanted as permanent contributors and reviewers. Prominent on the list were the non-Catholic Lewis and "Lewis's Oxford Group," better known as the Inklings, which included J. R. R.

---

[35]Kirk, *Eliot and His Age*, 231–2, 299–300; and Joseph Schwartz, "The Theology of History in T. S. Eliot's *Four Quartets*," *Logos*, vol. 2 (1999), 34.

[36]T. S. Eliot, "The Literature of Politics," *Time and Tide*, vol. 36 (April 23, 1955), 524.

[37]"Both very reserved" from Dawson's daughter, Julianna, quoted in Pearce, *Literary Converts*, 267. On Dawson writing fondly of Eliot, see his various letters to John Mulloy, in ND/CDAW.

[38]Alzina Stone Dale, *T. S. Eliot: The Philosopher Poet* (Wheaton, IL: Harold Shaw, 1988), 140.

[39]Record of Dawson Conversation, August 21, 1953, in Box 1, Folder 2, ND/CDAW.

[40]Havard, in James D. Collins, *C. S. Lewis at the Breakfast Table and Other Reminiscences* (New York: Collier, 1979), 223.

Tolkien, Charles Williams, and Owen Barfield.[41] And, in 1941, Lewis wrote to Dawson, "Dear Dawson (If we might both drop the honorific now?)."[42] In such a formal time, the dropping of the honorific meant something, and especially to Lewis, who did so only with those he greatly respected.[43] *Religion and Culture*, Dawson's first set of published Gifford Lectures, especially pleased Lewis. After praising the book and its "magnificent ending" in a letter of appreciation to Dawson, Lewis concluded, "Thanks very much: you have given me a great treat."[44] Lewis also invited Dawson to participate in his prestigious Socratic Club.[45]

The two disagreed on the meaning of history, though, and Lewis wrote his famous essay, "Historicism," in 1950, in part, to counter Dawson's philosophy of history. "I give the name *Historicism* to the belief that men can, by use of their natural powers, discover an inner meaning in the historical process," Lewis argued. Had the Ulsterman left his argument there, Dawson might not have disagreed. After all, as Dawson argued in his own Stoic, Augustinian fashion, all good comes from the One, the Creator of all. Further, when he, Dawson, discovered the truth of history, he believed he did so by grace alone. But Lewis took his argument further, giving examples of what he meant. "When Carlyle spoke of history as a 'book of revelations' he was being a Historicist. When Novalis called history 'an evangel' he was a Historicist."[46] These two examples were enough to include, by implication, Dawson. After Lewis sent Dawson an offprint of the article, Dawson returned the favor by writing two articles against Lewis's view, entitled "The Christian View of History" and "The Problem of Metahistory."[47] Dawson challenged Lewis directly in the former article and implicitly in the latter article. Dawson seems to have won this argument, though, as in *Mere Christianity* Lewis claimed to know "the key to history," a process by which the devil time and time again fools

---

[41] Untitled paper, list of possible *Dublin Review* contributors, in Box 14, Folder 117, UST/CDC. On Tolkien's intellectual relation to Dawson, see Bradley J. Birzer, *J. R. R. Tolkien's Sanctifying Myth: Understanding Middle-Earth* (Wilmington, DE: ISI Books, 2002); and John S. Ryan, *The Shaping of Middle-Earth's Maker: Influences on the Life and Literature of J. R. R. Tolkien* (Highland, MI: American Tolkien Society, 1992).

[42] Lewis, Magdalen College, Oxford, to Dawson, Oxford, August 20, 1941, in Box 15, Folder 32, UST/CDC.

[43] Conversation between present author and C. S. Lewis scholar Dr. Andrew Cuneo, Summer 2003.

[44] C. S. Lewis, Magdalen College, Oxford, to Dawson, September 27, 1948, in Box 15, Folder 32, UST/CDC.

[45] Pearce, *Literary Converts*, 227. Most likely, this event never occurred. See Dawson, Oxford, to Stella Aldwinckle, Oxford Socratic Club, May 5, 1942, in Box 14, Folder 20, UST/CDC.

[46] C. S. Lewis, "Historicism," in *Christian Reflections* (Grand Rapids, MI: William B. Eerdmans, 1967), 101.

[47] Mulloy, Record of Conversation with Dawson, August 25, 1953, in Box 1, Folder 1, ND/CDAW.

ordinary humans into doing the wrong thing.[48] Ironically enough, Dawson would not have disagreed with Lewis on this.

The founder of modern American conservatism, Russell Kirk, found much to his liking in Dawson's work. As early as in Kirk's second but most famous academic book, *The Conservative Mind*, originally published in 1953, he noted that the first problem conservatives must solve is the "problem of spiritual and moral regeneration." To support his first tenet of conservatism, Kirk cited Dawson approvingly.[49] Indeed, it is impossible not to notice Dawson's influence on Kirk's historical understanding throughout his many works and forty-three-year writing career.[50] Kirk first admitted to Dawson's influence on him in a 1984 review article in the *Chesterton Review*. "Dawson wrote many books, all of them important. In this perspective, it comes home to me that I have been saturated in Dawsonian historical studies, and that my own books reflect Dawson's concepts."[51]

In his autobiography, Kirk again revealed that, "strongly influenced by Christopher Dawson and Eric Voegelin, Martin D'Arcy and Mircea Eliade," he had "come to conclude that a civilization cannot long survive the dying of belief in a transcendent order that brought the culture into being."[52] At the time of his death in 1994, Kirk was planning to edit the collected works of Dawson, and he and his wife, Annette, had just returned from a trip to England, tracing Dawson's path there. "A historian endowed with imagination," Kirk wrote with great praise, "Christopher Dawson restored to historical writing both an understanding of religion as the basis of culture and a moving power of expression."[53]

Obviously, Dawson's influence went well beyond Kirk, Lewis, Eliot, Merton, Jones, and Griffiths, each of whom had developed his own reputation though a variety of means and works. But by the late 1950s, as noted above, Christopher Dawson was arguably one of the most influential Roman Catholic scholars and public intellectuals in the English-speaking world. With only a few exceptions, Dawson's mind rivaled any within the Roman Catholic Church.

---

[48]C. S. Lewis, *Mere Christianity* (New York: Collier Books, 1960), 54. I am indebted to my colleague Dr. Paul Moreno, an expert on historiography, for catching Lewis' slip.

[49]Russell Kirk, *The Conservative Mind*, 1st ed. (Chicago: Regnery, 1953), 414.

[50]For a full comparison and treatment of Dawson's and Kirk's intellectual sympathies, see Bradley J. Birzer, *Seeking Christendom: The Augustinian Minds of Christopher Dawson and Russell Kirk* (Norfolk, VA: IHS Press, forthcoming). See also James E. Person, Jr., *Russell Kirk: A Critical Biography of a Conservative Mind* (Lanham, MD: Madison Books, 1999), 58.

[51]Russell Kirk, "The High Achievement of Christopher Dawson," *Chesterton Review*, vol. 10 (1984), 436; and conversations between the author and Annette Kirk, Mecosta, MI, March 15, 2003.

[52]Kirk, *Sword of Imagination,* 474.

[53]Russell Kirk, "Introduction to the Transaction Edition," in Scott, *A Historian and His World*, 5.

Dawson's Contributions

"I have had to follow my own line of studies and plough a lone furrow for thirty-five years," Dawson told an audience in the early 1950s, "solely because the subject to which I have devoted myself—the study of Christian culture—has no place in education or in university studies."[54] Attempting to fulfill the purpose that he believed God had for him, Dawson wrote almost two hundred books and articles during his lifetime. His more famous books include *The Age of the Gods*; *Progress and Religion*; *The Making of Europe*; *Medieval Essays*; *Medieval Religion*; *The Judgment of the Nations*; *Religion and Culture*; *Religion and the Rise of Western Culture*; *Religion and the Modern State*; *The Division of Christendom*; and *The Formation of Christendom*.

While never the stylist that his American counterpart Russell Kirk was, Dawson always wrote with a verve and a purpose that has a charm all of its own. Stylistically, though, one should regard Dawson as the master of the conclusion, as his conclusions are as rhetorically persuasive as they are intellectually sound. Dawson also believed that his Roman Catholicism gave him a special purpose in writing. As the second world war took shape, Dawson wrote that as "the heirs and successors of the makers of Europe—the men who saved civilization from perishing in the storm of barbarian invasion and who built the bridge between the ancient and modern worlds," Catholics had a specific and unique purpose, given to them by God. In an Augustinian fashion, Dawson argued, Catholics always transcend the politics and ideologies of the day, representing, instead, the eternal supernatural realities which are "more organically united than any political body which possesses an autonomous body of principles and doctrines on which to base their judgments." So armed and commanded, Catholics must "maintain and strengthen the unity of Western culture." The forces arrayed against them desire nothing less than the total subversion and destruction of all that is True, Good, and Beautiful.[55]

Even if the forces waging the battle on behalf of Christendom fail, they will still serve a vital purpose, as "any Catholic who is intellectually alive and is at the same time obviously convinced of the truth of his religion administers a shock to [an ideologue's] preconceived ideas." He must not expect to "convert them," for they are entrenched in their own subjective realities. But by stating openly one's own beliefs and demonstrating one's faith publicly, the Catholic will certainly shake "their confidence in the inevitability of the secularist outlook and in the stupidity of the religious view of life."[56]

---

[54]Christopher Dawson, "Ploughing a Lone Furrow," in *Christianity and Culture,* J. Stanley Murphy, ed. (Baltimore, MD: Helicon, 1960), 17.

[55]Christopher Dawson, "Editorial Note," *Dublin Review,* vol. 207 (1940), 1.

[56]Christopher Dawson, *The Crisis of Western Education* (1961; Steubenville, OH: Franciscan University Press, 1989), 176.

Much of this was autobiographical for Dawson. In a speech delivered at a celebration for his seventieth birthday, Dawson revealed the reasons behind his decision to teach at Harvard and why he considered it the culminating moment of his scholarly life. "All my life for fifty years I have been writing on one subject and for one cause," he told those celebrating with him, "the cause of Christendom and the study of Christian culture."[57] Dawson held a very broad vision of the West. "I am still profoundly convinced of the importance of the need for the defence of the West," he wrote in 1942, "though it is important not to understand the expression in too narrow a political and geographical sense, as is often done. In my view the West is a cultural tradition like that of Hellenism and one which has an even wider and more universal mission."[58] For example, Dawson believed the Spartan defense of Hellas at Thermopylae had a serious spiritual significance, not just a military or a geopolitical significance.[59] Such a Greek proto-spiritualism and patriotism anticipated the true spiritualism of medieval Catholic Europe. And, by the time the world had reached the twentieth century, the true spiritualism had moved outside of and beyond Europe into the Americas, Africa, and Asia. The West's mission, properly understood, was truly universal. Indeed, Dawson argued the mission of the West is synonymous with the mission of the Church.

Things looked bleak during Dawson's own life. With the destruction wrought by the first and second world wars, the Cold War, the rise of nationalism, communism, fascism, the holocaust camps, the gulags, the killing fields, and the sheer mechanization and overwhelming destruction of human life in the twentieth century, western citizens wanted answers about the purpose of life and the necessity of the good life. Dawson willingly called western culture back to what he believed were first principles and right reason. With the world collapsing into ideological and mass democide, Dawson feared the "unloosing of the powers of the abyss." Indeed, he believed, "the dark forces that have been chained by a thousand years of Christian civilization . . . have now been set free to conquer the world."[60] The abyss competed with grace, and men and women began taking the easy route, the path of least resistance. At least, it seemed easy to them in the short run. In the long run, their poor choices would catch up with them, and the abyss would rule them, making them little more than pathetic slaves. Rather than celebrate the diversity of human persons created in the infinite image of the Creator, men instead seemed to be recreating a Babylon and imposing a strict, gray conformity.[61] Sadly, western civilization had entered the "Age of the Cinema—in which the

---

[57] Scott, *A Historian and His World,* 198.
[58] Christopher Dawson to Walter Zander, Gerrards Cross, Bucks, May 12, 1942, in Box 14, Folder 14, UST/CDC.
[59] Ibid.
[60] Christopher Dawson, "A Century of Change, 1840–1940," *Tablet* (1940).
[61] Ibid.

most amazing perfection of scientific technique is being devoted to purely ephemeral objects, without any consideration of their ultimate justification." Mechanical and created things had taken on a life of their own, and they were becoming the standard by which all of life was living. "It seems as though a new society was arising which will acknowledge no hierarchy of values, no intellectual authority, and no social or religious tradition," Dawson lamented, "but which will live for the moment in a chaos of pure sensation."[62]

The world, then, had to be sanctified, and Dawson believed in true Augustinian fashion that one could do that only by choosing to drain one's will, allowing God's grace to fill the vacuum and remake the person. Put another way, "the creative element in human culture is spiritual, and it triumphs only by mortifying and conquering the natural conservatism of man's animal instincts."[63] Indeed, history is nothing more than "the cumulative results of a number of spiritual decisions—the faith and insight, or the refusal and blindness, of individuals."[64] Man finds himself best through a non-mechanized order, a strong community (family and beyond), and the inculcation of the seven pagan and Christian virtues—prudence, justice, fortitude, temperance, faith, hope, and love.

As Dawson understood it, the Holy Spirit played the key role in his life as well as in his vision of history. He argued unceasingly that "the forces of evil cannot be successfully resisted without the power of the Spirit." The human person, then, exists as a potential vessel of grace—a noble and unique instrument—to reclaim the world for God. The Church exists as the "embryo" of the Kingdom of Christ.[65] "The Church is the divine organ of the Spirit in the world and the guardian and interpreter of the word of God," Dawson wrote in 1944. The Church's mission "is a universal mission to the whole human race, and it is therefore also her mission to enlighten and supernaturalize civilization."[66] Grace perfects nature through "the new creation which is the historic Church."[67] Dawson put this in philosophic terms in private, undated notes, entitled "Traditionalism and Rationalism."

> As language is essential to Reason, so the Word of God is essential to Faith. Granted the fact of Revelation, Reason is still insufficient as the vehicle of its transmission.

---

[62]Christopher Dawson, *Progress and Religion: An Historical Inquiry* (1929; Washington, D.C.: Catholic University of America Press, 2001), 176.

[63]Christopher Dawson, "Christianity and the New Age," in *Essays in Order,* Christopher Dawson and Tom Burns, eds. (New York: Macmillan, 1931), 238.

[64]Christopher Dawson, *The Historic Reality of Christian Culture: A Way to the Renewal of Human Life* (London: Routledge and Kegan Paul, 1960), 18, 20.

[65]Christopher Dawson, *Dynamics of World History*, John J. Mulloy, ed. (1957; Wilmington, DE: ISI Books, 2002), 260.

[66]Dawson, "Letter of Christopher Dawson to a Priest Critic of Certain Views of Dawson set forth in *The Judgment of the Nations*," dated April 10, 1944, in Box 1, Folder 16, ND/CDAW; and Dawson, "Catholicism and the Bourgeois Mind," *Colosseum*, vol. 2 (1935), 256.

[67]Dawson to Mulloy and *Commonweal*, March 5, 1955, in Box 1, Folder 16, ND/CDAW.

> For this it is necessary to have the Sacred Word of Scripture and the sacred society of the Church which is the bearer of the Sacred Tradition. The Holy Spirit in the Church is to the Word of God what human Reason in the tradition of culture is to the World of Man. The Spirit is the Interpreter as well as the verifier.[68]

For the Church to consider an alliance with secularism, therefore, would be a terrible betrayal of its mission, an almost pure "act of apostasy."[69]

One of the most important gifts offered by the Holy Spirit is the gift of creativity and imagination. "It is the nature of grace to be gratuitous, prevenient, and creative," Dawson wrote in 1955. "In this, it only carries on the process of natural creation."[70] The human person, made as *imago Dei*, must also act as a creator, but only to glorify God and creation. Only by allowing the Holy Spirit to work old truths into new forms—what John Henry Cardinal Newman called the "illative sense" and what T. S. Eliot called the "moral imagination"—could the world hope to overcome the ideologues, their false visions, and their massacres. Only the transcendent and a proper understanding of the economy of grace could renew the face of the earth. "It is a creative spiritual force," Dawson wrote, "which has for its end nothing less than the re-creation of humanity. The Church is no sect or human organization, but a new creation—the seed of the new order which is ultimately destined to transform the world."[71] Far from considering the imagination a hindrance to rationality or understanding, Dawson wrote, the Church "has always used imagination as the normal means of transforming the notional assent into a real one." Importantly, imagination "becomes a channel of the life of the spirit like the other powers of the soul."[72] Only the creativity of the Spirit will save civilization before it succumbs to self-destruction.[73]

---

[68] Dawson, unpublished notes, "Traditionalism and Rationalism," n.d., in Box 4, Folder 54, UST/CDC.

[69] Dawson to unknown correspondent, September 16, 1957, in Box 1, Folder 16, ND/CDAW.

[70] Dawson, "Memorandum," dated August 1, 1955, Box 1, Folder 15, in ND/CDAW; and *Historic Reality of Christian Culture,* 17.

[71] Dawson, "Christianity and the New Age," 227.

[72] Dawson, Oxford, to Frank Sheed, July 28, 1946, in Folder 12, Box 11, UST/CDC.

[73] Dawson, *Historic Reality of Christian Culture,* 93.

Chapter 1

Dawson the Convert

1889–1920

ON OCTOBER 12, 1889, MARY LOUISA AND HENRY PHILIP DAWSON GAVE birth to a son, Henry Christopher. The blessed event took place in a twelfth-century Welsh castle, known as Hay Castle, in the Wye Valley in Hereford-shire. Both the date and the place of his birth are auspicious, steeped in myth and tradition, and bringing together both sides of his family. October 12 was the Feast of St. Wilfrid, an eighth-century bishop of York, the ances-tral home of Dawson's father. St. Wilfrid famously stood by Roman Christian customs rather than Celtic ones and convinced many of his brother priests to do the same at a time when the two customs were stridently in opposition to one another. Legend records that St. Wilfrid converted the South Saxons to Christianity, freed numerous slaves throughout the British isles, founded several monasteries in Mercia, and patiently suffered much opposition from his enemies.

The Influence of Place and Family

The place is also important, as the castle is connected in popular Welsh mem-ory to a rather mysterious person known as Maude of St. Valery or Matilda of Hay, who supposedly built the castle in a single night while carrying the stones in her apron.[1] But whatever may have happened in the twelfth century, by the late nineteenth century, the castle belonged to Christopher's mother's fam-ily.[2] The men of his mother's side, of Welsh decent, had a long tradition of being High Church Anglo-Catholic clergymen, both priests and bishops. His

---

[1] Christina Scott, *A Historian and His World: A Life of Christopher Dawson* (New Brunswick, NJ: Transaction, 1992), 13–14.

[2] Dawson, Cambridge, MA, to Peter Feledick, Racine, WI, in Box 14, Folder 128, UST/CDC.

mother's family, therefore, had great standing in the region, which Dawson remembered as "a sort of Anglican theocracy" as "the landowners were largely
clergymen and the clergy were either landowners or brothers of landowners,
so that there was a complete unification of political, religious, economic and
social authority and influence."[3]

The rural culture into which Dawson was born was very traditional,
steeped in many layers of natural and inherited authority. Those around
young Christopher reverenced the role and tradition of family, the beauty
of nature, the Anglican Church, the Celtic saints and folklore, the Queen,
and God. Each of these "layers" represented an ever ascending level of natural authority. In their outlook, political views, cultural influences, and faith,
Dawson's family may have been more at home in the early eighteenth century than in the late nineteenth century. But in the late nineteenth century,
there was a still a purposefulness and security in the holding of such deep
and cherished traditions. "Never perhaps in the history of the world," Dawson reflected in 1926, "has there been a society more secure, more certain
of itself and more externally prosperous than that of England in the Victorian age."[4] By the 1940s, though, that security and purpose were gone, and
Dawson deeply regretted the loss of the world in which he was raised. "The
world and my childhood is already as far away from the contemporary world
as it was from the world of the middle ages—in many respects even further,"
Dawson lamented in the notes to his memoirs. He had been raised in a pre-
mechanical world, and, for the sake of the future, he felt compelled to record
his experiences as quickly as possible. "If we do not record a lot that used
to be taken for granted, it will be lost for good, and the understanding of
the past will become even more difficult than it is already," he feared. "Certain ways of human experience will become inaccessible, even to the historic
imagination."[5]

Dawson's beliefs went beyond mere nostalgia. Something had happened
between his childhood and the modern world of the early twentieth century.
There was at some point a "great divide," a break between the old world
and modernity. While ancient and medieval western men seemed to Dawson
noble and generally virtuous, modern western man was "an imperialist, a
capitalist and an exploiter."[6]

Dawson did not stand alone in these fears. Romano Guardini, a contemporary of Dawson's, recorded the same process at work while watching one area

---

[3]Christopher Dawson, *Tradition and Inheritance: Reflections on the Formative Years* (St. Paul, MN: Wanderer Press, 1970), 11.

[4]Christopher Dawson, "Why I am a Catholic," *Catholic Times*, May 21, 1926, 11.

[5]Dawson, "Manuscript Notes: Tradition and Inheritance" [1940s], in Box 4, Folder 94, UST/CDC.

[6]Christopher Dawson, *The Movement of World Revolution* (New York: Sheed and Ward, 1959), 99–100.

in Italy, Lake Como, change from a closely-connected rural community tied together by the Church to a region in which rising industry mechanized the community, atomizing one person from another, and destroying the organic nature of society. The greatest change, he argued, came from the modern desire to dominate and exploit nature rather than live with it. Ironically, the human attempt to dominate nature through mechanization had led to the loss of control. "It is destructive because it is not under human control," Guardini wrote. "It is a surging ahead of unleashed forces that have not yet been mastered, raw material that has not yet been put together, given a living and spiritual form, and related to humanity."[7] In his 1954 Cambridge inaugural address, C. S. Lewis said much the same thing. The rise of the machine had fundamentally changed the very nature of the relationship of man to man, man to the world, and man to God. In this brave new world, Lewis argued, "the new most often really is better and the primitive really is the clumsy." The machine, Lewis continued, takes on a religious significance to the poorly educated. "From the old push-bike to the motor-bike and thence to the little car; from the gramophone to radio and from radio to television; from the range to the stove; these are the very stages of their pilgrimage,"[8] the Cambridge don concluded. Dawson agreed with both of these sentiments. No person "can look at the history of western civilization during the present century without feeling dismayed at the spectacle of what modern man has done with his immense resources," Dawson wrote.[9] Like his fellow Christian Humanists, Dawson spent much of his scholarly work attempting to uncover and explain the reasons for the break with the past and the development of the modern western man.

Influenced by his mother's family, and especially by the deep respect he held for his mother, Dawson stood strongly entrenched in the Anglo-Catholic tradition before attending Oxford.[10] Still, he saw significant weaknesses in the Anglo-Catholic position. "It was lacking in authority," Dawson explained. "It was not the teaching of the official church but of an enterprising minority which provided its own standard of orthodoxy."[11] And though Dawson later converted to Roman Catholicism, he admired the Anglican Church for the remainder of his life, crediting it with teaching him the value of the liturgy and the weight of tradition. He once told his closest friend, E. I. Watkin, "that his Anglican education had enabled him to appreciate aspects of Catholicism he

---

[7]Romano Guardini, *Letters from Lake Como: Explorations in Technology and the Human Race,* trans. George Bromiley (Grand Rapids, MI: William B. Eerdmans, 1994), 79.

[8]C. S. Lewis, "De Descriptione Temporum," in *Selected Literary Essays,* Walter Hooper, ed. (Cambridge, England: Cambridge University Press, 1969), 11.

[9]Christopher Dawson, *Understanding Europe* (New York: Sheed and Ward, 1952), 3.

[10]Frank Sheed, "Frank Sheed Talks with Christopher Dawson," *The Sign,* vol. 38 (December 1958), 35.

[11]Dawson, "Why I am a Catholic," 11.

might have missed had he been what is now termed 'a cradle Catholic.'"[12] To an interviewer in 1961, he said, "Brought up an Anglo-Catholic, I was always familiar with Catholic books and ideas." While Anglo-Catholics remained distinct from Roman Catholics, seeing Roman Catholics as too fundamentalist, "they were even more completely separatist from the Protestant Nonconformists—The Dissenters."[13] And though the Roman and Anglo mind remained separated, the two had much in common, Dawson believed. One can find Dawson's greatest appreciation for Anglo-Catholicism in his 1933 centenary re-examination of John Henry Newman and his allies, *The Spirit of the Oxford Movement*.

Dawson's education was atypical and not always strictly formal. Movement within and exploration of the vast rural landscapes and countryside— especially its churches and shrines—shaped Dawson as much as did his voluminous reading. Indeed, as a young boy, Dawson claimed to have learned more "during my school days from my visits to the Cathedral at Winchester than I did from the hours of religious instruction in school."[14] The countryside came alive for him, as the mythic Celtic past seemed to weave itself through the land, the faith, and the books. "What David Jones called his 'Celticity,'" Dawson's close friend Harmon Grisewood remembered, "gave Christopher insights and a poetic appreciation both of nature and history which is often lacking in one whose ancestry is wholly English."[15]

From his mother's family, he inherited a love for myth, the tradition of the saints, and the necessity of beauty in its many forms. Dawson remembered that his mother repeatedly told the story of "Bran the Blessed, the mythical ancestor of the Holy Families of Wales—the story of the Lodestone river and the saying 'He who will be chief, let him be a bridge.'"[16] Though a giant, pagan king, Bran, whose name means "Raven," earned his title "the Blessed" as the one who, in many tales, first introduced Christianity to the Irish. Needless to say, Butler did not include an entry for Bran the Blessed in his multi-volume *Lives of the Saints*.

Dawson's mother's hagiographic and mythological stories must have shaped his outlook on the world profoundly. Even Dawson's first fictional story, written when he was only six, tellingly involved a battle between Christians and heathens.[17] This became a theme that would pervade every one

---

[12]E. I. Watkin, "Reflections on the Work of Christopher Dawson," *Downside Review*, vol. 89 (1971), 9.

[13]Aubrey Haines, "Catholic Historian at Harvard," *Voice of St. Jude* (1961), 30.

[14]Christopher Dawson, "Education and the Crisis of Christian Culture," *Lumen Vitae*, vol. 1 (1946), 208.

[15]Harman Grisewood, "Face to Faith: The Ideas of a Catholic Tiger," *The Guardian* (October 16, 1989).

[16]Dawson, *Tradition and Inheritance*, 12.

[17]Scott, *A Historian and His World*, 30. It should also be noted that one of the university papers Dawson kept from his Oxford days was a brilliant eighteen-page essay entitled "Early

of his non-fictional writings. From the mythical lives of heroes and gods, Dawson turned to the real lives of the Catholic saints. "From the time that I was thirteen or fourteen, I had come to know the lives of the Catholic saints and the writings of the medieval Catholic mystics," Dawson wrote, "and they made so strong an impression on my mind that I felt that there must be something lacking in any theory of life which left no room for these higher types of character and experience."[18]

More than anything else, though, Dawson felt the continuity of tradition and the far-reach of family on his mother's side. Such an intellectual and spiritual familial inheritance was a burden as much as a gift. This maternal patrimony would haunt and shape him all of his life. At Hay, Dawson felt "the immense age of everything, and in the house, the continuity of the present with the remote past, and the feeling was reinforced by the fact that nothing had changed since my mother had been a child in the same house and that all the family relations existed in duplicate, so that alongside of my parents, my nurse, and my uncles and aunts, I saw my mother's parents and her nurse and her uncles and aunts."[19] It should not surprise anyone a century later to recognize that when Dawson encountered the rapidly changing modern and urban world, in love with its own inventions and cleverness, he correctly believed himself a man displaced in time. Some scholars, not totally without justification, have accused Dawson of allowing nostalgia to color his history and philosophy. Certainly, Dawson must have longed at times for an ideal and mystical Celtic past. One can readily imagine not only Bran the Blessed and Saint Dafyd, the first bishop at Glastonbury, running through the faith and mythic scapes of young Christopher's mind, but a Celtic King Arthur as well.

If Christopher's mother provided the imaginative side, his father provided the discipline and intellect. Most of the men of his father's side, almost all from Yorkshire, had been military men. Patriotism and faith mingled comfortably in Dawson's family, and both sides were intellectually curious and acute. But this was especially true of Dawson's father, who had, for example, founded a Dante study group while in the Army. "His admiration for Dante had no limits," Dawson wrote. He considered him "the world's one perfect poet. This love of Dante no doubt stimulated his interest in Catholicism and helped to dispel the Protestant prejudices of his upbringing."[20] His father was also an adventurous soul, having traveled to South America when it was still

---

Welsh Literature." Dated 1909, it explores the extant sources of Celtic mythology and the bardic traditions, with a special focus on the connection of mythology to Catholic hagiography in the figures of St. Bridget and St. Columba. See "Early Welsh Literature," 1909, in Box 1a/Folder 51, UST/CDC.

[18] Dawson, "Why I am a Catholic," 11.

[19] Dawson, *Tradition and Inheritance,* 12.

[20] Ibid., 28.

a treacherous and undeveloped place and having served as the lead British officer in the famous 1882–1883 International Circum-Polar Expedition.[21]

An Unusual Education

Upper-middle class, both sides of Dawson's family deeply cherished tradition and conservatism, and both sides greatly valued rural and agrarian life. "Neither my parents nor their parents nor theirs—almost *ad infinitum*—ever lived in a town," Dawson wrote in the late 1940s, "and I find it exceedingly difficult, not merely uncongenial but unnatural, to do so myself."[22] Distrust of urban areas and masses of men would haunt Dawson for his entire life and greatly shape many of his views on culture, politics, and society. In 1961, he told a reporter that living in cities was dangerous for one's health and one's soul. The city merely distracts the person, Dawson believed. "A man has no room for a library in a city apartment and no time to use it if he had one." These distractions and desire for constant material gain force men to compete in "the rat race" of life and are "always tempted to conform to lower standards of secular culture that they see around them."[23] Indeed, his greatest regret in taking the job at Harvard in 1958, Dawson admitted, was leaving the rural countryside of England. "I've always been a countryman," he told a *Newsweek* reporter. "So was my father, grandfather, and great-grandfather. I shall hate to go."[24]

His parents initially sent him to a prestigious Anglican school, Winchester. Poor health got the best of Dawson, and his parents removed him from the school after only a brief stay. He also considered Winchester as a threat to his own family traditions, "hostile to culture and historic and religious tradition."[25] Further, the religion taught at Winchester, as opposed to that learned and gleaned in his own home, "was more ethics than religion, and a haze of vagueness and uncertainty hung around the more fundamental articles in Christian dogma."[26] Modernism had clearly infected the teachings at Winchester.

That aside, formal education never suited Dawson's restless and imaginative mind. "I got nothing from school, little from Oxford, and less than nothing from the new post-Victorian urban culture," Dawson wrote in the 1920s. "All my 'culture' and my personal happiness came from that much-derided

[21] E. I. Watkin, Part I of "Christopher Dawson, 1889–1970," *Proceedings of the British Academy*, vol. 57 (1971), 439–40; and Dawson, Devonshire, to Mr. Sheward Hagerty, London, April 30, 1958, in Box 15, Folder 72, UST/CDC.

[22] Dawson, *Tradition and Inheritance*, 10. Emphasis in original.

[23] Haines, "Catholic Historian at Harvard," 30.

[24] "The Catholic at Harvard," *Newsweek*, April 28, 1958, 58.

[25] Maisie Ward, "Dawson the Philosopher," *Duckett's Register*, vol. 4 (1949), 38.

[26] Dawson, "Why I am a Catholic," 11.

Victorian rural home life."[27] And, yet, his schooling must have left a certain impression on him, even if Dawson was too close to it to recognize it. Robert Speaight, Dawson's associate editor at the *Dublin Review* in the early 1940s, remembered Dawson in not always favorable terms. "Winchester and New College were written all over his scholar's stoop, tired intonations, and frail physique, and you were imperceptive if you did not discern an underlying toughness of mind and character."[28] Speaight had it wrong though, as Dawson studied at Trinity College, not New College. Still, the stereotype must have been evident in Dawson to some degree, or Speaight would not have remembered it twenty-five years later.

After the failure at Winchester, Dawson's parents had him schooled by a private tutor at Bletsoe in Bedfordshire, England, in 1905. This form of education seemed to suit Dawson much better. "He spent his time out of doors and in deep and varied reading," Maisie Ward wrote in a mini-biography of Dawson. "The tutor left his pupils largely to their own devices: he could hardly have done better."[29] A half century later, Dawson wrote that private tutoring must always be superior to high school. Many great thinkers, he must have noted with some satisfaction, had received a private or home-schooled education.[30] Perhaps most important, Dawson met his closest friend, E. I. Watkin, also privately tutored at Bletsoe.

At first, the two disliked one another vehemently. Dawson had entered a rationalist phase and, during an argument with the decidedly more Christian Watkin, Watkin lost his temper, and "forced the back of his garden chair down upon" Dawson's head.[31] Such passion, though manifested with boyish violence at first, soon proved the beginning of serious, intellectually-driven, life-long friendship. The two men, to varying degrees, would greatly influence one another for the entirety of their adult lives. As Dawson later remembered, he and Watkin were as two sides of the same coin: "I am a Latin, he is a Greek."[32] Watkin was impressed not only with Dawson's vast and penetrating intellect but also with Dawson's love of beauty, inherited from his Welsh ancestry.[33]

The two continued to strengthen their already rather deep friendship at Oxford and, for a time, even shared rooms together. Watkin remembered in his diary that the two often stayed up late into the night discussing any

---

[27]Watkin, Part I of "Christopher Dawson, 1889–1970," 440.

[28]Robert Speaight, *The Property Basket: Recollections of a Divided Life* (London: Collins and Harvill, 1970), 218. If Speaight is correct, perhaps Dawson absorbed the "New College" style from E. I. Watkin.

[29]Ward, "Dawson the Philosopher," 38.

[30]Dawson, Cambridge, MA, to Wesley Hartly, Santa Ana, CA, March 30, 1960, in Box 14, Folder 162, UST/CDC.

[31]Watkin, Part I of "Christopher Dawson, 1889–1970," 441.

[32]Maisie Ward, *Unfinished Business* (New York: Sheed and Ward, 1964), 117.

[33]Watkin, Part I of "Christopher Dawson, 1889–1970," 441.

and every thing of intellectual and poetic value.[34]   As they talked, Dawson's art collection—paintings of Christ, Socrates, and Charles I—watched
over them.[35]   During their many discussions, Dawson grew especially in-
trigued with Watkin's Roman Catholicism and the faith Watkin had accepted
in 1908.[36]   Dawson remembered the time and conversations with Watkin
as especially influential. "I'd always been fond of Dante. He was my father's favorite poet," Dawson stated in an interview in 1961. But through
conversation with E. I. Watkin, "I became absorbed in the theocratic philosophy of history—St. Augustine, Dante, and de Maistre."[37]   St. Augustine
provided Dawson with a theological and philosophical understanding of history; Dante provided Dawson with a mythical, metahistorical understanding
of the Church within western civilization; and Joseph de Maistre, a refugee in
Tzarist Russia, fleeing the French Revolution, taught Dawson the meaning of
organic community and fear of revolutionary and mass democratic fervor.

The Path to Conversion

Watkin was not the first person to introduce the depth and traditions of the
Roman Catholic religion to the budding scholar. Though reared in an upper
middle-class Protestant family, Dawson had first learned to respect the Roman
Catholic church from his rather open-minded father, who had taught him time
and time again about the great minds and artists of the Roman Catholic tradition. In particular, Dawson learned to love Dante, and most likely Virgil, from
his father. The deep Anglo-Catholic sympathies of his mother's side also led
to concerns Dawson had about the broader Anglican establishment. In 1961,
Dawson remembered his uncle becoming a bishop and feeling no sympathy
with non-Anglo-Catholics in the Anglican establishment. His uncle considered them "little better than infidels." But, Dawson continued, "I imbibed
my Catholic sympathies and my Catholic view of history from my father. In
my teens we were all enthusiastic readers of Robert Hugh Benson's novels—
despite the fact that he had left the Anglo-Catholics for Rome."[38] Benson, the
son of the Archbishop of Canterbury, was a famous early-twentieth century
English convert to Roman Catholicism. His conversion in 1903 deeply upset
the Church of England and all respectable Englishmen. That Dawson's family would still read him enthusiastically after such a controversial conversion
indicates how open and tolerant his father was. After becoming a Roman
Catholic priest, Benson wrote historical fiction dealing with various aspects of

---

[34]See Scott, *A Historian and His World*, chapter 3, on the discussions between Dawson and
Watkin.

[35]Scott, *A Historian and His World,* 44.

[36]Watkin, Part I of "Christopher Dawson, 1889–1970," 441.

[37]Haines, "Catholic Historian at Harvard," 30.

[38]Ibid.

Catholic persecution in England, as well as potent anti-Masonic science fiction novels anticipating the later dystopian novels of Aldous Huxley, George Orwell, and Ray Bradbury.[39]

Though the criticisms expressed by his mother's family helped move Dawson toward Rome, his mother never understood her son's eventual conversion, and it drove a painful wedge between them. Dawson lamented in a personal letter to a friend at the University of Notre Dame that his conversion "was a cause of separation and of suffering in regard to my mother."[40] The force of neither his family nor his best friend, E. I. Watkin, though, were enough to convert Dawson. Dawson was a man of the mind, deeply rooted in the traditions of Western Civilization, and it would take the powerful intellects and members of the community of souls to convince him of the truth of Rome. Most important for Dawson were St. Augustine, from whom Dawson derived his most original thoughts, including his entire philosophy of history and his theology of culture; the Oxford Movement's John Henry Cardinal Newman, another famous convert from Anglicanism to Roman Catholicism, whom Dawson considered his nineteenth-century counterpart; and the lives of the various saints and mystics, the men who, Dawson firmly believed, had really changed history by reflecting in their own personal lives the Light of the Logos. Looking back from 1958, Dawson explained the influences in an interview:

> St. Augustine's *City of God* affected me most powerfully. So did Harnack, a liberal Protestant, who never knew how much he contributed to the process of my conversion to the Church! . . . I was already an Anglo-Catholic before I went to Oxford. I had been brought up on the Oxford Movement. I was naturally much interested when Ronald Knox, still an Anglican, became the Chaplain at Trinity College while I was there; but he did not help in my conversion. Some of the men at Pusey House, the center of Anglo-Catholic life in Oxford, did. From them I learned a great deal of theology and patristics. Catholics who helped were Edward Watkin, whom I had known as a boy and who joined the Church a couple of years before I did; and Father Burdett, then a Jesuit; through him I came to know Stonyhurst.[41]

Three years later, again in a private letter, Dawson mentioned still others. "I would exclude Adam Muller, Othmar Spann and Maurras for whom I had no sympathy whatever, and perhaps Weber. Maurice Barres, Charles Peguy and Paul Claudel influenced me much during my undergraduate period and [Ernest] Troeltsch and [Frederic] LePlay soon after I became a Catholic."[42] In notes for his memoirs, written most likely in the late 1940s, he summarized the four major influences:

---

[39] Joseph Pearce, *Literary Converts: Spiritual Inspiration in an Age of Unbelief* (San Francisco, CA: Ignatius, 2000), 17–29.

[40] Dawson to Leo Ward, November 26 [no year given], in Box 15, Folder 176, UST/CDC.

[41] Sheed, "Frank Sheed Talks with Christopher Dawson," 35.

[42] Dawson, Cambridge, MA, to Peter Feledick, Racine, WI, in Box 14, Folder 128, UST/CDC.

I belong to the 1914 generation—converted 1913 rec. January 6, 1914. Influences (a) Anglo-Catholic (b) study of Catholic mysticism (Von Hugel, the Ecole Francaise, R H Benson (!) and personally through Father . . . Parker OSB and above all Father F. Burdett (then S.J.) (c) patristic and NT study especially . . . in St. Paul and St. Augustine (d) and from Catholic friends especially Burdett and E Watkin and my wife.[43]

Clearly, the companions—tangible and intangible—Dawson chose, were already Roman Catholic, if not in name, then in spirit.

Equally important, Dawson experienced a profound religious moment in Rome on Easter, 1909. The visit served "as a revelation . . . to a whole new world of religion and culture," his daughter Christina wrote.[44] On that day, Dawson stood at the Ara Coeli and had nothing less than a mystical revelation. There, his daughter later wrote, "he first conceived the idea of writing a history of culture" and, as he himself confided to his diary, "had great light on the way it may be carried out." The experience passed, but not his new conviction. "However unfit I may be," he wrote, "I believe it is God's will I should attempt it."[45] As Dawson put it in his 1926 autobiographical reflections on conversion, "It opened out a new world of religion and culture. I realised for the first time that Catholic civilisation did not stop with the Middle Ages and that contemporary with our own national Protestant development there was the wonderful flowering of the Baroque culture."[46]

Finally, in terms of influence and movement toward Roman Catholicism, there was also the love of Dawson's life, Valery Mills, a cradle Catholic whom he would marry on August 9, 1916, two years after his conversion. While the intellect led Dawson to the Church, his passion probably took him across the threshold. His actual decision to enter the Roman Catholic Church occurred in October 1913.[47] During this time of discernment, Dawson often stayed with his friend from Oxford, Father Burdett, a Jesuit in residence at Stonyhurst College, presumably discussing theology.[48] On the Feast of the Epiphany, 1914, Dawson officially entered the Church at St. Aloysius in Oxford. E. I. Watkin

---

[43]Dawson, "Manuscript Notes: Tradition and Inheritance" [1940s], Box 4, Folder 94, UST/CDC.

[44]Scott, *A Historian and His World,* 47.

[45]Ibid., 49.

[46]Dawson, "Why I am a Catholic," 11.

[47]Mulloy, Record of Conversation with Dawson, August 25, 1953, in Box 1, Folder 1, ND/CDAW.

[48]Dawson, Cambridge, MA, to Peter Feledick, Racine, WI, in Box 14, Folder 128, UST/CDC. In the same letter, Dawson wrote: "After my marriage, we lived for some time at the village of Wilshire, where [Burdett] was parish priest. Later on he was one of the priests at Oxford, but he finally left the Society [Jesuits] owing to ill health and became a secular priest, first as parish priest at Glasenbury and then in his last years, when his illness became more acute, he was in London where he died during the Second World War."

sponsored him, and Dawson took St. Augustine as his patron saint.[49] All of the conversations with his father, E. I. Watkin and his other friends, the writings of the Church Fathers and Doctors, as well as the examples of the saints and martyrs became a coherent and cohesive whole for Dawson as he entered the Church. The "doctrine of Sanctifying Grace" found in the New Testament and the writings of Sts. Augustine and Aquinas, Dawson admitted, "removed all my difficulties and uncertainties and carried complete conviction to my mind," he explained twelve years after his conversion. "It was no longer possible to hesitate, difficult though it was to separate myself from earlier associations and traditional ties." Equally important, Dawson "realised that the Incarnation, the Sacraments, the external order of the Church and the internal working of Sanctifying Grace were all parts of one organic unity, a living tree, whose roots are in the Divine Nature and whose fruit is the perfection of the saints."[50] Additionally, Dawson did not consider the saints as "a few highly gifted individuals." Instead, they are "the perfect manifestation of the supernatural life which exists in every individual Christian, the first fruits of that new humanity which is the world of the Church to create."[51] A man of deep convictions, Dawson saw himself not as rejecting the traditions of the Anglican Church, but instead as embracing those traditions that originally supported the Church of England, before its break from Rome in the sixteenth century. His new Roman Catholic theology, as he saw it, fulfilled rather than negated the Anglicanism of his youth.

Much of Dawson's logic in entering the Church was rigorous. In his famous early essay, "Nature and Destiny of Man," Dawson recorded ("almost precisely," as he told Maisie Ward) the thought process that culminated in his intellectual decision to convert.[52] The essay itself had found its way into print because of the enthusiasm of Maisie's brother, Leo.[53] It appeared in 1920 in a book edited by Capuchin Father Cuthbert, entitled *God and the Supernatural: A Catholic Statement of the Christian Faith*. Its authors included E. I. Watkin, Martin D'Arcy, and Father C. C. Martindale. In his own essay, Dawson described man as the *metaxy*, the "bridge" between the material and spiritual worlds. Like Bran the Blessed, man stood between two worlds, attempting to

---

[49] Scott, *A Historian and His World,* 62–65; and Gleaves Whitney, "Can Western Civilization Survive the Twenty-First Century? Some Dawsonian Considerations," paper delivered April 24, 1999, Philadelphia Society Annual Meeting, Philadelphia, PA. See also Pearce, *Literary Converts.*

[50] Dawson, "Why I am a Catholic," 11.

[51] Ibid.

[52] Maisie Ward, "The Case of Christopher Dawson," *The Catholic World,* vol. 169 (1949), 151. Dawson often referred to this essay as "my first published essay." See, for example, "Manuscript Notes: Tradition and Inheritance," in Box 4, Folder 94, UST/CDC. Two other essays, though, Christopher Dawson, "The Catholic Tradition and the Modern State," *Catholic Review* (1916), and Christopher Dawson, "Socialism, Capitalism, and the Catholic Tradition," *Universe,* April 11, 1919, had appeared earlier.

[53] Ward, "Dawson the Philosopher," 38.

act as a bridge and a balance. Only by properly ordering himself between the two extremes and demands of the physical and metaphysical can man fulfill his purpose for the "integration [of the material] in the universal order."[54] In other words, unless the physical world is sanctified by the individual, the individual—even if moved by grace—has little chance to sanctify the earth.

With the fifteenth-century Renaissance, Dawson lamented, scholars and philosophers moved away from the idea of the *metaxy*, focusing on the flesh alone. The Christian Renaissance of the Baroque period reversed this intellectual trend for a long period of time, but Charles Darwin again renewed the materialist idea of flesh alone in the *Origin of Species*.[55] Christ, ultimately, and Christ alone, Dawson believed "is the restorer of the human race, the New Man, in whom humanity has a fresh beginning and acquires a new nature."[56] Though Christ now sits at the Right Hand of the Father, the Holy Spirit—that is, the "Spirit of Christ"—working through the Sacraments and the Church, continues the work of the Incarnation of Christ throughout the remainder of time. "The Life of the Divine Trinity externalizes itself in the completed life of the Church, in humanity externally and immutably deified," Dawson wrote.[57] Charity replaces avarice, and the face of the world is renewed.[58] All things come originally from Christ, and all things must return to him. The language and power that connects man to God is Love, which Dawson defined as "man's participation in God's Will."[59] Hence, Dawson concluded, "to that end, the Church on earth moves infallibly, irresistibly. In the Sacraments, in the life of faith, in every act of spiritual will and aspiration of spiritual desire, the work of divine restoration goes ceaselessly forward. In that work is the whole hope of humanity."[60] Dawson's argument—the rigorous argument that led him to convert to Roman Catholicism—is profoundly Stoic and Augustinian. Augustine served not only as Dawson's scholarly exemplar, but also as his spiritual patron, as noted above.[61] Dawson admitted that nearly all of his ideas were "an attempt to reinterpret and reapply the Augustinian theory of history."[62] And, if Newman was Dawson's nineteenth-century counterpart, Augustine was Dawson's fifth-century counterpart. Like St. Augustine, who looked across the Mediterranean to see the Goths sack Rome, Dawson looked

---

[54]Christopher Dawson, "The Nature and Destiny of Man," in *God and the Supernatural: A Catholic Statement of the Christian Faith,* (London: Catholic Book Club, 1936), 57.

[55]Ibid., 58–9.

[56]Ibid., 69.

[57]Ibid., 84.

[58]Ibid., 70.

[59]Ibid., 76–7.

[60]Ibid., 84.

[61]C. J. McNaspy, S.J., Loyola University, New Orleans, to Dawson, Harvard, August 27, 1959, in Box 15, Folder 50, UST/CDC.

[62]Dawson, Oxford, to Professor Schlesinger, Notre Dame, IN, January 25, 1950, Box 15, Folder 124, UST/CDC.

across the English Channel, watching the new barbarians—the National Socialists, the Fascists, and the Communists—make their way into what was left of Christendom. Each of us, Dawson forcefully argued, must also act as St. Augustine did. "The only remedy is to be found in that spiritual force by which the humility of God conquers the pride of the evil one," he wrote. The majority of men will fight against the prophet or saint, and "he must be prepared to stand alone like Ezekiel and Jeremy." The world may very well shun or abuse him. Therefore, "he must take as his example St. Augustine besieged by the Vandals at Hippo, or St. Gregory preaching at Rome with the Lombards at the gates." Taking his argument from the Beatitudes, Dawson reminds us that Christ's words remain timeless. "For the true helpers of the world are the poor in spirit, the men who bear the sign of the cross on their foreheads, who refused to be overcome by the triumph of injustice and put their sole trust in the salvation of God," Dawson wrote.[63]

Dawson identified with Augustine as a man in a similar situation. Both faced barbarians, and each tried to preserve the best of the past to serve as an intellectual remnant for a Christian future. Each also embraced a common notion of the power of the imagination, the importance of the classical period, and the depravity of man. "Like St. Augustine," Frank Sheed wrote in his autobiography, "Dawson was a theologian of history. They both knew the beginning of the human race and its goal."[64]

In several important respects, though, Dawson had nothing in common with Augustine. Certainly Dawson gave far greater weight to the importance of the individual human person in shaping history than did St. Augustine. Equally important, Dawson never shared Augustine's Spartan view of aesthetics. Instead, Dawson was aesthetically a man of the Baroque.[65]

The Making of a Man of Letters

While at Trinity College, Oxford, Dawson's tutor had been the medievalist and political scientist Ernest Barker, with whom he maintained a life-long friendship. It was Barker who first introduced Dawson to medieval studies.[66] Barker had high praise for Dawson. In a letter of recommendation for his former pupil, Barker wrote, "I think he has the mind and the equipment of a philosophical historian above any other contemporary, or pupil, I have known."

---

[63]Christopher Dawson, *Religion and the Rise of Western Culture* (1950; New York: Image Books, 1991), 124.

[64]Frank Sheed, *The Church and I* (Garden City, NY: Doubleday and Co., 1974), 122. See also Scott, *A Historian and His World,* 45.

[65]This book will explore Dawson's Augustinianism in much greater depth in Interlude I.

[66]Dawson, Cambridge, MA, to Wesley Hartley, Santa Ana, CA, March 30, 1960, in Box 14, Folder 162, UST/CDC; and Wilfrid Sheed, "Introduction to Dawson," *Books on Trial* (March 1957), 296.

Further, Barker confided, though Dawson only earned a second class at Oxford in modern history, "in intellectual power, he stood alone among all the men I had ever taught. He has a subtle mind, in the deepest and finest sense of that word; he has a fine and instructive feeling for the profundities of thought; and he has followed the history of human culture, both in its material foundations and its spiritual aspirations throughout its sweep and course."[67] Dawson also held two of his other professors in high regard: Professor Firth, who led a seminar on the seventeenth century, and Edward Armstrong, a scholar of the Renaissance.[68] After earning an undergraduate degree at Oxford, Dawson studied briefly with the Swedish economist, Gustave Cassel, but returned to Oxford for graduate study in sociology and history.[69] Dawson dismissed his trip to Sweden as too short to be important, but his interest in economics certainly never waned, especially in the 1920s, as will be discussed further below. When the first world war broke out, British war officials deemed Dawson too sickly to fight, but he ably served in the civil service, aiding the war effort.

Over the next decade, Dawson read as widely and as deeply as possible, preparing for a writing career as a historian and general man of letters.[70] A voracious reader, even as a small boy, Dawson read everything he could, academic or otherwise. Much of his reading came from his uncle's vast library, a library he would one day inherit. In addition to his voluminous academic and scholarly reading, he loved Jane Austen, Henry David Thoreau, P. G. Wodehouse, Hilaire Belloc, G. K. Chesterton, H. G. Wells, R. H. Benson, Arthur Conan Doyle, and a huge selection of science fiction, historical fiction, American westerns, and English detective stories.[71] Chesterton especially influenced Dawson, as Dawson regarded him as "one of the greatest champions of Christian culture in our time."[72] Dawson appreciated Belloc's ability to write well, but believed him "very exclusive and one-sided."[73] Dawson also read a number of daily newspapers and listened to a variety of radio stations—English and foreign-language—to stay current on the world situation.[74]

A cursory examination of his notebooks from this important formative period of the early and mid-1920s—what Dawson called his "long period

---

[67]Ernest Barker, Cambridge, February 5, 1933, in Box 14, Folder 37, UST/CDC.

[68]Dawson, Cambridge, MA, to Wesley Hartley, Santa Ana, CA, March 30, 1960, in Box 14, Folder 162, UST/CDC.

[69]Dawson, Cambridge, MA, to Peter Feledick, Racine, WI, in Box 14, Folder 128, UST/CDC; Dawson resume, Box 15, Folder 29, UST/CDC; and Daniel Callahan et al., "Christopher Dawson: 12 October 1889–25 May 1970," *Harvard Theological Review*, vol. 66 (April 1973), 167.

[70]Sheed, "Introduction to Dawson," 296.

[71]Sheed, "Frank Sheed Talks with Christopher Dawson," 34; and Christina Scott, "The Meaning of the Millennium: The Ideas of Christopher Dawson," *Logos*, vol. 2 (1999), 79.

[72]Dawson to Mulloy, July 1, 1954, in Box 1, Folder 16, ND/CDAW.

[73]Dawson to Mulloy, January 18, 1958, in Box 1, Folder 16, ND/CDAW.

[74]Scott, "Meaning of the Millennium," 79.

of isolated study before I began my work"—reveals much about Dawson's reading habits. His notebooks include details from the writings of a number of important eighteenth- and nineteenth-century political and philosophical thinkers such as Friedrich Schiller (1759–1805), Johann Fichte (1762–1814), Friedrich Schelling (1775–1854), Joseph von Goerres (1776–1848), and Christian Krause (1781–1832). He also read Alfred Whitehead's *Science and the Modern World* (1926), Jan Christiaan Smut's *Holism and Evolution* (1926), and Charles E. Vaughan's *Studies in History of Political Philosophy Before and After Rousseau* (1925). Other influential writings included in his notes came from Plato's *Laws* and miscellaneous writings by Aristotle, Xenophon, Heraclitus, and Oswald Spengler. Additionally, Dawson took his notes in a variety of languages: English, French, Greek, and Latin.[75] In the same notebook, presumably after reading the above authors, Dawson concluded: "All the events of the last years have convinced me what a fragile thing civilization is and how near we are to losing the whole inheritance which our age might have acquired [sic] enjoyed." He noted that while visiting Austria in 1922, he "realized most intensely the value of the old baroque monarchies at which we used to sneer, and their infinite superiority to the sham democracies and ramshackle socialist republics which have taken their place." While the monarchies most likely were permanently dead, Dawson believed that "some new Augustan order must arise to take their place, if Europe is to survive. Christ needed Augustus as well as John the Baptist, and so it is in . . . our days with the Age of the Spirit."[76] The world, according to Dawson, had clearly changed with the Great War. In his vast reading during his preparation period, he was searching for the great divide, that which broke the ancient and medieval worlds from the modern one.

His reading and study paid off, as all of Dawson's numerous writings carry with them a feeling of extreme depth, historical insight, and wisdom. Even his most ardent critic never failed to recognize this. Dawson originally planned to write a massive and comprehensive five-volume world history of culture and religion. *Progress and Religion* (1929), Dawson's first book for the new Catholic publisher, Sheed and Ward, would have served as the theoretical introduction to the five volumes. His first published book, *The Age of the Gods* (1928), would have served as the first volume. The series would then have consisted of Vol. 2, *The Rise of World Religions*; Vol. 3, *The Making of Europe*; Vol. 4, *Medieval Religion*; and Vol. 5, *The Gods of Revolution*.[77] Dawson hoped

---

[75]Dawson, "Notebook 18," dated 1922–25, in Box 9, Folder 18, UST/CDC.

[76]Ibid. The strike-out is in the original.

[77]On Dawson's projected five-volume history, see E. I. Watkin, "Tribute to Christopher Dawson," *Tablet* (1969), 974; and Scott, *A Historian and His World,* 82–83. The introduction and four of the five versions came out in various forms during or immediately after Dawson's life. On the unpublished second volume, *The Rise of World Religions*, see Clement Anthony, "The Unpublished Second Volume," *Dawson Newsletter* (Spring 1990), 14–16.

to call the impressive project *The Life of Civilizations*.[78] Respectively, these books would have dealt with primitive man; the Chinese, Mediterranean, and Indian classical worlds; the early Middle Ages; the High and Late Middles Ages; and, finally, the rise of liberalism and revolution.

As it turned out, Dawson never published this as *The Life of Civilizations*. Instead, he published bits of it in various forms. Dawson seems to have addressed his own failure in 1954 in a review article for the *Tablet*. "Under the circumstances," he explained, "the history of a single civilization seems the most we can hope to achieve."[79] Even at the time he was writing most vigorously, Dawson believed that too little was known about non-European cultures for any one person or any group of dedicated scholars to tackle a real and comprehensive world history. Too many languages needed to be learned, and too many religions as well as too many cultural developments needed to be comprehended. Certainly the task proved impossible for Dawson. His close friend, E. I. Watkin, for one, expressed disappointment in Dawson's failure to complete the study. Such a comprehensive history, Watkin believed, would have given considerable academic credibility to Catholicism.[80]

Watkin's frustration with the publishing ventures of his friend raises an interesting question. Why did Dawson publish what he did, when he did? There is no doubt that Dawson was astonishingly prolific in his writing. As mentioned earlier, he published over twenty books, and hundreds of articles and individual chapters for various works. Even with his astounding literary output, his letters to his publisher Frank Sheed are filled with ideas for new books he wished to write but never did. Dawson proposed a sequel to *The Making of Europe*; another entitled *Religion in the Age of Revolt* (which probably became, at least in part, his posthumous *The Gods of Revolution*); a book entitled *European Revolution* (which also became a part of his posthumous *The Gods of Revolution*); a book outlining and analyzing the historical development of the common law and monarchical constitutionalism, entitled *English Tradition*; a biography of St. Paul; a full autobiography; a history of the Roman Catholic Church, simply entitled *The Church of Rome*; a comprehensive anthropological and theological book defining the differences between cultures and civilizations called *The Growth of Civilization*; and, finally, a book exploring the differences between Renaissance, secular, and Christian

---

[78] Scott, *A Historian and His World*, 82. Dawson's project significantly resembles Eric Voegelin's uncompleted five-volume *Order and History*. Voegelin was a historian and philosopher like Dawson. Unlike Dawson, though, Voegelin began life as a devout Lutheran but ended as what he called a "pre-Nicean Christian." On the differences in the importance of religion for the two men, see John Mulloy, "The Limitations of Eric Voegelin," in his *Christianity and the Challenge of History* (Front Royal, VA: Christendom Press, 1995), 269–75.

[79] Christopher Dawson, "Ages of Change: A Study of the European Inheritance," *Tablet* (May 22, 1954), 489.

[80] Watkin, "Tribute," 974.

humanism, entitled *The Age of Humanism*.[81] Sheed encouraged Dawson all he could, but as will be seen in the following chapters, Sheed experienced considerable frustration with Dawson's seeming inability to finish all that he started. Ultimately, of course, the decision of what to write and what not to write was Dawson's. But family, career, personal depression, and, by the end of his life, the demands of the market, all affected what Dawson wrote and published.

Sheed was not alone in attempting to prod Dawson to produce still more. Publisher Harcourt Brace, for example, asked Dawson to write a comprehensive western history text to be marketed to American Catholic colleges for introductory western civilization core classes.[82] An associate editor for Harcourt Brace estimated that the company could sell "between 20,000 and 35,000 of that total enrollment [at all Catholic colleges] of its first year of sale." Obviously the Catholic education market was blossoming.[83] Dawson's creativity and writing style alone, the editor at Harcourt Brace assured Dawson, would quickly allow the book to dominate the market. Dawson's reputation was such that anything he produced would "significantly supplant much of the market," as the current leader in the field was "comprehensive and dull." Such success in the Catholic market might open up the secular colleges as well.[84] While Harcourt Brace was deciding whether the Dawson text should appear as a 500-page paperback supplement to a western civilization course or as a full-blown 1,000 page "factual and interpretive text, complete with illustrations and factual data," the company also indicated its willingness—at Dawson's request—to publish a comprehensive history of the Roman Catholic Church and an interpretative book on the French Revolution.[85] Unfortunately, none of the three books ever appeared under Harcourt Brace. Dawson, however, left a title list of his twenty-two proposed chapters, many of which became the chapters of his last three manuscripts, derived from his Harvard lectures: *The Formation of Christendom*, the *Dividing of Christendom*, and the as-yet unpublished *Return to Christian Unity*.[86]

Despite the sheer volume of Dawson's output, he remained—to an astonishing degree—consistent in his ideas, thoughts, and arguments through-

---

[81] See various Dawson and Frank Sheed letters, in Box 11, Folders 1–25, UST/CDC; Tom Burns, London, to Dawson, Hartlington Hall, Skipton, Yorks, April 10, 1935, in Box 14, Folder 61, UST/CDC; and E. O. James, Oxford, to Dawson, January 24, 1962, in Box 15, Folder 6, UST/CDC. For a description of *The Growth of Civilization*, including the chapter list, see Dawson to Mulloy, July 10, 1954, in Box 1, Folder 15, ND/CDAW.

[82] Dawson, Cambridge, MA, to Mulloy, in Box 1, Folder 12, ND/CDAW.

[83] William B. Goodman, New York, to Dawson, Harvard, October 7, 1960, in Box 14, Folder 159, UST/CDC; and Dawson, Harvard, to Mulloy, September 28, 1960, in Folder 12, ND/CDAW.

[84] William B. Goodman, New York, to Dawson, Harvard, October 17, 1960, in Box 14, Folder 159, UST/CDC.

[85] William A. Pullin, New York, to Dawson, Harvard, December 15, 1960, in Box 14, Folder 159, UST/CDC.

[86] Dawson, "Harcourt Brace Book," ca. 1960, in Box 14, Folder 159, UST/CDC.

out the entirety of his writing career. He had already experienced a sort of epiphany at the Ara Coeli on Easter 1909, as a young man of twenty. It was then that he had envisioned a life dedicated to writing a history of culture. The remainder of his life, then, served as the fulfillment of the decision made in Italy. His ideas continued to evolve, but he certainly never experienced another such epiphany, intellectually or spiritually. Though Dawson considered "The Nature and Destiny of Man" his first significant publication, he published his first article, "Catholic Tradition and the Modern State," in 1916, when he was just 26. It was written only seven years after his intellectual breakthrough.

What is remarkable about this first publication is that Dawson outlines his entire theory of western history in this short article. The article, to be sure, is not Dawson's best. It is hastily written, full of giant leaps of intellect, and full of passion. It is Dawson as a young man, raw, pure, and angry. "It is not liberty, but power which is the true note of our modern civilisation," Dawson wrote in the venerable *Catholic Review*. "Man has gained in his control over Nature, but he has lost the control over his own individual life."[87] The present war was dramatically increasing the power of the state, and it, in turn, was turning the individual human person into nothing but a cog for its vast machine. "An official touches the handle of a great machine," Dawson lamented, "and from every corner of an empire millions of men move automatically, with an utter suppression of their own individualities, to the fulfillment of one gigantic task—a task that will bring wounds and death to millions, suffering and privation to all."[88]

Such changes in the twentieth century stemmed, first and foremost, from self-conscious changes of man in his relationship to God that began with the humanism of the Renaissance, a movement that, at least in 1916, Dawson regretted. The new relationship, though, was nothing more than the opening of Pandora's Box. It reintroduced the paganism that the Church had attempted to sanctify or suppress since the earliest moments of its history. The Reformation, then, in reacting against the new paganism, "fashioned a new Christianity—a transition religion—founded on private judgment and a new legalism." The Enlightenment also precipitated "a new outburst of Humanism of a definitely anti-Christian kind." Led by men such as Jeremy Bentham and, later, James and John Stuart Mill, it adopted the precepts and embraced the name of utility, making the individual person merely a means to an end. It also opened the way for the "sentimental naturalism" of Jean-Jacques Rousseau and the abhorrently violent French Revolution, ultimately attenuated by Catholic uprisings of "the Basques and the Tyrolese who were the real enemies of the new [utilitarian] spirit."

---

[87] Dawson, "Catholic Tradition and the Modern State," 24.
[88] Ibid., 25.

Finally, and perhaps most devastating for the young and anxious Dawson, English liberalism paved the way for industrialization. Industrial "development went on with the same reckless waste of human material that had marked Roman capitalism in the Iron Age of the Republic, and the mill towns and mining villages in England" had become "a byword through Europe for squalor and misery." Protestantism and liberalism tied so closely together that the former "tended more and more to make men conscientious members of the existing society—good citizens—and the supernatural character of religion gradually disappeared." Englishmen after the Reformation became, in Augustinian language, citizens of the City of Man rather than citizens of the City of God. Consequently, the works of men and the "spirit of Humanism"—whether in science or in the market—had, according to Dawson, almost become its own religion, with "the worship of success and of money, which last acquires an almost sacramental importance."[89]

Just as the influence and pressures of World War I are obvious in Dawson's first article, nothing influenced him and his decisions on what to write more than contemporary world events. Considering the tumults of his age, it is no small feat that Dawson was able to dedicate himself so unswervingly to the task of writing a comprehensive history of Christian culture. The rise of communism, the rise of fascism, World War I, World War II, and the advent of the Cold War are just five of the most important world-shaking events which occurred during Dawson's writing career. "I think you must distinguish between my historical and sociological books" and those "which were written in defense of the Catholic point of view in times of political crisis—such as *Religion and the Modern State*; *Beyond Politics*; *The Judgment of the Nations*; and many of the essays in *Enquiries*," Dawson explained in a personal letter to John Mulloy in 1953. The two sets of Gifford Lectures, *Religion and Culture* and *Religion and the Rise of Western Culture*, Dawson continued, "give the best general view of my ideas, but I also reckon *Progress and Religion* and *Understanding Europe* among my more important books and there is a good deal in *The Judgment of Nations* which I have not said elsewhere and which seem to me important."[90]

Dawson's writing can be broken into three phases, each representing a reaction to the moment's *zeitgeist*. Each phase, though, should be considered an evolution from the previous phase, never a break, never a repetition, and never an annihilation of what came before it. The first phase, temporally encompassed by the 1920s and the very early 1930s, includes his major works, the *Age of the Gods*, *Progress and Religion*, and *Enquiries into Religion and Culture*. Indebted to the sociological work of the LePlay House, each work in its own way attempted to rediscover the meaning and significance of culture in

---

[89]Ibid., 27–34.
[90]Dawson, Dorset, England, to Mulloy, February 22, 1953, in Box 1, Folder 4, ND/CDAW.

the face of post-war modernism. A self-taught counter-revolutionary French sociologist, Frederic LePlay had emphasized the necessity of understanding "work, place, and folk" in attempting to comprehend a people and its culture.[91] His work influenced late nineteenth-century Catholic social thought, and the LePlay House, located on Belgrave Road in Westminster, promoted his ideas. It also promoted Dawson and encouraged him to publish his burgeoning ideas. "The war and the peace, Communism and Fascism, Americanisation and Orientalism, the passing of Nordic man and the decline of Latin culture, Dadaism and cubism, the cinema and the negroid-American dance, Miss Gertrude Stein and Mr. Michael Arlen have all in turn been denounced as the causes or symptoms of this collapse" of western civilization, Dawson wrote in the late 1920s. "Only the most robust optimist can deny that a new barbarism, manifold and incoherent, is threatening not only the material order which was the work of the last century, but the whole intellectual and spiritual tradition on which Western culture has been based."[92] One may date the second phase from 1930, beginning with the publication of Dawson's first extensive analysis of politics and ideology, "Christianity and Sex," and ending in 1942, with the publication of *The Judgment of the Nations*, a call to nations to reclaim their Christian purpose and to fight the war and secure the peace on principles of human dignity and justice. In these twelve years, bolstered by the support of the *Order* men—a group centered around Tom Burns in Chelsea, London, and enthralled with Dawson's writings and thoughts— Dawson attempted to challenge the deadly ideologies spreading throughout the world.

The final phase began in 1948 with the publication of *Religion and Culture*, the first of the published Gifford Lectures, and ended with Dawson's death in 1970. While still dealing with ideological conflicts, this phase witnessed a return to the themes of the first phase, an even more in-depth exploration of the meaning and significance of history and culture. In the final phase of his writing career, Dawson propagated a program by which education could reclaim Christian Culture.

Despite considerable confidence in his ability to analyze the events around him, as well as the extensive means to communicate his ideas, Dawson was frustrated with his publishing efforts throughout most of his life. In a conversation with his close friend, the poet David Jones, Dawson complained, "I don't care what that wretched dean said about me—it's the kind of people

---

[91] Vivien M. Palmer, "Impressions of Sociology in Great Britain," *American Journal of Sociology*, vol. 32 (March 1927), 759; and *Critics of the Enlightenment: Readings in the French Counter-Revolutionary Tradition*, ed. and trans. Christopher Blum (Wilmington, DE: ISI Books, 2004), xxxv–xl.

[92] Christopher Dawson, *Enquiries into Religion and Culture* (London: Sheed and Ward, 1933), 42.

who read the *Daily Mirror* I would like to be read by."[93] He rarely sought academic appointments, as he did not want the pressure of academic publishing. Instead, he believed that his writing should be directed toward the well-educated, intellectually curious, non-academic public. "It is to this middle public that I have always directed my own work," Dawson admitted. "In fact I deliberately renounced any attempt to pursue research in order to cultivate this field which seems to me to be the area in which vital decisions will be reached."[94] In this vein, then, Dawson sought to publish his work wherever possible, rarely seeking to make a profit from his writing. "An agent inevitably thinks in terms of dollars, whereas what I am concerned about is teaching the right audience," Dawson explained, "and often this means publishing in small reviews that do not pay well."[95] Still, it seemed that he was not being read by the proper audience, as he complained in 1954 that "Catholics still seem extraordinarily vague about what they mean by culture."[96]

The lack of an academic appointment, though, necessitated the absence of an academic community and its concomitant moral, spiritual, and financial support. This proved the most frustrating part of Dawson's writing career, as he craved intellectual discussion and interaction. Equally important, his entire belief system informed him that while the individual human person, specifically the saint, did change history for the better, he did so as a part of—and within—much larger communities. At one level, those communities of the Church are rooted in a specific time, space, and culture. At another level, the most important community transcends time and space, calling all baptized souls as equals back to the One. Dawson knew he held full membership in the latter community.

One might also use Thomistic terms, labeling these respective communities accidental and essential. It was the former, the accidental communities, that seemed, often in his life, to elude and frustrate him. In a letter to Maisie Ward, Dawson confided that he wrote best when he felt himself a part of a purposeful community. "I have always felt the need of some common intellectual work for the church," Dawson wrote. "First of all we had *Essays in Order*, and later on the Sword of the Spirit which, though not exactly intellectual, performed the same function for me."[97] Indeed, looking back over Dawson's publishing history, he published his most and his best works when involved in some kind of purposeful community of friends and allies.

His earliest works appeared, for example, when he was both lecturing at Exeter and Liverpool and involved with Tom Burns and the many members

---

[93] Dawson quoted in Scott, *A Historian and His World,* 128.

[94] Dawson, Devon, to Mulloy, May 17, 1954, in Box 1, Folder 4, ND/CDAW; and Dawson, "Memorandum," dated June 1955, in Box 1, Folder 15, ND/CDAW.

[95] Dawson, Boars Hill, to Mulloy, October 3, 1953, in Box 1, Folder 4, ND/CDAW.

[96] Dawson to Mulloy, July 10, 1954, in Box 1, Folder 15, ND/CDAW.

[97] Dawson to Maisie Ward, October 13, 1953, in Box 11, Folder 18, UST/CDC.

of the *Order* crowd. His most interesting work, *The Judgment of the Nations*, was written when Dawson was Vice President of the Sword of the Spirit, the World War II ecumenical movement that attempted to force Americans and the British to fight the Germans on Christian grounds. The delivery of the prestigious Gifford Lectures in Scotland resulted in the publication of two of Dawson's best-known works, *Religion and Culture* and *Religion and the Rise of Western Culture*. During his four short years at Harvard, Dawson wrote five of his most important works. The "lack of personal and intellectual contacts," he continued in his letter to Maisie, "is an even more serious obstacle to original historical work. You see when I produced *The Age of the Gods* and *The Making of Europe* I had a job which gave one the necessary minimum of intellectual contacts and I had personal contacts with the Catholic world also." In the absence of such groups and support, Dawson continued, original research and writing proved nearly impossible. "One must have opportunities for the discussion and exchange of ideas, etc." he continued. "Otherwise my mind does not function freely.[98]

Dawson also believed that his work, what he often called metahistorical, offering a Stoic and Augustinian viewpoint through the lens of history, anthropology, philosophy, and sociology, was unique and hindered his success in the narrow fields of academia. "The difficulty of my job is that it has no recognised professional cadre, like art or poetry," Dawson wrote in the late 1930s. "One sees it clearly with Burke who was a dismal failure as a politician and who could never have been a professor of political philosophy, but whose work was none the less important, in spite of failing to conform to established categories."[99]

At times, though, Dawson recognized the advantage to what he called "Ploughing a Lone Furrow." When accepting the Christian Culture Award in 1951, he told his audience that as a single uninstitutionalized scholar, he could pursue humanistic studies, while the universities embraced the specializations and dangerous compartmentalizations inherent to modernity. "The old domination of classical humanism has passed away, and nothing has taken its place except the scientific specialisms which do not provide a complete intellectual education, but rather tend to disintegrate into technologies," he told his audience. Real education—that is a liberal education—is essential to the well-formed soul and intellect, but a "scientific specialist or a technologist who has nothing but his specialty is not an educated person." Because he knows only technical things, Dawson argued, he "tends to become merely an

---

[98]Ibid.

[99]Dawson to Harmon Grisewood, [1938 or 1939], in Box 2, Folder 2.5, Harmon Grisewood Collection, Georgetown University Archives, Georgetown, D.C. [hereafter GU/Grisewood].

instrument of the industrialist or the bureaucrat, a worker ant in an insect society."[100]

Ironically, for much of his life, the lone individual, Dawson, carried on the tradition of temporal and eternal communities. Certainly, Dawson had very little support from academic institutions. He served as a lecturer at Exeter from 1930–36 and at Liverpool University in 1934, two terms as the Gifford Lecturer at Edinburgh University, the 1946–1947 and 1947–1948 school years, and as the first Chauncey Stillman Chair of Roman Catholic Studies at Harvard University, 1958–1962.[101]

Dawson's Roman Catholicism, which had served him so well intellectually and spiritually, proved an additional hindrance prior to the second world war, as it had prevented him from obtaining a full-time academic position in England. When he applied for a full-time position at the University of Leeds, the blatantly anti-Catholic Dean Inge assured him, "I can think of no one more fitted than yourself to be a professor of the history and philosophy of religion. Your deep learning, your originality and lucidity of mind, and your power of making your subject interesting, seem to make it certain that you would have an enthusiastic following at Leeds." Still, Dawson's application would encounter great opposition because of his religion. "The one drawback is of course your religion. My distrust of the good faith of Roman Catholic scholars is almost as great as Dr Coulton's; but honestly I believe that you are quite straight."[102] Inge's consolation only went so far, and after an agonizing two-month debate, Leeds turned Dawson down because of his Roman Catholicism.[103] Most likely because of the influence of the prominent Inge, Dawson seems to have received the support of the local academic community. The opposition to his appointment came from an unexpected quarter. At the last moment, the local Anglican bishop intervened, claiming that Dawson's faith was antithetical to English culture and learning. The Anglicans, Dawson seethed, have "much the same attitude to Catholics as the Nazis have to the Jews!"[104]

His time residing just outside of Oxford in Boar's Hill in the 1930s, 1940s, and early 1950s only caused Dawson more spiritual and intellectual pain. When the London papers failed to review Dawson's 1952 book, *Understanding Europe,* he complained that "in this as in so much else the publicity one gets depends on the group you belong to, and the unorganized individual does not get a hearing."[105] In a conversation with John Mulloy, an American admirer

---

[100]Christopher Dawson, "Ploughing a Lone Furrow," in *Christianity and Culture,* J. Stanley Murphy, ed. (Baltimore, MD: Helicon, 1960), 18.

[101]J. J. Mulloy, Part II of "Christopher Dawson, 1889–1970," 443.

[102]W. R. Inge, King's College, Cambridge, to Dawson, [n.d.], Box 15, Folder 29, "Leeds University," UST/CDC.

[103]Scott, *A Historian and His World,* 110–11.

[104]Ibid., 111.

[105]Dawson, Oxford, to Harman Grisewood, June 11, 1952, in Box 2, Folder 2.2, GU/Grisewood.

of Dawson's, Dawson's wife Valery confided "that it was not well for him to be too much alone (there is that awful loneliness, is the manner in which she referred to life at Boar's Hill), and that she believed he should have more interest and contact with those interested in his work."[106] Being in Oxford and surrounded by academics only intensified Dawson's loneliness, as the Oxford dons treated his work with "comparative neglect" and he met with few of them socially or intellectually.[107] Even his own children provided little intellectual support. After all, there seemed "no prospect of the tradition of scholarship being carried on in the next generation, as none of his children are inclined in that direction, and he has only one unmarried sister in the direct line of the family."[108] As it turned out, one of Dawson's daughters, Juliana, became a nun and the other, Christina, became his biographer. His son, Philip, became a book dealer.

Dawson was also intensely shy and, often, personally insecure. This shyness, oddly enough, was probably most felt when he was with his friends, allies, and social equals. In a very pointed letter to Dawson in 1939, publisher Frank Sheed tried to explain to Dawson why he had few friends and felt isolated.

> That leaves the problem why you have not more Catholic contacts, which is part of the larger question. Why are you not in contact with more people of all kinds? Please don't be angry with me for what I am going to say. I don't say it is your fault, but I think the *cause* is mainly in you. And this primarily because of your health, for obviously it ties you down most maddeningly. One gets asked to do things and to meet people simply by being round where people are, and I know how difficult this is for you.[109]

Certainly, as Sheed noted, Dawson was rarely in good health. In fact, it is very difficult to find a letter to him in which the correspondent did not wish Dawson better health or one of Dawson's in which he did not complain about his health problems. Dawson seemed to be ill of one thing—psychologically and physically—or another throughout most of his adult life. One cannot, however, limit Dawson's social problems solely to his health. Though never openly ideological in his scholarship, Dawson could, at times, allow strict nuances in thought to divide him from his friends and his allies, who might slightly disagree on a minor point, here or there. "It seems to me that you shrink from meeting people with those views you are not fully in sympathy," Sheed continued. "Whereas one makes wide contacts only by taking peo-

---

[106]Mulloy, Conversation with Dawson, August 29, 1953, in Box 1, Folder 1, ND/CDAW.
[107]Ibid.
[108]Mulloy, Conversation with Dawson, September 1, 1953, in Box 1, Folder 2, ND/CDAW.
[109]Sheed, London, to Dawson, November 2, 1939, in Box 11, Folder 5, "Frank Sheed 1939," UST/CDC.

ple as they come. One meets everybody, likes some, is bored stiff by others, absolutely loathes a few—and so bit by bit one makes one's own circle."[110]

In a private letter written in 1989, several years after writing her father's biography, Christina Scott admitted that Sheed and Dawson had a strange relationship. "My father and Frank had a love-hate relationship and they needed each other in a way as sparring partners!" she wrote. "My father would ring him up at 6 a.m. after a sleepless night to talk about the sales of his books and perhaps no other publisher would have put up with that."[111]

None of this should suggest that Dawson did not have friends. He experienced numerous deep and profound friendships, mostly with writers, publishers, and editors. Several of his closest friendships were with Bernard Wall, Barbara Ward, E. I. Watkin, David Jones, Harmon Grisewood, and Tom Burns, just to name an important few. Despite his often intense loneliness, he also had a loving relationship with his wife and children. Though he belonged to several social groups, as will be discussed below, he preferred to meet his friends socially one on one, rather than in large groups. His life, as Sheed wrote in his autobiography, was almost completely the life of the mind. "He lived more wholly in the mind than anyone I ever met," judged Sheed.[112] When Dawson encountered another, he often did so mind to mind, despite an intensely held spirituality.

His shyness and anxiety extended to other areas as well. Importantly, for a writer who wanted to publicize his works, he believed himself a poor lecturer. To one invitation from Exeter in 1942, Dawson responded, not atypically, "I am very sorry that I cannot accept, but I am not a public speaker and rarely attempt it."[113] Sometimes shyness attacked Dawson so strongly that he would have his wife "read his lecture for him."[114] He also feared that many Catholics outside of his own limited social circles opposed him, his ideas, and his works. "I do feel there has been a distinctly unfriendly influence at work somewhere among Catholics with regard to my work," he wrote to Grisewood, "and I do not see how it can have been Sheed since it is against his obvious financial interests to interfere with my work."[115] Additionally, he worried and complained incessantly—but incorrectly—that the laity as well as

---

[110]Ibid.

[111]Christina Scott, London, to Harmon Grisewood, July 28, 1989, in Box 2, Folder 2.7, GU/Grisewood.

[112]Sheed, *The Church and I*, 124.

[113]Dawson, Oxford, to Rev. Reginald Sparrow, November 16, 1942, in Box 14, Folder 2, Dawson Collection, General Correspondence, 1940–1949, UST/CDC.

[114]Anne Freemantle, "Christopher Dawson Comes to Harvard," *Catholic Digest*, vol. 23 (1959), 51.

[115]Christopher Dawson to Harmon Grisewood, October [late 1930s] in Box 2, Folder 2.5, GU/Grisewood.

the institution of the Church itself failed to recognize his achievements.[116] "I move about among Catholics and I can say that I have never heard one word of criticism or dislike uttered about you by anyone—there is no other Catholic writer of whom I could say this," Sheed wrote to Dawson, attempting to calm his fears. "There is nothing but admiration—more unmixed in regard to you than to any other man in the intellectual world," Sheed continued. "Literally you only have to choose your paper—and there you will have a channel for anything you wish to write."[117]

But, even with the assurances of Sheed and the truth of Sheed's claims that he could publish with any Catholic periodical, Dawson never believed he was doing enough, or being effective enough in his writing and publicizing of ideas. When sending G. K. Chesterton a copy of his *Making of Europe* in 1932, Dawson thanked Chesterton for the "Ballad of the White Horse," but then wrote, "Unfortunately I am afraid that my book is in danger of falling between two stools—being too popular for the academic public and too abstruse for the general reader."[118] Perhaps these many insecurities drove him to write more and better. Tom Burns, his friend in the Chelsea circle, discussed in the next chapter, remembered each of Dawson's books as nothing less than a birthing struggle. "One had to play midwife to Christopher's books as they neared the end of their gestation. This involved trips to Devon," Burns complained, "giving encouragement and psychological energy which left one quite drained."[119] Sheed's letters reveal as much as those of Burns. Indeed, to read Sheed's letters to Maisie explaining the struggles with Dawson over getting a book ready for publication, one gets the impression that Sheed should at least get co-author status on many of Dawson's books.

The sheer amount of energy—anxious, grace-filled, or otherwise—that Dawson possessed often kept him up late into the night. He seemed to have suffered from chronic insomnia. "Just heard Kit [Dawson] put out his electric light. Poor Kit never sleeps without Sedormid & Co. [a sleep aid] and then hardly at all," his friend David Jones reported. "Even I seem a regular bruiser wid a fine swagger on me and a pipe in the hat of me compared with his health. I do wish he could be made well, he is so nice."[120] One daughter reported that Dawson's "active mind could take no rest."[121] There is no doubt as to the extensive activity of his mind. To write that it was highly gifted is trite

---

[116]Tom Burns, *The Use of Memory: Publishing and Further Pursuits* (London: Sheed and Ward, 1993), 49.

[117]Sheed, London, to Dawson, November 2, 1939, in Box 11, Folder 5, "Frank Sheed 1939," UST/CDC.

[118]Christopher Dawson, "Letter to G. K. Chesterton, June 1, 1932," *Chesterton Review*, vol. 9 (1983), 136.

[119]Burns, *Use of Memory*, 49.

[120]*Dai Greatcoat: A Self-Portrait of David Jones in His Letters*, René Hague, ed. (London: Faber and Faber, 1980), 73.

[121]Scott, *A Historian and His World*, 42.

and understated. "I won't say he knew everything," Frank Sheed conceded, "but there was nothing you could count on his not knowing."[122] His American patron, Charles Chauncey Stillman, believed that "Dawson's knowledge was the most encyclopaedic" he had "ever encountered" and understood Dawson to have a photographic memory.[123]

One of Dawson's most treasured possessions was the library he inherited from his uncle and then continued to build on his own. "The practice of having volumes—and such splendid ones—in every room is, I think, an altogether wonderful idea: one not only has the world of learning at one's fingertips, but at one's elbows, coat tails, and collar button," a visitor to the Dawson home wrote in 1954. "It is an old and hackneyed idea to have a library in one's house; it is a new and rewarding idea to have a house in one's library."[124] C. J. McNaspy, a Jesuit who had traveled to Oxford in the late 1940s and studied under Dawson, recalled that his home in Devonshire was "a living library, with tens of thousands of volumes—old and new—on all phases of religion, anthropology, sociology, ethnology."

Even more impressive to the young Jesuit, Dawson "seemed never to forget anything he read."[125] On their first encounter, October 29, 1947, McNaspy was attending a lecture and discovered the insatiable curiosity of Dawson, who had never been to the United States, but knew every nuance of its history. At the end of the lecture, McNaspy approached Dawson with some trepidation. "Oh, you're from Louisiana," Dawson said to the young priest. "Good. I've been wondering why it was that the see of the diocese moved from Natchitoches to Alexandria. Can you tell me?" Dawson asked. To which, McNaspy "gulped, muttered something," and then "admitted I didn't know, but thought it might be because Alexandria had become the larger city."[126]

Maisie Ward wrote: "From Chinese dynasties to American Indians, from prehistory to the Oxford Movement, from Virgil to the latest novel or even 'Western', Christopher can talk of anything."[127] When he did speak, Ward noted, one could publish his soliloquies exactly as they were delivered.[128] To his contemporaries, he seemed to have read anything and everything. David Jones visited Dawson, whom he called "Tiger," in the summer of 1942. "He

---

[122]Sheed, *The Church and I,* 123.

[123]Chauncey Stillman, "Christopher Dawson: Recollections from America," in *The Dynamic of Christian Character: Essays on Dawsonian Themes,* Peter J. Cataldo, ed. (Lanham, MD: University Press of America, 1983), 221.

[124]John L. Maddux, London, to Christopher and Valery Dawson, October 28, 1954, in Box 15, Folder 40, UST/CDC.

[125]C. J. McNaspy, "Christopher Dawson: In Memoriam," *America,* vol. 122 (June 13, 1970), 634.

[126]C. J. McNaspy, "Snippets from an Oxford Diary," *New Orleans Review,* vol. 6 (1979), 142. Impressed with McNaspy, Dawson, through the head of Campion Hall, asked him to be a student of his.

[127]Ward, *Unfinished Business,* 117.

[128]Ibid. This is true of many of his letters as well.

was funny in his own way. A bit severe and frightening in the way deep learning is apt to be," Jones reported. "What's he not read?"[129] Tom Burns remembered Dawson's study in Hartlington Hall in Yorkshire, the home he inherited from his father. "I can only remember cavernous cold rooms and a library where Christopher would sit most of the time in a high-backed armchair with books all round, knee-deep," Burns recalled. "The only light in the place was his wife Valery, tall and beautiful with unaffected charm. She ministered to husband, family and their guest with an easy devotion and would slip in and out of the pervading gloom at unexpected moments."[130] Dawson's poor skills in lecturing may have helped inspire his prolific literary output, as Dawson could also "reel off some twenty pages in one sitting," when writing.[131]

Anyone who met Dawson remembered the intensity of one-on-one conversation with him. He could bring out the best and worst in others. Maisie Ward remembered how powerfully a conversation with Dawson could affect those on the receiving end: "I have some delightful memories, especially of our visit to you in Yorkshire, when Frank, still full of conversational excitement had a road accident on the way back!"[132] Burns noted in his autobiography how Dawson disarmingly assumed "that one was as familiar with the piles of books that enveloped him as he was himself: an assortment ranging from St. Jerome to James Joyce."[133] The recipient gained much in a conversation with Dawson. David Jones said, "Other learned men make you feel ignorant, but Dawson made you realize that you knew more than you suspected."[134] On long walks with friends, Dawson pointed "out from his encyclopedic, finger-tip knowledge spots of prehistoric and historic interest," Father McNaspy wrote. "A walk with him was worth volumes."[135]

---

[129]Hague, *Dai Greatcoat,* 119–20.

[130]Burns, *Use of Memory,* 48.

[131]Claude Locas, "Afterthoughts of a Long Ago Dissertation on Christopher Dawson," *The Christopher Dawson Centre of Christian Culture Newsletter,* vol. 3 (July 2000). Dawson, though, considered himself a "slow writer at the best of times." See Dawson to Mulloy, July 10, 1954, in Box 1, Folder 15, ND/CDAW.

[132]Maisie Ward, New York, to Dawson, Harvard, 1961, Box 11, Folder 25, UST/CDC.

[133]Burns, *Use of Memory,* 48.

[134]Quoted in Pearce, *Literary Converts,* 355.

[135]McNaspy, "In Memoriam," 634.

Chapter 2

Little Platoons

1920–1930

DESPITE HIS PERSONAL INSECURITIES IN SOCIAL RELATIONS, DAWSON WORKED with others in a variety of small groups and in associations of friends, beginning in the early 1920s. One-on-one discussion or small-group discussion invigorated Dawson. Such interaction not only stimulated his own thought processes, but it also gave him a means by which to explore—in community—the various ideas he had developed while reading and researching on his own. Further, he believed group interaction necessary to provide a truly "catholic" experience of scholarship and the intellectual life. God desired community, not radical individualism, Dawson argued. Just as the Church—itself the Body of Christ—went forth into the world as community, so must its citizens. As Dawson saw it, God proved this in the scriptural passages found in St. Matthew's Gospel, known simply as the "Great Commission," to go forth two by two and preach the gospel. This need for community proved as true in the intellectual endeavors of the Church as it did in her specific liturgical endeavors.

LePlay House

The LePlay House of London offered Dawson his first post-Oxford membership in an intellectual group. Indeed, it proved to be importantly the first of many such groups. Frederic LePlay (1806–1882) had been a significant French counter-revolutionary sociologist, writing in the tradition of Edmund Burke, Joseph de Maistre, and Alexis de Tocqueville. Though a mining engineer by training and education, he turned his considerable intellect to the study of family, peasant life, and folk culture after the failed Revolution of 1830. A convinced agrarian, especially after traveling throughout Europe and interviewing numerous families, LePlay concluded that only private, familial ownership of small farms and homesteads could provide the necessary stability for a functioning and progressing society. His three famous factors in sociological study were: "work, place, and folk."[1] Though an agnostic most of his life, LePlay converted to Roman Catholicism just prior to his death, and his work indirectly influenced Pope Leo in the writing of his famous encyclical, *Rerum Novarum*.[2]

In the spring of 1920, English sociologist and philanthropist Victor Branford founded the LePlay House, dedicating it to the memory of LePlay and to furthering the pioneering work the French sociologist had begun.[3] Other prominent scholars and public intellectuals involved were Alexander Farquharson, who co-authored several important articles with Dawson, the American social critic Lewis Mumford, and the Scottish biologist Patrick Geddes. The group published the journal *Sociological Review* and hosted the meetings of the Sociological Society.[4] Dawson admired LePlay's writings, especially his six-volume *Les Ouvriers Europeans*. Indeed, toward the end of his own career, Dawson considered LePlay "one of the most original Catholic sociologists of the nineteenth century."[5] For Dawson, LePlay "shows how the different economic occupations and the natural environment influence the form of the family and hence the culture."[6]

Dawson credited his connection with the LePlay House as vital to his early writing and teaching career.[7] The friendships which developed through the group—especially Dawson's friendship with Victor Branford and Lewis Mumford—"encouraged me to begin writing." It also gave him connections to Exeter.[8] Most of Dawson's earliest writings appeared in the *Sociological Review* in the 1920s, and he continued to write for the journal through the first half of the 1930s. His first essay, "The Passing of Industrialism," appeared in 1920 and was reprinted in his 1933 Sheed and Ward collection, *Enquiries into Religion and Culture*. In this article Dawson continued the rather biting analysis begun in his first article, "Catholic Tradition and the Modern State," described in the previous chapter. Nineteenth-century England believed industrialization the "natural consequence of the freedom of society and trade,"

---

[1] Vivien M. Palmer, "Impressions of Sociology in Great Britain," *American Journal of Sociology*, vol. 32 (March 1927), 759.

[2] On LePlay, see the excellent and inspiring work cited above, *Critics of the Enlightenment: Readings in the French Counter-Revolutionary Tradition,* ed. and trans. Christopher Blum (Wilmington, DE: ISI Books, 2004), xxxv–xl.

[3] Christopher Dawson, "'He Gave...His Whole Self,'" *Sociological Review*, vol. 24 (1932), 24.

[4] Palmer, "Impressions of Sociology in Great Britain," 760.

[5] Christopher Dawson, "The World Crisis and the English Tradition," *English Review*, vol. 56 (1933), 251.

[6] Dawson, Cambridge, MA, to Col. Robert Patterson, Chicago, September 20, 1960, in Box 15, Folder 89, UST/CDC.

[7] Ibid.

[8] Dawson, "Manuscript Notes: Tradition and Inheritance" [1940s], Box 4, Folder 94, UST/CDC.

Dawson wrote. In reality, though, Dawson argued, "the note of the time was not freedom, but conquest and exploitation."[9] Laissez-faire industrialism proved to be nothing short of unbridled chaos. Rather than promoting order or freedom, it destabilized England. Out of the chaos of non-direction, a new mercantilism, in which each nation sought advantages for itself, arose. Though classical economics claimed that the result would be free trade, the opposite occurred. Each country erected increasingly steep protective trade barriers, isolating one country from another.

To feed this new mercantilism, industry turned to the new urban classes for its labor, resulting in "disaffection of the wage labourer" who, like a slave, was angry not so much at his low wages but rather at his lack of control over the end product of his labor. Like a slave, Dawson continued, the wage laborer was merely "instrumental. He possessed control neither over his work nor its fruit, but remained a human tool in the hands of the *entrepreneur* and the middleman."[10] While Dawson thus far reads like a number of anti-industrial critics from John C. Calhoun to Karl Marx, in actuality, he was following the Roman Catholic line of belief and argumentation, as expressed in the various papal encyclicals of the nineteenth and twentieth centuries. The worker is not initially a revolutionary, ready and willing to wage a class war of the poor against the rich. He only wants control over his own production. The anger and unrest of the laborer against the industrial machine is "rather an attempt to reverse the subordination of the human to the mechanical and the creative to the commercial function."[11]

Dawson's argument especially echoes those teachings expressed by Pope Leo in his famous 1891 encyclical, *Rerum Novarum*. After all, prior to the great divide separating the modern world from the medieval and ancient worlds, every man knew his place in the hierarchy of creation, Dawson believed. In the Middle Ages, especially, "social status was inseparable from function," he argued. "A man who had great wealth and no function was an anomaly, and so also to a lesser degree was the man who had a function and no means with which to fulfil it."[12] In eras of social stability, wealth serves merely as a means to some end. Properly used and understood, wealth helps maintain social stability rather than creating chaos. Society, after all, is a living organism, and the machine—defined by Dawson as that which mechanizes man, making him less than God intends him to be—is materialistic and, by necessity, avaricious. As an organism, though, a God-created and God-centered society extends over and through time.

---

[9]Christopher Dawson, "The Passing of Industrialism" in Christopher Dawson, *Enquiries into Religion and Culture* (London: Sheed and Ward, 1933),, 48.

[10]Ibid., 51–52.

[11]Ibid., 53.

[12]Ibid.

Here, Dawson echoed St. Paul's most common metaphor in the New Testament letters, the Church as a Body. Each person is distinguished not only by the time and place in which he is born, but also by the gifts given to him uniquely by God. God distributes these, then, according to His Will, through His economy of grace. "For just as in a single human body there are many limbs and organs, all with different functions," St. Paul wrote in his first letter to the Christian peoples of Rome, "so all of us, united with Christ, form one body, serving individually as limbs and organs to one another." Gifts such as teaching, counseling, or speaking "differ as they are allotted to us by God's grace, and must be exercised accordingly."[13]

Dawson's interest in economics as expressed in and around the theological arguments involving social stability and wealth—derived from his brief study in Sweden, his connection to LePlay's sociology, and his respect for Catholic social teachings—continued throughout the late 1910s and 1920s. His other economic articles appeared in the *Universe*, a Roman Catholic newspaper, and in *Blackfriars*, a journal of the English Dominicans. In each, Dawson argued for the private ownership of land by small farmers and peasants and a moral rather than utilitarian understanding of the market economy. The twin materialist philosophies of socialism and capitalism most threatened the institutions of property and the right to liberty, Dawson feared. "Socialism and Capitalism are, in fact, but two sides of the same development," he wrote. "They represent the last stages of that revolt against the Catholic tradition, which began in the sixteenth century, and which affected by degrees every side of European civilization."[14] Each "ism" is merely an attempt to replace the moral foundations of a spiritualized Christian society with the materialist laws of supply and demand, to make man economic rather than religious or cultural. Because God has given man dominion over the earth, even the material serves a spiritual and Godly purpose. Dominion, Dawson believed, does not mean domination and exploitation. Instead, man must act as a steward, receiving God's creation as a gift to better the fallen world, through grace. "There is a mystery in all the processes by which the earth is brought to bear fruit for the support of man, and the one great end of sacrifice and spell and purification is to cooperate with the forces of nature in producing good harvests, numerous flocks and favourable seasons," Dawson wrote.[15] To exploit the gifts of God is nothing less than the mockery of God and the arrogant denial of His authority and His wisdom.

As with the economy as a whole, wealth is morally neutral in and of itself. It must never become an end, but only serve as a means to something greater. Ultimately, Dawson believed, wealth is only good if one uses it "as a vehicle

---

[13]Romans 12:1–8.

[14]Christopher Dawson, "Socialism, Capitalism, and the Catholic Tradition," *Universe*, April 11, 1919.

[15]Christopher Dawson, "Catholicism and Economics," *Blackfriars*, vol. 5 (1924), 90.

of spiritual love."[16] One of the Church Fathers, St. Ambrose, had taken this argument to its logical conclusion. "What you give to the poor man is not yours but his. For what was given for the common use, you alone usurp. The earth is all men's and not the property of the rich."[17] Another Church Father, St. Basil, stated: "He who strips a man of his garments will be called a thief. Is not he who fails to clothe the naked when he could do so worthy of the same title? It is the bread of the hungry that you hold, the clothing of the naked that you lock up in your cupboard."[18] Each of these men followed the beliefs of the first Archbishop of Jerusalem, St. James. In his Catholic epistle, he wrote of the wealthy: "You have feasted upon earth: and in riotousness you have nourished your hearts, in the day of slaughter."[19]

Dawson, however, saw no contradiction between his views and those advocating a free society, properly understood. Capitalism, for Dawson, was not free. It meant the rule of the capitalists, businessmen who had gained control of the levers of political power. Instead, Dawson believed in the right to associate freely, one to another. "Economic life, as one of man's many activities, must find its own social expression and form its own organs," Dawson argued. "It must be ordered by the free association of individuals, not by a compulsory organisation proceeding from the centre of political authority."[20] Only this will allow true order, as ordained by God. For, Dawson wrote, should society divide itself between the rich and the poor, no hope can exist for an effective and stable social order in which the Church can thrive. "It is only by more light, by spiritual leadership, and by the diffusion of ideas that such a disaster can be averted. It is from Catholics, above all, that such enlightenment should come." Only Catholics have fully inherited the world reborn after the near death of the Graeco-Roman world. Catholics must "show the modern world that the true end of life for society, as for the individual, is something outside and above itself—the co-operation of spiritual beings in the service of God."[21]

Working with the members of the LePlay House, Dawson wrote several other articles on a surprisingly wide range of topics. With Farquharson, he wrote a two-part history of early Rome, focusing on the Latin love of order, the growth of cities in the Roman empire, and the virtues of the Roman family in the republic and the empire.[22] In the *Sociological Review*, he also wrote articles on primitive culture, foreshadowing much of what would appear in

---

[16] Ibid., 93.

[17] Ibid., 159.

[18] Ibid.

[19] James 5:5 (Douay-Rheims version).

[20] Dawson, "Catholicism and Economics," 213.

[21] Dawson, "Socialism, Capitalism, and the Catholic Tradition."

[22] Christopher Dawson and Alexander Farquharson, "Rome: A Historical Survey," *Sociological Review*, vol. 15 (1923), 132–47, 296–311.

his first book, *The Age of the Gods*; British cultural divisions in history; Oswald Spengler; theories of progress; cycles of civilization; morality; the secrets of the Orient; and European democracy. Overall, Dawson demonstrated a profound versatility, even as a relatively young scholar.

As mentioned above, it was also through Dawson's connections to the LePlay House that he obtained his first teaching post at the University of Exeter in 1925.[23] He held the title of "Lecturer on the History of Culture," a post he kept until 1933. His lectures, along with talks delivered at the LePlay House, proved a vital experience to the intensely shy Dawson. "The course of lectures I gave there in the middle and late '20s was of great value in helping me to present my ideas on the history of culture in a popular or relatively popular form," he wrote in the 1940s in his notes for his memoirs. Perhaps even more importantly, Dawson wrote, "after the *Age of the Gods* came out, I was encouraged to write in the same way for the Catholic public first by Leo [Ward] and then by Algar Thorold who shared my interests in mysticism and the *Ecole Francaise* and whose editorship of the *Dublin* was most helpful and stimulating to my work."[24] Clearly, his association with LePlay House had shaped and influenced the young Dawson significantly. It helped launch his writing and his brief academic career by providing a forum in which to discuss and publish his ideas. Alone, Dawson most likely would have simply continued to read and research in his study, his ideas trapped within himself. But in community, the young and aspiring Dawson thrived.

Order Men

As Dawson moved toward writing for a more popular audience regarding Catholic issues, a second group became even more important to his intellectual formation. At the end the 1920s, Dawson and several friends formed a journal called *Order: An Occasional Catholic Review*. The group of friends met often for social and intellectual interaction at the apartment of London socialite Tom Burns. The Chelsea group or *Order* men, as they called themselves, also included Jesuit scholar Father Martin D'Arcy, artist and poet David Jones, journalist Bernard Wall, Kierkegaard scholar Alexander (Alick) Dru, BBC announcer Harman Grisewood, and visionary artist and economic distributist Eric Gill. Others would attend the meetings infrequently, including actor Robert Speaight and poet W. H. Auden.[25] Many of the men—

---

[23]James Oliver and Christina Scott, "Chronology of the Life and Principle Works of Christopher Dawson," in Christopher Dawson, *Religion and World History: A Selection from the Works of Christopher Dawson*, Christina Scott and James Oliver, eds. (Garden City, NY: Image, 1975), 16.

[24]Dawson, "Manuscript Notes: Tradition and Inheritance," in Box 4, Folder 94, UST/CDC.

[25]Tom Burns, *The Use of Memory: Publishing and Further Pursuits* (London: Sheed and Ward, 1993), 42–43; and Robert Speaight, *The Life of Eric Gill* (New York: P. J. Kenedy and Sons, 1966), 199ff.

including Dawson—had known each other through visiting Gill at his famous distributist colony at Ditchling.[26] Indeed, it was most likely at Ditchling that Dawson came into contact with Burns, though he may have met him in his visits to Father D'Arcy in Oxford. But it was during the numerous discussions in Tom Burns's Chelsea apartment in London regarding the lack of beauty in the modern world—including, as they saw it, a decline in the beauty of the liturgy of the Roman Catholic Church—"that occurred the spontaneous generation of an idea for a review dedicated to reforming the Catholic Church."[27] The Church itself, these *Order* men believed, had become an obstacle to its own reform. They believed the Church, Burns recalled, to be "frail and flawed in many ways, almost an obstacle to faith."[28]

The discussions at his apartment usually began with arguments found in the French neo-Thomist Jacques Maritain's *Art and Scholasticism*.[29] Following the line of thought Maritain had presented in his book, at least as the *Order* men interpreted it, modern liberals had destroyed the concept of beauty by looking only at what was useful and to what extent it—whatever "it" might be—could be used. As a philosophical principle, utility could only lead to chaos and the destruction of the natural world and the uniqueness and dignity of the human person, the *Order* men argued. Dawson and the Chelsea group followed the writings and arguments of John Henry Cardinal Newman, rejecting all forms of utilitarianism, which they identified as the ultimate expression and fulfillment of English liberalism.[30] Grisewood, a very close friend of Dawson's, brilliantly expressed his political views in a manner that was indicative of the entire *Order* group. Though he had never consciously considered himself a conservative, he once had to sit under several portraits of famous Whigs and Liberals at a dinner party. At the end of the dinner, he commented, "I don't like sitting too close to" the Whigs and Liberals. They were, he added in all earnestness to his companion, "men who have done so much harm and who look so eager to do more. Next time do get a table at the other end—by the soldiers."[31]

Dawson would have been very comfortable with the sentiment expressed by his friend. John Mulloy remembered that Dawson "showed me a review from an American periodical which commended him as an English liberal, which amused him quite a bit, since neither he nor any of his forbears were

---

[26]Speaight, *Life of Eric Gill*, 137.

[27]Burns, *Use of Memory*, 42–43; and Bernard Wall, *Headlong into Change: An Autobiography and a Memoir of Ideas Since the Thirties* (London: Harvill, 1969), 51–52.

[28]Burns, *Use of Memory*, 44.

[29]Harman Grisewood, *One Thing at a Time: An Autobiography* (London: Hutchinson, 1968), 80.

[30]On Newman's understanding of liberalism as utilitarianism, see his "Liberalism," in his *Apologia Pro Vita Sua* (London: Penguin, 1994), 252–262.

[31]Grisewood, *One Thing at a Time*, 80.

Liberals."[32] As will be discussed in later chapters, Dawson and most of his circle considered liberals as simple-minded secularists and utilitarians who failed to understand truth, beauty, and goodness. Perhaps most damning from Dawson's view point, liberals lacked the power of imagination. They were quantifiers and calculators, sophisticated men of the world, but not of the soul. They had been duped by worldly wisdom.

Inspired by their many conversations regarding art and the lack of beauty in the world, the *Order* men took the journal title from two sources. First, they found inspiration in the Aristotelian/Thomist understanding of *order* as that which recognizes its specific end or purpose and places itself in its proper sphere in the Divine Economy. Tellingly, the masthead quoted St. Thomas Aquinas from his *Argument Against the Muslims*. "According to established popular usage, which the Philosopher considers should be our guide in the naming of things, those are called wise who put things into right order and control them well," the great medieval philosopher had written.[33] Therefore, the *Order* men argued, all things—no matter how high or low they might seem—have a vital place in the Divine Economy, and, if ordered properly, will fulfill a necessary, Godly purpose.[34] This, of course, would be God's "utility," as opposed to man's utility. God's utility inherently promotes the dignity and uniqueness of each human person, created as *imago Dei*, while man's utility merely serves the pleasure of the man or men in power. Nature, Aristotle wrote, makes nothing in vain. However, Aquinas added, only grace perfects nature. In other words, what God makes, God understands and loves. What man makes, man misunderstands and uses for his own purposes, purposes which at best are merely steps away from the diabolical.

Second, they took the idea of order from the eighteenth-century Anglo-Irish statesman and man of letters, Edmund Burke, who had stressed the need for the "moral imagination"—the ability to see clearly beyond the here and now into the reality of eternal forms—thus allowing one to order one's soul, one's present community, and one's soul to the eternal community.[35] Without the moral imagination, as Burke had argued, the human person lost his ability to order anything. Indeed, without the moral imagination,

> A king is but a man, a queen is but a woman; a woman is but an animal; and an animal not of the highest order. All homage paid to the sex in general as such, and without distinct views, is to be regarded as romance and folly. Regicide, parricide, and sacrilege, are but fictions of superstition, corrupting jurisprudence by destroying its simplicity. The murder of a king, or a queen, or a bishop, or a father, are only common homicide; and if the people are by any chance, or in any way gainers

---

[32]John J. Mulloy, Record of Dawson Conversation, August 21, 1953, in Box 1, Folder 2, ND/CDAW.

[33]Burns, *Use of Memory*, 46.

[34]Grisewood, *One Thing at a Time*, 107.

[35]Burns, *Use of Memory*, 46.

of it, a sort of homicide much the most pardonable, and into which we ought not to make too severe a scrutiny.[36]

The *Order* Men attempted to pull Burke's eternal understanding into created time. Beauty and imagination, they believed, led to truth. "We were up against, dismayed by, the hideous aesthetic expressions of modern religion," Burns remembered.[37] Though traditionalist and conservative in political, theological, and philosophical beliefs, the Chelsea group demanded radically new forms of art and expression. If all things, properly understood, had an end that was good, then all new forms of art must be embraced and sanctified for a Christian purpose. The traditional or modern form could continue, but its essence must come into conformity with grace.[38] This Burkean notion of the moral imagination and the rightly ordered soul, Burns remembered, first came to him through Maritain's *philosophia perennis*, "a living tradition, over and against materialism in its myriad forms."[39]

This combination of traditionalist and modern ideas espoused within the *Order* group would have distanced the members significantly not only from its more famous counterparts, the avant-garde and licentious Bloomsbury Group, but also from the utterly conservative and traditionalist group centered around J. R. R. Tolkien and C. S. Lewis, the Inklings.[40] The former, the Bloomsbury Group, was probably the most famous literary group of the early twentieth century. Between 1907 and 1930, its members included Virginia Woolf, Vita Sacksville-West, E. M. Forster, D. H. Lawrence, and John Maynard Keynes. It held a reputation for its radicalism in politics and its supposed adventures in sexuality. In almost every aspect of life, the members of the group attempted to defy all conventions and norms of their day. Strangely, the *Order* group was connected to the Bloomsbury Group through Tom's older brother, Charles, a professional psychiatrist. Charles specialized "at the Tavistock Clinic for nervous disease in Bloomsbury." When Tom first moved in with his brother, Bloomsbury "baffled rather than shocked me. I could make little of its denigrating approach to so many values that I held to be sacred." His many intellectual experiences in Paris, especially his friendship with Maritain, made him immune to the so-called "Bloomsbury intelligence."[41] Additionally, many initially thought Dawson was connected to Bloomsbury solely because of the beard he chose to wear, then seen as a radical statement. Many, iron-

---

[36] Edmund Burke, *Reflections on the Revolution in France* (Indianapolis, IN: Liberty Fund, 1999), 171.

[37] Burns, *Use of Memory*, 44.

[38] Grisewood, *One Thing at a Time*, 80.

[39] Burns, *Use of Memory*, 46.

[40] See Bradley J. Birzer, *J. R. R. Tolkien's Sanctifying Myth: Understanding Middle-Earth* (Wilmington, DE: ISI Books, 2002), chapters 3 and 6.

[41] Burns, *Use of Memory*, 41. For an excellent overview of the Bloomsbury Group, see Joseph Pearce, *Bloomsbury and Beyond: The Friends and Enemies of Roy Campbell* (London: HarperCollins, 2002).

ically, identified him, at least in looks, with D. H. Lawrence. The two men could not be more dissimilar.

On the other hand, the Inklings, driven by C. S. Lewis's personality and J. R. R. Tolkien's imagination, were full-blown conservatives in politics, religion, and art. The Inklings were, according to Inkling John Wain, a "circle of instigators, almost of incendiaries, meeting to urge one another on in the task of redirecting the whole current of contemporary art and life."[42] The *Order* men had some contacts with the Inklings, but no significant ones until the 1930s. Then, as noted earlier, Dawson formed friendships with several of the Inklings, including C. S. Lewis, Humphrey Havard, and Gervase Mathew, and he and Tolkien were both parishioners at St. Aloysius in Oxford. Robert Speaight would also work with another Inkling, Lord David Cecil, and David Jones would recognize J. R. R. Tolkien as a significant influence on his own work.

Adventuresome in art but not in politics, the *Order* men offered a middle way of looking at the world. And yet, for such a profound philosophical understanding of order, the writers and the writings for *Order* often possessed a very young, immature, and agitated disposition. They seem to have been the "angry young men" of their day. That which is not ordered properly, the young English Roman Catholics seemed to shout, would be badgered and harassed until ordered properly. In a disorderly fashion, they would promote order. Each article went unsigned, giving the impression of a collective mind, but it also allowed the individual author to speak as he so wanted. An Aristotle or a Burke might have approved the intent of the *Order* men, but certainly not their anxious will to action. "Once when I was trustful—and conceited—I nearly championed the obscene. Once I just failed to further a stupid attempt at revolution," the famous Dominican priest and distributist, Father Vincent McNabb, complained. "I can judge of the group that are behind *Order* only by hearsay, because their anonymity preference makes an impenetrable veil. Now, from what I hear of their views of Art, Morality, etc., I think I would as soon commit a canary to a cat as commit my name to the men (the young men?) behind *Order*."[43] Actor Robert Speaight only visited the Chelsea men once socially, but he left the luncheon "more feverish than when" he had journeyed there, dismissing them as "all th[o]se clever people." Still, he contributed to *Order*, all the while fearing that "the giovani of today would regard us as dilettante parasites on a society."[44]

The editors of *Order*—meaning, mostly, Tom Burns, but with the significant advice of Dawson—tried to make their position as clear as possible to

---

[42]John Wain, *Sprightly Running: Part of an Autobiography* (New York: St. Martin's, 1962), 181.

[43]Fr. Vincent McNabb, O.P., "Fr. Vincent McNabb, O.P., to Anonymity," *Order*, vol. 1 (August 1928), 54.

[44]Robert Speaight, *The Property Basket: Recollections of a Divided Life* (London: Collins and Harvill, 1970), 161–62, 164.

their readers. On the inside cover of issue number two, the editors stated their intentions in nine bulleted points. "We are Catholics, speaking to Catholics," read the opening line. The reading Catholic public, though, were not just the clergy, but also the laity. "We may be wise or foolish in these matters," stated point five. "Wise in proportion as we continually check and re-arrange ourselves and remember our end in view; foolish in proportion as we stampede, lose all idea of conscientious self-criticism and dwell continuously in present time." In point six, the editors admitted that they "indiscriminately admire one another," and promise to "pester with unholy zest whatever is left of Christianity and is not Catholic."[45] As Burns admitted in his memoirs, the Church "frail and flawed in many ways, [was] almost an obstacle to the faith."[46] The *Order* men wanted to change that, using the beauty and traditions of the Church to challenge what they considered the hollowness of modernity and the utilitarianism of the liberals.

In an unsigned eight-page "private and confidential" memo, dated October 19, 1928, Burns attempted to define the purpose of the journal to the various editors and contributors of *Order*. Apparently, after two issues, they still had not found their true voice or niche. First, the memo stated, the journal's audience included every Catholic person in England, regardless of social class. Indeed, the memo assured the editors and writers, each class of Catholics has its own role.

Second, *Order* should help prevent the continuing protestantization and secularization of the various Catholic peoples. Where there was ignorance in regard to protestantization and secularization, *Order* would bring it to light not only to those practicing falsely, but also to those outside of the practitioners who might be in a position to help correct the problem. Where there was apathy on the part of Catholics about such protestantization and secularization, *Order* wanted to prompt and prod Catholics into social and political action. Ultimately, *Order* desired "to form a Catholic mind," defined as:

> The development of personal and public moral qualities as necessary for the apperception of truth on most levels—vigilance; the discipline of a definite choice of end and the means proper to it (within the general choice of end and the means proper to it in general)—asceticism; a conscientious and commonsense recognition of a conflict between supernatural standards and quasi-natural, 'normal', standards and conventions, a continuous re-living of the Catholic choice in this, at the same time a constant recognition and encouragement to growth of religious truth.[47]

Three, *Order* wanted to propagate the truth militantly. In contrast to the Chesterbelloc view of Europe and the faith as inseparable and "Catholicism a jolly tavern," *Order* would attempt to build bridges to the Anglican Church,

---

[45]"Again the Idea of 'Order,'" *Order: An Occasional Catholic Review*, 1928.

[46]Burns, *Use of Memory*, 44.

[47]"Private and Confidential: From BM/Order London," October 19, 1928, in Box 15, Folder 82, UST/CDC.

and it would not shy from the truth, it claimed, even where the Roman Catholic Church was found wrong. In prodding the English Roman Catholics out of their complacency within established society and blindly accepting anti-Catholic discrimination, *Order* would "ridicule the *Tablet* [then a mainstream, conciliatory Catholic newspaper] until it bursts."[48] For the rest of the Catholic press, the memo simply used the words of Cato the Elder which began the Third Punic War, "*Delenda Est*."[49] It must be destroyed! *Order* would make a beautiful English Catholicism heard and respectable, by any means necessary.

In addition to their love of Aristotle, Aquinas, and Burke, the *Order* men also sought the approval and graciously accepted the influence of Dawson, already a member of their group, T. S. Eliot, and Jacques Maritain, each "of outstanding intellect and of enormous breadth in their reading."[50] These three thinkers, according to Grisewood, served as unofficial dons.[51] Of the three, Dawson played the only direct intellectual role in the *Order* movement. To his face, his friends called Dawson "Kit." After 1935, though, they gave him a rather unusual nickname. Rene Hague remembered that after a conversation with Dawson, a mutual friend, "overcome in those few minutes by the width of his learning, remarked, 'my God, what a tiger!'" From that point forward, Hague wrote, "'Tiger' Dawson became established, but not to his face."[52] Though his temper was different than that of such angry young men as Burns, Wall, and Grisewood, Dawson not only met with the *Order* men in intense discussions at Chelsea—"that never-ending party which went on at St. Leonard's Terrace"—but he also wrote at least three of the articles for the short-lived journal, though, as with all other articles in the four issues, they were unsigned.[53] The first was "Civilisation and Order" in the second issue, dated August 1928. The second was "The Psychology of Sex and the Catholic Order," in the third issue, dated March 1929. Dawson's final article for *Order*, entitled "The Idea of a Catholic Order," appeared in the fourth and final issue of the journal. The second article is an interesting analysis of Freud's, Huxley's, and St. Augustine's views of sex and the definition of the human person. In it, Dawson argued that man must be understood as the *metaxy*, neither fully spirit nor fully animal, but something in-between. His arguments were those first presented in his "Nature and Destiny of Man."

It is the first and third articles, "Civilisation and Order" and "The Idea of a Catholic Order," that are essential, though, to understanding the younger and

---

[48] Ibid. Ironically, Burns, and to a lesser extent Dawson, would later take over the editorship of the *Tablet*.

[49] Ibid.

[50] Grisewood, *One Thing at a Time,* 82–83.

[51] Ibid.

[52] René Hague, ed., *Dai Greatcoat: A Self-Portrait of David Jones in His Letters*, René Hague, ed. (London: Faber and Faber, 1980), 70, n. 17. The name most likely came from Blake's poem. See Speaight, *Property Basket,* 219.

[53] "Never-ending party," from Grisewood, *One Thing at a Time,* 83.

more anxious Dawson. Each is one of Dawson's most wide-reaching essays, serving as summaries for every single significant idea Dawson would pursue and develop throughout the rest of his writing career. In the first, "Civilisation and Order," Dawson argued that several scholars in the 1920s had identified the problems resulting from modernity justly. Still, these same scholars had failed to provide adequate solutions to the identified problems. Instead, too many scholars—most likely, Dawson was thinking of the Irving Babbitts of the world—were hoping for the establishment of an aristocratic humanism to reclaim civilization.

> If civilisation has nothing to do with morals and religion, if social justice and politi-
> cal liberty are matters of indifference to it, it can have but little contact with human
> life in its most universal aspects. It is an artificial growth, a hot-house plant which
> can only flourish in a world in which everyone is witty and well mannered and
> well dressed; where poverty and suffering are unknown. Such a society can never
> exist in its own right. It is the result of certain rare and transitory moments in the
> wider life of humanity. Its exquisite frivolity is powerless to withstand the hard
> facts of life.[54]

Such artificial civilizations, based on a second-rate aristocratic humanism, have existed throughout western civilization: "Horace rather than Virgil, Epicurus rather than Plato, Pope rather than Shakespeare," Dawson wrote.[55] True civilization results only when all of the elements of society understand their individual and unique places within the economy of grace, a divine republic that embraces a "profound harmony of every element in human life from the lowest to the highest."[56] Every civilization—Occidental, Asiatic, or otherwise—understands this at a most fundamental level, often calling it some variation of the natural law. Christians, Dawson claimed, understand it best.

Yet modern Catholics, who should have been leading civilization to moral order, had lost their way. Despite 1,900 years of Christian theology and philosophy, Roman Catholics had proven no more immune to the forces of modernity than non-Catholics. "Industrialism, compulsory education and military service, the popular press and party politics" assaulted Catholics from every side. A Catholic could find salvation in either Main Street or during the Passion Play at Ober Ammergau, "but for all that Babbitt is not Piers Plowman."

Still, Dawson argued, none of this was pre-destined. Only if Catholics were to reorder their educational system to teach children "a true following of wisdom, a science which is directed towards the vision of immutable truth,"

---

[54]Christopher Dawson, "Civilization and Order," *Order: An Occasional Catholic Review*, vol. 1 (August 1928), 42.

[55]Ibid., 43.

[56]Ibid.

could the Church serve as the proper and effectual *anamnesis* to reawaken the latent spirit of Western man and inspire a new Christendom.[57]

In the third article, "The Idea of a Catholic Order," Dawson continued the analysis of the humanist understanding of the world and its opposition to the understanding of the Catholic Church. The humanist and the humanitarian (Dawson used the terms interchangeably, though the humanists never did) seek a man-made order, but, he continued, "Catholicism is essentially the religion of Order." Even when the world falls apart, the Church remains solid, as it stands on eternal, Godly truth rather than temporary, man-made truth.[58]

Dominated intellectually by the quasi-religious humanist vision, the academic world of the 1920s viewed Catholicism as a threat to humanity, an ancient superstition still proclaiming sacrifice—of that which "makes life worth living"—a virtue. Jesus, such humanist scholars believed, was really "the supreme moralist, whose simple gospel of altruism and ethical perfection was perverted by the sinister activities of Saul of Tarsus into a mystery-mongering system of supernaturalism."[59] These humanists saw the Catholic as nothing more than a simple dualist, proclaiming the flesh against the spirit and the spirit against the flesh. In its own position, falsely understood and falsely represented by its enemies, Catholicism therefore found itself attacked on all sides. For opposite the humanists were the numerous Protestants, led by such important figures as Karl Barth, who rejected everything humanist and called for a recognition of the total depravity of the human person. Dawson rejected both objections as almost equally dangerous to a proper and necessary understanding of the human person.

Catholicism, he argued, once again recalling his own views in "Nature and Destiny of Man," has always embraced the human person as the *metaxy*, a being importantly made up of both spirit and flesh. "Catholicism has always affirmed the existence of the natural order and the good of human nature against the Marcionite, the Manichean, and the Calvinist," Dawson wrote. "Relatively speaking, the Catholic is a Christian humanist."[60] Unlike many of the heresies and heterodoxies, Catholicism does not reject the created order as tainted and, indeed, depraved, even after the Fall. Instead, it objects to an order of man as created by man, in which he uses the created goods of the material world for his own selfish or hedonistic visions. "Man alone is able to upset the balance and live, and thereby becomes the starting point of a movement of cosmic disorder, which affects the whole material world in so far as it is subordinate to him," Dawson argued. When man attempts to transcend or dominate the natural order, he can only "become the instrument

---

[57] Ibid., 44.

[58] Christopher Dawson, "The Idea of a Catholic Order," *Order: An Occasional Catholic Review*, vol. 1 (1929), 111.

[59] Ibid.

[60] Ibid.

of supernatural evil—the vice-regent of the Kingdom of Satan." Dawson did not believe the created world is evil, only man's incorrect use of it.

While man can bring disorder to the world, Dawson argued, in the vein of his intellectual and spiritual exemplar St. Augustine, he cannot order it properly. Only grace can reorder what man has destroyed. Such a reordering has been the task of the Church, Dawson believed, from its inception. "It can be healed only from outside by the re-ordering of humanity and, through humanity, of the material world to a supernatural end." Indeed, the primary role of the Church is to sanctify the world, and the individual human person—if properly ordered in his soul—plays the vital role in the process of sanctification. Slowly, through grace, each Christian is sanctified, the debris of the world being gradually removed from the order of his soul, and, then, the human as the *metaxy* serves as the bridge between the spiritual and material worlds. But man cannot "cannot live with the world or without it," Dawson wrote. "He is always in danger of falling into two opposite errors."[61] The Christian, therefore, is constantly tempted to either the humanist extreme or the Puritan extreme. From the very beginnings of the Church, most heresies have come from the inability to walk between the two extremes. Heresies, more often than not, take one truth at the expense of all others. It should surprise no Christian that in 1929, with the world disordered ideologically, politically, and sexually, the temptations of the heresies were as great then as they ever were, if not far greater.

While under attack from the world, Dawson feared, the Church in its present condition only worsened the situation. First, the Roman Catholic press in England seemed to be failing miserably, as it had paradoxically embraced both extremes. "It manages to be entirely out of touch with the real world—to live in an atmosphere of the sacristy—and yet at the same time to be thoroughly unsupernatural and even materialistic," Dawson continued.[62] Second, the Catholic Church, though never a mere sect according to Dawson, had most recently been acting as one. This seemed to Dawson most obvious in its present understanding of art. "The vice of Catholic art is not so much that it is ugly or commercialised as that it is *ecclesiastical*." That is, Dawson continued, Catholic art had become separated from the life of the average Catholic. "This unwholesome isolation of Catholic art is but a symptom of the spirit of sectarianism which infects almost every side of Catholic social and intellectual activity," Dawson concluded. Art and liturgy introduced the average person into the mysteries of the Church, as will be explored later. For the average man to contemplate the beautiful and mysterious within the Church, he must first be taught what is beautiful, through word and deed. Without these

---

[61] Ibid., 112.
[62] Ibid., 113.

moorings, the average Catholic will become alienated first from the Church and second from the universe and creation itself.

Despite his intense criticisms of the world and the Church, Dawson concluded his last *Order* article on an optimistic note. The world, he argued, must be sanctified, just as it had been in the early Church and the medieval period. The Church must take the worldly order and spiritualize it. Grace had so moved Christian individuals in the past, such as a St. Benedict, that it must do so again, and men must willingly accept the grace given to them to transform the world. "A Catholic has only to *be* in order to change the world in which he lives, but in that act of being there is contained all the mystery of the supernatural life," Dawson argued. "It is a function of the Church to sow the divine seed—to produce not merely good men but spiritual men—that is to say super-men." The true Catholic must ignore or bypass the "unspiritual Catholic" who must be recognized as "the most abject of all failures." For he is neither good "for the Church nor for the world—in the words of the Gospel neither for the land nor for the dunghill. He is fit only to be trodden on."[63] Angry and anxious, Dawson called a spade a spade. Such was the mission of the faithful Christian in extraordinary times.

With such innovative—if somewhat angry—traditionalists as Dawson, the first issue of *Order* did exceedingly well, selling out the initial 2,000 copies of its first edition almost immediately after its June 1928 release. It had to be reprinted to meet the demand.[64] Grisewood believed, in hindsight, that the importance of *Order* came not from the articles themselves but from the response to the articles—by both the public and the writers. "*Order* was a bombshell—as it was meant to be," Grisewood remembered. "Its importance was not the explosion but the crater which remained," he continued. It "drew to its rim a circle of people who for the next few years met together often to discuss certain manifestations of the twentieth century in relation to the abiding truths of Christianity."[65] Still, the group only published a total of four issues, with issue four published in November 1929. Burns, as late as the fall of 1930, still hoped to produce one final issue of *Order*, a capstone of the entire effort.

> I oscillate between (1) silence (2) small cheap, quick, critical, all-round and often (3) large, expensive, general, quarterly, solid, clanical [sic] (4) One vast, chaotic, omnium-galtiarum *interim*, transitional, [?], irresponsible, undiluted, unrestrained number all written off my own bat. What do I do? Work multiplies—silence is easier. But there's lots to say and few saying it.[66]

In the end, Burns left *Order* as it was, four solid if anxious issues, and he turned his energy to another project, a book on D. H. Lawrence, and,

---

[63] Ibid., 114, 115.

[64] Burns, *Use of Memory*, 45.

[65] Grisewood, *One Thing at a Time*, 79.

[66] Burns, London, to Dawson, September 3, 1930, in Box 11, Folder 31, UST/CDC.

of course, to his full-time job as an editor at Sheed and Ward.[67] He never completed the Lawrence book, and he left Sheed and Ward after only a few years in their employ.

Robert Speaight tried to explain the reasons for *Order* being short lived. "The mystique of 'order' was worked for considerably more than it was worth," he argued, "with an illegitimate extrapolation from the theological to the political field." In fairness, it should be noted that Speaight was never a part of the social aspect of *Order*, and he later believed that the *Order* crowd had been too soft on fascism.[68] While the world was collapsing into political and moral chaos, Speaight feared, the *Order* man simply discussed aesthetics and literature. In his own beliefs, Speaight, knowingly or not, was attacking the very essence of the *Order* men, the idea of the supremacy of culture over all things and the importance of the liberal arts and a group of men of letters dedicated to bringing beauty to the world.

But Dawson and Wall would never recant the emphasis on culture and literature over politics. The culture preceded the political system, Dawson thought. Any attempt to change culture through politics would end in failure or disaster. Indeed, one of the lures of *Order* as a group—along with the popular appeal of the Inklings—came from its emphasis on literature, theology, and culture as driving forces in society, bypassing the seductive lure of politics and political systems and power. The ideas and consequences of a Benito Mussolini, a Sigmund Freud, a D. H. Lawrence, or a Karl Marx could not be defeated with a new law, tariff, or tax break. Instead, one could only defeat such heresies through a proper understanding of the order of Creation—specifically through religious and cultural ideas of beauty, truth, and goodness.

Though they had originally wanted to address problems only in the British Isles, the *Order* men made contact with their counterparts in Paris: philosopher Jacques Maritain; novelist George Bernanos; philosopher and historian Etienne Gilson; philosopher and poet Francois Mauriac; and Russian philosopher and historian Nicholas Berdyaev.[69] The Paris group, oddly enough, centered around Berdyaev, a Russian émigré who desired the intellectual nourishment such a group could offer. He first invited Jacques Maritain, who decided to join the budding group only after Berdyaev promised that no Protestants would be invited. The meetings alternated between Berdyaev's home in Clarmart and Maritain's home in Meudon. The latter was especially attractive to Parisian Catholic intellectuals as the local bishop had given the Maritains permission to have a chapel with the Blessed Sacrament present in their home.[70]

---

[67]Ibid.

[68]Speaight, *Property Basket,* 164ff.

[69]Burns, *Use of Memory,* 46. Burns claims that there were four issues of *Order,* Grisewood remembers five. See Grisewood, *One Thing at a Time,* 79.

[70]Donald A. Lowrie, *Rebellious Prophet: A Life of Nicholai Berdyaev* (Westport, CN: Greenwood Press, 1974), 200; and John Hellman, "The Humanism of Jacques Maritain," in *Understanding*

Berdyaev held mixed beliefs regarding Maritain. He greatly respected him as a friend and as a person, but he distrusted Maritain's neo-Thomism. "I could not help regarding his 'Christian philosophy' as a superstructure on a basis of Aristotelian rationalism," Berdyaev wrote of Maritain.[71] Still, to Maritain's credit, Berdyaev thought, he is a "rare phenomenon, a Frenchman in whom there is not the slightest sign of national exclusiveness."[72] Such an openness, of course, would prove vital to the English *Order* men who desired to bring non-English Roman Catholic ideas to their homeland to serve as a needed leaven. And, indeed, the introduction to non-English ideas would greatly increase the scope, ideas, and influence of the *Order* movement. Burns, himself, was versatile in his attractions. "He was equally at home among the Maritains at Meudon and in the household of James Joyce," Grisewood wrote.[73] Speaight described Burns as "agog with continental notions."[74]

These groups—in England and abroad—needed an institution to give their Christian humanist movement cohesion, sustained purpose, and longevity. That institutional support came from a brand-new publishing firm, Sheed and Ward. It was Sheed and Ward that recognized the power and potential of the now-international *Order* movement. The firm absorbed most of the *Order* men and their ideas by the earliest part of the 1930s. It was, however, Dawson who had originally taken the idea to Sheed and Ward, to form a partnership with the *Order* men, when he joined them for the publication of his *Progress and Religion* in 1929. Tom Burns had joined Sheed and Ward as one of the firm's main editors in 1926.[75] Frank Sheed, a Catholic from Australia, was first impressed with Burns when the two met in the London branch of the Catholic Evidence Guild.[76] Additionally, Sheed found Dawson's first major essay, "The Nature and Destiny of Man," simply "overwhelming."[77] To combine Dawson's brilliant mind with Burns's ability to organize and edit must have seemed ideal for Sheed. The Australian was no stranger to controversy and he relished a good fight in the public sphere. "Today is the 15th anniversary of my landing in England," Sheed recalled in 1935. "Guy Fawkes is avenged."[78] Sheed had, after all, no less a goal than the complete domination of Roman

---

Maritain: Philosopher and Friend, Deal W. Hudson and Matthew J. Mancini, eds. (Atlanta, GA: Mercer University Press, 1987), 124.

[71] Nicholas Berdyaev, *Dream and Reality: An Essay in Autobiography* (New York: MacMillan, 1951), 261.

[72] Ibid., 262.

[73] Grisewood, *One Thing at a Time,* 79.

[74] Speaight, *Property Basket,* 161.

[75] Burns, *Use of Memory,* 31.

[76] Ibid., 30.

[77] Maisie Ward, "Dawson the Philosopher," *Duckett's Register,* vol. 4 (1949), 38.

[78] Sheed to Maisie, November 5, 1935, in Box 1, Folder 4, in Sheed and Ward Family Papers, University of Notre Dame Archives, Notre Dame, IN (hereafter ND/CSWD).

Catholics in the English intellectual scene.[79] The alliance between the *Order* men and Sheed and Ward proved successful for each party. For, with the collaboration between *Order* and Sheed and Ward, the ideas of the *Order* men took on an significant aura of respectability. Rather than remaining in journal form, *Order* became Sheed and Ward's highly charged and intellectual series, *Essays in Order*, edited by Christopher Dawson and Tom Burns. In most cases, Dawson chose the authors, and Burns edited the manuscripts.[80]

The first such "Essays in Order" did not bear the name of the series title. Instead, three men—Burns, Dawson, and Father John-Baptiste Reeves, O.P.—worked together to compile and edit a volume of essays, entitled *A Monument to St. Augustine*. Published in 1930, its makeup certainly foreshadowed what was to come with the officially named *Essays in Order*. Contributors included Dawson, Father D'Arcy, Father Reeves, E. I. Watkin, Maurice Blondel, Etienne Gilson, Jacques Maritain, C. C. Martindale, Erich Przywara, and Bernard Roland-Gosselin. In essence, *A Monument* was a compilation of ten *Essays in Order*. Its importance goes well beyond its foreshadowing of the powerfully-charged series. This coming together of such an eminent group of minds was in and of itself nothing short of astounding. These various authors would, in large part, make up a considerable contingent of the twentieth-century Catholic Literary Revival. Perhaps the most important aspect of the *Monument* is its revelation of the importance of St. Augustine to the thought of Dawson, Sheed and Ward, and the Roman Catholic Literary Revival of the interwar period. As Burns noted, "a collection of essays could be formed at once unified within itself and approaching the special needs and interests of its readers—who might thus read it, indeed, as written: in personal sympathy, in commemoration." Further, Burns admitted, the "present volume rightly comes first as its attempts to evaluate the general influence which St. Augustine has had in Western thought and culture and his meaning for us at the present day."[81] The book, for reasons that elude the extant paper trail, took considerable time to get through the Roman Catholic censor. When it did make it through his grasp, Burns breathed a huge sigh of relief. "At last it's got thro' the Censor," he wrote to Dawson. The censor "had written to me (Did I tell you?) saying that it bristled with Immanence and other sticky subjects! You can imagine how frightened I was."[82] It was neither the first nor the last time Dawson would have run-ins with censors. As one reviewer perceptively noted, any book in the current Thomist revival would demand

---

[79]Sheed, somewhere in the Atlantic Ocean, to Maisie, January 2, 1933, in Box 1, Folder 3, ND/CSWD.

[80]Christina Scott, *A Historian and His World: A Life of Christopher Dawson* (New Brunswick, NJ: Transaction, 1992), 97.

[81]Tom Burns, "Compiler's Note," in *A Monument to Saint Augustine: Essays on Some Aspects of His Thought Written in Commemoration of His 15th Centenary*, Tom Burns, ed. (London: Sheed and Ward, 1945).

[82]Burns, London, to Dawson, August 8, 1930, in Box 11, Folder 31, UST/CDC.

a *Nihil obstat,* for "it would seem that Augustinianism has been in unofficial 'exile,' owing to its incompleteness." Further, as "a philosophical instrument it cannot compare with the systematic perfection of Thomism."[83]

Regardless, the book made it through, and it proved a success. So much so, that Sheed and Ward approved *Essays in Order,* and another phase of Dawson's life began and his productivity continued unabated.

---

[83] Gerald Sykes, "A Monument to St. Augustine (review)," *Bookman,* vol. 73 (June 1931), 438.

Interlude I

An Augustinian Vision of History

IT WOULD BE HARD TO FIND A GREATER INFLUENCE ON CHRISTOPHER DAWSON than St. Augustine. One only has to employ the imagination to jump back fifteen centuries to see the parallels. On August 24, 410, at midnight, Alaric and his Gothic warriors entered the gates of Rome and sacked the city. They raped, pillaged, and murdered for nearly three straight days. As they understood it, Alaric and his men were loyal Romans and only desired formal recognition as legitimate armed forces. They wanted Rome to bestow upon them pensions and formal titles.[1] Though the empire had been crumbling for years due to cultural, political, and economic decadence, the actual breach of Rome's walls stunned and shattered the western world. Rome, the common thought ran throughout western civilization, was to last forever. Through the mouth of Jupiter, Virgil had promised as much in the *Aeneid*, and such faith had taken on a life of its own. Indeed, the pagan stoics themselves, and especially Marcus Aurelius, had assumed that the Roman Empire was the Incarnate Logos.

"When the brightest light on the whole earth was extinguished, when the Roman empire was deprived of its head and when, to speak more correctly, the whole world perished in one city," wrote St. Jerome, expressing the common sentiment, "I was dumb with silence, I held my peace, even from good, and my sorrow was stirred."[2] Such a catastrophic event had seemed inconceivable even to those living under the waning protection of the Roman empire. And yet it had happened. The great symbol of the vast Roman empire, though no longer the capital, had fallen to invasion. True, many Christians and their basilicas were spared, but the city had fallen nonetheless.[3] The ruin continued, St. Jerome lamented, throughout much of the empire.

---

[1] Warren Thomas Smith, *Augustine: His Life and Thought* (Atlanta, GA: John Knox Press, 1980), 145.

[2] St. Jerome quoted in Daniel Boorstin, *The Creators* (New York: Random House, 1992), 59.

[3] Smith, *Augustine: His Life and Thought,* 145–47.

For twenty years and more Roman blood has been flowing ceaselessly over the broad countries between Constantinople and the Julian Alps where the Goths, the Huns and the Vandals spread ruin and death....How many Roman nobles have been their prey! How many matrons and maidens have fallen victim to their lust! Bishops live in prison, priests and clerics fall by the sword, churches are plundered, Christ's altars are turned into feeding-troughs, the remains of the martyrs are thrown out of their coffins. On every side sorrow, on every side lamentation, everywhere the image of death.[4]

The failure to turn back one invasion led to numerous others. The failure to protect the rights and property of some citizens led to the insecurity of the rest.

Though also reeling from the onslaught of the barbarians, St. Augustine stood firm in his opposition to the pagans who believed Rome had fallen because it had ignored the old gods. Gracefully, St. Augustine turned the evil of the destruction of the barbarians into something good. His defense came in the form of one of the most important and influential works in the history of Christianity, the *City of God* (413–426). It would be difficult to exaggerate the importance of this work, as it became the theological, social, cultural, and political guidebook for the Middle Ages.[5] For one thousand years, only Scripture was regarded by western Christians as a more authoritative text.

Through the writing of the *City of God*, St. Augustine also came to realize that though Rome may have fallen, Christianity stood strong. "Though he was a loyal Roman and a scholar who realized the value of Greek thought, he regarded these things as temporary and accidental," Christopher Dawson explained. "He lived not by the light of Athens and Alexandria, but by a new light that had suddenly dawned on the world from the East only a few centuries earlier."[6] The essence of Christianity remained, no matter how the accidents appeared. Truth is eternal, but cities, kingdoms, and civilizations are fleeting. For St. Augustine, Rome represented the City of Man, in its paganism, decadence, and torture of Christians; Jerusalem represented the City of God.[7] While the City of Man might take many forms, the Church, united by the sacraments across time, would take a form counter to the ways of the world. The Church, the embryo of the City of God, would prevail in the end.

Like St. Augustine, Christopher Dawson looked out over a ruined world. On one side, Dawson viewed a world controlled by ideologues, and, consequently, a world of the gulag, the Holocaust camps, the killing fields, and total war. On the other side, he saw a world of the pleasures of the flesh,

---

[4]St. Jerome quoted in Christopher Dawson, *Enquiries into Religion and Culture* (London: Sheed and Ward, 1933), 221.

[5]Christopher Dawson, *Religion and the Rise of Western Culture* (1950; New York: Image Books, 1991), 68; and Dawson, *Enquiries into Religion and Culture,* 199.

[6]Christopher Dawson, "The Hour of Darkness," *Tablet* (1939), 625.

[7]Ibid.

ad-men, and what C. S. Lewis labeled the democratic "conditioners," found especially in bureaucracies and institutions of education.[8] Both East and West had become dogmatically materialist, Dawson argued, though after radically different fashions. The West pursued material greed and embraced avarice, while the East made anything spiritual illegal and immoral.

Each side, Dawson believed, mechanized men, making them less than what God or nature desired them to be. In almost every way, the devastation of Dawson's twentieth-century world was far greater than that of St. Augustine's fifth-century world. At least barbarian man believed in something greater than himself. One could confront him as a man, a man who knew who he was and what he believed, however false that belief might be to Christians. Modern and post-modern men, Dawson feared, tend to accept readily, and perhaps insatiably, the false, substitute religions offered by corporations and tyrants. If modern men reject Christianity, Dawson argued, they will readily grasp for anything proclaiming truth that comes their way: fascism, National Socialism, communism, or materialist capitalism.

Fifteen centuries after St. Augustine, Dawson believed, the barbarians stood again at the gates, and the world faced a similar crisis. There "are moments when the obscurity of history seems to be suddenly illuminated by some sign of divine purpose," Dawson wrote in 1959. "These are the moments of *crisis* in the literal sense of the word—times of judgment when the powers of this world are tried and condemned and when the course of history suddenly flows into a new channel." Devastation is the result, Dawson argued, using very Hebraic covenantal language. "Such was the age of the Hebrew prophets, such was the age of St. Augustine, and such is the age in which we have the privilege and misfortune to live today."[9]

And, like his patron St. Augustine, Dawson wanted to employ his energy and imagination—a freely-given gift from the Holy Spirit, he argued—to bring the world back to right reason and first principles. As Dawson wrote of St. Augustine: "To the materialist, nothing could be more futile than the spectacle of Augustine busying himself with the reunion of the African Church and the refutation of the Pelagians, while civilisation was falling to pieces about his ears." To Augustine, the destruction of political institutions meant very little in the long run. The venerable scholar and saint "looked beyond the aimless and bloody chaos of the world to the world of eternal realities from which the world of sense derives all the significance it possesses."[10] In this passage, Dawson could easily have been writing about himself and his role in the twentieth century, confronting the newly emerging technological and secu-

---

[8]C. S. Lewis, *The Abolition of Man: Or Reflections on Education with Special Reference to the Teaching of English in the Upper Forms of Schools* (1943; New York: Touchstone, 1996).

[9]Christopher Dawson, *The Movement of World Revolution* (New York: Sheed and Ward, 1959), 102.

[10]Dawson, *Enquiries into Religion and Culture*, 222.

larized world ruled by the ideologues left and right. As Aidan Nichols, O.P., has recently observed, Dawson's body of work is itself "best thought of as a latter-day *City of God*."[11]

Indeed, one of the most neglected topics of the Catholic Literary Revival of the twentieth century is the role St. Augustine played. Most scholars have focused on the importance of Pope Leo's 1879 encyclical on the necessity of reviving the thought of St. Thomas Aquinas, *Aeterni Patris* ("On the Restoration of Christian Philosophy"), and the subsequent development of neo-Thomism as led by such powerful intellects and personalities as Jacques Maritain. They especially influenced the proceedings and documents produced by the Second Vatican Council.[12] The neo-Thomists tended to believe that any religious emotion was dangerous, while reason was an essential pre-cursor to faith. All reason, they believed, would lead back, inevitably, to God, a belief that Dawson found simply wrong.[13]

As will be examined in greater detail later in this chapter, Dawson believed that every philosophy was culturally specific. Philosophy serves, then, as the highest and best expression of a particular people, nation, or time. The neo-Thomists, therefore, erred in being too western, Dawson noted. "The Thomists in particular have until recently ignored the problem of the diversity of cultures and have shown no interest in Indian and Chinese philosophy," Dawson wrote in private. Indeed, rather than attempting to sanctify all cultures to Christianity, the neo-Thomists have simply attempted to adapt "Thomism to modern European science or to meeting the challenge of modern systems of philosophy which are themselves purely Western: more Western, in fact, than Thomism itself," he continued.[14] "Thomism may represent the *philosophia perennis* of the Western world, and it may be potentially the *philosophia perennis* of the whole world," Dawson claimed. "But it is not so actually, and it cannot become so until it has incorporated the philosophical traditions of the rest of the world in the same way that it incorporated the philosophical traditions of Hellenism."[15]

A true philosophy of culture, Dawson argued, must walk a path between "the absolutism of the Neo-Thomists and the relativism of the moderns," and

---

[11] Aidan Nichols, O.P., "Christopher Dawson's Catholic Setting," in *Eternity in Time: Christopher Dawson and the Catholic Idea of History,* Stratford Caldecott and John Morrill, eds. (Edinburgh, Scotland: T&T Clark, 1997), 34. See also Ernest L. Fortin, "A Note on Dawson and St. Augustine," in *The Birth of Philosophic Christianity: Studies in Early Christian and Medieval Thought,* Brian Benestad, ed. (Lanham, MD: Rowman and Littlefield, 1996), 115–122.

[12] See especially Tracey Rowland, *Culture and the Thomist Tradition: After Vatican II* (London: Routledge, 2003).

[13] James Hitchcock, "Postmortem on a Rebirth: The Catholic Intellectual Renaissance," *American Scholar,* vol. 49 (1980), 216.

[14] Dawson, "The Relation of Philosophy to Culture," September 7, 1955, in Box 1, Folder 15, ND/CDAW.

[15] Ibid.

fall more in line with the "tradition of the medieval English scholasticism—a theological absolutism combined with a philosophical relativism ... it is also the tradition of the French Catholic traditionalists like Bonald and de Maistre."[16] Such a vision of culture, most likely taken from Book XIX, chapter 17, of the *City of God*, bridges the universal with the particular. "This heavenly city, then, while it sojourns on earth, calls citizens out of all nations, and gathers together a society of pilgrims of all languages, not scrupling about diversities in manners, laws, and institutions," St. Augustine had written. "It therefore is so far from rescinding and abolishing these diversities, that it even preserves and adapts them, so long only as no hindrance to the worship of the one supreme and true God is thus introduced."

In other words, as Dawson saw it, since philosophy served as the highest form of expression for any single culture, it must be an expression unique to that group. But since there is one God and one truth, theology must be absolute. So several cultures might worship the one God and one truth in a variety of ways. But each culture had to acknowledge the one God and one truth, not confusing its particular manifestation of worship with the universal and absolute truth.

Other differences existed between the Augustinians and the neo-Thomists. First, twentieth-century Augustinians such as Dawson and Russell Kirk held no fondness for mass, twentieth-century democracy, while Maritain and the neo-Thomists were adamantly pro-liberal and pro-democracy.[17] In this, the twentieth-century Augustinians sided with important western men, Plato and Edmund Burke, to name two, seeing much of mass democracy as nothing more than unrestrained mob action. As discussed briefly in chapter three, Dawson thought Maritain's scholarly output declined after 1936, the year in which Maritain declared himself a man of the Left.

> [Maritain] has made too much emphasis on political issues, in the former, he has become quite a poor prose writer, obscurity replacing his former clarity. Earlier Maritan of Three Reformers and Religion and Culture (in Essays in Order) is one Dawson liked. True Humanism [1936] is on the border between the earlier and later Maritain, and contains examples of both good and bad styles. Dawson prefers Gilson to Maritain, and believes the former is a much clearer and better writer.[18]

In his private notes, Dawson considered *True Humanism*, perhaps Maritain's most famous work, too dualistic, offering the Christian only the stark contrast

---

[16]Dawson to Mulloy, January 19, 1957, in Box 1, Folder 9, ND/CDAW. Romano Guardini may have offered the best bridge between the Augustinians and the neo-Thomists. In his book *The Conversion of Augustine* (Westminster, MD: Newman, 1960), Guardini wrote that Augustine, untempered, leads to Calvinism and Lutheranism. Only when one takes the thoughts of Aquinas and Augustine together, can one fully understand Augustine. In other words, Aquinas offers the proper and logical conclusion to Augustine.

[17]Hitchcock, "Postmortem," 219.

[18]John J. Mulloy, Record of Dawson conversation on August 19, 1953, in Box 1, Folder 2, ND/CDAW.

of St. Thomas and Karl Barth.[19] Second, just as Dawson thought the neo-Thomists were too abstract and theoretical—if not outright ideological—the neo-Thomists thought little of Dawson, considering him a "mere" historian, a recorder, and a glorified scribe.[20] Most of Dawson's criticisms of Maritain and the neo-Thomists remained private, however. Only on occasion, such as in Dawson's 1960 *Thought* article, "The Study of Christian Culture," did he criticize the neo-Thomists in print, and even then, the criticism was relatively tame. "Catholic education is being pushed in the opposite direction toward metaphysical absolutism so that you will get two mutually exclusive and incomprehensible universes of discourse," Dawson wrote, echoing the late medieval Christian Platonist Petrarch.

> The student is bound to take Thomism largely on faith since there is no competition of rival schools, as in the medieval university, and so one is in danger of having a solid monolithic structure of infallible knowledge which includes philosophy as well as theology and treats the two as coequal, so that Catholic education becomes identified with an authoritarian ideology, like Marxism.[21]

With students, he would be more open about his beliefs. Historian John Hellman remembers tea with the Dawsons in the early 1960s.

> The most memorable part of the conversation was when Dawson, frowning at discovering what I was being taught by the Thomist legion at Marquette, went over to his bookshelves and took down a volume of Bonaventure (in Latin) which he passed on for me to leaf through, a practical antidote to the tunnel visions of those Gilson-formed scholastics from St. Michael's College, Toronto, working to build the New Middle Ages in middle America.[22]

Though Hellman does not state it explicitly, it would be fair to write that Dawson believed one should understand Thomism through the eyes of Bonaventure.

Few scholars have written on Augustinianism in the twentieth century, yet it would be difficult to overemphasize the saint's importance. In his 1956 work, *Beyond the Dreams of Avarice*, for example, Russell Kirk wrote that the modern traditionalist must view the world as did St. Augustine. "We have the high duty of keeping alight amid the Vandal flood, like Augustine of Hippo, the spark of principle and conscience."[23] Indeed, Russell Amos Kirk became

---

[19]Dawson, N.D., no title, in Box 9, Folder 22, UST/CDC.

[20]Hitchcock, "Postmortem," 220. Dawson admitted that much that passed for history was also too culturally specific. Few men could abstract themselves from their own time or beliefs to describe effectively the past or an alien people, he argued. See his "Introduction," xiii, in *Celtic Peoples and Renaissance Europe*.

[21]Christopher Dawson, "The Study of Christian Culture," *Thought*, vol. 35 (1960), 485–93.

[22]John Hellman, "Christopher Dawson, The New Theology, and Harvard in the 1960s," *The Christopher Dawson Centre of Christian Culture Newsletter*, vol. 2 (July 1999).

[23]Russell Kirk, *Beyond the Dreams of Avarice; Essays of a Social Critic* (Chicago: Regnery, 1956), x. Dr. Kirk's wife, Annette, confirmed her husband's Augustinianism in conversation with the present author, March 15, 2003.

Russell Amos Augustine Kirk when he formally entered the Roman Catholic Church in 1964.[24] Only three years after his marriage and conversion, Kirk wrote in the columns of *National Review* that "Augustine, so neglected today, perhaps has more to teach this age than has any other philosopher."[25] In his autobiography, Kirk wrote of himself, "Reading the fathers of the Church, Augustine and Gregory and Ambrose especially, Kirk gave up his previous spiritual individualism." St. Augustine's words made Kirk realize the value of community: "'The calm judgment of the world is that those men cannot be good who, in any part of the world, cut themselves off from the rest of the world.' Therefore, the Church had been raised up."[26]

Dawson had written something similar nearly a decade earlier. Only humility can defeat pride. In particular, only the sacrifice of Christ can defeat the machinations of the devil. The true religious reformer will be treated like a prophet of old: distrusted and despised by the world. "He must be prepared to stand alone like Ezekiel and Jeremy," Dawson wrote. "He must take as his example St. Augustine besieged by the Vandals at Hippo, or St. Gregory preaching at Rome with the Lombards at the gates. For the true helpers of the world are the poor in spirit, the men who bear the sign of the cross on their foreheads, who refused to be overcome by the triumph of injustice and put their sole trust in the salvation of God."[27] For Dawson and Kirk, St. Augustine served as both the lodestar in confronting the evils of the world and as a means by which the modern traditionalist should navigate in turbulent ideological waters.

As Dawson's publisher and friend, Frank Sheed, wrote in his own autobiography, St. Augustine should take his place as one of the six most important thinkers in the twentieth-century literary revival. Sheed's other five were Dawson, Belloc, Chesterton, C. C. Martindale, and Ronald Knox. St. Augustine, perhaps more than any other Christian thinker, emphasized the power of human imagination, guided by the Holy Spirit.[28] In this, St. Augustine anticipated Newman's "illative sense," T. S. Eliot's and Russell Kirk's "moral imagination," J. R. R. Tolkien's idea of "sub-creation," and Dawson's desire to re-invigorate the world with imagination in his own work. Further, Augustine was not important just for his own age, but for all ages throughout western civilization. He is, after all, "one of the key figures of all history," Sheed argued. "Every man living in the Western world would be a different man if Augustine had not been, or had been different."[29] He was, in many ways, as

---

[24]Conversation with Annette Kirk, March 6, 2004.

[25]Russell Kirk, "Beginning in Doubt," *National Review*, vol. 19 (March 21, 1967), 306.

[26]Russell Kirk, *The Sword of Imagination: Memoirs of a Half-Century of Literary Conflict* (Grand Rapids, MI: William B. Eerdmans, 1995), 231.

[27]Dawson, *Religion and the Rise of Western Culture,* 124.

[28]Frank Sheed, *The Church and I* (Garden City, NY: Doubleday and Co., 1974), 110, 128.

[29]Frank Sheed, ed. and trans., *Confessions,* by St. Augustine (Indianapolis, IN: Hackett, 1993), xxvii.

Sheed and Dawson believed, a nexus in the world. He not only served as a geographical nexus, bridging Africa with Rome, Europe, and the Holy Land, but he was, more importantly, a nexus between the classical and the medieval worlds. Like Plato, Aristotle, and Cicero, he came at the end of his own civilization, and he recorded all that he could of what had come before him, allowing a remnant to benefit from such understandings.

An Augustinian Metahistory

Dawson's thought also reflects that of St. Augustine in his desire to see all things in a quasi-dualistic fashion. This dualism stems not only from St. Augustine's original heretical beliefs in Manicheism, but also from his Platonism. Indeed, one of St. Augustine's greatest accomplishments was the sanctification of Plato's understanding of the two realms: the perfect Celestial Kingdom and the corrupt copy, based on the ideal forms of the True, the Good, and the Beautiful. One finds a similar tension and conflict between this world and the next in all of Dawson's ideas and works. "Christian culture is always in conflict with the world," Dawson wrote directly.[30] The "conception of the sacred and the secular manifests itself at every stage of culture from the primitive to the most highly civilized and in every form of religion."[31]

For Plato, the two realms never meet, except on rare and mystical occasions when the person finds, through the practice of the virtues, the "mind beside itself," a form of divine madness, as he explained in his *Phaedrus* (sections 249–250). For St. Augustine and for Christopher Dawson, though, one cannot readily separate the two cities, the City of God and the City of Man, in any strict dualism or profound opposition. "In truth," St. Augustine wrote, "these two cities are entangled together in this world, and intermixed until the last judgment effect their separation."[32] While the two cities do not meet spiritually, they intermingle physically.[33] As Dawson argued,

> We must remember that behind the natural process of social conflict and tension which runs through history there is a deeper law of spiritual duality and polarization," Dawson argued in no uncertain terms, "which is expressed in the teaching of the Gospel on the opposition of the World and the Kingdom of God and in St. Augustine's doctrine of the two cities Babylon and Jerusalem whose conflict run through all history and gives it its ultimate significance.[34]

---

[30]Dawson to Mulloy, November 11, 1957, in Box 1, Folder 16, ND/CDAW.

[31]Dawson, "Notes on Secularism," dated December 18, 1953, in Box 1, Folder 15, ND/CDAW.

[32]St. Augustine, the *City of God*, Book 1, Section 35.

[33]Christopher Dawson, *Dynamics of World History*, John J. Mulloy, ed. (1957; Wilmington, DE: ISI Books, 2002), 315.

[34]Christopher Dawson, "The Social Factor in the Problem of Christian Unity," *Colosseum*, vol. 4 (1938), 14; and "Is the Church Too Western to Satisfy the Aspirations of the Modern World?" in *World Crisis and the Catholic: Studies Published on the Occasion of The Second World Congress for the Lay Apostolate (Rome)*, (New York: Sheed and Ward, 1958), 168.

Christians live in the City of Man, Augustine argued, but sojourn as pilgrims in this world as citizens of the City of God. "The City of God is a real society with its roots in eternity and its development in time and history," Dawson wrote.[35] Love separates the two cities. That is, a proper understanding of sacrifice for others as well as a prideful, false understanding of the nature and significance of love as sacrifice to self divides this world from the next. "Two cities have been formed by two loves: the earthly city by the love of self, even to the contempt of God; the heavenly by the love of God, even to the contempt of self," St. Augustine argued. "The former, in a word, glories in itself, the latter in the Lord."[36] This profound dualism—between the City of God and the City of Man—lasts as long as time itself. Each new generation must accept its place in history and struggle for the Good, the True, the Beautiful, and, ultimately, the One. "There is no aspect of human life and no sphere of human action which is neutral or 'secular' in the absolute sense," Dawson contended.[37] Instead, all things are subject to such dualism, and all material forces must be sanctified and properly spiritualized.

Unlike the abstract Celestial King of Plato's metaphysics, a wholesome, beneficent, and totally sovereign God intertwined and intertwines Himself in history. God acts personally not only through the deepest profundity of the death and resurrection of the Incarnate Word, but also through the actions of angels and men, creatures chosen by God to do His will and perform His miracles. Sometimes He acts directly, but more often than not, He asks His creatures to act lovingly in His Name. But, as noted earlier, it is the Incarnation that serves as the middle point of history, the center of God's story within time. For after the Incarnation, Dawson argued, eternity and time readily mix, especially through and within the sacraments of the Church. "For the Christian view of history is not merely a belief in the direction of history by divine providence," Dawson explained. "It is a belief in the intervention by God in the life of mankind by direct action at certain definite points in time and place."[38] For Christ has already shown us the way, and His actions have altered history and nature itself: we are to humble ourselves, to give up our selfish wills, and to become His instruments, both St. Augustine and Dawson argued. Just as Christ humbled Himself on the cross, so do we to the Maker of all. "Thy will be done" were the words that Christ taught us to speak to Abba, a form of address as intimate as "papa." In the words of Augustine:

> Choose now what you will pursue, that your praise may be not in yourself, but in
> the true God, in whom there is no error. For of popular glory you have had your

---

[35] Dawson to Mulloy and *Commonweal*, March 5, 1955, in Box 1, Folder 16, ND/CDAW.

[36] St. Augustine, *The City of God,* trans. Marcus Dods (New York: Modern Library, 1993), Book 14, Section 28.

[37] Christopher Dawson, "The Problem of Christ and Culture," *Dublin Review*, vol. 226 (1952), 64.

[38] Dawson, *Dynamics of World History,* 247.

share; but by the secret providence of God, the true religion was not offered to your choice. Awake, it is now day; as you have already awaked in the persons of some in whose perfect virtue and sufferings for the true faith we glory: for they, contending on all sides with hostile powers, and conquering them all by bravely dying, have purchased for us this country of ours with their blood; to which country we invite you, and exhort you to add yourselves to the number of citizens of this city.[39]

The Church, as St. Augustine knew well, was built on the blood of the martyrs who followed Christ's example. Martyrs such as Sts. Perpetua, Felicity, Boniface, Sir Thomas More, John Fisher, Maximilian Kolbe, and Blessed Miguel Pro have shown the way throughout the two-thousand year history of the Church. They have challenged respectively Roman oppression, German ignorance, Anglican nationalism, National Socialism, Mexican secularism, and global communism. The foe is ever the same, merely taking a different name and appearing in a somewhat different guise.

Yet martyrdom is not the only thing that separates these men and women from the rest of humanity. All true Christians humble themselves to God and to God's task for themselves, even if it leads them to physical death. But, love, the highest of virtues, comes in many forms, and one may justly sacrifice a part of himself—his time, his talent, etc.—without actually physically dying. Martyrdom is simply the highest form of love. Man, then, must order himself to the will that has created all, for his job is to bring all things back into the divine order. Dawson saw that man's "whole destiny depends on the proper co-ordination of" the matter and the spirit, "for since he is a bridge, the lower world is in some sense dependent on him for its spiritualization and its integration in the universal order."[40] Dawson accepted the Augustinian answer as to how one conforms one's self to the order of creation. This can only be accomplished, he argued, through the draining of one's will and the acceptance of God's grace, which fills the void of the individual human will.

In Dawson's Augustinian vision, not only are individual persons important, but humanity as a whole is vital to the work of creation. "There is a point at which the world of spirit comes in conscious contact with the world of matter," Dawson wrote. "That point is man."[41] Man, then, serves as the *metaxy*, a being who is neither wholly spirit nor wholly animal, but an essential bridge between the two. Language, as will be discussed later in this chapter, allows us to be the *metaxy*, the nexus of spirit and flesh, just as Christ was the Incarnate Word, the nexus between God the Father and humanity. The idea of *metaxy* also allows one to dismiss either extreme spiritualism or extreme materialism. "Man is not saved *from* the body, as the Gnostics taught, but *in* the body," Dawson wrote, reflecting St. John's teachings regarding Christ in the

---

[39] Augustine, *City of God,* Book 2, Section 29.

[40] Christopher Dawson, "The Nature and Destiny of Man," in *God and the Supernatural: A Catholic Statement of the Christian Faith,* (London: Catholic Book Club, 1936), 57.

[41] Ibid., 63.

first chapter of his gospel. "The gift of the Spirit was fulfilled in the body, as the work of the Incarnation was contained and completed in the Church."[42] A Christian must allow the Spirit to sanctify the material, something done on an everyday level in culture and tradition. It is most often done through the power of language, allowing one generation to pass its beliefs on to the next. "Language enlarges the physical inheritance of the blood by a spiritual inheritance of memory and tradition," Dawson argued, echoing the work of Aristotle in his *Politics*, "which makes the community conscious of its existence in the past, of its historic continuity and experience."[43]

Sainthood, the abandonment of self-love and the acceptance of the Divine Order, represents the highest form of perfected nature in this fallen world.[44] "I realized that the Incarnation, the Sacraments, the external order of the Church and the internal working of sanctifying grace were all parts of one organic unity, a living tree, whose roots are in the Divine Nature whose fruit is the perfection of the saints," Dawson explained in 1926. "The saint is the perfect manifestation of the supernatural life which exists in every individual Christian."[45] Several years earlier, he had written that "Only in the saints, with whom the process is exceptionally advanced, is the whole external life conformed to the new inward principle." For most Christians, Dawson continued, "the natural life goes on almost unchanged, based on its principle and following its own laws." But grace can and may change all things. "Behind all this the supernatural principle carries on its seminal activity and forms the embryonic life," Dawson wrote, "which is destined eventually to absorb into itself and remake the whole nature, mental and physical, with all its vital activities."[46]

Dawson credited St. Augustine as "the founder of the philosophy of history."[47] Unlike the Greeks, who had a more cosmological perspective, St. Augustine believed that history itself had a spiritual meaning. That God chose an obscure nomadic tribe to be his "Chosen Nation" proves the point, Dawson thought. The Christian recognizes that the Jews "had been made the vehicle of an absolute divine purpose, [and] was to him the very centre of his faith." As opposed to the mythologies of the Greeks and of the East, the Christian believes in the purpose of history as God's sacred instrument. Indeed, Christ came not at any point, but in the "fullness of time," (Galatians 4:4) when three distinct cultures intersected with one another, again proving that history was vital to God's plan. Because of Alexander the Great's conquest of

[42]Christopher Dawson, *The Formation of Christendom* (New York: Sheed and Ward, 1967), 108.

[43]Ibid., 34.

[44]Dawson, *Dynamics of World History*, 252.

[45]Christopher Dawson, "Why I am a Catholic," reprinted in *Chesterton Review* (May 1983), 112–113.

[46]Dawson, "Nature and Destiny of Man," 82.

[47]Dawson, *Dynamics of World History*, 311.

the Holy Land, and guerilla leader Judah Maccabees' invitation to the Roman Republic to intervene and remove the Hellenstic rulers, Jesus of Nazareth was born into a Hellenistic Jewish culture, controlled militarily and politically by the Roman Empire, and divided, theologically, among several Jewish schools of thought.[48]

The simultaneous dualism and importance of history presents a significant dilemma for every Christian. While we are already citizens of Heaven, we must live in the earthly City of Man. "The earthly city," St. Augustine reminds us, "which does not live by faith, seeks an earthly peace, and the end it proposes, in the well-ordered concord of civic obedience and rule, is the combination of men's wills to attain the things which are helpful to this life."[49] Therefore, the City of Man attains greatness and decline in never-ending cycles. In the earthly city, "the princes and the nations it subdues are ruled by the love of ruling."[50] A Christian must never fully trust a government, which is, more often than not, St. Augustine argued, nothing more than a gang of thieves and robbers that has bested all other gangs of thieves and robbers. When justice dissolves—and justice is a gift from God, not a gift from the world of men—"what are kingdoms but great robberies? For what are robberies themselves, but little kingdoms? The band itself is made up of men; it is ruled by the authority of a prince, it is knit together by the pact of the confederacy; the booty is divided by the law agreed upon."[51]

We see this clearly in St. Augustine's view of the Roman empire. "Rome is to him always, 'the second Babylon,'" Dawson explained, "the supreme example of human pride and ambition, and he seems to take a bitter pleasure in recounting the crimes and misfortunes of her history."[52] The Incarnation allows the Church, the representative of the City of God on earth, as John Henry Cardinal Newman put it, "to gather His Saints."[53] Christian loyalty, then, can be to no nation, but to the one, Universal, Catholic Church.[54]

The vision of history espoused by St. Augustine and Dawson, then, is not strictly history in the modern, professional sense of the term. The *City of God*, Dawson explained, was "a vast synthesis which embraces the history of the whole human race and its destinies in time and eternity."[55] Larger than a study of mere fact or a laying out of a sequence of names and dates, St. Augustine's *City of God* is "metahistory." For metahistory "is concerned with the

---

[48] Ibid., 313.

[49] Augustine, *City of God,* Book 19, Section 17.

[50] Ibid., Book 14, Section 28.

[51] Ibid., Book 4, Chapter 4.

[52] Dawson, *Enquiries into Religion and Culture,* 237.

[53] Newman quoted in Dawson, *Dynamics of World History,* 314.

[54] Dawson, *Dynamics of World History,* 315.

[55] Christopher Dawson, "St. Augustine and His Age," in *A Monument to Saint Augustine: Essays on Some Aspects of His Thought Written in Commemoration of His 15th Centenary,* Tom Burns, ed. (London: Sheed and Ward, 1945), 43.

nature of history, the meaning of history and the cause and significance of historical change," Dawson wrote. "The historian himself is primarily engaged in the study of the past. He does not ask himself why the past is different from the present or what is the meaning of history as a whole. What he wants to know is what actually happened at a particular time and place and what effect it had on the immediate future."[56] Unlike history, metahistory posits a truth about philosophy and theology. It attempts to find an essence at the heart of the various accidents of history. Dawson believed that in addition to St. Augustine, Alexis de Tocqueville was one of the greatest of metahistorians. His "profundity is due to the breadth of his spiritual visions and to the strength of his religious faith."[57] As with language, a metahistory has a sense of poetry to it. The "mastery" of professional historical methods and "techniques will not produce great history, any more than a mastery of metrical technique will produce great poetry." The true historian, or the metahistorian, will recognize that "something more is necessary—intuitive understanding, creative imagination, and finally a universal vision transcending the relative limitation of the particular field of historical study."[58] The historian, like the poet, should be divinely inspired, accepting the creativity offered by the love of the Holy Spirit, the source of all creativity and imagination. So armed, the historian should recognize the Creator and glorify the creation. The professional historian, Dawson claimed, will often fall into the trap of antiquarianism, thus diminishing the profundity of history as a divine instrument.[59] He will, then, forget the higher purpose of history as ordained by God and explore only the trinkets created, time and time again, by man.

Homo Religiosus

Dawson's understanding of culture stood at the heart of all of his beliefs regarding history, anthropology, and sociology. His serious interest in the intersection of religion and culture began in 1907, as a freshman at Oxford, while reading the medieval Icelandic sagas.[60] Whether individual human persons or cultures recognized it or not, he realized, religion shapes almost all norms and mores, language, and family structure. Even material things, such as food ways and courtship customs, ultimately have a religious basis. A culture that has by and large rejected its religion or secularized itself has merely substi-

---

[56]Dawson, *Dynamics of World History,* 303. For a critique of Dawson's position, see Hayden White, "Religion, Culture and Western Civilization in Christopher Dawson's Idea of History," *English Miscellany,* vol. 9 (1958), 247–87.

[57]Dawson, *Dynamics of World History,* 309.

[58]Ibid., 309–10.

[59]Ibid., 304.

[60]Frank Sheed, "Frank Sheed Talks with Christopher Dawson," *The Sign,* vol. 38 (December 1958), 35.

tuted some false religion—most likely an ideology of some kind—for its lost faith.

Once this is understood, Dawson argued, the process of a man fulfilling his destiny is rather obvious: God calls each person; each person has the natural law written on his heart; and each human person best expresses his religiosity within the natural and inherited community. Real community is not based on some freely-entered social contract between equals, but instead is natural, organic, hierarchical, and driven and governed by proper authorities. The community in which a person's religiosity is best expressed could be rooted in the here and now, or it could transcend the particular, partaking of the universal, much like the Burkean community of the dead, the living, and the yet unborn. Both forms of community are equally valid and necessary in God's economy of grace. Each plays its own role, and each person is called to play a unique role within each. "The Catholic conception of society is not that of a machine for the production of wealth," Dawson wrote in 1933, "but of a spiritual organism in which every class and every individual has its own function to fulfil and its own rights and duties in relation to the whole."[61]

At the root of every society lies the *cultus*, defined as the group of people, usually based on kinship, who band together to worship the same deity or deities. "Therefore from the beginning the social way of life which is culture has been deliberately ordered and directed in accordance with the higher laws of life which are religion," Dawson explained.[62] Culture "is essentially a vital phenomenon—a way or order or pattern of social living. It is a way of gaining, preserving, and extending life."[63] Further, it is a "network of relations," again, in the Burkean sense, connecting person to person, in and across time.[64] Economics, politics, and law proceed from the culture. American cultural critic Russell Kirk, influenced by Dawson in a variety of ways, explained Dawson's views well:

> A cult is a joining together for worship—that is, the attempt of people to commune with a transcendent power. It is from association in the cult, the body of worshippers, that community grows.... Once people are joined in a cult, cooperation in many other things becomes possible. Common defense, irrigation, systematic agriculture, architecture, the visual arts, music, the more intricate crafts, economic production and distribution, courts and government—all these aspects of a culture arise gradually from the cult, the religious tie.[65]

---

[61] Dawson, letter to the *Cambridge Review*, dated February 17, 1933, reprinted in the *Chesterton Review,* vol. 23 (November 1997), 530.

[62] Christopher Dawson, "The Relationship between Religion and Culture," *Commonweal*, vol. 49 (February 25, 1949), 489.

[63] Dawson, "Culture, Religion and Ethics," dated January 19, 1957, in Box 1, Folder 15, ND/CDAW.

[64] Dawson to Mulloy, May 24, 1960, in Box 1, Folder 16, ND/CDAW.

[65] Russell Kirk, *Redeeming the Time*, Jeffrey O. Nelson, ed. (Wilmington, DE: Intercollegiate Studies Institute, 1996), 7.

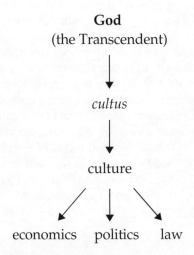

Christopher Dawson's understanding of culture

Further, "religion is the key to history," Dawson claimed. "We cannot understand the inner form of a society unless we understand its religion."[66] "A social culture is an organized way of life which is based on a common tradition and conditioned by a common environment," Dawson wrote in 1949. "It is therefore not identical with the concept of civilizations, which involves a high degree of conscious rationalization nor with society itself, since a culture normally includes a number of independent units."[67]

Since the worship of the same divinity ultimately shapes and defines a culture, the loss of religious faith necessitates the eventual destruction of the culture. "The society without culture is a formless society—a crowd or a collection of individuals brought together by the needs of the moment—while the stronger a culture is, the more completely does it inform and transform the diverse human material of which it is composed," Dawson wrote in *Religion and Culture*.[68] A culture without a common faith may linger for a while, but eventually it must dissolve, for all other bonds between men, especially political bonds, are tenuous at best without a common faith. In other words, there is no such thing as a culture that is secular. A secular culture would, by definition, mean the absence of a culture.

---

[66]Dawson, "Relationship between Religion and Culture," 489. See also Dawson to Father Ward, November 30, 1956, in Box 1, Folder 2, in Leo Ward Papers, University of Notre Dame Archives, Notre Dame, IN (hereafter, ND/CLRW).

[67]Dawson, "Relationship between Religion and Culture," 488.

[68]Christopher Dawson, *Religion and Culture* (London: Sheed and Ward, 1949), 48.

Rather than embracing Hobbes, Locke, or Rousseau, Dawson sided with de Maistre and Burke in rejecting all social contract theory. Culture is organic, developing slowly over time. It must be cultivated, Dawson argued, not abstracted, contracted, or decreed. "Culture does not arise spontaneously from the soil," Dawson explained. Instead, culture "is an artificial growth which has been diffused from its original source in the Eastern Mediterranean by a complex process of transplantation and has been gradually made to bear fruit in a new soil by a long process of careful cultivation." Further, Dawson wrote, "drama and prose are like the vine and the olive, and they are derived from the same homelands."[69] Following the thought of Edmund Burke in his various works against the French Revolution, Dawson believed that cultures were delicate at best. Drastic change, then, must necessarily result in the death of culture, for the fabric of culture remains fragile, and its delicate threads may become undone at any moment. What might take 1,000 years to build can be destroyed in days.

And yet, no culture can remain isolated from every other culture. Almost every culture, Dawson argued early in his writing career, must evolve in a nuanced, complicated, three-part process when it encounters an alien culture. First, when two cultures come into contact with one another, there is a process of cross-fertilization of ideas, biology, and religious beliefs. Second, as the two cultures become accustomed to one another, the synthesized culture grows dramatically. The third part of the process is the most unstable and potentially the most dangerous to the longevity of the culture. This third stage represents a period of maturity, "when either the new elements are completely assimilated and the original culture tradition once more becomes dominant, or when a complete fusion of the two elements takes place and the new type of culture becomes stabilized and permanent."[70] If things fail in stage three, the culture breaks apart. Dawson noted that this was the cause of the Greek breakup in the fifth-century B. C. "Hellenic civilization collapsed not by a failure of nerve but by the failure of life," Dawson wrote.[71]

Further, every culture has both a "moral" and a "scientific" element, to use Dawson's terminology.[72] The former informs the norms and mores, the practical arts, the ethics, and the organization of the community through the culturally dependent legal and political institutions. The latter, the "scientific" as Dawson called it, is the traditional, that which is inherited and observed from one's ancestors and maintained for one's posterity. Oral or written com-

---

[69]Christopher Dawson, "Christianity and the Humanist Tradition," *Dublin Review*, vol. 226 (1952), 6.

[70]Christopher Dawson, *Progress and Religion: An Historical Inquiry* (1929; Washington, D.C.: Catholic University of America Press, 2001), 57–58.

[71]Ibid., 59.

[72]Christopher Dawson, "The Modern Dilemma," *Cambridge Review*, February 17, 1933, 36.

munication is the vital element in transmitting this second aspect of culture.[73] The moral aspect of culture is subjective, while the scientific aspect of culture is objective. This strictly follows Dawson's own dualistic personal beliefs, for, as mentioned earlier in this chapter, he described his own thinking as "a theological absolutism combined with a philosophical relativism."[74]

In addition, Dawson argued, all "religion is based on the recognition of a superhuman Reality of which man is somehow conscious and towards which he must in some way orientate his life. The existence of the tremendous transcendent reality that we name GOD is the foundation of all religion in all ages and among all peoples."[75] Religion serves, then, as a bridge between the spiritual and the physical.[76] Dawson claimed that one could, as in the moral aspect of culture mentioned above, study the phenomenology of religion. That is, one could readily observe the rituals and experiences of individual persons or generations of persons. Importantly, phenomenology only reveals the subjective truths of religion. To complete the picture, one must also consider the objective, pure Being, the Author of creation. Specifically, a scholar must study rules governing human-God relations as well as human-human relations. Only by studying both the experience of religion and the objective rules of God can one discover the truths of various cultures, the human person, and eternity. The true scholar, as in Dawson's scientific aspect of culture mentioned above, must accept the reality of the Divine, allowing theology as an objective discipline to "retain its primacy and its autonomy."[77]

History—defined by Dawson as the past, present, and future, the continuity of time itself, created in eternity by God—serves as one of the most important bridges between the subjective ethics of human cultures and persons and objective rules of the Transcendent. "The whole history of Christendom is a continual dialogue between God and man, and every age of the Church's life, even the most remote and obscure, has some important lesson for us today,"[78] Dawson argued.

As a discipline, history can offer much more to an understanding of anthropology and theology than can philosophy. Philosophy, as described earlier, "belongs to its culture in some respects more intensely and intimately

---

[73]Dawson, "Culture, Religion and Ethics," dated January 19, 1957, in Box 1, Folder 15, ND/CDAW; and Mulloy, "Record of Dawson conversation," August 19, 1953, in Box 1, Folder 2, ND/CDAW.

[74]Dawson to Mulloy, January 19, 1957, in Box 1, Folder 9, ND/CDAW.

[75]Dawson, *Religion and Culture*, 25.

[76]Christopher Dawson, "Religion and Culture: The Problems of Cultural Relativity in so far as it affects religion" dated September 10, 1955, in Box 1, Folder 15, ND/CDAW.

[77]One may find Dawson's most important and extensive discussion of "phenomenology" in "A Definition of Religion" in Christopher Dawson, *Religion and World History: A Selection from the Works of Christopher Dawson*, Christina Scott and James Oliver, eds. (Garden City, NY: Image, 1975),, 33.

[78]Dawson to Mulloy and *Commonweal*, March 5, 1955, in Box 1, Folder 16, ND/CDAW.

than any other forms of intellectual activity."[79] In other words, philosophy represents the highest form of cultural expression, but, for the most part, it cannot escape its cultural context. History, though, is the vehicle through which the Divine interacts with cultures and peoples. "For while philosophy and theology occupy different spheres, theology and history do not, except in so far as history is purely factual or united to special aspects of culture. Christian theology is a theology of Incarnation and of the successive stages of revelation," Dawson wrote in 1953.[80] Additionally, Dawson argued, theology and Christianity happen "*inside* history in a way that they do not with philosophy."[81] Theology, after all, studies "the creation, the fall and the restoration of human nature in Christ." Therefore, theology is a part of history, certainly "far more historical than philosophical."[82] Philosophy can rarely be more than "the most elaborate of cultural constructs," Dawson argued.[83] It is, ultimately, "a rational reflection on the whole of this cultural experience."[84]

Though man can escape philosophy, he can never escape history. Dawson found the idea of the abstract individual absurd, for each person is born into a certain time, a place, a family, a language, a religion, a culture, and an ethnicity. History and one's inheritance, genetic or otherwise, shape and inform all that he is and, more often than not, delimit what he can become. History is usually not a "dead weight but an active force that impels him forward along the path he has to travel," though in places like ancient Egypt, it became a stagnant and regressive force.[85] Significantly, civilization arises with the historical interaction of cultures through trade, war, and conquest.[86] But, Dawson warned, the interaction of the spirit, the material, culture, and history, is a difficult one to study. "We cannot understand a religion or even a philosophy unless we understand how it has been conditioned by social and historical factors," Dawson wrote in 1933. "Ideas and beliefs ally themselves with social forces and become fused with them in such a way that it is often difficult to disentangle them."[87]

Only the Divine fully understands the purpose and meaning of history, for He is the Author of it, and He uses it as His vehicle for His will. Man can

---

[79]Dawson, "Culture, Religion and Ethics," dated January 19, 1957, in Box 1, Folder 15, ND/CDAW.

[80]Dawson, "Theology and the Study of Christian Culture," August 22, 1953, in letter to John Mulloy, in Box 1, Folder 2, ND/CDAW.

[81]Ibid.

[82]Dawson to Mulloy, January 6, 1955, in Box 1, Folder 16, ND/CDAW.

[83]Dawson to Mulloy, August 31, 1955, in Box 1, Folder 15, ND/CDAW.

[84]Dawson, "The Relation of Philosophy to Culture," dated September 7, 1955, in Box 1, Folder 15, ND/CDAW.

[85]Christopher Dawson, *Religion and World History: A Selection from the Works of Christopher Dawson*, Christina Scott and James Oliver, eds. (Garden City, NY: Image, 1975), 269.

[86]Dawson, "Culture, Religion and Ethics," dated January 19, 1957, in Box 1, Folder 15, ND/CDAW.

[87]"Introduction" in Dawson, *Enquiries into Religion and Culture*, ix.

only glimpse a part of its significance, and a continuity of men in a culture can gain a greater appreciation of the purpose of history over generations, should they choose to preserve and build upon the understandings gleaned from their forefathers. Even the most primitive man, though, is aware not only of history's power but also of the Author of history's power. Primitive and pre-modern man attempts, usually through ritual, to understand and worship what he can of the Divine.[88] His ritual stems from what he has inherited from his ancestors and what he will pass on to his progeny. History connects him with all others. Like all societies, even primitive ones must "establish working relations with external reality and this reality is spiritual as well as material, so that their total structure of relations includes the whole of reality so far as they see it and understand it."[89] The relationship and parallels between high and low cultures remain, for each must first understand or order itself to the order of creation and find its place in the economy of grace and its reflection in the Great Chain of Being.

> The world of culture is a moral universe which extends downwards to the most primitive forms of social life and upwards to the higher ethical systems. And all cultures from the lowest to the highest are similar in their essential structure. That is to say they all depend on religious or spiritual sanctions; they are all rooted in particular material circumstances—economic, geographical and biological, and they themselves represent the patterns of social and moral behaviour by which these two factors are coordinated. Of these factors, the first is the concern of theology, comparative religion and moral philosophy, the second is dealt with by physical anthropology and to a great extent by sociology and economics, while the last is the proper study of social anthropology.[90]

While the material is always an important aspect of the individual human person and culture, every culture must first understand its relationship to the spirit before it can appreciate and understand its material needs. "The creative force of a culture always comes from the mind of the spiritual side," Dawson wrote in the introduction to his unpublished book, *The Rise of the World Religions*. The "material environment or the material circumstances of life only condition the form of its expression."[91]

Certainly, Dawson stressed, the historian of culture can never neglect the material aspects of a culture or of an environment. To focus only on the spiritual aspect of culture, Dawson feared, was just as ineffective and dangerous as focusing on the material alone. "Nevertheless, the limitations imposed on the freedom of the individual by the limitations of the social environment and tradition are facts of experience which the Christian, no less than the secular historian, is bound to take account of, and we cannot escape them by shutting

---

[88] Dawson, *Religion and World History*, 269.

[89] Dawson to Father Leo Ward, October 24, 1956, Box 1, Folder 2, ND/CLRW.

[90] Dawson to Father Leo Ward, November 20, 1956, Box 1, Folder 2, ND/CLRW.

[91] Dawson, Introduction to "The Rise of the World Religions," unpublished, in Box 1, Folder 15, ND/CDAW.

our eyes to their existence," Dawson wrote. "For human freedom is not the freedom of a pure spirit, it is the difficult freedom of a creature bound to his body, his country, and his people, the member of a society unable to disembarrass himself of the inheritance of the past and the countless limitations that are inseparable from the conditions of material existence."[92] Political philosopher Eric Voegelin, a generation younger than Dawson, rightly noted that to privilege either the spiritual or material at the expense of the other is to verge into a modern form of Gnosticism. Dawson best expressed this same belief in his profound essay, the "Nature and Destiny of Man." In it, Dawson wrote: "By the vital activity of the Spirit of Christ working through the Church and the Sacraments, mankind is remoulded and renewed; the disorder and weakness of human nature is overcome, and the domination of charity in spiritual love is substituted for the blindness of physical impulse and the narrowness and evil of selfish desire."[93] Though it is the spirit that is immortal, the spirit resides in the temple of the body, at least while it is within time. Christ was not the Word that *entered* flesh, but the Word that *became* flesh.

Though history is the bridge between the objective and the subjective, it is merely a tool, and it has no moral or independent agency in and of itself.[94] After all, Dawson contended, the Christian understands history as "a contemplation of the divine interposition in time," which remains "inaccessible to scientific history."[95] The Spirit—governed by its own will—sanctifies the material. "It is all a question of the continuity of the Incarnational process," Dawson wrote. "It is the mission of the Church to transform human life like a leaven, and to transform all forms of life, i.e. all cultures."[96] The Christian historian, therefore, undertakes a more difficult task in interpreting history than does the mere rationalist, materialist, or ideologue.[97] To clarify his position, Dawson offered the image of an iceberg, of which only a small portion can be seen. "What we see in history is only a partial and uncertain manifestation of the spiritual activity which is taking place at once below and above the level of historical study," Dawson explained. "No doubt you can have a comparative study of cultures on a purely rational plane, but since such a study is incapable of discrimination in spiritual values, it is unable to

---

[92]Christopher Dawson, "The Frontiers of Necessity: The Social Factor in Religious Belief," *Tablet* (1938), 697.

[93]Dawson, "Nature and Destiny of Man," 69–70.

[94]Dawson, *Religion and World History,* 272. For a relatively complete view of Dawson's understanding of the meaning of history, see Dawson, *Dynamics of World History.*

[95]Dawson, "Theology and the Study of Christian Culture," August 22, 1953, in letter to John Mulloy, in Box 1, Folder 2, ND/CDAW.

[96]Dawson to Mulloy, January 15, 1958, in Box 1, Folder 16, ND/CDAW.

[97]Dawson, "Theology and the Study of Christian Culture," August 22, 1953, in letter to John Mulloy, in Box 1, Folder 2, ND/CDAW.

discern the spiritual movement of history and the meaning of history."[98] To ignore the spiritual is to ignore the most important part of reality.

In truth, only an academic without an academic position could have argued such a thing and have the argument carry weight in the secular twentieth century. Rationalists, materialists, and ideologues often outright rejected Dawson's demand to study the spiritual aspect of man. One standard objection from twentieth-century scholars was that Dawson's theological reasoning was circular and tautological, that it could not be proven. Dawson's history, the criticism ran, was instead wishful thinking and mere assertion. Though Dawson's arguments might be beautiful, they remained false nonetheless. After all, to take Dawson's position, one had to assert that God existed, that scripture is true, that there is something beyond what we can prove with our five senses.

To these accusations, Dawson simply acquiesced. He fully admitted that he did assert the truth of God, the truth of scripture, and a belief in mysteries beyond the proof of our finite science. Dawson offered two lines of defense for his position. First, he argued, one can never understand religion as a scholar without looking at it from the inside. "For religion has its origins in the depths of the soul," Dawson argued, "and it can be understood only by those who are prepared to take the plunge."[99] Second, only we moderns have discounted religion. Therefore, not to take religion seriously is to negate the vast majority of human experience. Ultimately, to embrace such a belief would be to embrace chronological snobbery, the idea that one's generation is better than another. "It is, however, a well-known fact that many philosophers in all ages have asserted not only that a real knowledge is possible on this deeper level of consciousness but that this is the highest and most genuine form of knowledge accessible to man," Dawson argued. Further, almost all traditional philosophies, regardless of their origin point in the world, agree with this.[100] Every culture has been shaped by a religion, as has been proven by the anthropological evidence. Cultural rules and norms in ancient Confucian rituals, Dawson argued, are not simply "a matter of social etiquette; they are nothing less than the external manifestation of that eternal order that governs the universe, which is known as the Tao, the Way of Heaven." In India, one can translate the rules of ethics as "Order or Right."[101] In the western tradition, Aristotle, the Stoics, and the eclectic Roman republican Cicero uncovered the eternal rules of God and Nature, labeling them "right reason" or "first principles."

It is we moderns who are fooled into believing only in our private judgment and our individual senses. We modern sophists, Dawson argued, are the

---

[98] Ibid.
[99] Dawson, *Religion and Culture,* 33.
[100] Ibid., 34.
[101] Dawson, *Progress and Religion,* 100-01.

ones being unscholarly in discounting a higher power, a power unseen and un-known through our five physical senses, but recognized by all human cultures prior to the advent of modernity. Indeed, anthropologists believe that in ev-ery pre-twentieth century society, religion played a vital role in the history and development of a people, even if the same anthropologists dismiss the spiri-tual desires as mere justifications and rationalizations for materialist longings and acquisitions. Once a common worship and an understanding of theology develops or has been discovered, Dawson claimed, a common culture devel-ops. The "movement of introversion, by which man attains a consciousness deeper than that of his discursive reason but no less real," Dawson argued in the Gifford Lectures, "appears to be a universal human experience, common to almost all forms and stages of human culture."[102]

Language, Profane and Mundane

While Dawson dealt with the issue of culture in all of his major writings, beginning in his first book, *The Age of The Gods*, a study of primitive religions and cultures, Dawson offered his most developed understanding of culture in his Harvard University lectures. Published in part in the mid-1960s as *The Formation of Christendom*, Dawson drew on his own lifetime of scholarly thought and research and embraced a solidly Aristotelian view of the social world. Aristotle had famously written in his *Politics* that man is by nature a social animal, meant to live in community. To leave community, a man must become either a beast or a god, but he can no longer remain human. A man may not live outside his cultural inheritance, Dawson wrote, paraphrasing Aristotle, without becoming an "idiot, living in a private world of formless feelings, but lower than the beasts."[103] Not even offering the Aristotelian alternative of becoming a God, Dawson further noted that culture is the means by which "men have learned from the past" through "the process of imitation, education and learning and to all that they hand on in like manner to their descendants and successors."[104]

With St. John, Dawson proclaimed the importance of the Word to the human person as well as to history and culture. As "little words"—that is, human persons as *imago Dei*—humans pass on their civilization through the rational use of language. Language allows human societies to inherit and then transmit what is known and what is believed. Against those who see war as the great precipitator of cultural evolution, Dawson claimed all true progress comes from the proper use of language. "The word," he wrote, "not the sword or the spade, is the power that has created human culture."[105] The

---

[102]Dawson, *Religion and Culture,* 35.
[103]Dawson, *Formation of Christendom,* 31.
[104]Ibid.
[105]Ibid., 33.

sword protects the word, Dawson claimed, and the spade supports the word. Just as God spoke the universe into existence, man, created in His image, speaks culture into existence, tying the generations within time, but simultaneously also across time. Only through language can man store wisdom and understanding, building upon what was learnt and uncovered by previous generations, passing it on to future generations. "Language is the foundation of social life," Dawson wrote.[106]

An intimate relationship, of course, exists between language, tradition, and reason. "Language, which is essential to Reason," Dawson explained, "is itself essentially traditional, and I should say that it is in the creation of tradition, unless indeed it is a miraculous gift or invention," an idea which Dawson would not dismiss.[107] Language provides a framework for reason. Specifically, God communicates through tradition, a gift that proves "inaccessible to Reason." In addition, argued Dawson, "the individual who denies the authority of language and the other fundamental forms of human culture is thereby debarred form the use of reason, which is essentially bound up with communication. He is," Dawson concluded, "an idiot."[108] Further, as

> language is essential to Reason, so the Word of God is essential to Faith. Granted the fact of Revelation, Reason is still insufficient as the vehicle of its transmission. For this, it is necessary to have the Sacred Word of Scripture and the sacred society of the Church, which is the bearer of the Sacred Tradition. The Holy Spirit in the Church is to the Word of God, what human Reason in the tradition of culture is to the Word of Man. The Spirit is the Interpreter as well as the verifier.[109]

Throughout history, one finds a correlation between God's revelation and man's development of language. Dawson therefore concluded that the order of grace and the order of nature are intimately connected.[110] Following Aquinas, Dawson argued that grace remakes and perfects nature. "The Christian concept of Revelation does not simply involve the intelligibility of a spiritual reality but a change in the nature of the creature which renders divine communication possible," he argued in 1959.[111] Because each culture and person represents a singular image of God and God's revelation, reason unaided can never be universal, but, instead, must be culturally specific. "In every culture men possess the power of reasoning as they possess the power of speech, but the content of their reasoning is different as the knowledge

---

[106]Dawson, "Culture and Language," not dated, in Box 1, Folder 15, ND/CDAW. Owen Barfield, nearly a decade younger than Dawson, made similar arguments in his brilliant *Poetic Diction: A Study in Meaning* (1928; Hanover, CT: Wesleyan University Press, 1984).

[107]Dawson, "Memorandum," dated July 11, 1959, in Box 1, Folder 14, ND/CDAW.

[108]Ibid.

[109]Ibid.

[110]Ibid.

[111]Dawson, to Ruth Anshen, November 7, 1959, in Box 14, Folder 29, UST/CDC.

that they possess depends on the culture to which they belong," Dawson argued.[112]

Language also enables man to wield his most powerful tool for survival as a species, that is, through the imagination of the culture and the individual human person, as best expressed in myth. "I believe the old myths are better not only intrinsically, but because they lead further and open a door into the mind as well as into the past," Dawson noted in his autobiographical writings, entitled "Tradition and Inheritance." Myth, Dawson forcefully argued, "was the old road which carries us back not merely for centuries but for thousands of years; the road by which every people has traveled and from which the beginnings of every literature have come."[113] When discussing the best historiographical methods to understand pre-Norman England, for example, Dawson argued in favor of giving the Celtic legends their due. "It is true that considerable difference of opinion exists as to the date and historical value of the oldest Welsh poetry, but even if we put them at the lowest, there can be no doubt that they embody an ancient and genuine folk tradition which had its origin in the dark age of post-Roman Britain," he wrote in a critical book review. "These relics of a submerged tradition are no less worthy of our historical study than the remains of Saxon cemeteries and village sites, and the more so in that they are a faint but living voice from a lost world, which brings to us an echo of the impression that the events of the age of conquest left in the memory of the British people."[114] If archeological evidence allows one to study the material side of man's nature, the mythological allows one to comprehend, at least in substantial part, his spiritual nature. Myth, properly defined, is simply the supernatural working in history. Additionally, myth is a universal truth that repeats itself in some form or particular variation for every people and every time. History, Dawson conceded, is "not a flat expanse of time, measured off in dates, but a series of different worlds." Each world possesses its "own spirit and form and its own riches of poetic imagination."[115] One should not be surprised, Dawson concluded, that the British people chose Arthur, not Alfred or Harold, as "the central figure of national heroic legend."[116] After all, Dawson believed, the British love lost causes and extreme opposition in the face of doing what is right; it remains a fundamental part of their national character.

One sees the importance of myth and language not just in stories, but in names and in the naming of things. In *Genesis*, for example, God gives man

---

[112]Dawson, "The Relation of Philosophy to Culture," dated September 7, 1955, in Box 1, Folder 15, ND/CDAW.

[113]Christopher Dawson, *Tradition and Inheritance: Reflections on the Formative Years* (St. Paul, MN: Wanderer Press, 1970), 32.

[114]Christopher Dawson, "The Making of Britain," *Tablet* (1936), 782.

[115]Christopher Dawson, "Backgrounds and Beginnings," *A.D.*, vol. 1 (1951), 110.

[116]Dawson, "The Making of Britain," 782.

alone the ability to name things on this earth, to categorize, and to serve as a steward over creation. From a Jewish or Christian perspective, naming is synonymous with controlling. One also finds this outside of the Judeo-Christian tradition. In many primitive religions, for example, especially among Native Americans, shamans usually considered the knowledge of names as equivalent to the control over the things named. In fact, such an understanding of names can be found in almost every culture throughout world history.

Language also serves as the unifier not only of a people over time, but also for an immediate and generational community as well. Hellas provides a good example in the larger abstract understanding of the importance of language as a unifier. It was through language that the Mediterranean became Hellenized, adopting Greek culture, art, philosophical abstractions, and cultural symbols.

Jesus of Nazareth, the Word Incarnate in Christian theological terms, was born into this language and culture. But it was also a culture of many cultures, in flux. As a Jew, Jesus lived in a world controlled militarily and dominated economically by the Roman Empire, itself significantly Hellenized. Even the name "Jesus" was a Greek name, for example, the equivalent of the Aramaic Joshua. Jesus' most traveled disciple, St. Paul, walked safely on Roman roads and spoke Greek, spreading the new religion throughout the Mediterranean, specifically in the Greek isles and throughout the Roman boot. When St. John wrote his Gospel, he used the Stoic concept, the Logos, the burning fire, love, or word, at the heart of all things, to describe the Divine Savior. In a letter discussing the implications of the Protestant Reformation and its dislike of the Greek and Roman inheritance, Dawson wrote:

> It is certainly desirable that we should learn to know more about the ancient philosophical systems of China and India, but this does not mean that we should try to undo the work of the Fathers and of St. Thomas by divesting the original Hebrew thought of Our Lord of its rationalist 'Greek dress'. For where are we to begin? The Church used the categories of Greek thought to define the dogmas of the Faith and the Gospel itself has been transmitted to the world in a 'Greek dress.' It is the mission of the Church to teach all nations, but she cannot disavow her own part and start her mission all over again. That was the great error of the Protestant Reformation, which attempted to abolish a thousand years of Catholic development and to construct a new model of evangelical Christianity on exclusively scriptural foundations.[117]

Therefore, the informed Christian must think beyond the mere Hebraic. To limit the Christian inheritance to the Jews and the Jews alone would be to retard the true development and very purpose of Christendom. "We do not believe, like the Protestants (or some Protestants) that the Bible is the only record of these dealings," Dawson wrote. "On the contrary, the whole history of Christendom is a continual dialogue between God and man, and every age

---

[117]Dawson, Hermitage, to unknown recipient, January 6, 1956, in Box 14, Folder 108, UST/CDC.

of the Church's life, even the most remote and obscure, has some important lesson for us today."[118]

No one person or generation—or even all persons and generations combined—has a full understanding of God's purpose or of the Divine Economy. Yet each manifestation of God's grace offers a new piece of the puzzle, worth studying. Each person is a new and unique reflection of God, and each culture—as a network of minds—is a reflection of the Logos and the power of imagination. Each new created thing reveals more about the nature and Being of God. Not just the Jews, but the Greeks, Romans, and all other peoples, are worth studying, as they, in their finite ways, reveal some singular aspect of the Infinite.

The Catholic understanding of the Divine Economy "is the acceptance of an organic world of spiritual realities into which man obtains entry not by his own right, but by 'grace,'" Dawson wrote in 1933. As a member of the Church, the Christian sees only the historic manifestation of Christ's grace. Beyond the physical, earthly Church is the much greater part, not visible to our eyes. Hence, Roman Catholicism "attaches such immense importance to the doctrine of the Communion of Saints, the solidarity of the living and the dead in the common life of the One Body," Dawson continued.[119] The dead share in the communion with the living. "The men who died for the faith in third-century Rome or sixteenth-century Japan are still partners in the common struggle, no less than those who are the leaders of Christian thought and action in our own days," Dawson explained.[120]

A negation or attenuation of this belief of continuity would also destroy the concept of mystery—intimately related to poetry, art, myth, and literature—which is central to the continued viability of any culture. Indeed, the first fruits of any proper culture are music and poetry.[121] Poetry, especially, "is in its origins inseparable from prophecy, and among every people we find the figure of the inspired mantic poet at the threshold of its literary tradition."[122] Though art often appears as abstract, Dawson claimed, a scholar can learn far more about a society and a people through a study of its arts than by all the economic statistics available. Quantifying is nothing more than a conglomeration of raw, disinterested, dry numbers and figures. And yet humans are diverse, unique, full of zest and passion. "We can learn more about mediaeval culture from a cathedral than from the most exhaustive study of constitutional

---

[118]Christopher Dawson, "Communications: Christian Culture," *Commonweal*, vol. 61 (April 1, 1955), 678.

[119]Christopher Dawson, "The Future Life: A Roman Catholic View," *The Spectator*, vol. 151 (1933), 889.

[120]Christopher Dawson, "Christian Culture: Its Meaning and Its Value," *Jubilee*, vol. 4 (1956), 37.

[121]Christopher Dawson, *Education and the Crisis of Christian Culture* (Chicago, IL: Henry Regnery Company, 1949), 10–11.

[122]Dawson, *Religion and Culture*, 67.

law," Dawson wrote, adding that "the churches of Ravenna are a better introduction to the Byzantine world than are all the volumes of Gibbon."[123] Even the farmer had traditionally been an artist. There is, after all, an "intimate communion of human culture with the social in which it is rooted," and this becomes manifest "in every aspect of material civilization—in food and clothing, in weapons and tools, in dwellings and settlements, in roads and methods of communication."[124] "To cultivate" and "agriculture" obviously have their roots in the culture. We moderns, though, Dawson feared, have become so used to a fragmented world that we see art as something high and high alone, to be placed in galleries, separated from work and ordinary life. It is therefore difficult for present-day scholars to conceive of art as anything more than exploitation and leisure for the elites.[125]

Education through myth, poetry, and art into one's culture traditionally has provided an initiation into the divine mysteries, especially of the Divine Economy and the communion of the living and the dead. "It is only in the poetic imagination which is akin to that of the child and the mystic that we can still feel the pure sense of mystery and transcendence which is man's natural element."[126] Such a religious ordering, alone, allows us to order "life as a whole—the moulding of social and historical reality into a living spiritual unity."[127] It forces man to recognize that something greater than himself exists. It forces man to realize that he is a creature, not the Creator. It necessarily humbles man.

Traditionally, the best means of Christian education and initiation has come through the liturgy, which combines the myth, poetry, and art of the Church into a drama, presented before the members of the Body of Christ.

> In Christianity, on the other hand, the liturgy was the center of a rich tradition of religious poetry and music and artistic symbolism. In fact, the art of Christendom in both its Byzantine and medieval phases was essentially a liturgical art which cannot be understood without some knowledge of the liturgy itself and its historical origin and development. And the same is true to a great extent of popular and vernacular culture. The popular religious drama, which had such an important influence on the rise of European drama as a whole, was either a liturgical drama in the strict sense, like the Passion plays and Nativity plays, or was directly related to the cult of the saints and the celebration of their feasts. For the cult of the saints, which had its basis in the liturgy, was the source of a vast popular mythology, and provided a bridge between the higher ecclesiastical and literary culture and the peasant culture with its archaic traditions of folklore and magic.[128]

---

[123] Dawson, *Dynamics of World History,* 72.

[124] Dawson, *Progress and Religion,* 54.

[125] Dawson, *Dynamics of World History,* 72.

[126] Dawson, *Religion and Culture,* 29.

[127] Christopher Dawson, "Introduction," in Carl Schmitt, *The Necessity of Politics: An Essay on the Representative Idea in the Church and Modern Europe* (London: Sheed and Ward, 1931), 10.

[128] Christopher Dawson, "The Institutional Forms of Christian Culture," *Religion in Life,* vol. 24 (1955), 376.

The other means, almost as important as liturgy, was monasticism, in which "religion and culture attain their complete fusion."[129]

Dawson, therefore, argued that the Protestant overemphasis on the Judaic inheritance was dangerous on many levels. It focused too much on the worldly and on a non-complicated linear history, thus attenuating the levels of hierarchy and mystery in Creation. It centered us too much in time. The Judaic was vital, of course, but so was the Greek and the Roman. "The history of the Jews is bound up with the history of the world, not with that of any single political or territorial unit," Dawson understood, speaking before a largely Jewish audience at Brandeis University. "In every age they have had a particular task to perform, but this task is to be seen in relation to the world situation rather than as part of a continuous national tradition."[130] But the earliest council, the Council of Jerusalem, presided over by Archbishop James, and the discussions of St. Paul in his letters to the earliest Christian churches, prove the need to move beyond the merely Jewish origins of Christianity and to embrace and sanctify all cultures. "For as many of you as were baptized into Christ have put on Christ," St. Paul wrote to the Christians of Galatia. "There is neither Jew nor Greek, there is neither slave nor free, there is neither male nor female; for you are all one in Christ Jesus."[131] Following these new, universal teachings, Christianity very quickly moved away from Jerusalem and a Jewish culture base.

> In the West early Christian culture was predominately Greek. The Latin Christian culture was largely the creation of Africa—Tertullian, Cyprian, Augustine. Here as in Asia Minor, there was a strong undercurrent of oriental culture (Punic) which was only extinguished by the growth of Christian culture, but in this case it was Latin not Greek that became the dominant element. So too in Gaul, the vernacular Celtic language of the Christian writers like Irenaeus. It was not till the Fifth century that Gallic Latin culture produced its characteristic literature, and by that time the Germanic peoples had become the ruling race, so that the Latin Christians in Gaul (and Spain) were in somewhat the same sociological position as the Syriac speaking Christians in the East.[132]

Further, the Jewish revolts of 66–70, 115–117, and 132–135 eroded the historic and theological ties between Judaism and Christianity. Christianity, then, does not just proceed from Judaism in some direct line; it explodes from Judaism, becoming universal.

---

[129]Ibid., 377. This subject is covered in depth in Chapter 3.

[130]Christopher Dawson, "On Jewish History," *Orbis*, vol. 30 (1967), 1248.

[131]Galatians 3:27–28 (RSV).

[132]Dawson to Mulloy, June 20, 1960, in Box 1, Folder 12, ND/CDAW.

Sanctifying the Pagan

The Christian must redeem not just one person or one culture, but all persons, cultures, times, and places. Christianity must never be exclusive or particular, but instead welcoming and universal. Christianity was, Dawson explained, "not conceived as a human society but rather as a new creation, reborn in Christ and destined to extend beyond the boundaries of Israel to the Gentiles and the whole human race."[133] Dawson's central theological tenet came from St. Paul's Letter to the Colossians, the first chapter, in which he explains that all things come from the One, and all things must be sanctified and brought back to right order, in conformity with the One. "He is before all things, and in him all things hold together. He is the head of the body, the church," St. Paul wrote. For "he is the beginning, the first-born among the dead, that in everything he might be pre-eminent. For in him all the fullness of God was pleased to dwell, and through him to reconcile to himself all things, making peace by the blood of his cross."[134] Indeed, Dawson argued, only in God exists pure Being. All other being reflects the pure Being of God, in some way, shape, or form. "Thus the whole universe is, as it were, *the shadow of God* and has its being in the contemplation or reflection of the Being of God," Dawson explained in 1930. "The spiritual nature reflects the Divine consciously, while the animal nature is a passive and unconscious mirror."[135] In these arguments, Dawson significantly resembles his nineteenth-century exemplar, John Henry Newman. "There is in truth a certain virtue or grace in the Gospel which changes the quality of doctrines, opinions, usages, actions, and personal characters when incorporated with it," Cardinal Newman wrote, "and makes them right and acceptable to its Divine Author, whereas before they were either infected with evil, or at best but *shadows of the truth*."[136]

The complete sanctification of the pagan is the end result of the Christianization of the world. As the Christian moves forward, empowered by the Holy Spirit and the sacraments, he takes the pagan and changes the essence not only of the individual pagan, but of the pagan culture itself. Just as the physical person remains the same during baptism, but his soul is purified and the direction of his desires changes, so too with culture. "In fact the development of Christian culture and the progress of Christianity in the individual soul are in many ways parallel," Dawson explained. "For the history of Christianity is essentially that of the extension of the Incarnation; and the study of culture shows the same process at work in history that may be seen in detail in the

---

[133] Dawson, *Formation of Christendom*, 86.

[134] Colossians 1: 17–20 (RSV).

[135] Christopher Dawson, "The Dark Mirror," *Dublin Review*, vol. 187 (1930), 177; emphasis added.

[136] John Henry Cardinal Newman, *An Essay on the Development of Christian Doctrine* (Garden City, NY: Image Books, 1960), 348; emphasis added.

lives of individuals."[137] A culture may keep its pre-Christian forms, but the essence of the culture—its stories, myths, symbols, etc.—become Christian in meaning and purpose. "The cult of the saints and the holy places consecrated the whole historical and geographical context of culture," Dawson wrote, "and gave every social relation and activity its appropriate religious symbolism."[138] Dawson argued that this was an extension of the "Aristotelian principle of matter and form."[139] Even against and within the modern, totalitarian state, the Spirit can work.

> The Church remains what she has always been, the organ of the Divine Word and the channel of Divine Grace. It is her mission to transform the world by bringing every side of human existence and every human activity into contact with the sources of supernatural life. Even the modern State, that new Leviathan, that 'King over all the children of pride,' is not irrelevant to the work of grace nor impenetrable to its influence. If it does not destroy itself, it must be transformed and reconsecrated, as the power of the barbarian warrior became transfigured into the sacred office of a Christian king.[140]

Therefore, even in the twentieth century, against the brutal mechanized ideologies, man had a chance to redeem the world through the Spirit, Dawson argued.[141]

In these beliefs, Dawson follows a long tradition of western theology and especially of the Christian Humanists. In his "On Christian Doctrine," St. Augustine wrote that if philosophers "have said aught that is true and in harmony with our faith, we are not only not to shrink from it, but to claim it for our own use from those who have unlawful possession of it." In much of the *City of God*, St. Augustine uses Cicero and Plato to support his argument that a thriving Christianity was compatible with a stable post-Roman world. "Human institutions such as are adapted to that intercourse with men which is indispensable in this life—we must take and turn to a Christian use."[142]

Clement of Alexandria, living in the late second and early third centuries, presaged Augustine's argument. Pre-Christian faiths, he argued in his *Miscellanies*, served as a "preparatory teaching for those who [would] later embrace the faith." Additionally, he speculated that philosophy was given to the Greeks as an introduction to Christianity. For philosophy, Clement concluded, "acted as a schoolmaster to the Greeks, preparing them for Christ, as the laws of the

---

[137]Dawson, "The Leavening Process in Christian Culture," dated August 7, 1955, in Box 1, Folder 16, ND/CDAW.

[138]Christopher Dawson, "Education and the Crisis of Christian Culture," *Lumen Vitae*, vol. 1 (1946), 209.

[139]Dawson to Mulloy, August 27, 1954, in Box 1, Folder 15, ND/CDAW.

[140]Christopher Dawson, "Church, State, and Community: Concordats or Catacombs?" *Tablet* (1937), 910.

[141]See especially his book *The Judgment of the Nations* (New York: Sheed and Ward, 1942).

[142]St. Augustine, *On Christian Doctrine*, Book II, Chapter 40.

Jews prepared them for Christ."[143] That is, Plato and Aristotle served to prepare the way for Christianity philosophically in a manner similar to the way
Abraham and Moses had done so legally and theologically.

The belief in the sanctification of the pagan is undergirded by the belief
that one can demonstrate the continuity of time and space, as it has been
sanctified by the Incarnation, Death, and Resurrection of the Logos. For truth
belongs to God, Dawson argued, whether codified in scripture or nature or
even within elements of paganism. With the creation of the world, the natural
law reveals much, though certainly not as much as direct revelation.

> Natural Law provides a good example of what I mean by the comparative study
> of values. Our conception of Natural Law is peculiar to our own culture and rep-
> resents a synthesis of Hellenic and Christian elements. But we can find parallel
> conceptions in the other cultures—notably in China, where the Confucian concept
> of nature and law and virtue provides a remarkable analogy. So too in India we
> have the ancient Vedic concept of rita, which parallels the Hellenic idea of Dike,
> and the later concept of Dharma, which has points of resemblance with the me-
> dieval concept of canon and natural law.[144]

By being the Author of all societies and of the plethora of cults/cultures,
Dawson argued, God placed a part of His Truth in each culture. Therefore,
as each non-Christian culture encounters Christianity, it has some piece of
the larger truth, allowing it to accept the full Truth of Christ's Incarnation,
Death, and Resurrection. Even "primitive religion is essentially an attempt
to bring man's life into relation with and under the sanctions of, that other
world of mysterious and sacred powers whose actions is always conceived as
the ultimate and fundamental law of life." Sin, especially, and the need for
redemption or purification manifest themselves strongly in primitive cultures,
Dawson argued.[145] Or, as Dawson's fellow Augustinian, C. S. Lewis, explained
with his usual succinctness, "Paganism does not merely survive but first really
becomes itself in the v[ery] heart of Christianity."[146] Further, Dawson noted,
because history remains such a mysterious thing to man, "we must believe
that every period of history and every human race and culture has its part to
play in the progressive development of this process of spiritual creation."[147]

Historically, one can find this understanding of paganism throughout the
history of Christendom. Cardinal Newman offered several examples in his
Essay on the Development of Christian Doctrine.

> The use of temples, and these dedicated to particular saints, and ornamented on
> occasions with branches of trees; incense, lamps and candles; votive offerings on

---

[143]Clement of Alexandria, *Miscellanies.*

[144]Dawson, "Memorandum," dated July 25–28,1955, in Box 1, Folder 15, ND/CDAW.

[145]Dawson, "The Dark Mirror," 184.

[146]C. S. Lewis, Magdalen, to Dom Bede Griffiths, November 1, 1956, CSL Letters to Dom Bede
Griffiths, Letter Index 36, in Wade Center Inklings Papers, Wheaton College, Wheaton, IL.

[147]Dawson, "Memorandum," dated August 1, 1955, in Box 1, Folder 15, ND/CDAW.

recovery from illness; holy water; asylums; holidays and seasons, use of calendars, processions, blessings on the fields; sacerdotal vestments, the tonsure, the ring in marriage, turning to the East, images at a later date, perhaps the ecclesiastical chant, and the Kyrie Eleison, are all of pagan origin, and sanctified by their adoption in the Church.[148]

Perhaps the best scriptural example of the sanctification of the pagan comes from St. Paul in his attempt to convert the Athenians. While standing on Mars Hill, he congratulated the Athenians for being religious. Specifically, he noted how he was impressed with their statue to the "unknown God." Christ, he told them in no uncertain terms, was their unknown God. All of their religion, philosophy, and culture had pointed them to Christ. Paul even quoted approvingly, though sanctifying the meaning, two pagan philosophers and poets, Aratus and Cleanthes, in Acts 17:28: "In him we live and move and have our being" and "For we are indeed his offspring."[149]

Other examples of sanctification, following St. Paul's attempt at Mars Hill, include St. Augustine's sanctification of Plato, Aristotle, and Cicero in the *City of God*; St. Thomas Aquinas's sanctification of Aristotle; and even the Christian monks who built their monastery on top of the highest mound/temple in Cahokia, Illinois, the former site of the priest-king of a vast Indian Empire. The monks of Cahokia were, themselves, following a very old western tradition, as churches throughout Europe and North America sit on formerly sacred pagan sites. They, in essence, baptized the suspect ground, just as Augustine and Aquinas baptized pagan ideas.

Two problems, Dawson noted in his Gifford Lectures, could arise with the sanctification of the pagan. First, the reliance on natural revelation, natural theology, and the natural law may lead one—the human person or an individual culture—astray. One cannot accept natural theology, after all, as a guide that is as sure as the truths revealed in scripture or through tradition. At the beginning of his Gifford lectures, for example, Dawson cites William Blake's apocalyptic poetry approvingly. If man "has not the religion of Jesus, he will have the religion of Satan, and will erect the synagogue of Satan, calling the Prince of this World, 'God', and destroying all who do not worship Satan under the name of God.... Deism is the worship of the God of this World by the means of what you call Natural Religion and Natural Philosophy, and of Natural Morality or Self-Righteousness, the selfish virtues of the Natural Heart. This was the religion of the Pharisees who murdered Jesus. Deism is the same, and ends in the same."[150] On the following page Dawson wrote, "Religion is feeling and imagination: not reasoning and demonstration." Dawson's fear of natural theology also reflects St. Augustine's fear of

---

[148] Newman, *An Essay on the Development of Christian Doctrine,* 373.

[149] Scriptural commentary and analysis from The Navarre Bible, *Gospels and Acts* (Princeton, NJ: Scepter, 2002), 832–35.

[150] Dawson, *Religion and Culture,* 10.

embracing too wholeheartedly that which came before Christianity. Many of the ancient gods, the venerable North African argued in the *City of God*, were actually demons disguised to fool men into making mischief.[151]

Second, the Christian may fail to sanctify the pagan person, ritual, or culture fully. For Dawson, this became most obvious at the end of the medieval period, when the Church had failed to rid the barbarians (now Germans) of their nationalistic notions. Ultimately, the Germans were left with the choice presented so ably in the Arthurian legends: to choose the Grail or Guinevere, the continuation of the Word Incarnate or the lesser desire of the flesh, to be Galahad or Lancelot. With the Reformation and the destruction of Christian universalism, Dawson argued, Lancelot won. And, as a result, Germanic nationalism reared its frightful head and spread throughout Protestant Europe.[152]

But no matter the dangers—and all actions in this world are potentially fraught with danger, Dawson believed—one must continue to sanctify the pagan, to redeem the time, and to remake the world for God's Kingdom. For Dawson, this was the job of the Christian Humanist and the modern saint. As opposed to the Renaissance or secular Humanist, the Christian Humanist recognizes the profundity of Eternity entering Time, the Incarnation and the change in the nature and destiny of man. Secular humanism seeks to glorify man as the highest being in the universe. "The men of the Renaissance had turned their eyes away from the world of the spirit to the world of colour and form, of flesh and blood," Dawson wrote. "[T]hey set their hopes not on the unearthly perfection of the Christian saint, but on the glory of Man—man set free to live his own life and to realize the perfection of power and beauty and knowledge that was his by right."[153] The Christian Humanist differs dramatically from the secular humanist. Rather than placing man at the center of the universe, he instead desires to identify the proper place for man in the universe. The Christian Humanist, therefore, asks two fundamental questions: 1) what is the role of man within God's creation; and 2) how does man order himself within God's creation? "Humanism was a real historical movement, but it was never a philosophy or a religion," Dawson explained. "It belongs to the sphere of education, not to that of theology or metaphysics. No doubt it involves certain moral values, but so does any educational tradition. Therefore it is wiser not to define humanism in terms of philosophical theories or even of moral doctrines, but to limit ourselves to the proposition that *humanism is a tradition of culture and ethics founded on the study of humane letters*."[154] It is, Dawson argued, the combination of Greek and Christian thought, taking the best of Aristotle and showing its continuity in St. Paul. The Church em-

---

[151] Augustine, *City of God,* Book 2, Chapter 10.

[152] Dawson, *Religion and the Rise of Western Culture,* 157.

[153] Dawson, "Nature and Destiny of Man," 58.

[154] Dawson, "Christianity and the Humanist Tradition," 3.

braced Christian humanism at the Council of Jerusalem in 50 A.D. "The real decision was made by the apostolic Church when it turned from the Jews to the Gentiles, from the closed world of the synagogue and the law to the cosmopolitan society of the Roman-Hellenistic world," Dawson explained. It was St. Paul, though, "the first Christian humanist," who provided the blueprint for the Church and the sanctification of the pagan at Mars Hill in Athens. "Humanism and Divinity are as complementary to one another in the order of culture, as are Nature and Grace in the order of being," Dawson concluded.[155]

It is the Spirit, though, that animates all life and culture. "The vital and creative power behind every culture is a spiritual one. In proportion as the spiritual element recovers its natural position at the centre of our culture, it will necessarily become the mainspring of our whole social activity," Dawson wrote at the conclusion of his second book, *Progress and Religion*. "Since a culture is essentially a spiritual community, it transcends the economic and political orders. It finds its appropriate organ not in a state, but in a Church."[156] The only true progress comes when man recognizes himself as the *metaxy*, spirit and flesh, and the culture as the joint product of Divine and human labor. "The process of redemption consists in grafting a new humanity on to the old stock," Dawson explained, "and in building a new world out of the debris of the old."[157]

---

[155]Ibid., 8–11. Dawson was significantly influenced by the Russian theologian and philosopher, Nicholas Berdyaev, and especially his book *The Meaning of History*, trans. George Reavey (1923; Cleveland, OH: World Publishing Company, 1969).

[156]Dawson, *Progress and Religion*, 192.

[157]Dawson, *Enquiries into Religion and Culture*, 242.

Chapter 3

Essays in Order,
Humanism, and Moots

1931–1940

Essays in Order

WITH THE SUCCESS OF A MONUMENT TO ST. AUGUSTINE, THE FOUR ISSUES of *Order*, and the strong working relationship of Burns and Dawson, Sheed and Ward decided to publish an entire series under the title "Essays in Order," to be jointly edited by Dawson and Burns. Pan-European in its Catholic authorship, *Essays in Order* "led the way in the work of the spiritual regeneration of culture," historian and theologian Aidan Nichols explains. The writers for the series "would clarify—in the sense of purify—the waters of culture which, though life-giving of themselves, have become muddied and insanitary."[1] The series not only included the ideas of the English *Order* men, such as those of Dawson, but also branched out to include the Parisian Christian counterparts, such as Nicholas Berdyaev and Jacques Maritain. In turn, the French counterparts had German counterparts, such as Peter Wust and Theodor Haecker, and Sheed and Ward included them in their roster as well.[2]

Indeed, Burns saw the series as a defense of the West, calling on the Holy Spirit to cleanse and sanctify what had been dirtied—or never baptized—from ancient Greece to the present.[3] The series tackled the complicated issues of so-

---

[1] Aidan Nichols, O.P., "Christopher Dawson's Catholic Setting," in *Eternity in Time: Christopher Dawson and the Catholic Idea of History,* Stratford Caldecott and John Morrill, eds. (Edinburgh, Scotland: T&T Clark, 1997), 35.

[2] Tom Burns, *The Use of Memory: Publishing and Further Pursuits* (London: Sheed and Ward, 1993), 48. Alick Dru also had significant connections to Haecker. See Burns, London, to Dawson, October 17, 1930, in Box 11, Folder 31, UST/CDC.

[3] Burns, *Use of Memory,* 51.

ciology, hagiography, history, philosophy, psychology, evolution, and theology. And though written by intellectuals, the books were aimed at the average, intelligent reading public. Each "essay" was roughly 100 pages in length— about fifteen to twenty thousand words—too long for an article, but too short for a proper monograph.[4] Of the fourteen contributions, only E. I. Watkin's deeply philosophical *Bow in the Clouds* exceeded the normal page limit. The advertising slogan for the series was: "If you cannot read *Essays in Order*, you cannot read."[5] New books in the series would also appear as regularly as possible, so as "to keep you [Dawson] in the public mind and help" with the sales of "the larger books" of Sheed and Ward, Burns admitted.[6]

The relatively extensive extant correspondence between Burns and Dawson, unfortunately, reveals little in the way of the profound ideas that went into developing and guiding the series. It does, importantly, reveal the desire of Dawson and Burns to find the best persons possible to write such essays on a variety of important topics. Their most important concern, interestingly enough, was their inability to find an Englishman to represent Catholicism properly. "I think there ought to be at least one Englishman among the first lot," Burns requested of Dawson. In his personal notes on *Essays in Order*, sent to Dawson, Burns wrote, "We want social thinkers," but "none of our people have guts."[7] When a suitable candidate could not be found, the two editors decided Dawson should be among the writers in the first batch of *Essays* to be published.[8]

Not surprisingly, they also wanted a big name for the first number, to give the series *gravitas* and legitimacy as well as to have something of a model to send out to prospective authors.[9] To the relief of Dawson and Burns, a figure no less eminent than Jacques Maritain agreed to write the first number. Burns wanted to temper Maritain's influence on the series as well, requesting Dawson write at least a 2,000–4,000 word essay to accompany the Maritain volume. Burns offered Dawson specific recommendations on what to write: "I should say: you might sketch (1) general scheme of series (2) position of Thomism in this (3) of Maritain in Thomism (4) and explain some of his scholastic" ideas used.[10] Clearly, *Essays in Order* would not become merely a neo-Thomist series. More practically, Maritain's essay came in at only 12,000 words, roughly 3,000–8,000 words too short. A longish introduction by Dawson would make up for its brevity.[11]

---

[4]Burns, London, to Dawson, September 13, 1930, in Box 11, Folder 31, UST/CDC.

[5]Maisie Ward, *Unfinished Business* (New York: Sheed and Ward, 1964), 119.

[6]Burns, London, to Dawson, February 6, 1931, in Box 11, Folder 31, UST/CDC.

[7]Burns, notes for *Essays in Order*, sent to Dawson. Dated October 14th, 1930, in Box 1a, Folder 38, UST/CDC.

[8]Burns, London, to Dawson, September 3, 1930, in Box 11, Folder 31, UST/CDC.

[9]Burns, London, to Dawson, September 13, 1930, in Box 11, Folder 31, UST/CDC.

[10]Burns, London, to Dawson, October 30, 1930, in Box 11, Folder 31, UST/CDC.

[11]Burns, London, to Dawson, February 6, 1931, in Box 11, Folder 31, UST/CDC.

In the end, there were fourteen volumes total in the first series of *Essays in Order*:

1. Jacques Maritain, *Religion and Culture*

2. Peter Wust, *Crisis in the West*

3. Christopher Dawson, *Christianity and the New Age*

4. E. I. Watkin, *The Bow in the Clouds*

5. Carl Schmitt, *The Necessity of Politics*

6. Nicholas Berdyaev, *The Russian Revolution*

7. Michael de la Bedoyere, *The Drift of Democracy*

8. Christopher Dawson, *The Modern Dilemma*

9. Rudolf Allers, *The New Psychologies*

10. Ida Coudenhove, *The Nature of Sanctity: A Dialogue*

11. Herbert Read, *Form in Modern Poetry*

12. Gerald Vann, O.P., *On Being Human: St. Thomas and Mr. Huxley*

13. Thomas Gilby, O.P., *Poetic Experience: An Introduction to the Thomist Aesthetic*

14. Theodor Haecker, *Virgil, Father of the West*

The list certainly represented an impressive and diverse group of scholars and poets. Some of these authors were well established. Other authors, such as Ida Coudenhove, became established after publishing in *Essays in Order*. Some became very controversial in the 1930s. Carl Schmitt, for example, was a Professor of Political Theory at the University of Berlin when he wrote his *Essays in Order* book in 1930 and 1931. In May 1933, however, he and philosopher Martin Heidegger joined the National Socialist Party. Maritain, though, went the other direction, embracing the theory of natural rights and a more liberal politics, becoming the foremost Thomist of the twentieth century. By 1936, Maritain proclaimed himself a man of the Left.[12] A contributor to the "New Series" of *Essays in Order*, discussed below, Francois Mauriac, won the Nobel Prize in Literature in 1952. Had the series continued, there would have been more prominent contributors, as Dawson and Burns had originally

---

[12]Ralph McInerny, *The Very Rich Hours of Jacques Maritain: A Spiritual Life* (Notre Dame, IN: University of Notre Dame, 2003), 132–33.

projected a much larger roster. The frontispiece of the first book in the series, Maritain's *Religion and Culture*, promised future "Essays in Order" from Father Martin D'Arcy, Charles Du Bos, Eric Gill, Ronald Knox, Gabriel Marcel, John-Baptist Reeves, and Douglas Woodruff.[13] In their private correspondence, notes, and discussions, Dawson and Burns also revealed their desire to have figures such as Frank Sheed, Richard Sullivan (an expert on natural law), Yves Simon, and G. K. Chesterton write for *Essays in Order*.[14] Dawson and Burns also wanted to cover divorce, the living wage, censorship, and eugenics as specific issues. None of these, however, ever appeared in print under the moniker of *Essays in Order*.[15]

In the first volume, *Religion and Culture* by Maritain, Dawson followed Burns's advice and outlined the themes of and need for *Essays in Order*, but he did so in a far more scholarly voice than had existed in the journal from which the series had taken its name. Still, even Dawson's more scholarly voice was unmistakably filled with anxiety. "The old order is dead," he stated bluntly in the "General Introduction."[16] Modernity had shattered the world, dividing everything into small, disconnected compartments, and then dividing them yet again into even smaller, more isolated units. The world had begun a process of inevitable and imminent decay, Dawson warned. In the world of ideologies, Catholics might at first feel lost. After all, no Catholic plan existed—or should exist—to compete with the utopian fanaticism of the various ideologues of the Left and the Right. Roman Catholicism "has no *policy* nor can the Catholic compete with the Marxian Socialist in offering the modern world a panacea for its material ills." The Protestant—or, the "sectarian Christian," as Dawson labeled him—"can isolate himself from the age in which he lives and construct a private world in harmony with his religious convictions."[17] The Catholic has no such choice, for he must encounter and interact with the time and place into which he has been placed and born. He has been put there for a reason, according to the divine plan; each person has a unique role in the economy of grace.

The Catholic must, above all, be patient, recognizing that all matter and all spirit are connected and that each good and created thing has its place in the divine order. Nature, as Aristotle once wrote, makes nothing in vain. "The Catholic conception of society is not that of a machine for the production of

---

[13] Jacques Maritain, "Religion and Culture" in *Essays in Order, vol. 1–3,* Christopher Dawson and Tom Burns, eds. (New York: Macmillan, 1931), frontispiece.

[14] Sheed, New York, to Maisie, April 29, 1935, in Box 1, Folder 4, in ND/CSWD; and Burns/Dawson, *Essays in Order*, "State of Affairs," December 30, 1930, in Box 11, Folder 31, UST/CDC.

[15] Burns/Dawson, *Essays in Order*, "State of Affairs," December 30, 1930, in Box 11, Folder 31, UST/CDC.

[16] Christopher Dawson, "General Introduction," in *Essays in Order,* Christopher Dawson and Tom Burns, eds. (New York: Macmillan, 1931), v.

[17] Ibid., vi.

wealth, but of a spiritual organism in which every class and every individual has its own function to fulfil and its own rights and duties in relation to the whole," Dawson wrote in 1933.[18] The Catholic seeks what is catholic, that is, that which is universal, not the temporary or the faddish. Further, he must, through grace, attempt to bring all things back to right order, to the unity of the One, the Creator.

The ideologues and materialists will declare the Catholic to be merely escapist, Dawson warned. Indeed, the assault on the Catholic came from all aspects of modernity, he lamented. The most prominent social philosophers of the previous two centuries—the Rousseaus, the Kants, the Benthams, and the Spencers of the world—had assaulted the very foundations of "the absolutism and realism of Catholic philosophy."[19] Additionally, the outlandish reverence for science had allowed for more brutal and inhumane killing, machinery that "leads to over-production and unemployment," and capitalism which "involves exploitation and social unrest." The only solution that prevented complete annihilation by what Dawson called the forces of the "machine" would come from the recognition of an order that is, at once, both in time and eternal: "Order and guidance are necessary if disaster is to be avoided, for civilisation is not the result of a natural process of evolution, it is essentially due to the mastering of Nature by the human mind. It is an artificial order, governed and created by man's intelligence and will." Dawson, not atypically, saw the situation dualistically. On the one side, the Americans had embraced a new material order of economic exploitation and radical individualism. On the other side, many in Europe had embraced the false spiritualism of nationalism.

The Catholic, caught between "subjective idealism and moral pragmatism," had been forced into exile, awaiting the destruction of the world while seeking refuge and accepting penance in the desert wasteland. The Catholic had, in short, acted as a Protestant, seeking refuge from a world that despised him. One could justify such actions, Dawson believed, but such a defensive attitude would ultimately prove counterproductive. While the Catholic may have remained aloof from the moral and intellectual bankruptcy of modernity, he now found himself in the moral and imperative position of bearing truth to a shattering world. It is, to put it simply, the burden and the duty of the Catholic.

Additionally, Dawson found a model for such actions in the past. Just as the scholars of the Reformation and Counter-Reformation had done, present-day scholars must recreate a Republic of Letters. "It is necessary for all of us to do what is in our power to restore the intellectual community of European culture," Dawson wrote, "and for Catholics before all, since they stand almost

---

[18] Christopher Dawson, "The Modern Dilemma," *Cambridge Review*, February 17, 1933.
[19] Dawson, "General Introduction," x.

alone to-day as the representatives of a universal spiritual order in the midst of the material and external uniformity of a cosmopolitan machine-made civilization."[20]   Once unified intellectually, if not in the liturgy or the episcopate, Catholics and Protestants could strengthen each other morally and challenge the reigning materialisms of the world. The two sides, Dawson would later argue, had much to learn from one another.

In his personal notes for the introduction, which did not make it into print, Dawson wrote that the Church suffered from two significant defects. Just as he had written in his final essay for the journal *Order*, Dawson noted first the problem of the Church hierarchy and its failure to understand the laity. Simply put, the hierarchy was woefully out of touch with folk culture, and it had no idea how to bridge the gap between itself and the main church body. In other words, it failed to lead properly because it did not understand its followers. Similarly, even the more active and intellectual of the church body, such as those who advocated distributism, were too "partial and narrow" in their views. They failed to see the bigger picture of the Church universal and focused only on their little corner of the universe.[21]   Only a very few non-Catholics would ever comprehend the meaning of the faith or the Church.

> It is useless to preach to the general public that society will find the solution of all its difficulties in the Faith—for they interpret that as an obscurantist attempt to return to an unintelligent medievalism. They have no comprehension of the vital element in Catholicism—the supernatural. Nor can we prove the supernatural to them by an appeal... which they didn't realize.[22]

Second, and perhaps more important, Catholics possess no monopoly on the truth, and they must avoid the arrogant assumption that they do. But one particular truth—a proper understanding of the human person in the created order—they understood unreservedly and better than all competitors, Christian or not. Recognition, explanation, and application of this one truth would give them the upper-hand in the coming struggle between tradition and modernity, Dawson believed. Equally important, the Catholic knows well that man is not the creator. God is, and He is sovereign. Only such humility on the part of humanity will allow grace to reorder the world.

Despite the dour picture Dawson presented in his introduction, the English Catholic also saw significant signs of hope. Prior to World War I, Dawson noted, two Frenchmen, Charles Peguy and Paul Claudel, had initiated a Catholic Literary Revival. Peguy (1873–1914), a supporter of nationalism and socialism as a young man, converted to Catholicism in the 1900s and dedicated his writings to the faith.[23] A poet like Peguy, Claudel (1868–1955)

---

[20]Ibid., xi, xii, xvi, xix–xx.

[21]Dawson, "Introduction to ESSAYS IN ORDER—Notes," n.d., in Box 4, Folder 26, UST/CDC.

[22]Ibid.

[23]Roger Kimball, "Charles Peguy," *The New Criterion*, vol. 20 (November 2001).

embraced Catholicism at the age of eighteen and spent his professional life as a diplomat. Unlike Peguy, Claudel rejected all forms of socialism as demonic. Thinkers such as Maritain, Etienne Gilson, and Pierre Rousselot, S.J., had followed their lead and had produced outstanding works of scholarship. In Germany, Erich Przywara, Carl Schmitt, Theodor Haecker, and Peter Wust had offered scholarship of commensurate quality. Even men such as Max Scheler—whom Dawson thought flawed—had contributed to the revival. The goal of *Essays in Order*, then, was to bring these thinkers and their thoughts together, to bring the English Roman Catholics in line with the continental ones and to initiate a new Catholic Republic of Letters, Dawson argued. Dawson and Burns desired nothing less than an intellectually-reformed Christendom, profoundly united even while ethnically, liturgically, and philosophically diverse.

With Dawson's introduction for Maritain's book—and, hence, for the series—completed, the question of Dawson's first book in the series became very important to the two editors. After considerable discussion on the matter, Dawson and Burns finally decided that his first *Essay in Order* should deal with the issue of humanism.[24] Though at first the two thought Dawson's friend, E. I. Watkin, to be in the better position to write on the topic, it became obvious in the correspondence between them that Dawson was the best choice. Dawson had, after all, already somewhat tackled the issue in his very first published essay, fifteen years earlier, continuing the development of his ideas for and against humanism in his three articles for *Order*, his second book, *Progress and Religion*, and in his most recent articles in T. S. Eliot's *Criterion* and Arnold Lunn's *Dublin Review*. The latest two, "The End of An Age" and "The Dark Mirror," each published in 1930, served as chapters one and two, respectively, of the four-chapter *Christianity and the New Age*, the third volume of *Essays in Order*.

Humanism, as a philosophical issue, was in its waning days of popularity when Dawson wrote his first *Essay in Order*. But in the 1910s and 1920s, it had played a crucial role in philosophical, cultural, and social discourse. The personalities and works of Irving Babbitt and Paul Elmer More served as the touchstones for the first generation of American humanists, while T. E. Hulme served as the equivalent in England and Nicholas Berdyaev, exiled from Russia, in France. T. S. Eliot, Christopher Dawson, and Jacques Maritain were second-generation humanists, though each held great reservations regarding the humanist project. Russell Kirk was a third-generation humanist, while present-day scholars such as political philosopher Claes Ryn and literary critic George A. Panichas can be considered the fourth generation of humanists.

As the leader of the American humanists, Babbitt stood squarely in the American conservative tradition of John Adams and Nathaniel Hawthorne

---

[24]Burns, London, to Dawson, February 6, 1931, in Box 11, Folder 31, UST/CDC.

and drew upon the greats of world civilization for his arguments: Socrates, Plato, Cicero, Virgil, Confucius, and Horace. Dawson was quite familiar with Babbitt's writings, though he ultimately rejected the American's views. Babbitt, following the classical tradition, viewed the human person as comprised of three parts:

> I have tried to show elsewhere, on the degree to which he establishes a correct relationship between the part of himself that perceives, the part that conceives, and the part that discriminates. The part that conceives, that reaches out and seizes likenesses and analogies, may be defined as imagination; the part that discriminates and tests the unity thus apprehended from the point of view of its truth may be defined as analytical reason; the part that perceives is, in the case of the humanist, primarily concerned with the something in man that is set above the phenomenal order and that I have already defined as the power of control.[25]

To be well ordered—that is, to be fully human—man must balance the various disparate parts. To ignore the will, as modern man was doing according to Babbitt, meant the destruction not just of civilization but of humanity, for the animalistic part can only survive if governed by the will. Even more important, only by conforming one's will to the law of nature and creation can man find peace and civilization. The gift of free will, Babbitt believed, allowed one to attain true happiness by conforming the will to the higher law. All come together in work, a "labor of the spirit" which is "self reform."[26] According to Babbitt, three philosophies threaten a proper understanding of the human person: utilitarianism, which views man as a means to an end and focuses on the animalistic side of sensate pleasure; humanitarianism, which also subordinates the will to the materialist and appetitive desires; and pragmatism, which regards as legitimate only that evidence gleaned from the senses.

American critic Paul Elmer More agreed (more or less) with his close friend, Irving Babbitt, in his understanding of humanism. A discussion that took place along North Avenue in Cambridge, England may best explain their differences. They were discussing a matter, "when suddenly [Babbitt] stopped short, faced about upon me, and, with both hands rigidly clenched, ejaculated: 'Good God, man, are you a Jesuit in disguise?'"[27] More failed to recall the exact topic of conversation, and he may merely have been Jesuitical in his argumentation, but the comment reveals a significant difference between the two men. Though both had been raised in New England Calvinist tradition and among Puritan stock, More re-embraced his Christianity, however heterodox a few of his views may have been. More's good friend, T. S. Eliot, teased him in correspondence:

---

[25]Irving Babbitt, "Humanism: An Essay at Definition," in *Humanism and America: Essays on the Outlook of Modern Civilisation,* Norman Foerster, ed. (New York: Farrar and Rinehart, 1930), 43.

[26]Russell Kirk, *The Conservative Mind*, 1st ed. (Chicago: Regnery, 1953), 372.

[27]Paul Elmer More, *On Being Human* (Princeton, NJ: Princeton University Press, 1936), 27.

But having refused this, how much else of orthodox theology do you refuse? What about the Angels and Archangels and the Saints and the Patriarchs? And devotions of Our Lady? And I do not forget that an eminent friend of ours has called you a *binitarian contra mundum*. No, sir, I call upon you to demonstrate your orthodoxy; or alternatively, to demonstrate that you are the *only* Catholic living. What are your views now on the Marriage at Cana, and the Loaves and Fishes?[28]

More had no real answer for Eliot. And to the question raised by Babbitt, More only wrote: "I have never been able to answer the question satisfactorily."[29] Maybe he was a Jesuit after all.

Though T. S. Eliot had been a member of the Bloomsbury Group as well as a disciple of Irving Babbitt's, when he became a Christian in 1927, he grew increasingly skeptical of the humanism of Babbitt. In a letter to the editor of the conservative and humanist *Bookman*, Eliot wrote:

> May I state that for the teaching of Babbitt himself I have the greatest admiration; and to Mr. Babbitt the deepest gratitude. My own position seems to me to be very close indeed to that of Mr. More; for example as put in his admirable essay in your same number. What differences there are between Mr. More and myself are all on our own side of the fence, do not concern the general issues of humanism and would appear to most humanists to be trivial theological details. My chief apprehension about 'humanism' has been lest the teachings of Mr. Babbitt should be transformed, by a host of zealous disciples, into the hard and fast dogma of a new ethical church, or something between a church and a political party.[30]

Ultimately, Eliot feared, a humanism not tied to an orthodox Christianity would become nothing more than a liberal Protestantism or, worse, a new "'Ethical Culture Society,' which held Sunday morning services."[31] Most importantly, without an orthodox Christian grounding, the humanists would ignore original sin, believing—however indirectly—"that man is either perfectible, or capable of indefinite improvement."[32] Instead, as Dawson would also argue in his last *Order* piece, published in the same year as Eliot's piece, humanism and Christianity need each other.[33]

While men such as Babbitt were merely skeptical of the supernatural elements of Christianity and More was, at least until the last decade in his

---

[28]T. S. Eliot, London, to Paul Elmer More, August 30, 1930, in Box 3, Folder 3, Paul Elmer More Collection (C0054), Princeton University Department of Rare Books and Special Collections (hereafter PEM/Princeton).

[29]More, *On Being Human*, 27. As to More's orthodoxy or heterodoxy, see the excellent correspondence between More and T. S. Eliot, dated Shrove Tuesday, 1928, through January 11, 1937, in Box 3, Folder 3, PEM/Princeton.

[30]T. S. Eliot, London, to the editor of the *Bookman*, March 31, 1930, copy in Box 3, Folder 3, PEM/Princeton.

[31]T. S. Eliot, "Second Thoughts About Humanism," *Hound and Horn*, vol. 2 (June 1929), 342. See also T. S. Eliot, *Essays Ancient and Modern* (London: Faber and Faber, 1936), 82–83; and T. S. Eliot, "Religion without Humanism," in *Humanism and America*, 105–112.

[32]Eliot, "Second Thoughts About Humanism," 349.

[33]Eliot, "Religion without Humanism," 105–112.

life when he embraced Christian orthodoxy, simply heterodox, others such as Columbia University's educational philosopher John Dewey initiated a truly anti-Christian form of humanism. Dewey "commenced with a thoroughgoing naturalism, like Diderot's and Holbach's, denying the whole realm of spiritual values," in which "nothing exists but physical sensation, and life has no aims but physical satisfaction," Russell Kirk wrote in 1953. "He proceeded to a utilitarianism which carried Benthamite ideas to their logical culmination, making material production the goal and standard of human endeavor; the past is trash, the future unknowable, and the present gratification the only concern of the moralist."[34] Along with several other prominent thinkers, Dewey signed the "Humanist Manifesto" of 1933.[35] The manifesto argued that theistic institutions should conform to the concerns of human life *qua* human life.

> Religious humanism [meaning a religion worshiping humanity] maintains that all associations and institutions exist for the fulfillment of human life. The intelligent evaluation, transformation, control, and direction of such associations and institutions with a view to the enhancement of human life is the purpose and program of humanism. Certainly religious institutions, their ritualistic forms, ecclesiastical methods, and communal activities must be reconstituted as rapidly as experience allows, in order to function effectively in the modern world.[36]

Further, society must lose its emotionalism, as manifested in theistic religion. Science should determine all that is to come, the Deweyites argued:

> Humanism asserts that the nature of the universe depicted by modern science makes unacceptable any supernatural or cosmic guarantees of human values. Obviously humanism does not deny the possibility of realities as yet undiscovered, but it does insist that the way to determine the existence and value of any and all realities is by means of intelligent inquiry and by the assessment of their relations to human needs. Religion must formulate its hopes and plans in the light of the scientific spirit and method.[37]

Ultimately, the thirty-four signers of the Humanist Manifesto concluded, "the time has passed for theism." Should it continue, it must do so in a manner that, as they argued, speaks to problems of the twentieth century, places man at the center of existence, and uses the scientific method. Religion, they concluded, serves only a utilitarian function, a "means for realizing the highest values of life."[38]

---

[34]Kirk, *Conservative Mind,* 365.

[35]W. F. Albright, *History, Archaeology, and Christian Humanism* (New York: McGraw Hill, 1964), 7.

[36]"A Humanist Manifesto: Twenty Years Later," *The Humanist* (1953), 60.

[37]Ibid., 59.

[38]Ibid. On the differences between the American Humanists and the Roman Catholic Church, see Lisa Moreno, "The National Catholic Welfare Conference and Catholic Americanism, 1919–1966," dissertation, University of Maryland, 1999, 165–66.

One of Dewey's present-day admirers and disciples, Richard Rorty, continues the secular humanist tradition at the end of the twentieth-century and beginning of the twenty-first century. For Rorty, America is the great democratic and liberal experiment. He views this democratic experiment as one in which institutions promote "co-operation" instead of embodying "a universal and ahistorical order."[39] Any attempt to bring God back in, or, as he puts it, to "re-enchant" the world, would be folly.

Though Dawson had written sporadically on humanism, it was his 1931 book, *Christianity and the New Age* that placed him squarely in the debate. Indeed, Dawson's contributions in *Essays in Order* #3 earned him a permanent place in the history of humanist thought. As a reviewer for the *New York Times* wrote in 1939, "This is the theme recurring in much of the writings of some of the foremost thinkers of our day, such as the late Irving Babbitt and Paul Elmer More, and Berdyaev, Christopher Dawson, and T. S. Eliot."[40] Though these five differ in their religious outlook, they perfectly form a continuity: Babbitt, the agnostic; More, the skeptical Anglican; Berdyaev, the heterodox Orthodox; Dawson, the Augustinian Catholic; and Eliot, the orthodox Anglican. Certainly, even the most cursory glance at the several American and British humanist publications—such as the *American Review*, the *Bookman*, and the *Criterion*—reveals how much the humanists relied upon one another for support and disagreement.

The reviewer for the *New York Times* might also have added the name of T. E. Hulme, a young, rising philosopher who had been killed in World War I. His *Speculations: Essays on Humanism and the Philosophy of Art*, published in 1924 and edited by Herbert Read, was regarded by the humanists and non-humanists alike as a critical work in the history of humanism and philosophical thought. Dawson especially appreciated Hulme's insights into original sin and the changes in the new understandings of man coinciding with the rise of Copernican thought.[41] As to the former, the agnostic Hulme believed that one must accept original sin for a proper understanding of man. As to the latter, Hulme had contended that with the writings of Copernicus, many scholars and intellectuals began to think of man as the center of the universe.[42] In other words, Copernicus became the nexus between the medieval and the modern in the view of man.

In the four succinct chapters of *Christianity and the New Age*, Dawson offered a *tour de force* on the significance of humanism, properly and improperly understood. He also still revealed a very angry, anxious side, one that

---

[39] Richard Rorty, "Priority of Democracy to Philosophy," in *Reading Rorty: Critical Responses to Philosophy and the Mirror of Nature (and Beyond),* Alan R. Malachowski, ed. (Oxford: Basil Blackwell, 2002), 295.

[40] Dino Ferrari, "New Essays on the Humanities," *New York Times*, February 5, 1939, BR10.

[41] Dawson, "Notes on T. E. Hulme, SPECULATIONS, 1924," n.d., in Box 5, Folder 10, UST/CDC.

[42] Ibid.

would not disappear until the 1950s when Dawson was in his sixties. His analysis, significantly influenced by the work of Hulme, Eliot, and Berdyaev, began with a brief history of the West through the Protestant Reformation and the Enlightenment. In a theme Dawson had already developed, he argued that the Enlightenment attempted to create "a completely secularised culture." Protestantism remained, but the predominant modern culture had relegated it to a few hours on Sundays and so could "not interfere with the reign of Mammon."[43]

Lacking spiritual leadership, the so-called men of letters of the late nineteenth century—so-called, for they were followers rather than leaders and hence not men of letters at all—turned to whatever allowed "a means of escape from reality" in the nineteenth century. "That was the meaning to many of the catchword, 'Art for Art's sake.' Symbolism and aestheticism, the Ivory Tower and the Celtic Twilight, Satanism and the cult of 'Evil,' hashish and absinthe," Dawson wrote. "All of them were ways by which the last survivors of Romanticism made their escape, leaving the enemy in possession of the field."[44] Few thinkers understood the larger movements in society, Dawson believed. Instead, the nineteenth century witnessed the reign of small-minded and provincial thought.

One broad-minded nineteenth-century philosopher whom Dawson surprisingly admired was Friedrich Nietzsche. Though far from being a humanist, Nietzsche critically understood the importance of religion and spirituality to a people and to the history of the West. Dawson evidently approved of a false spirituality over a false de-spiritualized materialism. Another was the aforementioned T. E. Hulme, "an exceptionally original mind" that "could free itself from the influence of Liberal dogma" and recognize that Europe was not "progressing" as the H. G. Wells and George Bernard Shaws of the world assumed, but was instead passing into something new and dark. Nicholas Berdyaev proved even more important than either Nietzsche or Hulme. In *The Meaning of History,* the Russian exile argued effectively—at least to Dawson—that the humanism of the Renaissance began the decline in real progress. While Medieval man had spent his intellectual and spiritual energies pursuing "an intuition of the eternal verities which is itself an emanation of the Divine Intellect," the Renaissance thinkers became fascinated with themselves, humans *qua* humans, and fascinated with the world as the place in which humans play and live.[45]

This loss of the importance of the transcendent deeply concerned Dawson. The fascination with the self, combined with the scientific revolution of the sixteenth and seventeenth centuries and the rise of capitalism, made man "a

---

[43] Christopher Dawson, "Christianity and the New Age," in *Essays in Order,* Christopher Dawson and Tom Burns, eds. (New York: Macmillan, 1931), 157.

[44] Ibid., 158.

[45] Ibid., 159, 170, 161.

subordinate part of the great mechanical system that his scientific genius has created." Everywhere in science, culture, and politics, the machine ruled, and humans became merely cogs within it. To make matters worse, as Dawson saw it, "the new bureaucratic state, that 'coldest of monsters'" developed and presided over it all.[46]

One finds the ultimate development of the machine and its control over and mechanization of humanity in the purely materialist ideas of Karl Marx, Dawson continued. "All other things—religion, art, philosophy, spiritual life—stand on a lower plane of reality," in the thought of Marx. "They are a dream world of shadows cast on the sleeping mind by the physical processes of the real world of matter and mechanism."[47] And yet, even this materialistic philosophy, by necessity, takes on an aura of religiosity, having its own martyrs, prophets, and saints. "We are faced with the disturbing spectacle of Communists who preach the dismal gospel of Marxism with an enthusiasm and devotion which is rare among Christians," Dawson lamented in a 1934 article dealing with humanism and the cultural and historical thought of St. Augustine.[48] But, the Marxist is not alone in his materialism. The capitalist—especially as developed after the Civil War in America—is a materialist as well. "The Communists may have deified mechanism in theory," Dawson wrote, "but it is the Americans who have realised it in practice."[49] In America and all truly capitalist societies, Dawson feared, the soul has all but died, and the "ordinary man gets more satisfaction from his cinema and his daily paper than from grand opera or classical literature."[50]

Still, one must temper Dawson's views here. While he distrusted the capitalism of the nineteenth-century liberals and utilitarians as ultimately destructive, he understood the materialism of the Marxists to be far worse. For, as Dawson believed, the American or British capitalist was genuinely concerned with the increase of happiness and prosperity of society. Further, the capitalist materialism was never totalitarian, allowing for the rise of numerous cultural and religious reform movements, some of which directly challenged the morality of capitalism. But communism is totalitarian, and "it does not tolerate the existence of any other spiritual ideal or any autonomous religious activity."[51]

For any properly ordered soul or society, Dawson continued, man must recognize his true place in the universe, and he must acknowledge the supremacy of the Creator:

---

[46] Ibid., 161, 162.

[47] Ibid., 165.

[48] Christopher Dawson, "Civilization and the Faith," *Theology*, vol. 28 (1934), 76.

[49] Dawson, "Christianity and the New Age," 167.

[50] Ibid., 168–69.

[51] Christopher Dawson, "Marx's Materialism," *Church Times*, June 1, 1934.

God is the one Reality. Apart from Him, nothing exists. In comparison to Him, nothing is real. The universe only exists in so far as it is rooted and grounded in His Being. He is the Self of our selves and the Soul of our souls.[52]

In very Platonic and Stoic language, Dawson wrote, "Thus the whole universe is, as it were, the shadow of God, and has its being in the contemplation or reflection of the Being of God." And, reflecting rather strongly the Jewish *Book of Wisdom*, Dawson wrote: "The spiritual nature reflects the Divine consciously, while the animal nature is a passive and unconscious mirror."[53] All created life, therefore, is an extension of God, and humans are dark mirrors, poorly reflecting the Pure Image of God. Humans represent a bridge between the material and the spiritual. Unlike the angels or the animals, humans possess both the physical and the soul. Man, then, must order himself to the Will that has created all, for his job is to bring all things back into the Divine Order. The predominately spiritualist—or what a Catholic would call the mystic—is as rare as the pure materialist, Dawson believed. The vast majority of men are somewhere in between the pure materialist and the mystic. Throughout human history, Dawson stressed, human societies have always recognized the supremacy of a Being or beings who transcend, limit, and give guidance (or hindrance) to humans. Such a rule applies equally to primitive man and civilized man.[54]

How then, asked Dawson in the *Essay*, should man order himself? In contrast to the private judgment and individualism of Protestantism, the Roman Catholic must recognize that if God is the Beginning and the End, and if all things come from and through the Word, then man receives all of his life and his gifts from the Divine. God is sovereign, and man is derivative, a creature rather than a creator. All creation, though, forms a part of an organic whole, with a distinct beginning—the Word creating the Universe; a middle—the Incarnation, Death, and Resurrection of the Word; and an end—the Apocalypse in which the Word brings all things back to right order. While Dawson's ideas match those found in Scripture, they are equally rooted in the ancient Greek thought of Heraclitus and Thales and the others who attempted to solve the problem of the One, the Many, and the One. The Protestant Reformers—consciously or not, Dawson argued—attempted to destroy the organic unity of creation and time. The Reformers separated dogma from intellect, thus resulting in "the dissolution of dogma itself in the interests of that moral pragmatism which is the essence of modern Protestantism." By divorcing the cult from the culture, Dawson argued, Protestants took away that which makes

---

[52]Dawson, "Christianity and the New Age," 201. In this passage, it should be noted that Dawson is talking specifically about Asian Indian religion, but also showing the similarities to Christianity. Hence, this passage applies to the Christian understanding of God as well as to the Indian conception.

[53]Dawson, "Christianity and the New Age," 176.

[54]Ibid., 178ff.

life worthwhile. For all intents and purposes, Protestantism de-spiritualizes life and the world. Consequently, "religion loses all contact with absolute truth and becomes merely an emotional justification for a certain behavior."[55]

But, Dawson further posited, even if one considers only history and ignores theology, one must recognize the organic whole of God's plan and the place of humanity within it. After all, Dawson argued, even before the Word became flesh, "The One God had chosen for Himself one people and had bound it to Him by an eternal covenant." After the Incarnation, Death, and Resurrection of the Word, God created the Church with the power of the Holy Spirit, thus continuing the organic unity—and beginning the healing of the disunity caused by the choices and institutions of man—of all Creation. "For the possession of the Holy Spirit was the essential characteristic of the new society," Dawson wrote, and its creation, the Church, "enjoyed supernatural powers and authority." Ultimately then, within the organic unity of existence, the "Church was itself the future kingdom in embryo."[56]

The writings of St. John thoroughly informed Dawson's articulation of the organic unity of society and the Christian inheritance. With "St. John's identification of the Logos and the Messiah in the prologue to the Fourth Gospel," Dawson argued, Jesus "was not only the Christ, the Son of the Living God; He was also the Divine Intelligence, the Principle of the order and intelligibility of the created world." Further, Christ serves as the nexus between the human and the Divine. "In Him God is not only manifested to man, but vitally participated," Dawson wrote, elaborating on John 1:9. "He is the Divine Light, which illuminates men's minds, and the Divine Life, which transforms human nature and makes it the partaker of Its Own supernatural activity."[57] Cultural order, in other words, was participation in a Divine reality, itself designed for the good of mankind.

Importantly, Dawson ended his first *Essay in Order* by noting that all such changes and sanctification of the world came only through the Church by the power of the Holy Spirit. "The Church is no sect or human organisation, but a new creation," Dawson wrote in the final chapter. The Church is "the seed of the new order which is ultimately destined to transform the world." Further, Dawson argued, "the creative element in human culture is spiritual." All progress, rightly understood, comes from man's proper ordering of the soul to God, and that can be done only through the grace imparted to the Church through the sacraments. Only such an understanding can defeat the collectivist, man-made ideologies that lead only to the machine and the mechanization of man and the destruction of the human person. Unlike the skeptical humanism of a Babbitt or the atheistic humanism of a Dewey, Dawson's humanism demanded a proper understanding of the human person, not as the

---

[55] Ibid., 210–11.
[56] Ibid., 216, 219, 220.
[57] Ibid., 222.

highest being in the universe, but as a being created in the Image of God, born in a certain time and place, tainted by original sin, but given the grace to be a being of Heaven. He finds his true self only when "united in a direct and personal relation with the Divine Word."[58]

Dawson concluded *Christianity and the New Age* with one of the most powerful paragraphs he ever produced. "Every Christian mind is a seed of change so long as it is a living mind, not enervated by custom or ossified by prejudice," he wrote. "A Christian only has to *be* in order to change the world, for in that act of being there is contained all the mystery of supernatural life." God has ordained the Church, through the grace of the sacraments, to "produce not merely good men, but spiritual men—that is to say, supermen."[59] In this function, the Church acts as the vital agent of the Love that created and moves the universe, an organic unity of matter and spirit, of heaven and earth, and of time and eternity. The Church, guided by the Holy Spirit, continues as well as it transforms the organic unity of Creation. "The spirit breathes and they are created and the face of the earth is renewed."[60]

The *Essays in Order* series proved a success in terms of sales, critical reception, and its ability to unite English and continental Roman Catholics into a cohesive movement. Both the secular and the Catholic press praised *Essays in Order*. "This book of Catholic apologetic, written by three remarkably able men, is of exceptional value to all students of our times who would understand one of the most striking phenomena of present history, the deepening conviction of Catholicism that she is to be the savior of a shattered and bankrupt world," a reviewer for the *New York Herald Tribune* wrote of the first three *Essays in Order* by Maritain, Peter Wust, and Dawson. "This is more than a pious wish or a mere surge of zealous hope. It is reasoned persuasion based upon a profound analysis of our ills and upon a remembrance of mighty victories in other ages of crisis."[61] In a review article entitled "A Roman Catholic Offensive," the reviewer for England's Protestant *Church Times* conceded that "these essayists are far less obscurantist and far more reasonable than used to be the case with Roman Catholic apologists. Instead of retiring within the fortress of Infallibility, only issuing thence to make sallies against Christians of another complexion, they come into the open, in the spirit of peace and sweet reasonableness." After especially praising *Christianity and the New Age*,

---

[58] Ibid., 227, 238, 240. Dawson was not alone in his beliefs. As already has been noted, Eliot argued along similar lines at the same time as Dawson. Paul Elmer More eventually accepted this position as well, a view which became a staple of much Catholic thought in the twentieth century. One can find it in the writings of Hans Urs von Balthasar, Henri de Lubac, Pope John Paul II, and Pope Benedict XVI. See, for example, the interview with Tracey Rowland, "Benedict XVI, Vatican II, and Modernity," *Zenit.org* (July 24–25, 2005), parts 1 and 2.

[59] Dawson, "Christianity and the New Age," 242–43.

[60] Ibid., 243.

[61] William L. Sullivan, "The Church and the World: Essays in Order," *New York Herald Tribune*, July 19, 1931.

the reviewer concluded, "Mr. Dawson does not mention the English Church, and treats of Protestantism without derision."[62] Elated, a reviewer for the *Catholic Times* of London wrote that Dawson's *Christianity and the New Age* "has shown that England still has its Defender of the Faith."[63]

For reasons that are not completely clear in the archival or published materials, Burns quit his managerial position at Sheed and Ward toward the end of 1934. His decision, though, came after the firm's owner and director, Frank Sheed, refused to make Burns a full partner. "I asked to be taken into partnership but Sheed told me that he wished to keep the firm 'a family concern,'" Burns wrote in his autobiography. "We parted in friendly fashion—at least to all appearances—in January, 1936."[64] Burns's memory failed here. The letters of the Sheeds clearly indicate that Burns was gone by the spring of 1935.[65] Burns and several others took control of the *Tablet*, the paper so vilified in the issues of *Order*, in 1936. Burns seems also to have believed that Sheed and Ward was not entirely stable financially. "I can only say that I do not think it [should] be taken for granted that the stool marked S&W will ever remain fixed firmly on four legs, as solid as ever it was."[66] Additionally, Burns thought very little of Sheed as a person. In 1989, Dawson's daughter Christina wrote in a private letter to Harman Grisewood, Burns "thought I was too generous in my remarks about Frank Sheed who as you know he loathed."[67]

One sore point between Burns and Sheed after Burns left was control over *Essays in Order*. Burns wanted to continue editing it with Dawson at whatever firm he arrived, but Sheed clearly wanted to keep the series with Sheed and Ward. Dawson wrote to Burns, trying to explain the situation and his desire to keep editing the series with Sheed and Ward. Dawson compared the separation of Burns and *Essays in Order* to the custody of a child after a divorce. Dawson, though, thought the greater threat came from the possibility of the destruction of the series itself. Dawson feared "the ideas for which I have been working would fall between the two stools of Sheed" and Burns's new employer, "which would be a disaster."[68]

Dawson was not about to give up *Essays in Order*, which he considered essential to the continuance of the Catholic Literary Revival. When Burns began to disassociate himself from Sheed and Ward, Dawson turned to his friend and disciple from the Chelsea Group, Bernard Wall. Burns approved of Wall as his successor, but asked Dawson to "inaugurate ESSAYS IN ORDER NEW

---

[62]"A Roman Catholic Offensive," *Church Times*, April 17, 1931.

[63]"Essays in Order," *Catholic Times*, December 1, 1931.

[64]Burns, *Use of Memory*, 55.

[65]Sheed, NY, to Dawson, Exeter, March 8, 1935, in Box 11, Folder 1, UST/CDC.

[66]Burns, Chelsea, London, to Dawson, March 4 [1935], in Box 11, Folder 32, UST/CDC.

[67]Christina Scott, London, to Harman Grisewood, August 21, 1989, in Box 2, Folder 2.7, GU/Grisewood.

[68]Dawson, Devon, to Burns, London, March 3 [1935], in Box 11, Folder 32, UST/CDC.

SERIES with BW as [your] assistant (if he wants the job)."[69] It would have been hard for Dawson to find a better partner than Wall, at least in terms of intellectual compatibility. Though only aged 25, Wall had just founded the anti-Communist, pro-Catholic journal, *Colosseum*. Certainly, Wall was brilliant. He had spent a considerable amount of time with the *Order* men, while still attending Oxford, having lived with Burns in Chelsea, and he had a deep intellectual and spiritual drive. Wall's friend Rene Hague remembered him as "a great extender of horizons."[70] Another friend, artist and poet David Jones, recalled in 1974, "His proficiency in modern languages was considerable, but the popular nature of much of his published work kept him from being appreciated in the academic world."[71]

Colosseum

Equally important, Wall saw himself as Dawson's protégé. In an obituary of Dawson, Wall admitted that "Christopher was a full twenty years older than I which is the right distance between a master and an inept pupil." And referring to the *Order* men, Wall wrote movingly, "A little group of intimate friends, whom Christopher has now left behind him, has often mourned his illness: for he was our prophetic and natural leader—of a stature to head the way through the chaos of half-truths and half-knowledge in religion and culture through which we still have to live."[72] Wall not only excelled at languages, but he and his wife, Barbara, also traveled constantly throughout Europe during the late 1930s, and his correspondence, articles, books, and memoirs provide some of the best insight into European culture and politics of that time period. He is probably one of the most important unknown figures of the Catholic Literary Revival of the previous century.

The list of contributors and friends of Wall's *Colosseum* was a "who's who" of the prominent European Christian Humanists of the 1930s. Dawson, E. I. Watkin, Nicholas Berdyaev, Jacques Maritain, and Erik von Kuehnelt-Leddihn all wrote path-breaking articles for *Colosseum*. The review greatly resembled Burns's original conception for *Order* rather than the more respectable *Essays in Order* of Sheed and Ward. Indeed, there can be little doubt that Wall's *Colosseum* continued the ideas of the Chelsea group, but in a more dogmatic and polemical form than the now respectable *Essays in Order*

---

[69]Burns, Chelsea, London, to Dawson, March 4 [1935], in Box 11, Folder 32, UST/CDC.

[70]René Hague, ed., *Dai Greatcoat: A Self-Portrait of David Jones in His Letters*, René Hague, ed. (London: Faber and Faber, 1980), 41.

[71]William Blissett, *The Long Conversation: A Memoir of David Jones* (Oxford: Oxford University Press, 1981), 141.

[72]Bernard Wall, "Christopher Dawson—A Lion in Fight Against Half-Truth," in Box 1a, Folder 2, UST/CDC.

allowed.[73] Despite the clear anxiety found not only in the title and the articles of the journal, Wall believed the new effort to be an attempt "to keep one's head clear in the tumult of passions."[74] The traditional western and Roman Catholic view, he thought, was the one objective voice in a sea awash with ideologies, Left and Right. And, just as with the original *Order*, *Colosseum* was hated by numerous Catholics, both on the more modernist and more conservative sides of the faith.[75] Unlike the original *Order*, though, *Colosseum* represented a pan-European Christian humanism, rather than an English one. Wall even edited the journal from various European cities—Fribourg, London, and Paris.[76] Throughout the journal's five-year run, Wall relied on Dawson's advice, support, and articles, though Dawson never served in any official capacity on the journal.[77]

The title of Wall's journal revealed much, as he viewed Roman Catholics of the twentieth century as being in the same position as the martyrs under the iron fist of imperial Rome. But in case readers missed the intent of the title, Wall's opening pages of the first issue revealed everything about his goals. "The *Colosseum* will not be a polite review," Wall conceded. "We hold that in our time silence would be inexcusable; and our belief in what we intend to say is too sincere for us to sit back and pay scholarly compliments." Further, Wall argued, following Dawson in *Christianity in the New Age*, true Catholic scholars must no longer hide in the monasteries or accept penance in the desert. Instead, they must fight against the "shrieking contradictions of Capitalism, Bolshevism, Yogi, Democracy, Usury, Determinism, Freudianism, Starvation and Advocates of Poison Gas." The human person "has been defaced and is now exploited and commercialized." The world of the 1930s, shaped and delimited by the ideologues and their creation of the machine to mechanize man, offered only the false Manichean choice of "the sub-human mediocrity of the bourgeois world" and the false errors of the Bolshevists and Fascists, Wall argued. Because of the errors of the modern world, "crooks and demagogues like Stalin, Göring and Goebbels are enabled to exploit it."

To counter these falsehoods and the propagators of ideologies, Wall continued, Dawson, Maritain, Watkin, and the other writers of *Colosseum* would fight for a proper definition of the human person. Man, they argued, finds himself only in a religious and familial context. The twentieth-century Catholic must recognize the beginning of modern errors—that is, the new,

---

[73]Elizabeth Ward, *David Jones: Mythmaker* (Manchester, England: Manchester University Press, 1983), 45.

[74]Bernard Wall, *Headlong into Change: An Autobiography and a Memoir of Ideas Since the Thirties* (London: Harvill, 1969), 76.

[75]Ward, *David Jones: Mythmaker,* 46.

[76]Wall, *Headlong into Change,* 76.

[77]Wall wrote a volume of stunningly beautiful and perceptive letters to Dawson while he was watching the rather nasty events unfolding in 1930s Europe. See Wall Correspondence, Folder 174, Box 15, in UST/CDC.

elevated understanding of man in the Renaissance—and attempt to push him back into his proper place in the "hierarchy of beings."[78]   Dawson thrived within the format of the journal, and he wrote some of his most innovative and, not surprisingly, most pointed and incisive pieces for *Colosseum*, each following one of Wall's most significant themes and ideas for the journal. He wrote, for example, articles on Catholicism's relationship to liberalism, the meaning of pacifism for the Catholic, and the need for—but also the barriers to—a reunion of Christian branches and denominations.

But the events of the day overtook the intentions of Wall and Dawson as realized in both *Colosseum* and *Essays in Order, New Series*. Though continuing the tradition of building a "Republic of Letters" between English and Continental Catholics, this second series only saw the publication of two works: Francois Mauriac's *God and Mammon* (1936) and the German liturgical reformer Johannes Pinsk's *Christianity and Race* (1936). There were numerous problems with the New Series. First, with the editorial assistance of Burns missing, Dawson was at an almost total loss. Dawson was the ideas man, and he needed an effective organizer. As brilliant as Wall was, he was too extended in his own personal obligations, especially in his extensive traveling and already-established commitment to editing *Colosseum*. Even alone, the job of editing the journal proved itself nearly impossible, and Wall simply shut down *Colosseum* in 1939. He had gone into considerable debt to keep the journal going, and he was very keen on getting someone to relieve his financial burden.[79] Second, events in Europe were so tumultuous in the second half of the 1930s that it became difficult to recruit continental Catholics to write for the English series. Third, simple health problems prevented the series from taking shape.

Dawson, for example, had attempted to recruit C. C. Martindale and Eric Gill to write for the New Series, but each became too ill to do so.[80] Dawson had also hoped to enlist Maritain for a second book as well as enlist books by Erich Pryzwara and Dietrich Bonhofer, thus extending the Catholic Republic of Letters to Protestants with the latter choice.[81] Finally, Sheed complained that Dawson and Wall lacked tenacity and fortitude. "It is not unthinkable that they might get bored with the whole show after a few years," Sheed wrote to his second in command, E. H. Connor, when Dawson and Wall proposed a new series for Sheed and Ward in 1944. "That indeed was the sole reason why the *new Essays in Order* petered out."[82]

---

[78]Bernard Wall, "Programme," *Colosseum*, vol. 1 (1934), 5.

[79]Wall, Paris, to Dawson, [December 1938 or January 1939], in Box 15, Folder 174, UST/CDC; and Wall, Paris, to Dawson, February 22 [1939], in Box 15, Folder 174, UST/CDC.

[80]Michael Trappes-Lomax, Sheed and Ward, London, to Dawson, Hartlington Hall, February 25, 1936, in Box 11, Folder 26, UST/CDC.

[81]Dawson, notes for Essays in Order, n.d., in Box 4, Folder 26, UST/CDC.

[82]Sheed, New York, to Connor, London, March 17, 1944, in Box 11, Folder 40, UST/CDC.

A New Review

With the failure of *Colosseum* and *Essays in Order, New Series*, Dawson attempted to create a replacement—a quarterly review—but it never got off the ground. In a letter to Sheed in February 1939, Dawson outlined its purpose and proposed that Sheed and Ward finance the project. *"The Colosseum* should be transformed into a new quarterly dealing with Western culture which should be historical and sociological rather than theological," to be called *Europe: A Preview of Western Culture*.[83] Wall and Dawson also considered *The European Review* or simply *West* as titles.[84] Dawson and Wall were to be the co-editors, with Dawson handling English matters and authors, and Wall dealing with the continental Catholics. Additionally, Dawson believed it "desirable to find a non-Catholic subordinate, whether sub editor or secretary, who would help us get in touch with possible non-Catholic contributors in this country."[85] While Sheed remained unconvinced about the final point regarding non-Catholic contributors, he had advocated the merging of *Colosseum* and *Essays in Order, New Series*, since the spring of 1937.[86] At the very least, should *Colosseum* continue, Sheed, whose firm had bought *Colosseum* in the Spring of 1937, wanted Dawson to help Wall co-edit it.[87]

Dawson, hoping for a united Christendom, wanted the new journal to serve as an opening in a new Christian Republic of Letters, but within certain limitations. "The reviews should be open to non Catholic contributors (writing of course on non Theological subjects) on equal terms with the Catholic contributors."[88] When Anglican T. S. Eliot's *Criterion* collapsed in late 1938, for example, the American turned Englishman showed interest in joining Dawson and Wall as a partner in the new journal. It is unclear if he would have done so if the journal were to be financed by Sheed and Ward. Eliot may well have hoped that his own firm, Faber and Faber, might provide the financial backing.[89] Additionally, Dawson and Wall simply believed there were too few English Roman Catholics who could write well enough to contribute to the journal.[90] "I am still utterly puzzled to find a Catholic in England who can be asked to write for the first number," Sheed confided to Dawson.[91] Dawson did, however, find two English Roman Catholic allies and potential contributors in his friends David Matthews, a secular priest and future bishop, and Thomas Gilby, a Dominican priest, both of whom showed

---

[83]Dawson, Cambridge, to Sheed, London, February 6, 1939, in Box 11, Folder 5, UST/CDC.
[84]Wall, Paris, to Dawson, [December 26, 1938], in Box 15, Folder 174, UST/CDC.
[85]Dawson, Cambridge, to Sheed, London, February 6, 1939, in Box 11, Folder 5, UST/CDC.
[86]Sheed, London, to Dawson, March 23, 1937, in Box 11, Folder 3, UST/CDC.
[87]Sheed, London, to Dawson, September 4, 1938, in Box 11, Folder 4, UST/CDC.
[88]Dawson, Cambridge, to Sheed, London, February 6, 1939, in Box 11, Folder 5, UST/CDC.
[89]Wall, Paris, to Dawson, [December 1938 or January 1939], in Box 15, Folder 174, UST/CDC.
[90]Wall, Paris, to Dawson, February 22 [1939], in Box 15, Folder 174, UST/CDC.
[91]Sheed, London, to Dawson, Cambridge, March 30, 1939, in Box 11, Folder 5, UST/CDC.

great interest in the new journal.[92] Tom Burns, now a director of the *Tablet*, also showed considerable interest in the new project. "I do not believe that even a quarterly could survive if it had to carry overheads and to be run on a strictly commercial basis," Burns cautioned Dawson, "but I think that a group of writers could be got together who would take on the job in a missionary spirit and would work on a rate which would not be commensurate with the standard of work involved."[93]

Three other problems arose for the collaborators. First, Wall and Dawson had a difficult time defining the West, especially as it applied to the meaning of the new review. Dawson thought in broad, inclusive terms of what was once Christendom in the Middle Ages and what could again be Christendom, but Wall thought almost exclusively of the Anglo-Saxon worlds of the United Kingdom, the United States, Canada, Australia, and New Zealand. "The English-speaking world seems to me almost (sometimes) a thing of its own, like Bolshevism or Nazism," Wall wrote to Dawson.[94] Ultimately, Wall told Dawson, the decision would be Dawson's as to how the West should be defined. Dawson should decide the scope of the journal and write the program for it.[95]

The second problem came from the perceived lack of public interest in a quarterly. "I rather feel in my bones that the day of the quarterly is over in the traditional sense," Wall admitted.[96] Simply put, no audience for a new Catholic journal existed. The final problem came when the *Tablet*, to the great surprise of Dawson, Sheed, and Wall, leaked the news that the *Colosseum* was folding before anything definite had been decided or a replacement established. "Maisie and I have been giving much thought to the problem of the quarterly, she having been much worried at the stupid announcement" in the *Tablet* about "the closing of *Colosseum*," Sheed wrote. Frank and Maisie wanted *Colosseum* to continue. "We feel that it would be a tragedy to let a healthy paper simply die; it is still the only platform for the expression of your and our outlook; and if there were at all a long gap it might be difficult to get the *Colosseum* subscribers to start all over again when you think the time is ripe for the new paper."[97] Dawson, too, was angry with the *Tablet*, and wrote to the editor, Douglas Woodruff. "It is true that I have been discussing with Wall and Sheed for some time the idea of a new review to be called *Europe* (or some such name) and would incorporate *Colosseum* and of which I should be coeditor and I may have mentioned this to you in private conversation. But

[92]Dawson, Cambridge, to Wall, Paris, May 28 [1939], in Box 15, Folder 174, UST/CDC.

[93]Tom Burns, London, to Dawson, April 12, 1939, in Box 14, Folder 61, UST/CDC.

[94]Wall, Paris, to Dawson, [December 26, 1938], in Box 15, Folder 174, UST/CDC.

[95]Wall, Paris, to Dawson, [February or March 1939], in Box 15, Folder 174, UST/CDC.

[96]Wall, Paris, to Dawson, February 22 [1939], in Box 15, Folder 174, UST/CDC.

[97]Sheed, London, to Dawson, April 20, 1939, in Box 11, Folder 5, UST/CDC.

nothing has been definitely settled and so far as I know nothing has ever been announced with regard to the stoppage of *Colosseum*."[98]

But the events of the world intervened in a more important way than had the *Tablet's* unfortunately premature announcement. With the invasion of Poland in 1939, Wall's life changed considerably, as would Dawson's. First, Wall had to flee Paris in 1940, and he "escaped through Calais after the fall of France at the very last minute."[99] He spent much of the war working for British intelligence and counter-espionage. Second, the tensions of the time trapped Wall in his own obscure dualist tendencies, and he broke his friend- ships and alliances with anyone who deviated from his own particular views of the world. "But my closest associate as regards ideas at this tragic time was Christopher Dawson. This association eroded my friendship with Eric [Gill] and also with Maritain," Wall admitted in his autobiography. Dawson, "with his vast knowledge of world cultures, his special studies in European history, mediaeval and modern, seemed to me far better equipped to give an all round picture of our condition than Eric who was a stone-carver or Maritain who was a philosopher."[100] Wall especially hoped and believed that Dawson's influence would prevent America from accepting a pro-Fascist po- sition.[101] Maritain, however, Wall suggested, had little real power in France, though he seemed to be causing difficulties in America, "stirring up trouble amongst Catholics there."[102] Therefore, Wall reasoned, Maritain was some- where between an insignificant and a dangerous ally. "I am *so* glad you liked the reviews," Wall wrote to Dawson in February 1939. "I wanted to put old Maritain in his place, with all his manifestos of intellectuals, etc!"[103] Only a month later, Wall wrote, "However, I wish I felt more certain in Rome they will shortly either take the *Action Francaise* off the Index, or put Maritain on it. Either of these measures would please me."[104] The *Action Francaise* had been put on the Index for its possible fascist leanings.

Wall's decision to side with Dawson over Maritain proved perplexing to Dawson, as the English historian saw no need for a choice to be made in the matter. While Dawson did not agree with Maritain on many important things, he certainly respected him as a scholar, especially in the early part of the 1930s. 1936, however, proved to be the year that Dawson began to see Maritain as something other than an ally. In a conversation held in 1953 with John Mulloy, Dawson said that he believed that Maritain's "residence in the United States has spoiled both his language and his thought. In the latter, he

---

[98] Dawson to Woodruff, March 30, 1939, in Box 11, Folder 5, UST/CDC.

[99] Blissett, *The Long Conversation,* 141.

[100] Wall, *Headlong into Change,* 89.

[101] Wall, Paris, to Dawson, December 12 [1938], in Folder 174, Box 15, in UST/CDC.

[102] Ibid.

[103] Wall, Paris, to Dawson, February 1939, in Folder 174, Box 15, UST/CDC.

[104] Wall, Paris, to Dawson, March 3, 1939, in Folder 174, Box 15, in UST/CDC.

has made too much emphasis on political issues, in the former, he has become quite a poor prose writer, obscurity replacing his former clarity." Dawson liked Maritain's writings for *Essays in Order* and before, and he thought Maritain's 1936 book on humanism, *Integral Humanism,* a blend of the good and the bad. For Dawson, the work certainly foreshadowed a less interesting Maritain.[105] In his own personal notes, Dawson criticized Maritain's *Integral Humanism* as falsely dualistic. "It is a mistake to take Barth and St. Thomas as the 2 Christian positions, for the contrast can be marked equally well *within* the two religious divisions of Christendom," Dawson wrote. "In Catholicism we have the contrast [of] Augustinism–Thomism, and in Protestantism that of Luther–Melanchthon or Barth–? It narrows the isms unduly if we make St. Thomas the only Catholic and Barth the only Protestant."[106] Certainly, the Augustinian Dawson would not appreciate Thomism as the only Catholic tradition.

The Moot

Maritain's influence, though, could be felt in yet one other Christian group in which Dawson was involved in the 1930s and 1940s, the aforementioned Moot, founded by English Quaker J. H. Oldham and T. S. Eliot. Oldham hoped to create some kind of Christian Party or fraternity to operate behind the political scene to counter the various socialist parties as well as the socialist tendencies in the non-socialist parties in Britain.[107] Each of the founders had hoped to bring together the greatest Christian minds of the time to counter the threats of the ideologues, and Dawson was one of Eliot's first choices. Oldham wanted a specific and concerted plan of action to develop:

> In the light of this consideration of fundamental attitudes we might attempt to draw up, or make a beginning in the attempt to draw up, a systematic outline of the tasks which ought to be undertaken by the members of the Moot, but of the most urgent tasks to which Christian thought as a whole should address itself and in the carrying out of which as many of the best Christian minds as possible should be enlisted. Any provisional outline which the Moot might prepare might be submitted either after this meeting, to a number of other thinkers for criticism and comment. In this way a programme of work might evolve, in the carrying out of which an increasing number of able minds might be enlisted.[108]

Unlike the other groups to which Dawson belonged, the Moot was heavily Anglo-Catholic. Impressively, the Moot included men such as Karl Mannheim, Reinhold Niebuhr, John Baillie, and Michael Polanyi.[109] Speaking at the first

---

[105]Mulloy, Record of Dawson conversation on August 19, 1953, in Box 1, Folder 2, ND/CDAW.

[106]Dawson, Notes on Maritain and Integral/True Humanism, in Box 9, Folder 22, UST/CDC.

[107]Roger Kojecky, *T. S. Eliot's Social Criticism* (New York: Farrar, Straus, and Giroux, 1971), 170–171.

[108]Oldham, London, to Members of the Moot, October 18, 1938, in Box 15, Folder 80, UST/CDC.

[109]Kojecky, *T. S. Eliot's Social Criticism*, 237–39.

meeting, Dawson advocated a "totalitarian Christianity." It would not be "totalitarian" in the sense of fascism and communism. Instead, it would be totalitarian in that it would affect every aspect of one's life. It should, Dawson argued in a very Augustinian manner, reflect the two communitarian orders of the Middle Ages, the various religious orders as well as "the natural community of the peasant society based on blood and soil and incorporated in and subordinated to the Church through an hierarchy." This, Dawson concluded, much to the chagrin of the fellow members of the Moot, was "obviously the solution . . . a totalitarian Christian Order, but this would be the Kingdom of God—a very long range policy."[110]   Christ, after all, "claims the total allegiance of Christians."[111]   Eliot later accepted many of Dawson's points as presented at the first meeting, as witnessed in his own books on Christian culture. The Moot, though, to a great extent, sided at the time with Maritain's more Thomistic conception of Christian humanism, formulated in Maritain's *Integral Humanism* (1936).[112]   And Eliot himself, while an advocate of the Catholic conception of natural law, rejected any notion of a return to medieval Catholicism as "too abstract."[113]

Dawson only attended a few meetings of the Moot, though he and Oldham corresponded frequently during its existence, and Oldham did much to promote Dawson's works and the World War II Sword of the Spirit movement in the Moot newsletter, the *Christian News-Letter*. The Anglicanism and the Thomism may have proven overwhelming to Dawson. More likely, the group was simply too large, abstract, and impersonal. He preferred his groups intimate and dedicated to spontaneous intellectual discussion. In a rather biting fashion, Dawson responded to one of Oldham's letters, criticizing the purpose of the Moot, which he seems to have believed desirous of politicizing Christianity:

> But I am not sure that the sentence 'all life is meeting' adequately expresses the central issue . . . you have only to add a single letter and it expresses just the opposite—the swamping of spiritual action and personal relations by proliferation of social activities and organization—all life is meetings, Cabinet meetings, departmental meetings, board meetings, social meetings, congresses, conferences, committees, 'the sound of all the soulless things that sing the soul to sleep.'[114]

As World War II progressed, Oldham wanted to focus the discussion of the Moot on practical ideas and possibilities, and Dawson wanted to discuss theology and the movements of the Holy Spirit.[115]

---

[110]Ibid., 164.

[111]Christopher Dawson, "The Problem of Christ and Culture," *Dublin Review*, vol. 226 (1952), 66.

[112]Kojecky, *T. S. Eliot's Social Criticism*, 168.

[113]Ibid., 177.

[114]Dawson to J. H. Oldham, March 27, 1942, in Box 15, Folder 80, UST/CDC.

[115]Dawson to J. H. Oldham, April 18, 1942, in Box 15, Folder 80, UST/CDC.

Still, the late 1920s through the mid 1930s must have been a golden period for Dawson. Though the western world was collapsing, Dawson was fighting the good fight, and he had numerous companions—intelligent, dedicated men, Catholic and non-Catholic—who looked to him for his scholarly analysis and intellectual guidance. A very shy but brilliant man who worked in isolation but throve on discussion and interaction with others, Dawson wrote prolifically during this time. And yet, as the events of 1939 would prove, all of Dawson's words and works with *Order*, *Colosseum*, and the Moot seemed for naught. Dawson's *Order* friend Harman Grisewood expressed the fears and the defeats well. Ideological wars soon consumed the light and beauty of an Eliot, a Maritain, and a Dawson, he wrote.

> The bitter frosts that followed the war were to finish the job. Scientific humanism at a crude level trampled the ground which had been leveled and seeded by philosophers of another sort. Politics ate up the autonomy which the arts had won. None of this did I foresee at the time, but I did see a turning point had been reached and I knew that for me personally the turn things took was for the worse. The kind of people who were now to be in the ascendancy would not be the sort of people we liked. We would be, culturally, in opposition. In the middle ages we would have gone into exile with the King.[116]

But it was not the Middle Ages, and there was no king with whom to go into exile. Every Englishman, Dawson had once argued, loves a lost cause.[117] And, Dawson was certainly no exception. He might go down and western civilization might go down, but neither would do so easily.

---

[116]Harman Grisewood, *One Thing at a Time: An Autobiography* (London: Hutchinson, 1968), 105.

[117]Christopher Dawson, "The Making of Britain," *Tablet* (1936), 782.

Chapter 4

Against the Ideologues

1930–1942

DESPITE THE BEST EFFORTS OF DAWSON AND HIS CHRISTIAN HUMANIST ALLIES
in *Order, Essays in Order, Colosseum,* and the Moot, the disorder of the world
and the arrogant brutality of the ideologues proceeded at an astounding pace
throughout the 1930s. To help counter this fall into the abyss, Dawson wrote
some of his most penetrating and compelling work between 1930 and 1942.
So, on one hand, Dawson wrote about humanism, culture, history, and religion. On the other hand, he entered into the debate over current politics.
He most likely would have preferred to continue to write about culture and
religion, but he believed that as a traditionalist conservative and an Augustinian, he had a duty to enter into the realm of the political and ideological
wars. Since the various ideologues had replaced the Christian catechisms with
creeds and propaganda in the first third of the twentieth century, the conservative must also "develop a similar intellectual propaganda," Dawson wrote
in his personal notes. For the fight had gone well beyond the civility of the
ballot box and had, instead, become a "battle of ideas and beliefs. Practical
politics are not enough," Dawson continued. "We need a conservative sociology to set against the socialist theory of society, and a conservative spiritual
ideal of order to meet the idealism of revolution."[1] This became Dawson's
mission for roughly a twelve-year period.

Beginning with his booklet for T. S. Eliot, "Christianity and Sex," Dawson
continued his analysis of the ideological situation in several books throughout the 1930s: *The Modern Dilemma* (1932); *Religion and the Modern State*
(1935); and *Beyond Politics* (1939).[2] In each, Dawson used his consider-

---

[1] Dawson, "Conservatism," unpublished manuscript dated June 1932, in Box 3, Folder 38,
UST/CDC.

[2] Dawson also wrote *The Spirit of the Oxford Movement* in 1933, but it dramatically stands
apart from this series of political works.

123

able skills as a sociologist, anthropologist, and historian to analyze the crises caused by the ideologies. "The fact that we have lost confidence in the ship's officers is no reason for entrusting its navigation to people who believe in wrecks as a matter of principle or who make a business of piracy," wrote Dawson with a rare bit of humor in volume eight of *Essays in Order, The Modern Dilemma*.[3] The leaders of the previous century—the liberals—had allowed a century of materialism to flourish at the expense of the spirit, and the ship had gone adrift. As each person and society longed for the spirit, liberalism's neglect of the spirit allowed at least two false spiritualisms to arise: nationalism and socialism. Real unity could only be found in the organic history of the western tradition—which all ideologues abhorred, mutilated, and attempted to annihilate. Like the Roman Republic, Dawson wrote, modern Europe had "conquered and organised the world and lost its own soul in the process."[4] As Dawson viewed it, the world seemed to have lost its soul in the "mass civilisation that is coming to birth in Moscow and Detroit."[5]

Religion and the Modern State and *Beyond Politics* continued the same analysis. Dawson, in a rather scholarly and even-handed fashion, described the rise of fascism while labeling the rise of the New Deal in America as a benign form of dictatorship. "It is in fact a constitutional dictatorship," Dawson wrote bluntly.[6] Further, he noted, to abandon the free market, as the Americans had done, would lead to the abandonment of other American liberties. "We shall also have to abandon political individualism and the right to criticize and oppose the Government," Dawson predicted.[7] Rooted in the Burkean tradition of organic common law and constitutional medievalism, Dawson believed that all liberties were wrapped together, inseparable one from another. A people discovered and earned their rights over time. One could not simply declare as an abstraction this or that right. Instead, specific rights must develop through tradition, as had the English rights from early Anglo-Saxon common law through the Magna Carta to the present. In both *The Modern Dilemma* and *Religion and the Modern State*, Dawson criticized mass democracy. It must fail as a political system, he argued, for democracy creates a situation in which citizenship becomes a duty and a burden rather than a right and a privilege. Perhaps more troubling, mass democracies more often than not allow bureaucracies and selfish interests to assume control, forcing all things to become political and politicized.[8] This is true especially in the democratic welfare state, which will ultimately not just give away things to its

---

[3] Christopher Dawson, "The Modern Dilemma," *Cambridge Review*, February 17, 1933, 10.
[4] Ibid., 22.
[5] Ibid., 28. See also his "Europe: Its Tradition and Its Future, Cultural and Religious," *Christendom*, vol. 12 (1942), 144–56.
[6] Christopher Dawson, *Religion and the Modern State* (New York: Sheed and Ward, 1936), 23.
[7] Ibid., 24.
[8] Ibid., 38–45.

subjects, Dawson warned, but will also mechanize its citizens, making them something less than human. "It may be harder to resist a Totalitarian state which relies on free milk and birth-control clinics than one which relies on castor oil and concentration camps," Dawson feared.[9]

Unfortunately, as the world disintegrated, so did Dawson's psychological and physical health. Dawson frequently suffered from deep bouts of depression during his life, and he referred to them as "Uncle Paul" in correspondence with his close friend, E. I. Watkin.[10] A serious attack of depression and insomnia hit Dawson terribly hard during the late 1930s, seeming to last for nearly three years.[11] When Burns left Sheed and Ward for the *Tablet*, Dawson invested a considerable amount of money in the new venture and hoped to become a director as well as a full-time writer for the Catholic newspaper. Burns accepted Dawson's investment, but he refused to allow Dawson to write regularly because of his health. "In your present state of health I think it would be unfair to you and to the *Tablet* to fix an annual salary in return for definite work," Burns wrote in 1936. "It would be better to pay for things piecemeal." Further, Burns added, "it is awful to think of this insomnia continuing: surely you ought now to put your health before everything, come to London and see the best man available and go rigorously through his treatment."[12]

There can be little doubt that Dawson's health affected his writing in this period. One only has to give the most cursory glance to Dawson's bibliography and publication dates to see that the period from 1936 to 1946 reveals relatively little written output compared to the ten years prior to 1936. In 1938, Burns's former employer, Frank Sheed, became so irritated with Dawson's inability to produce his next book that he wrote: "But owing to your quite unforeseen unwellness, the arrangement has worked out to be a solid loss for us, and the loss would continue to increase in the absence of a new book."[13] As will be shown in a much more detailed manner in chapter five, Sheed and Dawson's friendship almost ended several times between the late 1930s and 1946. In those years, Dawson seems to have carried the weight of the world, and the urgency and anxiety he felt may, ironically, have prompted some of his most profound thoughts, even as it hindered his ability to write. Whatever caused his restlessness, it did result, ultimately, in great productivity of mind and soul, which offered him purpose again and allowed him to escape his depression. Most importantly, with each new work, he increasingly

---

[9]Ibid., 108.

[10]Christina Scott, *A Historian and His World: A Life of Christopher Dawson* (New Brunswick, NJ: Transaction, 1992), 42. The name "Uncle Paul" came from a Belloc poem.

[11]Ibid., 127ff.

[12]Tom Burns, London, to Dawson, Hartlington Hall, Skipton, Yorks, February 4, 1936, in Box 14, Folder 61, UST/CDC.

[13]Sheed, London, to Dawson, May 12, 1938, in Box 11, Folder 4, UST/CDC.

called for a return to traditional theology and an openness for the citizens of Christendom to prepare themselves for the grace of the Holy Ghost.

"Age of Propaganda"

"We live in an age of economic and social panaceas—the Five Years' Plan, Technocracy, Social Credit, Economic Autarchy, and the rest," Dawson wrote in 1935. "[T]he most successful governments are not those that govern best, but those which are able to generate the most unbounded faith in their own particular nostrum."[14] The twentieth century was quickly becoming the "Age of Propaganda," Dawson believed. Propaganda served as one of the worst means by which any power could attempt to mechanize the mind of man. Utilitarian at its most basic level, it inherently destroyed the imagination of the human person, asking him to absorb and obey without criticism. "In the war of ideas, it is the crudest and the most simplified ideology that wins,"[15] Dawson argued. Indeed, the rise of propaganda alarmed Dawson terribly in the 1930s. As the propaganda increased in intensity and sophistication, the English scholar's writings took on a corresponding air of profound urgency in the 1930s.

As early as 1928, Dawson had worried about the seemingly inevitable seismic cultural and philosophical shifts in the world. The civilized world seemed hopelessly fragile, and it stood over a fault line, ready to collapse at the slightest provocation. Perhaps even a gentle nudge might push it over.[16] By the early 1930s, the western world was, with nearly unstoppable rapidity, becoming politicized at the expense of culture and religion as well as at the expense of the dignity of the human person. Most terrifyingly for a Christian Humanist like Dawson, various ideologies were attempting to implement their particular visions of utopia. And the results—to any right-thinking person—were predictable. "The nightmares of the hive—the insect society—or Leviathan— the monstrous social organism—nightmares which have so long haunted the imagination of men of letters—seem to be passing from the sphere of phantasy to the world of every day experience," Dawson feared.[17] "Thanks to science, there is no longer any limit to the amount of power which the state can exercise."[18]

---

[14]Christopher Dawson, "The Future of National Government," *Dublin Review* (1935), 237.

[15]Christopher Dawson, *The Movement of World Revolution* (New York: Sheed and Ward, 1959), 100.

[16]Christina Scott, "The Meaning of the Millennium: The Ideas of Christopher Dawson," *Logos*, vol. 2 (1999), 67.

[17]Christopher Dawson, "Religious Liberty and the New Political Forces," *The Month*, vol. 183 (1947), 44; and C. J. McNaspy, "A Chat with Christopher Dawson," *America*, vol. 106 (October 28, 1961), 120.

[18]Dawson, "Religious Liberty and the New Political Forces," 44.

In hindsight, the twenty-first century historian cannot easily avoid the gaze of the nearly 200 million murdered from the previous century. Their ghostly eyes stare at us, asking us to write their testimonies and memorials. We, for the most part, ignore them, choosing to call the previous century a century of progress and liberation. But, one must ask, who was liberated? Certainly not the twenty-one million murdered in National Socialist work camps or the sixty million worn down to nothing in the Soviet Gulags.

Much to Dawson's surprise, human nature seemed far more malleable than he would first have imagined. If agrarian man easily became proletarian man under industrialization, Dawson asked, why could not proletarian man become simplified, technologically-controlled, mass man?[19] Each step away from man farming the created earth seemed to make him less human and less animated. Instead, man became increasingly mechanized as technology advanced and bureaucracy grew. Worse, man seemed not to protest too much his own mechanization. Utopia, impossible to create and fantastic in its desire for escape from true reality, would naturally become dystopia.[20] The totalitarian results were horrifying, especially after the relative peace of the nineteenth century: mass murder; loss of all freedoms; and wars among the ideologues, internally and externally. After all, Dawson believed, World War II had been first and foremost a war of ideas, similar to the wars surrounding the French Revolution.[21] Under the inspiration of Edmund Burke, especially as articulated in his *Letters of a Regicide Peace*, the British had fought vigorously and unceasingly against the French and demanded a complete victory over the Gallic ideological and dictatorial forces. Unlike the British victory in 1814, however, the end of World War II brought no century of lasting victory and peace. Instead, by the end of 1946, the war of ideas and ideologies turned into a cold war between the two materialist powers, the United States and the U.S.S.R. No permanent peace seemed in sight, and Christian principles of war and peace, as they had been in 1919 and 1920, were simply set aside for an odd combination of idealistic and *realpolitik*.

The new ideological states promoted the so-called progressivism of the early twentieth century, which was rapidly revealed to be a bloody progress, trampling on human dignity in the name of some amorphous abstractions.[22] The modern state—whether democratic, fascist, or communist—promoted universal education to shape the youth, and, once those youth had been formed, into universal military service they marched. To pay for universal education and universal military service, the state confiscated private prop-

---

[19]Christopher Dawson, "The Foundations of Unity," *Dublin Review*, vol. 211 (1942), 98.

[20]Christopher Dawson, "Religion and the Life of Civilization," in *Religions of the Empire: A Conference on Some Living Religions within the Empire*, William Loftus Hare, ed. (London: Duckworth, 1925), 467.

[21]Dawson, "Foundations of Unity," 97.

[22]Dawson, *Religion and the Modern State*, xii.

erty, denying its protection as an inherent, God-given right.[23] Dawson chided all ideologies as mechanistic and ultimately pagan. "Communism in Russia, National Socialism in Germany, and Capitalism and Liberal Democracy in the Western countries are really three forms of the same thing," Dawson argued. Each moves along "different but parallel paths to the same goal, which is the mechanization of human life and the complete subordination of the individual to the state and to the economic process."[24] Coming to fruition in the nineteenth-century, neither liberal Capitalism nor Marxian Socialism offered a solution to the needs of man, properly understood as "a free personality, the creature of God and the maker of his own destiny."[25]

In his personal notes written in the 1930s, Dawson summed up the five most important threats to liberty.

1. The danger to political freedom from the growth of bureaucratic control over the machinery of government.

2. The danger of the mechanization of society by the centralization of economic organization.

3. The danger to intellectual freedom and liberal culture from the domination of the specialist and the technician.

4. The danger to spiritual freedom from the control and manipulation of public opinion by the totalitarian psychological techniques.

5. The danger to national freedom and to international peace from the unlimited aggression and violence of the new mass-tyranny.[26]

Consequently, Dawson directed most of his energy, time, and considerable talents to explaining in a rather nuanced fashion—historically, sociologically, theologically, and culturally—the rise of the myriad of ideologies and their takeover and consolidation of numerous nation-states in the twentieth century. With the breakdown of the philosophical, cultural, and political unity of Christendom during the sixteenth-century, nation-states were free to form at will. The most effective form of nationalism, Dawson argued, embraces an ideology which allows it to homogenize the cultural, religious, and ethnic differences of its people. "Nationalism tends to turn into barbarianism," Dawson explained in an interview. "The real heart of nationalism is tribalism, the feeling that 'we're all the same blood, we must stick together.'"[27] Or, as Dawson put it more succinctly in his unpublished "Memorandum on

---

[23]Ibid., 46.

[24]Ibid., xv.

[25]Dawson, "Future of National Government," 250–51.

[26]Dawson, "An English Political Tradition," [1930s], in Box 1a/Folder 58, UST/CDC.

[27]McNaspy, "A Chat with Christopher Dawson," 122.

Culture and Ethics," the "modern cult of nationalism" is nothing more than "an idealization of cultural particularism."[28] In his argumentation, Dawson follows the lead of one of the most important nineteenth-century historians, Lord Acton. "Christianity rejoices at the mixture of races," Acton had written in his famed essay, "Nationalism." Paganism, however, "identifies itself with their differences, because truth is universal, errors various and particular."[29] From Dawson's standpoint, modern nation-states clearly embraced the pagan particularism as opposed to the Church's universalism. Through a common liturgy and a common liturgical and intellectual language, the Church had attempted to suppress the barbarian nationalism throughout its one-thousand year hegemony during the Middle Ages.[30] But the Church had failed in its greatest mission, that is, keeping together the Body of Christ. It failed to sanctify the pagan fully, Dawson argued, thus allowing the German nationalists to arise and reshape German culture and politics at the beginning of the sixteenth century.[31]

Dawson found nationalism to be a latent force in the western character. It could and did emerge in a number of different ways throughout the history of western civilization. The Germanic barbarian nationalism stood ready to emerge at any time it found opportune, especially if Christendom became divided against itself. Christendom certainly disintegrated because of the barbarian propensity for nationalism, but not all at once. It was also not unique to the Germans in the western tradition, as Hellas may have experienced a prototype of nationalism after the Persian Wars. For the modern world, though, the process began in earnest in the early fourteenth century and continued through the present day. The French first experienced a budding nationalism in 1302 and then again during the French Revolution.[32]

The rise of a nation-state and its ideological propaganda must by necessity witness the corresponding decline of religious influence and thought, Dawson argued. Christianity, through grace and mercy, especially embraces the universal rather than the particular, as Lord Acton had correctly stated. The nation-state, though, demands a different unity of thought, culture, and politics, seeing in the Church a rival faith. "And in each case what we find is a substitute religion or counter religion which transcends the juridical limits of the

---

[28]Dawson, "Memorandum on Culture and Ethics," November 22, 1956, in Box 1, Folder 15, ND/CDAW.

[29]John Emerich Edward Dalberg-Acton, *Essays in the History of Liberty* (Indianapolis, IN: Liberty Fund, 1986), 409–33. On the various views of Dawson's debt to Lord Acton see Joseph Pearce, *Literary Converts: Spiritual Inspiration in an Age of Unbelief* (San Francisco, CA: Ignatius, 2000), 333; and Scott, *A Historian and His World,* 35, 49. Dawson, at least in private, claimed that Acton had little effect on him. See Mulloy, "Record of Conversation with Dawson, August 24, 1953," in Box 1, Folder 2, ND/CDAW.

[30]Dawson letter to E. I. Watkin in 1953, quoted in Scott, *A Historian and His World,* 207.

[31]Christopher Dawson, "On Nationalism," *Tablet* (April 13, 1940), 349.

[32]Ibid. Also see his *The Dividing of Christendom* (New York: Sheed and Ward, 1965), 21.

political State and creates a kind of secular Church," Dawson maintained.[33] Nationalism, then, unifies its disparate peoples and cultures through an ideology, expressed through propaganda, which takes "the place of theology as the creator of social ideals and the guide of public opinion."[34]

The Enlightenment and the French Revolution completed the work begun in earnest by the Reformation, Dawson argued. The Enlightenment, after all, witnessed more neglect and attenuation of Christian ideals and more selling of church property than any other time in the history of western civilization. The Enlightenment, in essence, extended the worst desires of the Reformers even into the cultural and geopolitical areas that had resisted the Reformation of the sixteenth and seventeenth centuries.[35] It should not surprise the modern mind, Dawson claimed, that the philosophies of the Enlightenment helped spawn both liberalism and communism. Each rejected the intellectual contributions of Christendom and instead embraced materialist understandings of the world. Each also employed propaganda as a means of undermining the "social order and traditional morality." Both the Liberals and the Communists understood the spiritual underpinnings of Europe even better than did the European Christians of Dawson's day. "Christianity is everywhere the first object of Communist attacks," the English historian lamented.[36] Hence, each ideological group attempted to undermine the Christian understanding of spirituality. These groups initially hoped that Christians would embrace Christ as a political revolutionary. Finally, each ideological group also destroyed culture, tradition, and civilization without rebuilding anything of note.[37]

The undermining of the spiritual bond of Europe and its substitution with ideologies has had numerous profound effects on European culture, lamented Dawson.[38] First, it has led to substitute, false religions. God created man to find religion, to find Him, and man without true religion is empty. He finds himself devoid of something, but that something remains elusive. He will seek until he finds either true religion or a substitute that temporarily fills the void. "The ordinary man will never stand for nihilism: it is against all his healthier instincts," Dawson wrote in 1955.[39] To find his substitute, man turns in many

[33]Christopher Dawson, "Education and the State," *Commonweal*, vol. 65 (January 25, 1957), 425.

[34]Christopher Dawson, "Christianity and Ideologies," *Commonweal*, vol. 64 (May 11, 1956), 139.

[35]Ibid., 140.

[36]Christopher Dawson, "The New Decline and Fall," *Commonweal*, vol. 15 (1932), 320, 322.

[37]Christopher Dawson, "Birth of Democracy," *Review of Politics*, vol. 19 (1957), 50.

[38]Dawson, "New Decline and Fall," 322.

[39]Dawson, Devon, England, to Father Leo Ward, Notre Dame, IN, February 20, 1955, in Box 1, Folder 5, ND/CDAW; and Dawson, "The Victorian Background," 246.

directions: utopianism, drugs, and cults, "leaving the enemy in possession of the field."[40]

Second, the substitute of ideology for true religion has yielded to the unwieldiness and ultimate tyranny of science and technology. If Christianity cannot delimit the growth of technology, providing the scientists with an ethical understanding of the world, technology soon masters man. Man "becomes a subordinate part of the great mechanical system that his scientific genius has created," Dawson lamented. "In the same way, the economic process, which led to the exploitation of the world by man and the vast increase of his material resources, ends in the subjection of man to the rule of the machine and the mechanisation of human life."[41] German-Italian theologian Romano Guardini (1885–1968) explained the problem of a technological order equally well. With the rise of modern technology, man could choose to work with nature, or he could seek to dominate nature. In the first relationship of man to technology, "the aim is to penetrate, to move within, to live with," Guardini argued in 1922 in his reflections on man and technology, *Letters from Lake Como*. This first type, according to Christian Humanists like Dawson, Guardini, or J. R. R. Tolkien, exists according to the scriptural commands as found in Genesis to have stewardship over the earth. "The other, however, unpacks, tears apart, arranges in compartments, takes over and rules."[42] The dominating kind of technology soon takes on a life of its own, and man loses his control over it and becomes subsumed by it. "It is destructive because it is not under human control," Guardini concluded. "It is the surging ahead of unleashed forces that have not yet been mastered, raw material that has not yet been put together, given a living and spiritual form, and related to humanity."[43]

Unrestrained science and technology has resulted not only in mechanized man, but also in bureaucratized government, Dawson argued. Bureaucratic states—whether democratic or tyrannical—are the "coldest of cold monsters."[44] Certainly, this was true for the totalitarian states, Dawson believed. To him, for example, one could not readily separate National Socialism from International Socialism. "Marxian Socialism is not the only form of Socialism extant," Dawson wrote to the *Catholic Times*. "There is, for example, National Socialism, which is the official title of German Fascism."[45] One is, in essence, related intimately to the other, whatever their accidents may

[40]Christopher Dawson, "Christianity and the New Age," in *Essays in Order*, Christopher Dawson and Tom Burns, eds. (New York: Macmillan, 1931), 158.

[41]Ibid., 162. See also his "European Democracy and the New Economic Forces," *Sociological Review*, vol. 22 (1930), 33.

[42]Romano Guardini, *Letters from Lake Como: Explorations in Technology and the Human Race*, trans. George Bromiley (Grand Rapids, MI: William B. Eerdmans, 1994), 43.

[43]Ibid., 79.

[44]Quoted in Dawson, "Christianity and the New Age," 162.

[45]Dawson, to the editor, *Catholic Times* (May 11, 1934), in Box 16, Folder 17, UST/CDC.

appear. As we discussed earlier, Dawson took these comparisons even further, likening capitalism and liberal democracy to communism and National Socialism. He concluded cautiously, "Of course I do not mean to say that they are absolutely equivalent, and that we have no right to prefer one to another. But I do believe that a Christian cannot regard any of them as a final solution of the problem of civilization, or even a tolerable one."[46] Eight years later, Dawson argued that Soviet Communism, German National Socialism, and America's New Deal were all variants of a theme, each ruling through a centralized bureaucracy.[47] Each saw the individual human person as nothing more than a means to an end, and each sacrificed true religion to the needs of the nation-state. In the end, Dawson believed, each of the three nation-states represented a radical form of materialism. Ultimately, Dawson claimed, the alliance of science, ideology, and political power was forcing humanity "helplessly towards the abyss."[48]

To overcome and adulterate tradition, faith, and local communities, various ideologues created a left-right tension. Indeed, as Dawson viewed it, the left-right dichotomy was a necessary ruse to advance any ideology. "The revolutionary forces which inspire the two rival extremisms of the Left and the Right are both alike the enemies of Europe, and they have far more in common with each other than with either the conservative or democratic elements in Western society, with which each respectively attempts to form a common front," Dawson wrote.[49] Fascism, Dawson argued, especially understood the need for creating the left and the right. Of all the twentieth-century ideologies, it best "carried the technique of total war into the political forum," intentionally creating false tensions and divisions, forcing an extreme resolution, rather than a prudent one.[50] Such a division negated the vertical axis of grace and sin, and put everything on the horizontal, worldly axis. "Evil has become, as it were, depersonalized, separated from individual passion and appetite, and exalted above humanity into a sphere in which all moral values are confused and transformed."[51] Ultimately, Dawson noted, ideologies serve as nothing more than addictive drugs for decadent and lost peoples, and no true Catholic could accept the left or the right.[52]

---

[46]Christopher Dawson, "Man and Civilization," in *God and the World: Through Christian Eyes (Second Series)*, Leonard Hodgson, ed. (London: Student Christian Movement Press, 1934), 38; incorporated later into *Religion and the Modern State*, xv.

[47]Christopher Dawson, *The Judgment of the Nations* (New York: Sheed and Ward, 1942), 114.

[48]Ibid., 6.

[49]Dawson, quoted in John C. Heenan, *Cardinal Hinsley* (London: Burns, Oates and Washbourne, 1944), 184–85. See also Christopher Dawson, "The Left-Right Fallacy," *Catholic Mind*, vol. 44 (1946), 251–53.

[50]Dawson, "Foundations of Unity," 103.

[51]Christopher Dawson, "The Hour of Darkness," *Tablet* (1939), 626; and his "Parties, Politics, and Peace," *Catholic Mind*, vol. 43 (1945), 370.

[52]Christopher Dawson, "The New Community: Fascism, Democracy, and the English Tradition," *Tablet* (January 7, 1939), 5.

The only real solution to the hydra-headed monster of ideology, nationalism, social engineering, and domineering science was a return to Christendom. The Catholic Church had, after all, always upheld the *Christiana Res Publica* as the highest form of government and civilization. Simply because it had not openly advocated it recently, did not mean that it had given up the ideal. Instead, as Pope Leo XIII had said, the Church's position at the end of the nineteenth century was not at that moment in time to promote the return to Christendom, but instead to "set itself as a wall and a bulwark to save human society from falling back into barbarism." In other words, the Church had gone into a defensive mode.[53] It needed to prevent too much decay before advocating a return to true civilization.

No matter how great the decay around and within the world, the Church has three significant advantages over the destruction caused by the seemingly unrelenting "Progress." First, it concerns itself with human salvation, not with worldly things. Second, its entire history had been based on a rise, corruption, a fall, and reform. Institutionally, it understands the need to "redeem the time." Indeed, it is the very decay of Christendom, Dawson argued, at least its ostensible decay, that can lead to its restoration. "The apparent apostasy of Christendom and the social and political catastrophes that have followed do not destroy the possibility of restoration," Dawson contended. Instead, "they may even prepare the way for it by bringing down the walls and towers that man has constructed as refuges of his selfishness and the fortresses of his pride."[54] Further, because the Christian order rests on the natural law—unalterable by man—the foundation exists, no matter how deeply buried or covered with man's works and sins.[55] Catholics have a unique Godly duty to perform, as "they are the heirs and successors of the makers of Europe—the men who saved civilization from perishing in the storm of barbarian invasion and who built the bridge between the ancient and modern worlds."[56]

In their battle against the ideologues, Catholics would also find aid in the inevitable reassertion of human nature, at least at some point. While the ideologue may offer a religious substitute for the purpose of life to the average person, technology would ultimately fail to satiate human desires. "I think an entirely technological culture would be an entirely barbarous culture," Dawson wrote. "Even if, *per impossiblile*, all the spiritual traditions of culture could be temporarily suppressed, it could only lead to a nihilist revolution which would destroy the technological order itself."[57] The Catholic,

[53] Quoted in Dawson, *Judgment of the Nations,* 144.

[54] Dawson, *Judgment of the Nations,* 145.

[55] Christopher Dawson, "The Restoration of Natural Law," *The Sword* (May 1946), reprinted in *Dawson Newsletter* (Fall 1990), 14–15.

[56] Christopher Dawson, "Editorial Note," *Dublin Review*, vol. 207 (1940), 1.

[57] Dawson to Mulloy, January 29, 1955, in Box 1, Folder 15, ND/CDAW.

therefore, must be ready for the fall of technological civilization, prepared to offer the lost soul a home and a purpose.

The First Institution: Family

Much taken with Dawson's works in the 1920s, T. S. Eliot invited Dawson in August 1929 to write anything of interest to the English Roman Catholic.[58] In December of that same year, Eliot specified what he wanted from Dawson: an analysis of the ideological assault on marriage. "The views of a practising Catholic layman about marriage reform, birth control, the relations of the sexes in general in the modern world; would I am sure attract much interest and compel much respect; and so much is being said on the opposite side that I should myself be very glad to have such a statement," Eliot wrote.[59] In the consequent "Christianity and Sex," Dawson warned that a culture can undergo much political and economic change and survive intact. But the "breakdown of the traditional morality is undoubtedly the most important, for it involves a profound biological change in the life of society."[60] The family, according to Genesis and to every non-western society that Dawson could identify, is the first institution.[61] It precedes the state. It serves, therefore, as the fundamental unit of any society, providing the moral framework and the tightest social bonds possible. "The institution of the family inevitably creates a vital tension which is creative as well as painful," Dawson wrote. Culture arises not from instinct but from thought, art, and work. "It has to be conquered by a continuous moral effort, which involves the repression of the natural instinct and the subordination and sacrifice of the individual impulse to the social purpose."[62] Further, Dawson argued, the best form of family was the patriarchal family, itself the norm for most of western and Chinese civilizations. It most efficiently protects society from the whims and desires of human nature. "It requires chastity and self-sacrifice on the part of the wife and obedience and discipline on the part of the children," Dawson argued, while "the father himself has to assume a heavy burden of responsibility and submit his personal feelings to the interests of the family tradition." As opposed to the matrilineal, matriarchal, and earth-fertility goddess societies, the patriarchal family of the western and Chinese traditions first advanced the ideas of chastity, honor, and piety, the basis of western social stability. The

---

[58]T. S. Eliot, London, to Christopher Dawson, through Sheed and Ward, London, August 16, 1929, in Box 14, Folder 120, UST/CDC.

[59]T. S. Eliot, London, to Dawson, December 10, 1929, in Box 14, Folder 120, UST/CDC.

[60]Christopher Dawson, *Christianity and Sex* (London: Faber and Faber, 1930), 7.

[61]Ibid., 18. In his *Politics*, Aristotle argued that the Polis was superior to the family, but the family came first. Family is the first community, and further communities develop as ever expanding concentric circles.

[62]Dawson, *Christianity and Sex*, 19–20.

patriarchal family alone allows for the perpetuation of the species through its primary material function, procreation. If it collapses, society must collapse or change in a fashion so drastic as to be no longer recognizable. The failure of the patriarchal family to adapt to and survive urbanization in ancient Hellenistic civilization accounts for the decline of both ancient Greece and Rome. In the ancient world, Dawson noted, men wanted only small families, and they turned to prostitutes, slaves, and homosexuality to make up for the loss of family life.[63]

Another such radical change was occurring, Dawson believed, in both the United States and, to a much greater extent, in the Soviet Union, in the twentieth century. In each regime, materialism and ideology were drastically altering the makeup of the family. The Soviet state took this argument to its extreme, claiming that families proved incompatible with communism. As the institution of the family diminished, the power of the state increased.[64] In the United States and the West, though, the situation was not much better. "The family is steadily losing its form and its social significance, and the state absorbs more and more of the life of its members," Dawson observed. The state replaces the heads of the houses, and the home "has become merely a sleeping place for a number of independent wage-earners." If one divorces procreation from the essence of the family and if the state begins to define morality, "the final stage in the dehumanization of culture will have been reached," Dawson feared. Such a moment will demonstrate "that mankind is not the crown of creation," but instead nothing more than "an intermediate stage in the evolution of an ape into a machine."[65] Without the institution of the family, Dawson concluded, man cannot reach his full potential as a being created in the image of God.

The Particular or the Universal

The Modern Dilemma: The Problem of European Unity first appeared in 1932. It was Dawson's second major contribution to Sheed and Ward's *Essays in Order*. A short 113 pages, *The Modern Dilemma* was volume 8 of the series and came from a number of talks Dawson had given for the BBC and that had originally been published in the BBC's *Listener*.[66] In it, Dawson offered his first truly sustained argument against nationalism, a subject he had decried in all of his previous writings, but never to the extent he did in this work. Indeed, he believed, most modern political and economic evils derived from modern nationalism and the outmoded nation-state. Nationalism attacked

---

[63] Ibid., 20–22.
[64] Ibid., 6–9.
[65] Ibid., 26, 29.
[66] Scott, *A Historian and His World,* 100.

the very foundation of the cultures that made up the great civilizations. Europe cannot stand divided, and modern "nationality is regarded not merely as a political fact, but as a cultural ideal," Dawson wrote. "It has captured both loyalties—the simple tribal loyalty of blood and race, and the higher loyalty of civilisation and spiritual unity."[67] Nationalism creates false absolutes, demands much of its citizens, and wages intensely violent wars. Because of nationalism, "modern war partakes at once of the nature of a racial struggle, a crusade and a conflict of cultures, and owing to conscription and the mobilisation of public opinion it acquires an absolute and almost universal character."[68] It creates a false cult and subsumes all things in life to its desires and whims.

Outside of and within Europe, the results seemed equally devastating, as the West had traditionally provided the world with the ideals of social justice and liberty. Yet with Europe divided, it could no longer serve as the touchstone for the world, and the world, rather than looking to the successes of Europe, looked instead to its scandalous division. Thus, the world not only rejected Europe, it also rejected the ideals of the West as failed and chaotic. Such failure of nerve returns to plague the West, Dawson warned. "Western civilisation is morally discredited, and even the Western peoples themselves no longer possess any faith in its spiritual values." With the spirit dead, the West is left with nothing more than a "purely material effort of economic exploitation and predatory imperialism." The Europe of the 1930s, Dawson believed, faced the same fate as Republican Rome in 43 B.C. It would either die, or it would remake itself under a centralized government. In either case, it would never find any meaningful spiritual fulfillment. Though he dreamt of utopia, modern man merely "built a slum and a factory and a cinema and a giant hotel."[69]

As the world becomes mechanized and men lose their individuality, Dawson argued, they would seek spiritual fulfillment in some way. Even the Soviets have a spiritual side—albeit false—in their stated desires for equality and social justice. Communism in the Soviet Union is "an attempt to restore order on the basis of a definite creed; a new Communist orthodoxy has taken the place of the old religious orthodoxy that was the foundation of Holy Russia."[70] Indeed, Dawson warned, modern states often take on the role of religious guardian. "The moment that a society claims the complete allegiance of its members, it assumes a quasi-religious authority," Dawson argued. "For since man is essentially spiritual, any power that claims to control the whole of man

---

[67]Christopher Dawson, *The Modern Dilemma: The Problem of European Unity* (London: Sheed and Ward, 1932), 13; and *Christianity in East and West* (La Salle, IL: Sherwood Sugden, 1981), 214.

[68]Dawson, *Modern Dilemma,* 14.

[69]Dawson, "The Modern Dilemma," 21–22, 28, 38.

[70]Ibid., 40.

is forced to transcend relative and particular aims and to enter the sphere of absolute values, which is the realm of religion."[71]

Many in the West, Dawson believed, sought purpose in economic productivity and a Puritan-style work ethic. No people ever established a great civilization based on economic principles alone. Properly understood, economics serves only as a means to an end. True creativity comes from spiritual efforts, not economic ones. Without such spiritual creativity, the world loses its purpose and falls into decadence.[72] Only in the long struggle of history and culture, with a recognition that true freedom resides in the realm of the spiritual, did some peoples arrive at true and purposeful freedoms. "Unfortunately, they are not the natural birthright of the human race, as the early Liberals used to believe," Dawson wrote. "They are the culmination of a long process of social development—the flower of an advanced civilization."[73]

Instead, just as the ancient world found its only true fulfillment in Roman Catholicism, so the modern western world can survive only if it rediscovers Catholicism, the foundation of Europe itself. The West will find fulfillment in neither an ideology nor avarice. One can never know the specifics of the future, as it rests "in the hand of God and in the heart of man, and both are hidden," Dawson feared.[74] Still, even if Europe stands "under sentence of death," Dawson believed, "Christianity will not perish with it."[75] Additionally, Dawson cautioned, one must not look for a return to the Middle Ages, for that period served its purpose in God's economy of grace. Instead, one must, by surrendering one's will to grace, accept whatever age God gives the world.[76] Trust in God and His providence remains essential, Dawson maintained throughout his works. God "is more real than the whole external universe," Dawson wrote. "Man passes away, empires and civilisations rise and fall, the stars grow cold; God remains." Christ is the only true reality that men have known, and he is the bridge from this shadow world to the true world of pure forms and pure existence.[77]

Beyond Liberalism: The New Leviathan

Dawson wanted to entitle his 1935 book *The New Leviathan*. Frank Sheed adamantly opposed Dawson's title. "I still feel an absolute conviction that 'The New Leviathan' would sink the book," he wrote to Dawson. Dawson

---

[71]Ibid., 95. See also his "Fascism, Democracy, and the English Tradition," 5–7; and "Church, State, and Community: Concordats or Catacombs?" *Tablet* (1937), 909.

[72]Dawson, *Modern Dilemma,* 42–3.

[73]Dawson, "The Modern Dilemma," 54.

[74]Ibid., 47.

[75]Ibid., 31.

[76]Ibid., 101.

[77]Ibid., 106–7.

had defended the title, stating that Americans were not completely ignorant of the meaning of Leviathan. "When you say that the meaning of the word 'Leviathan' cannot be entirely unknown even in America, you are telling the literal truth. It is not *entirely* unknown: but you will never win the great public with a word whose meaning is not entirely unknown."[78] Dawson finally acceded to Sheed's wishes, entitling the book, rather blandly, *Religion and the Modern State*.

Here, for once, Dawson's judgment was absolutely correct, and Sheed was dead wrong. First, *Religion and the Modern State* is a title that tells the reader very little. Second, and perhaps most important, a book in the 1930s with the title *The New Leviathan* might have had real staying power, being seen as a contemporary of Aldous Huxley's *Brave New World* and a vital forerunner to such timeless books as Friedrich Hayek's *The Road to Serfdom*, George Orwell's *1984*, or Lewis's *That Hideous Strength*. Instead, the book, itself brilliant, has become lost in the myriad of "Religion and ——" titles of Dawson's other works. Third, *The New Leviathan* would have rather pointedly clarified Dawson's always strongly anti-authoritarian views. As it was, the general public improperly understood this book, along with an article Dawson wrote in 1934, and gave the historian the unsubstantiated title of "Fascist," a charge that was thrown around readily in the polarized 1930s and, unfortunately, continues to this day.[79] "In discussing the nature of this State Mr. Dawson states the favourable opinion of Fascism," the reviewer for the *Times Literary Supplement* stated bluntly. In *Religion and the Modern State*, the *TLS* reviewer continued, Dawson "contemplates with equanimity the substitution of strong public controls for the individual liberty dear to English tradition, appreciates a polity which is both hierarchical and authoritative, and clinches his argument with quotations from Papal encyclicals which have a definitely Fascist ring."[80]

Following up on the themes presented and addressed in *The Modern Dilemma*, *Religion and the Modern State* argued that the new Leviathan of the 1930s promoted mass organization as a means to rival religion, viewing the latter as a competitive force. This state of affairs should not surprise someone trained in the Augustinian tradition. St. Augustine had warned poignantly and brilliantly that the state and the Church, each representing two cities, one of man, the other of God, would always war with one another.[81] In keeping with his inheritance from St. Augustine, Dawson defined totalitarianism succinctly in 1942, outlining its dangers: Totalitarianism "seeks to transform

---

[78]Frank Sheed, London, to Christopher Dawson, March 11, 1935, in Box 11, Folder 1, UST/CDC.

[79]See Scott, *A Historian and His World,* 122–24; and Patrick Allitt, *Catholic Converts: British and American Intellectuals Turn to Rome* (Ithaca, NY: Cornell University Press, 1997), 258.

[80]"The Christian and the World," *Times Literary Supplement*, August 22, 1935.

[81]Dawson, *Religion and the Modern State,* xix–xxi, 77–85, 113, 142–154.

human nature from without by physical and psychological conditioning." It promises much by taking much. "It absorbs the individual personality into the life of a unified mass organism in which and for which alone he exists," Dawson continued, and it "offers men deliverance from insecurity, deliverance from responsibility, deliverance from the burden of freedom."[82]

And yet the modern state could not exist without Christianity and Christendom. Not only did medieval Christendom serve as the highpoint of western civilization, it also created the culture in which the modern state had arisen. In part, nationalism had its origins in Christianity's demand for a mystical and sacred people, bonded by the Spirit and willing to sacrifice their gifts and very lives for Christ's Army. Socialism derives its force from the Christian and Jewish demand for social justice and the equal rights for the poor.[83] In other words, nationalism and socialism are each modern heresies. They each appropriate a great truth of Christianity, but they do so by excluding a multitude of other truths. They remove a piece from the whole, and the whole suffers, while the piece is exaggerated.

Liberalism is also a heresy, Dawson argued in the 1930s, as it takes from Christianity the dignity and celebration of the uniqueness of each human person. At the same time, liberalism neglects "the immense burden of inherited evil," and consequently plans "an imaginary world for an impossible humanity."[84] Dawson found that modern secular liberals even had their own saints and martyrs. "Western secularization has its own idealism. It is essentially the transposition of Christian moral idealism to a purely this-worldly end, and to a rationalized or materialist conception of reality," he wrote in a private letter, dated 1954. "This is found typically in the liberal idealism of the 19th century (and of the 18th) which had so many marks of a religion and which produced its saints, like J. S. Mill, and its martyrs."[85] This tradition, begun in Christendom and inherited by the liberals, would continue with even greater force in fascism and communism.

Dawson especially attacked liberalism in *Religion and the Modern State* as being the unwitting vehicle for tyranny. By liberalism, Dawson meant a type of anti-religious, anti-clerical political belief. He separated the secular tradition from the Anglo-Saxon and Germanic barbarian heritage of parliamentary systems. The latter arose in an organic Burkean fashion, based originally on barbarian law and the northern witan. Parliaments, Dawson believed, came

---

[82]Dawson, "Foundations of Unity," 100.

[83]Dawson, *Religion and the Modern State,* xxi; and his "Introduction," in Carl Schmitt, *The Necessity of Politics: An Essay on the Representative Idea in the Church and Modern Europe* (London: Sheed and Ward, 1931), 27.

[84]Christopher Dawson et al., "Christianity and War: A Symposium," *Colosseum,* vol. 4 (1937), 35.

[85]Dawson, Devon, England, to Mulloy, February 25, 1954, in Box 1, Folder 4, ND/CDAW.

out of the common law tradition. Specifically, they arose with the aristocracy's resistance to monarchical and centralized power.

As a subset of liberalism, modern democracy was also a flawed system, Dawson claimed. First, once everyone can vote, voting becomes meaningless, destroying the prestige of citizenship. Second, democracy allows political machines and bureaucracies to dominate political life, again destroying the prestige of leadership. Finally, and perhaps most important, democracy allows for special interests to rule, becoming the "tools of sordid and selfish interests."[86] After a century of material prosperity, Dawson argued, liberalism had found itself unable to cope with the disasters of the first world war and then the Great Depression of 1929–1933. Because liberalism rejected leadership in all areas of political life—hence, its "colourless neutrality"—the world found itself adrift at the beginning of the twentieth-century. Devoid of western leadership for nearly a century, many political thinkers turned to communism and various ideologies, finding absolutes and pretenses of truth, where liberalism had offered none, or, at best, subjective platitudes.[87] Its *laissez-faire* attitude has proven irresponsible, Dawson claimed, and democratic liberalism has merely allowed the ideologies to move in and set up camp. With its new mass organization and scientific techniques in management and psychology, Dawson feared, liberalism might "easily become the vehicle of spiritual forces which claim to dominate not only the State or the economic order but the human soul itself."[88] After witnessing the ideological powers war with one another for five years, Dawson concluded that a "godless civilization is a civilization without law and without truth, a kingdom of darkness, and the whole vast mechanism of human science and power becomes an engine of destruction driving violently forward to the abyss."[89]

Most democracies that lose their purpose, though, will veer toward fascism rather than communism, Dawson thought. "They will be replaced not by Communism but by some form of Fascism," Dawson explained, "since the latter is more able to secure a relatively high degree of political efficiency and economic control without involving the complete destruction of the existing social structure."[90] One of fascism's most important features, Dawson believed, was its ability to assimilate and co-opt rather than destroy the middle class. Such a potential alliance, Dawson argued, gave fascism an advantage

---

[86]Dawson, *Religion and the Modern State,* 39–40.

[87]Ibid., 3. See also his "The Significance of Bolshevism," *English Review*, vol. 55 (1932), 239–48.

[88]Dawson, *Religion and the Modern State,* vii–viii, xiv.

[89]Christopher Dawson, "Foundations of European Order," *Catholic Mind*, vol. 42 (1944), 314–15.

[90]Dawson, *Religion and the Modern State,* 14; "Fascism and the Corporative State: A Reply by Christopher Dawson," *Catholic Herald*, August 3, 1935; and "The Significance of Fascism," unpublished ms. dated [1933], in Box 4, Folder 155, UST/CDC.

over communism, as communism simply attempted to destroy the entrenched upper and middle classes, dismissing them as bourgeois.

Still, the communists had also inflicted much damage on the liberal capitalists. Indeed, the communists and their socialist allies had effectively painted capitalists as exploitative and liberal parliaments as the toadies of the capitalists.[91] Liberal capitalists, in turn, did nothing to promote virtue or a satisfying way of life. Instead, Dawson thought, liberal capitalists did little more than pursue the dreams of avarice.[92] Dawson never wavered in his belief that liberalism was hollow because of its neutrality. The nineteenth-century capitalists, therefore, neither promoted good nor evil. Indeed, if they did unwittingly sanction some evil, they did so merely as fallen creatures. "Even in its darkest days," Dawson wrote, "capitalist England produced the Oxford Movement, and Primitive Methodism, and the Salvation Army, not to mention the various movements of humanitarian reform."[93]

Devoid of imagination, the liberals unwittingly allowed communism, a philosophy "more suitable to gorillas than to human beings," to flourish. Many Communists in the 1930s espoused humanitarian ideals, but Dawson warned, this was merely a trick, as the Communists "are anxious to find allies in Western democracy against enemies no less ruthless than themselves."[94] Dawson believed that communism itself posed no direct threat to the West, as most westerners would never take it seriously. The real danger to the West came from the liberal tolerance of the communists. According to the modern twentieth-century liberals, Dawson feared, "Bolshevism is a great social experiment, not perhaps wholly suited to English conditions, but nevertheless deserving of our general appreciation and sympathy."[95] Such "sympathy," though, allowed the Communists to murder dissidents in their own countries with little protest in the West, regarding liquidation "as a necessary step towards the creation of a new order which will put an end to the exploitation of man by man."[96]

In *Religion and the Modern State*, Dawson attempted to envision what an Anglo-Saxon tyranny might look like. As just noted, it would certainly be more fascistic than communist. Further, Dawson was convinced that the United States was on a more dangerous path toward totalitarian government than was Great Britain. For while Dawson did not label the American New Deal as fascist, he did call it a "constitutional dictatorship."[97] The future for

---

[91] Dawson, *Religion and the Modern State,* 6.

[92] Ibid., 71.

[93] Christopher Dawson, "Marx's Materialism," *Church Times,* June 1, 1934.

[94] Christopher Dawson, "Not Christianity and Not Communism," London *Catholic Herald* (November 8, 1936).

[95] Dawson, "Introduction," in Schmitt, *Necessity of Politics,* 15.

[96] Ibid., 21.

[97] Dawson, *Religion and the Modern State,* 23.

the United States, Dawson feared, is a nationalist and socialist state that is neither fascist nor communist, but something still, at least nominally, rooted in the Anglo-Saxon tradition. Though it will profess and maybe even practice humanitarian and liberal principles, "it will be equally [to Nazi Germany and the USSR] unwilling to tolerate any division of spiritual allegiance." It will develop a cradle-to-grave welfare state, and the school will replace the Church, Dawson believed. The mass of men will learn mass culture through the cinema, radio, and the press. With the centralized control of information to its citizens, the modern state will never attack religious institutions outright, but will instead present its own side and ultimately outweigh any credibility religion might maintain.[98]

"Progressive" National Socialism and the Abyss

Espousing a false religion, the National Socialists of Germany openly embraced the pagan. Their "race mysticism" tapped into the " 'dark' forces that underlie the rational surface of life," Dawson argued.[99] In a speech given on November 14, 1932, in Italy, to a room full of European diplomats and leaders, including Italian fascists and German National Socialists, Dawson warned: "The relatively benign Nationalism of the early Romantics paved the way for the fanaticism of the modern pan-racial theorists who subordinate civilization to skull measurements and who infuse an element of racial hatred into the political and economic rivalries of European peoples."[100] Dawson gave Hitler considerable credit for his ability to recognize the movement of these dark forces in the world and to capture the new spirit for his own purposes. Dawson believed that Hitler's lack of liberal education and political experience gave him an immense advantage in the turbulent world situation of the 1930s. When other politicians and statesmen were looking to antiquated models, Hitler brought something seemingly fresh—or dank and very old and pagan, as the case may be—to the table. Hitler ably identified "himself with the forces that lay beneath the political surface and [was able] to render them politically conscious."[101] Dawson found Hitler's *Mein Kampf* an especially stunning and disturbingly important work. In it, Hitler bluntly laid out his plan of action. The German dictator wanted to reverse the imperial policy of the Second Reich and instead focus on the medieval German policy of expansion into the Slavic lands as quickly as possible. Profoundly anti-western, Hitler attempted to revive Prussian notions of the state and expan-

---

[98] Ibid., 54–57.
[99] Ibid., 18.
[100] Quoted in Scott, *A Historian and His World,* 106.
[101] Christopher Dawson, "Hitler's 'Mein Kampf,' " *Tablet* (1939), 373.

sion. As leader of the National Socialists, Hitler recreated "the old militarist power-state in a new modernized streamlined mechanized form."[102]

Because Hitler had little regard for Judeo-Christian norms or recent history, he refused "to regard political frontiers as anything more than the temporary limit of continually changing natural forces."[103] Hitler tapped into something deeper and darker than Judaism or Christianity could imagine. After all, Dawson argued, if the ordinary man fails to find purpose in the traditions of Christendom, itself radically divided after the Reformation, or in the pursuit of profit in the market, he will turn to the nearest ideology that promises truth. Hitler, unfortunately, understood this well.

In the mid-1930s, Dawson believed that some of Germany's remilitarization was justified, as the country had been treated horribly by the allied victors of the First World War.[104] But when National Socialist Germany annexed Austria, Dawson lamented that "no Catholic can regard the passing of Austria with indifference." For nearly a thousand years, it had stood as a bulwark of Christianity against the Reformation and the Turks. It had been "the embodiment of Catholic culture in Central Europe" and with its demise, "a whole epoch in the history of Christendom has ended."[105] In many ways, the fall of Austria represented the final demise of whatever remnant of medieval Christendom still existed. Echoing Burke in his *Letters on a Regicide Peace*, Dawson argued that "there is no virtue in a peace which consists in sitting still till our enemies are strong enough to destroy us."[106] Hitler's takeover of Austria may warrant war, Dawson concluded in 1938.

As mentioned previously, Dawson's intense criticism of democracy in *Religion and the Modern State* and his rather abstract examination of National Socialism earned him the title of "fascist." Indeed, by 1939, four full years after the publication of *Religion and the Modern State*, it was almost a consensus among Dawson's critics that he had embraced some form of fascism. A reviewer for the typically pro-Dawson publication, *Commonweal*, complained that Dawson's "conception of dictatorship as precursor of something better than present democracies is at once fantastic and repellent."[107] That summer, the same publication printed a letter from a reader with an even more blunt appraisal: "Christopher Dawson seems to be going fascist on us."[108] Michael Williams, an editor of *Commonweal*, retorted in the following issue that "we may or may not agree with what such a competent and moderate thinker

---

[102] Christopher Dawson, "Christian Culture in Eastern Europe," *Dublin Review*, vol. 224 (1950), 29–30.

[103] Dawson, "Hitler's 'Mein Kampf,'" 373.

[104] Christopher Dawson, "The Re-Making of Europe," *Tablet* (1936), 428.

[105] Christopher Dawson, "The Moral of Austria," *Tablet* (1938), 358.

[106] Ibid.

[107] James N. Vaughan, "Mr. Dawson after Munich," *Commonweal*, vol. 29 (April 21, 1939), 723.

[108] James D. Collins, "Mr. Dawson after Munich," *Commonweal*, vol. 30 (July 28, 1939), 336.

as Christopher Dawson brings forward as proof of the inner weaknesses and technical faults of the liberal and democratic systems of England and France and the United States; but it is no answer to him, or any other competent critic, to dismiss him as a fascist."[109] The Reverend J. C. Hardwick feared that Dawson "preaches a return to discipline and authority." Dawson, along with T. S. Eliot and Nicholas Berdyaev, was following the political trends of the day, as "a definite reaction away from democracy and towards fascism."[110]

Unfortunately, this judgment of Dawson as a fascist has continued to the present day.[111] The first substantial accusation in recent years has come from Kevin Morris, in a controversial article in the *Chesterton Review*, entitled "Fascism and British Catholic Writers, 1924–1939." In it, Morris claims that one should not be surprised that many fascists saw Dawson as a "fellow traveler" after reading his *Religion and the Modern State*.[112] Strangely, Morris begins his section on Dawson by calling him a "liberal intellectual," two words Dawson would have never have accepted for himself. Despite his supposed liberality, Morris continues, "Dawson was an original thinker, clearer and more analytical than [other Catholic fascists], so that his book provides an important and lucid marker of how Catholics could have leaned toward Fascism." Morris's wording is telling, as it provides a marker of how Catholics *could* have approved of fascism. But, of course, Dawson did not approve of fascism. Morris may twist his understanding of Dawson all he wants, but he cannot make Dawson approve of fascism or make him a "fellow traveler." Dawson noted some of fascism's strengths in *Religion and the Modern State*, and he strongly criticized democracy for being spiritually empty. It was a critique he shared with Plato, Cicero, Edmund Burke, and Alexis de Tocqueville. In his autobiography, Bernard Wall attempted to explain why so many thought he and Dawson were fascists. "This confusion arose because in the general hysteria of the time," he wrote, "Christopher went on calmly disentangling the sociological threads in Europe."[113]

Finally, Morris claims that Dawson was a fascist because he supported Franco in the Spanish Civil War. In this accusation, Morris gets something right. Dawson did support Franco, as did most English Roman Catholics, but he did so very reluctantly and with great reservations. Wall attempted to justify this stance in his biography. "Franco was not a Fascist, though he had Fascist support (the Falangists), but a traditionalist general."[114] Joseph

---

[109] Michael Williams, "Views and Reviews," *Commonweal*, vol. 30 (August 4, 1939), 355.

[110] J. C. Hardwick, "The Intellectuals in Retreat," *Modern Churchman*, vol. 24 (1935), 631.

[111] John J. Mulloy, Conversation with Christopher Dawson, August 29, 1953, in Box 1, Folder 2, ND/CDAW.

[112] Kevin L. Morris, "Fascism and British Catholic Writers, 1924–1939," *Chesterton Review*, vol. 25 (1999), 33.

[113] Bernard Wall, *Headlong into Change: An Autobiography and a Memoir of Ideas Since the Thirties* (London: Harvill, 1969), 89.

[114] Ibid.

Pearce has answered this critique better than anyone. "The Communists and the Anarchists who made up the bulk of the Republican forces, fanatically anti-clerical and anti-Christian, were responsible for the murders of numerous priests, monks, and nuns and for the burning and looting of hundreds of churches throughout Spain," Pearce writes. "Before the Civil War was over twelve bishops, 4,184 priests, 2,365 monks, and about three hundred nuns had been killed."[115] Support for Franco did not mean so much a love for Franco as it did a revulsion of the so-called "republicans." As Dawson himself conceded, even using the word fascism was "like a red tag to a bull."[116]

Even more recently, Jay P. Corrin of Boston University in his well-respected and generally well-reviewed *Catholic Intellectuals and the Challenge of Democracy* (2002), also misjudges Dawson's position regarding fascism. Corrin has taken most of his arguments regarding Dawson from, not surprisingly, *Religion and the Modern State*. Like Morris, Corrin claims that the English Roman Catholic believed that Catholic social ideals "were more in line with Fascism than with either liberalism or socialism."[117] Corrin again affirms Dawson's supposed faith in fascism, writing that Dawson argued "that the Church is naturally more comfortable with fascist forms of governance than with democratic parliamentary ones." Corrin especially laments Dawson's influence on the present-day Church historians, who Corrin believes have uncritically agreed with the English intellectual that the Catholic Church collaborates with dictators. But only thirty-some pages before the initial accusation of Dawson's supposed fascism, Corrin writes that many opposed Dawson's refusal to accept fully the supposed standard and thoughtless pro-Franco line, and, thus, he was dismissed as editor of *The Dublin Review*.[118] Again, in the footnotes, Corrin contradicts himself by correctly claiming that Dawson served as one of the leaders in the Catholic fight against an alliance with fascism.[119] Though Corrin is of many minds regarding Dawson, the reader is left with the impression that Dawson, the great Christian Humanist, was a simple-minded Catholic proponent of authoritarian systems. For Corrin, as with many modern scholars, to be anti-communist and also critical of aspects of democracy is to be pro-fascist. Such a simplistic analysis, of course, disregards the importance of the Catholic cultural bias against communism, especially after Pope Leo XIII's horrifying visions of Satan laying waste to the earth in the twentieth century and the Marian vision at Fatima which stated that communism was the greatest threat to the Catholic Church. Corrin also equates Dawson's distrust of

---

[115]Joseph Pearce, "Chesterton and Fascism," *Chesterton Review*, vol. 25 (1999), 75; and "Spirit of the Times," *Review of Politics*, vol. 5 (2003), 292–93.

[116]Christina Scott, "Christopher Dawson's Reaction to Fascism and Marxism," *Chesterton Review*, vol. 25 (1999), 405.

[117]Jay P. Corrin, *Catholic Intellectuals and the Challenge of Democracy* (Notre Dame, IN: University of Notre Dame Press, 2002), 381.

[118]Ibid., 382–83, 354.

[119]Ibid., 442, n. 33.

democracy with a distrust of liberty. In fact, Dawson greatly cherished liberty, properly understood. But he argued in a Burkean fashion that true liberty derives from generations of finely-honed tradition, not simply from pulling the lever in a voting booth.

As mentioned previously, Dawson did everything possible to negate the so-called left-right divide in politics in the 1930s and 1940s. It served as a mere trick of the ideologues, Dawson argued. "The tactics of totalitarianism are to weld every difference of opinion and tradition and every conflict of economic interests into an absolute ideological opposition which disintegrates society into hostile factions bent on destroying one another," he wrote in 1946.[120] These were important words in what were possibly the two most polarized decades of the twentieth century. "The one thing that Dawson did, for me and others, was to emphasize that there is a great constitutional position between the extreme right and the extreme left." Barbara Ward stated in an interview. "This was a tremendously important point in the '30s. You remember that, at that time, the feeling was that if you weren't a Communist you had to be a Fascist, and if you weren't a Fascist, you had to be a Communist. Dawson kept alive the constitutional center with its natural law basis."[121] Stated differently, Dawson's center was always "Christian humanism, the Christian Center."[122] He argued that liberalism failed to produce a spiritual ideal for the human person or human society, thus leading to the idealism—however false—of fascism and communism.[123] But Dawson himself was never a fascist. It was an absurd charge in the 1930s, and it is even more absurd at the beginning of the twenty-first century.

No Fascist: Beyond Ideologies

Though many of his friends encouraged Dawson to revise *Religion and the Modern State*, editing out or explaining the parts that seemed fascistic, he refused to do so. In those heated and polarized days, one seemed to be either an extremist of the Right or of the Left, and Dawson was tired of such hyperbole. Stubbornly, he believed that to revise his book would be the equivalent of admitting either error or defeat. If he clarified his position, he would do so in his next work, *Beyond Politics*. Certainly, *Religion and the Modern State* sold well, and the possibility existed for Dawson to revise it several times, but he con-

---

[120]Dawson, "The Left-Right Fallacy," 252.

[121]Barbara Ward, "Christian Woman of the World," *Our Sunday Visitor*, vol. XLVIII, no. 3 (May 17, 1959).

[122]Anne Freemantle, "Christopher Dawson Comes to Harvard," *Catholic Digest*, vol. 23 (1959), 53.

[123]Dawson, Oxford, to Bruno Schlesinger, Notre Dame, IN, January 24, 1950, in Box 15, Folder 124, UST/CDC.

tinued to refuse to do so, much to the chagrin of his editor, Frank Sheed.[124] As late as 1952, Sheed wanted Dawson to revise and republish *Religion and the Modern State*, but Dawson refused. "I said if he'd bring it out now it might have some effect on the way" world events of the Cold War crystallize, Sheed wrote in 1952. However, Dawson "was not moved by this."[125]

Dawson rejected all totalitarian systems as man-made instruments used to attack God's Truth and the Church. He also repeatedly cautioned that the western states must not adopt the methods of the communists or fascists in attacking either. "As soon as men decide that all means are permitted to fight an evil," he wrote in 1940, "then their good becomes indistinguishable from the evil that they set out to destroy."[126]

Dawson was a traditionalist and conservative who favored ordered liberty. "Our parliamentary institutions are not the artificial creation of liberal idealism, as in so many countries; they are an organic part of the life of the nation, and they have grown up century by century by the vital urge of social realities," he explained in some of his most Burkean language.[127] Dawson defined liberty: it "is not the right of the mass to power, but the right of the individual and the group to achieve the highest possible degree of self-development."[128] Liberty, he argued, must be earned, not decreed, and the English had earned it over centuries of struggle, following the Anglo-Saxon traditions of common law and the Christian tradition of natural law. The strongest society, as represented by the best of the Anglo-Saxon cultural tradition, embraced what Edmund Burke called the "little platoons," the subsidiary institutions that make life worth living. Family, church, and local community each socialize the human person to the larger needs of the community, but each does so without the totalitarian spirit.[129] Indeed, England was not only decentralized socially, but also politically. "In reality England consisted of thousands of miniature monarchies—often highly autocratic ones—ruled like the medieval State by the temporal power of the squire and the spiritual authority of the parson," Dawson continued.[130] True community and natural bonding among men come not from ideas and ideologies or even from social contracts and treaties. "Men are not tied to one another by paper and seals," but instead "are led to associate by resemblance, by conformities, by sympathies." Such a truth, Dawson argued, works for individuals as well as for countries. Two countries will find amity not because of utopian visions—which would

---

[124]Scott, *A Historian and His World,* 126.

[125]Frank Sheed, London, to Maisie, October 24, 1952, in Box 1, Folder 10, ND/CSWD.

[126]Christopher Dawson, "The Threat to the West," *Commonweal,* vol. 21 (February 2, 1940), 318.

[127]Christopher Dawson, *Beyond Politics* (New York: Sheed and Ward, 1939), 13.

[128]Ibid., 46.

[129]Ibid., 51–53.

[130]Ibid., 69. See also his "World Crisis and the English Tradition."

polarize one from the other—but from a "correspondence in laws, customs, manners and habits of life."[131]

Real unity—that is, for Dawson, organic unity—came not only from tradition, but from the symbol of the king, who "represents the whole. He is in a real sense the common possession of the nation." Indeed, conservatism's greatest contribution to England "has been the preservation of this older and more organic conception of the representative principle throughout the process of political rationalization that transformed the English constitution" in the nineteenth century.[132] Conservatism, especially as embodied in the Burkean, Anglo-Saxon tradition, "stands above all for the preservation of the inherited traditions of our civilization and the defense of the higher cultural values in society against the new mass movements that threaten Europe with a return to barbarism."[133] Conservatism's conception of the whole differs little—if any—from the Catholic conception of the economy of grace. "Each member . . . is spiritually equal, but differentiated by its function," Dawson explained. Therefore, there exists an "organized hierarchy of classes each with its specific function in the life of the whole. The merchant who provides for the economic needs of society may well be richer than the priest who provides for its spiritual needs, the soldier who defends it, the peasant who feeds it."[134]

Unfortunately, since the French Revolution—which stood for everything the Anglo-Saxon tradition despised, as Dawson argued—ideologies had spread throughout the world like a drug. Sweeping away history and everything else, ideologies offered "a drastic simplification of the problems," Dawson wrote. They " 'liquidated' every social and ideological element which could not be brought into immediate harmony with the dominant party and its creed."[135] Every battle of ideologues—because everything becomes involved and politicized in a given society—must end in nothing less than dictatorship, with one vision completely uprooted by another.[136]

As the title of Dawson's fourth major work on political theory, *Beyond Politics*, suggests, society must focus on the religious and the cultural underpinnings of society, resisting the trend to politicize all things. To follow the course of the ideologues, Dawson feared in 1938, would only end in the "mechanical monster," and the regulation and de-personalization of every aspect of life. Such mechanization would homogenize every human person and every individual culture into one cosmopolitan, bland mess. Already, modernity had brought about horrible mechanization. Even something as seemingly in-

---

[131] Christopher Dawson, "European Unity and the League of Nations: European Unity and International Order," *Tablet* (1939), 741.
[132] Dawson, "Conservativism," unpublished ms. dated June 1932, in Box 3, Folder 38, UST/CDC.
[133] Ibid.
[134] Ibid.
[135] Dawson, *Beyond Politics,* 36.
[136] Ibid., 40.

nocuous as the automobile, meant to make life more convenient, had done nothing but "bring mutilation and death to large numbers of harmless people. We see it on a large scale in the way that the modern industrial system, which exists to serve human needs, nevertheless reduces the countryside to smoking desolation and involves whole populations in periodic troughs of depression and scarcity," Dawson lamented. "But we see it in its most extreme and devilish form in modern warfare which has a nightmare quality about it and is hardly reconcilable with a human origin or purpose."[137] Mass society will lead to the destruction of true individuality, and society will "dissolve into a human herd without personality."

The result of such conformity, Dawson argued, would be "the Kingdom of Antichrist." After all, the new ideological states are "inevitably contaminated with all sorts of impure elements and open to the influence of evil and demonic forces."[138] The situation was as bleak as could be imagined:

> For the first time in the world's history the Kingdom of the Anti-Christ has acquired political form and social substance, and stands over against the Kingdom of God as a counter-church with its own creed and its own moral ideals, ruled by a centralized hierarchy and inspired by an intense will for world conquest.[139]

---

[137]Ibid., 5–6.

[138]Ibid., 79, 113, 132. See also his "Hour of Darkness," 625.

[139]Quoted in "Christopher Dawson in an Article in the London Catholic Times," *Ave Maria*, June 2, 1934, 695.

Interlude II

What is the West?

DAWSON BELIEVED THAT ONE COULD NOT SIMPLY EQUATE CHRISTENDOM WITH the medieval period, though many of his critics claimed that he did. Every phase of history has its singular role within time, within the Divine Economy itself. The medieval period proved vitally important to the history of Christendom, but no more so than the eras of the ancient past, of the present, or of the future. The West—within which Christendom first arose but to which it can no longer be confined—began long before Europe, as the West "has come into Europe and has passed beyond it."[1] In other words, the West, especially in its classical and medieval phases, served as "the vehicle for the world diffusion of the Church and the Christian faith."[2] The medieval West preserved the classical tradition, satiating its deepest longings and answering its most difficult questions. In almost unbroken continuity, Dawson believed, the medieval flowed from the classical, especially in terms of scholarship and philosophy. But as with all societies and cultures in a fallen world, the medieval had served its purpose—a purpose, Dawson believed, that now had ended.

The modern scholar incorrectly equates Europe with Christendom because "it was as Christendom that Europe first became conscious of itself as a society of peoples with common moral values and common spiritual aims."[3] Europe, after all, is not even really a continent, but instead "an historical creation, an invention of the Greeks, who adapted a myth in order to express their sense of independence towards the civilization of Asia and their struggle for freedom against Persian imperialism."[4] Europe, then, became the preferred term in

---

[1] Christopher Dawson, *Understanding Europe* (New York: Sheed and Ward, 1952), 26.
[2] Dawson to Mulloy, January 6, 1955, in Box 1, Folder 16, ND/CDAW.
[3] Dawson, *Understanding Europe*, 26.
[4] Christopher Dawson, "Europe—a Society of Peoples," *The Month*, vol. 181 (1945), 311.

the Renaissance, as a means to "distinguish the new *orbis terrarum* from the old."[5] "Europe" serves as a term of convenience, rather than as an absolute.

Certainly, Dawson experienced frustration as scholars continued to label him Euro-centric. "There is a small but rather fierce group who are so violently anti-Chesterbelloc that they are averse to anything which connects Europe with the Faith," Dawson complained in 1955. "I have never been a Bellocite and my view of Western culture is quite different from 'Europe is the Faith.' But this group lumps me with the followers of Belloc, none the less."[6] As one writer complained in the *Catholic World*, "When Mr. Dawson speaks in detail of the study of Christian culture, he assumes that it is almost exclusively concerned with the Middle Ages and Western Europe."[7] While defending his own beliefs in the *Catholic World*, Dawson wrote that "the world mission of Christianity is based on its conception of a spiritual society which *transcends all states and cultures* and is the final goal of humanity."[8] Properly understood, history is "not a flat expanse of time, measured off in dates, but a series of different worlds and . . . each of them had its own spirit and forms its own riches of poetic imagination."[9] Further, while the Incarnation remains the center of all of history, as Dawson argued throughout his life, even the "world kingdoms—Assyria, Babylon, Persia, Macedonia, Rome—have their place in the development and dispensation of Revelation."[10] Those empires around the time of Christ were especially important to the history of the world as they served as a chain of islands and safe havens for civilization running from Rome to China. In between the two poles of West and East stood Persia and India. On either side, north and south of the line, barbarians preyed upon the civilized.[11]

Equally important, the western Church never held an official policy of Europeanizing the world. Instead, the Church celebrated the diversity of cultures and often incorporated specific things from the various cultures that it found to be good, true, and beautiful. "All this does not mean that the Church ought to adopt a crude Europeanizing policy in the mission field: that it ought to ignore the special goods of other cultures and not welcome as generously as possible all the cultural values and aptitudes with which they can enrich the universal Catholic tradition," Dawson wrote in a private letter in 1947. "But

[5]Christopher Dawson, "Ages of Change: A Study of the European Inheritance," *Tablet* (May 22, 1954), 489.

[6]Dawson to Mulloy, April 19, 1955, in Box 1, Folder 16, ND/CDAW.

[7]Sr. Marie Corde McNichols, R.S.M, "Western Culture and the Mystical Body," *Catholic World*, vol. 186 (1957), 170.

[8]Dawson to the *Catholic World*, dated November 11, 1957, in Box 1, Folder 16, ND/CDAW.

[9]Christopher Dawson, *Tradition and Inheritance: Reflections on the Formative Years* (St. Paul, MN: Wanderer Press, 1970), 31.

[10]Dawson, "Memorandum," dated August 1, 1955, in Box 1, Folder 15, ND/CDAW.

[11]Christopher Dawson, ed., *Mission to Asia* (1955; Toronto: University of Toronto Press, 1998), vii.

after all that has been the traditional attitude of the Church in the past and it was by this assimilation of diverse culture elements that Western Christian culture was built up."[12] The western Church assimilated and sanctified what it found rather than crushing it. The West has roots well beyond Europe. "Western culture had to undergo a long process of development until it finally became a suitable vehicle for the Christian dynamic impulse," Dawson wrote. "I think one might apply the Aristotelian principle of matter and form to the process."[13] In other words, the essence of these cultures changed, while the forms of these cultures remained the same. Therefore, Dawson argued, one may find significant roots of western civilization in a number of specifically non-European places; in the Mediterranean, in North Africa, and in western Asia, to name a few.

> This tradition is entirely different from the influence of the pagan culture, which continued to exist in a submerged subconscious form; for it affected those elements in Christian society which were most consciously and completely Christian, like monasteries and the episcopal schools. Consequently it is impossible to study Christian culture without studying classical culture also. St. Augustine takes us back to Cicero and Plato and Plotinus. St. Thomas takes us back to Aristotle. Dante takes us back to Statius and Virgil, and so on, throughout the course of Western Christian culture. And the same is true of Eastern Christendom in its Byzantine form, though this only reaches Russia ... second hand and infrequently. But the same is true of theology, at least its more advanced study. The whole of the old theological literature of Catholic Christendom, both East and West, is so impregnated by classical influences that we cannot read the Greek and Latin Fathers, or even the Scholastic and 17th-century theologians without some knowledge of classical literature and philosophy.[14]

Many things came together to precipitate the formation of the West, thus allowing the initial spread of Christianity.

As discussed in Interlude I, theology guided history, and history served as the vehicle for the Divine to interact with humanity. If one accepts that God with absolute sovereignty created the universe, as Dawson believed, then one must also accept that every culture comes originally from God and, therefore, reflects God in some fashion, however obscure, fallen, and difficult to find. This argument is at once Stoic, Jewish, Christian, and specifically Augustinian. Since each culture comes from *the* source of all truth, it must also hold within it an element of the truth. Indeed, for a culture to be entirely false, according to Dawson's theological understanding, it would cease to exist. For only love—Divine Truth itself—animates all things. This applies to individual souls as well as to particular cultures.

Dawson's understanding is Stoic as well as Christian and Boethian. Evil is the absence of good; it is untruth itself. Even the devil must have some

---

[12]Dawson, Oxford, to Reverend Father, March 24, 1947, in Box 15, Folder 192, UST/CDC.

[13]Dawson to Mulloy, August 27, 1954, in Box 1, Folder 15, ND/CDAW. See also "Christianity and the Western Tradition," *The Listener*, vol. 39 (1948), 742–43.

[14]Dawson to Mulloy, January 6, 1955, in Box 1, Folder 15, ND/CDAW.

truth and love within him—although it must also be almost inconceivably and infinitesimally small—or he would simply cease to exist. Even the most depraved and anti-life culture in the world must have some truth in it. But such cultures rarely exist for long, as the natural law is universal and recognizable by most peoples. Untruth ultimately collapses in upon itself.

Those movements, therefore, which do not fall neatly into the scheme of western Christendom—Islam, Byzantium, Chinese and Indian cultures, and even the native peoples scattered throughout the world—must be studied accordingly. All peoples and all cultures play a role in the history of Christendom. For whatever reason—known to God alone—He "chose Rome instead of India as the temporal vehicle of [His] purpose and caused Catholicism to express itself through the medium of Western cultural forms."[15] Just as the Christians baptized Greek philosophy, Roman polity, and Germanic heroic virtues and notions of kingship, so they must transform the essences of all world cultures and all human persons. Through the grace of the Holy Spirit, Dawson argued, Christians must sanctify the world.

The Birth of the West: Greece and Rome

The advent of the West began with the Persian Wars, according to Dawson.[16] In particular, the Battle of Thermopylae in 480 B.C. must rank as one of the most important in world history, for it reshaped the world itself. Herodotus described the escalation of the conflict beautifully:

> But Xerxes was not persuaded any the more. Four whole days he suffered to go by, expecting that the Greeks would run away. When, however, he found on the fifth that they were not gone, thinking that their firm stand was mere impudence and recklessness, he grew wroth, and sent against them the Medes and Cissians, with orders to take them alive and bring them into this presence. Then the Medes rushed forward and charged the Greeks, but fell in vast numbers: others now took the places of the slain, and would not be beaten off, though they suffered terrible losses. In this way it became clear to all, and especially to the king, that though he had plenty of combatants, he had but very few warriors.[17]

The Greeks—organized in units by their respective towns—continued to fight, despite suffering severe wounds and being greatly outnumbered. After days of battering, the Greeks decided to break up their defense. Some stayed, others returned to their respective city-states to warn them and to help them prepare for a defense. The Spartans, under the leadership of King Leonidas, decided to stay. The Oracle had prophesized either greatness or ruin for them, and they believed they would attain the former through sacrifice. Should they flee

---

[15] Christopher Dawson, *The Modern Dilemma: The Problem of European Unity* (London: Sheed and Ward, 1932), 32.

[16] Dawson, *Understanding Europe,* 27.

[17] Herodotus, *History*, Book VII.

to defend their homes, Leonidas believed, all would be lost. Allied with the
Thespians, who refused to abandon the Spartans, Leonidas and three hundred
men made their last stand. They drove themselves to the heart of the narrow
pass at Thermopylae. There, the Greeks freely collided with the Persians,
mostly conscripts, being forced to fight by bullwhips at their backs. Leonidas
threw himself into the invading force and died quickly.

> Drawing back into the narrowest part of the pass, and retreating even behind the
> cross wall, they posted themselves upon a hillock, where they stood all drawn up
> together in one close body, except only the Thebans. The hillock whereof I speak
> is at the entrance of the straits, where the stone lion stands which was set up in
> honour of Leonidas. Here they defended themselves to the last, such as still had
> swords using them, and the other resisting with their hands and teeth; till the
> barbarians, who in part had pulled down the wall and attacked them in front, in
> part had gone round and now encircled them upon every side, overwhelmed and
> buried the remnant which was left beneath showers of missiles.[18]

Overwhelmed by the numbers of Persians, the Greeks fell quickly. As they did,
they continued to fight, inspired by one officer declaring "If the Medes darken
the sun, we shall have our fight in the shade."[19] The mission at Thermopylae
was vital to the defense of Hellas itself. For as Leonidas and his three-hundred
Spartans sacrificed their lives, attempting to hold the pass at Thermopylae
against the horde of Persian invaders, Athens had time to prepare a defense.
When the last Greek died, the West was born.

That the West began in an act of heroic sacrifice should not surprise anyone, Dawson thought. Such sacrifices, the surrender of will and ego, would
shape much of the West's history. The sacrifices at Thermopylae began the
tradition, thus preparing the way for the Christian martyrs in Roman arenas
and the knights defending Christendom against the infidel invaders. Indeed,
sacrifice may be the most powerful weapon humans possess this side of eternity. In Dawson's Augustinian understanding, the sacrifice of the will is what
allows grace to fill us and God to make us who we are meant to be and best
serve Him. By penetrating all of creation and time, the Light of the Logos
could inspire those before and after the Incarnation.

In the sacrifices made at Thermopylae, the Spartans identified with the
Athenians, the universal overcame the particular, and Greek patriotism first
took hold. "But we must surely admit that there were spiritual issues in the
struggle between the Persians and the Greeks," Dawson wrote in 1942, "and
so it is today, though the issues for us are not so simple as for the men who
fought at Thermopylae and Plataeae."[20]

---

[18]Ibid.

[19]Ibid.

[20]Christopher Dawson to Walter Zander, Gerrards Cross, Bucks, May 12, 1942, in Box 14,
Folder 14, "General Correspondence, 1940–1949," UST/CDC.

While the numerous Greek city-states were different, one from another, they shared certain general features. First, each community was independent from others and could act in an autonomous fashion. "It was as 'free men,' as members of a self-governing community, that the Greeks felt themselves to be different from other men," Dawson wrote in *Understanding Europe*, "and it was as members of the wider society of Hellenism which embraced a hundred cities and was in contact with every part of the Mediterranean world that they developed their co-operative work of thought and rational enquiry which was the source of western philosophy and science."[21] Second, the Greeks brought together the concepts of patriotism, freedom, and the classical virtues, thus creating not only the liberal arts but also, consequently, the first true humanist culture.[22] This new form of education allowed the Greeks to maintain unity and pass their traditions and culture from generation to generation. As Dawson explained in his posthumously published Harvard lectures, from its very beginning, Greek philosophy encouraged freethinking and open inquiry. "Ionian philosophy is marked by a spirit of free enquiry and true scientific curiosity that is utterly unlike the strict traditionalism of oriental thought," Dawson wrote.[23] The Greeks sought a "sacred order" governed by a "higher principle."[24] In the end, many of the most important Greek philosophers arrived at something like monotheism because of this search. The highest achievement, according to Dawson, came from Plato. "For it was in the philosophy of Plato that the theory of a transcendent reality attained its classical expression in the West," Dawson wrote. "The vision of Eternity that had so long absorbed the mind of the East, at last burnt on the Greek world with dazzling power. With Plato, the Western mind turns away from the many-coloured changing world of experience to that other world of eternal forms."[25] In other words, Plato spoke deeply and strongly of an objective reality, subject neither to man's whims nor to his passions. In this respect, Dawson believed, Plato anticipated Christian theology and the sovereignty of the Divine.

The greatness of Greece, though, passed quickly. Several things contributed to this decline. Tragically, especially given the sacrifices at Thermopylae, the Greeks never overcame their own jealousies and suspicions of one another, resulting in the brutal civil wars only half a century after the successes of the Persian Wars. "The free cities were torn asunder by mutual hatred and by class wars," Dawson explained in *Progress and Religion*. "They

---

[21]Dawson, *Understanding Europe*, 28.

[22]Ibid.

[23]Christopher Dawson, *Religion and World History: A Selection from the Works of Christopher Dawson*, Christina Scott and James Oliver, eds. (Garden City, NY: Image, 1975), 93; and *Understanding Europe*, 28.

[24]Dawson, *Religion and World History*, 94.

[25]Ibid., 100. Also see "Religion and the Life of Civilization," in *Religions of the Empire: A Conference on Some Living Religions within the Empire*, William Loftus Hare, ed. (London: Duckworth, 1925), 462.

found no place for the greatest minds of the age—perhaps the greatest minds of any age—who were forced to take service with tyrants and kings."[26] Dawson, of course, is referring to Socrates, Plato, and Aristotle, the real founders of western philosophy. Each of the great philosophers described and defended the best of what had come before them, fully realizing that the glory days of Greece were long past. Each served, vitally, as an *anamnesis*—a reminder of right reason and first principles. Though their spirit failed to reawaken Hellenic patriotism, it did preserve it for the inspiration of later generations and cultures.

Taking advantage of this chaos and tumult of the Greek city-states, Philip of Macedon and his son, Alexander, spread Hellenism through most of the known world, creating a "real world-wide civilization which influenced the culture of all the peoples of Asia as far east as North-West India and Turkestan."[27] As the influence spread, the culture became decentralized and, in many ways, dead. "Hellenic civilization collapsed not by a failure of nerve," Dawson concluded, "but by a failure of life."[28] Its philosophy and theology no longer meant anything to its people, and when the root of any culture fails, the culture must die quickly thereafter. The farmer "citizen soldier" stood at the very heart of Hellenic culture at the momentous battles of Thermopylae and Marathon, Dawson argued. The average Greek preserved patriotism, a love of local community and family, seeing his land and religion as "inseparable from the family tombs and the shrine of the local hero." The culturally decadent—the businessman seeking only profit or the unmanly men who played games all day in an urban setting—replaced the citizen soldier in the Hellenistic period, Dawson lamented.[29]

Hellenistic culture continued to flourish in the Roman Republic and Empire. Dawson considered Rome's most important dates to be from the reign of Alexander the Great to Constantine's conversion. During this time, Rome developed from an agrarian republic to an urban empire. "For the first and last time in the history of Western culture the whole civilized world [west] of Persia and India was united by a common law and defended by a uniform military system."[30] In almost all ways—in philosophy, art, and politics—the Romans were inferior to the Greeks, Dawson claimed. Rome's strength came from the sheer endurance and fortitude of her citizens. "The foundation of her power and of her very existence was the peasant citizen-soldier," Dawson wrote in *Progress and Religion*.[31] While the Greeks went to places

---

[26]Christopher Dawson, *Progress and Religion: An Historical Inquiry* (1929; Washington, D.C.: Catholic University of America Press, 2001), 59.

[27]Dawson, *Understanding Europe*, 28–29.

[28]Dawson, *Progress and Religion*, 59.

[29]Ibid., 60.

[30]Dawson, *Understanding Europe*, 29.

[31]Dawson, *Progress and Religion*, 166.

that were already peopled, the Romans peopled new lands and "drove their roads like a plough through the virgin soil of Western Europe."[32] According to Dawson, this achievement of the Romans was the "indispensable continuation and completion of the achievement of Hellenism."[33] The Romans, in essence, developed the physical, linguistic, legal, and educational infrastructure that would allow the highest achievements of the Greeks to spread—albeit in simplified and diffused form—into barbarian Europe.

If the Romans were inferior to the Greeks in culture, they were superior to them in engineering, the great feat that allowed them to unify much of the western world. "Owing to its geographical character," Dawson wrote in one of his first published essays, "Italy never possessed the possibility of internal cultural unity, until the Roman engineers had succeeded in supplying the country with a system of artificial communications more perfect than anything the world had known before the 17th century."[34] The Romans soon misused the freedom the republic offered them, and, according to Dawson, the republic degenerated into misrule by exploitative capitalists and malcontent, power-hungry military officers.[35] Only the establishment of the empire under Julius and Augustus averted complete Roman collapse. Indeed, Augustus oversaw a golden age, but one that degenerated even more quickly than had the republic. Still, no matter what their successors did with their inheritance, Julius and Augustus accomplished much. Julius, for example, began the serious incorporation of Western European peoples into the empire, while Augustus viewed himself "as the conscious champion not only of Roman patriotism, but of specifically Western ideals."[36] Like those valiant Greeks who sacrificed themselves for the greater good during the Persian Wars, Augustus would protect the West from the despotisms of the East.

And yet it was not enough to protect from enemies abroad, for a corrupt people cannot protect themselves. Centered around decadent, unproductive urban civilization and centralized state socialism, the "Roman Empire and the process of urbanization which accompanied it were, in fact, a vast system of exploitation which organized the resources of the provinces and concentrated them in the hands of a privileged class."[37] Dawson explained this exploitation succinctly in *Progress and Religion.* Augustus "could not restore the citizen farmer in the place of the slave, nor could he cope with the cosmopolitan urban development of the city of Rome itself." Rome, for all intents and pur-

---

[32]Dawson, *Understanding Europe,* 30.

[33]Ibid.

[34]Christopher Dawson and Alexander Farquharson, "Rome: A Historical Survey," *Sociological Review,* vol. 15 (1923), 133.

[35]Christopher Dawson, *Enquiries into Religion and Culture* (London: Sheed and Ward, 1933), 202.

[36]Christopher Dawson, *The Making of Europe: An Introduction to the History of European Unity* (1932; Washington, D.C.: Catholic University of America Press, 2003), 19.

[37]Dawson, *Enquiries into Religion and Culture,* 210.

poses, committed suicide. The great capital city of the Empire had nothing in common with its predecessor, the capital of the Republic. "It served no social function, it was an end in itself, and its population drawn from every nation under heaven existed mainly to draw their Government doles, and to attend the free spectacles with which the Government provided them." Inevitably, the capital under the late Empire proved itself to be "a vast, useless burden on the back of the empire which broke at last under the increasing strain."[38] Further, as the state grew in size and scope, it soon determined every aspect of life, subsuming the individuality of its citizens in the collective mentality of the bureaucracy and imperial court.[39]

Temporary but vital moments of respite existed, of course, throughout the overall decline of the Empire, Dawson argued. He especially singled out the importance of the second-century "Flavian and Antonine emperors" who had established a world that had never "seemed more prosperous, more civilised, or more peaceful."[40] In the long run, despite their best efforts, these emperors merely slowed down the decay, as the army, the bureaucracy, the capitalists, and the engineers continued to spread Rome throughout Europe, adding new territories and new peoples ripe for exploitation.[41] And yet, no matter what its successes or failures, Rome in all of its manifestations played a vital role in God's Divine Economy. Approvingly quoting Prudentius, Dawson explained that Rome laid the foundation for the forthcoming universal Christian religion. All peoples subsequent to Rome "cherished the memory of the universal peace and order of the Roman Empire, with its common religion, its common law and its common culture."[42]

As with all things in God's providence, the efficiency of the soulless Roman Empire worked in favor of the coming formation of Christendom. In chapters 10 and 11 of *The Making of Europe*—which many regard as Dawson's greatest work—Dawson convincingly argues that the Hellenistic culture the Romans had inherited no longer provided the answers a person or a culture asks about his or its origins, meaning, and significance. "The cities were still being built with their temples and statues and theaters as in the Hellenistic age," Dawson explained, "but it was a sham façade that hid the decay within." The desire for universality among the Romans continued throughout the age of the empire, as they believed themselves destined to rule the world. But they lost their reasons as to why they should rule the world. Power and exploitation simply begat more power and exploitation, but purpose faded. In history, Dawson explained, "there is in it always a mysterious and inexplicable element, due

---

[38] Dawson, *Progress and Religion*, 166–67.
[39] Dawson, *Enquiries into Religion and Culture*, 212.
[40] Dawson, *Making of Europe*, 22.
[41] Dawson, *Modern Dilemma*, 21–23.
[42] Dawson, *Making of Europe*, 32.

not only to the influence of chance or the initiative of individual genius, but also to the creative power of spiritual forces."[43]

The Christian church became the new *polis*, but it was charitable rather than jealous and universal rather than nationalist. But the early church never desired to be a state in and of itself. Instead it viewed its place "if not [as] a state within the state, at least an ultimate and autonomous society."[44] Not surprisingly, the Roman state feared the competition. The empire's persecution of Christianity only nurtured the soil in which the seeds of the new faith could develop and grow. According to Dawson, the martyrs of the second and third centuries became "the complete Christians," an inspiration to a decadent population, devoid of any higher understanding, but still seeking something higher than itself.

One sees this perhaps most clearly in the story of St. Perpetua. Carthaginian guards imprisoned Perpetua only days after her baptism in 202. Estranged from her father, Perpetua kept her infant son with her in prison, and she attempted to impart strength to her brother, also a recent convert. The Holy Spirit, Perpetua believed, gave her fortitude as well as a number of intense and detailed visions that offered her hope for eternal citizenship in the next world. No matter what beasts would tear at her, she assumed, she would actually be fighting with the devil in disguise. When a gladiator approached her in the arena, Perpetua "took the gladiator's trembling hand and guided it to her throat." The commentary in the ancient "Martyrdom of Perpetua" concludes:

> O brave and fortunate martyrs, truly called and chosen to give glory to our Lord Jesus Christ! And anyone who is elaborating upon, or who reverences or worships that honor, should read these more recent examples, along with the ancient, as sources of encouragement for the Christian community. In this way, there will be new examples of courage witnessing to the fact that even in our day, the same Holy Spirit is still efficaciously present, along with the all powerful God the Father and Jesus Christ our Lord, to whom there will always be glory and endless power. Amen.[45]

Indeed, the saints became the dying witnesses to a purpose in this life and the life beyond. Their blood led to mass conversions among a lost Roman people.

Not only did the idea of martyrdom and the communion of saints play vital roles in the formation and continuation of Christ's one body, transcending time, but it also demonstrated the triumph of life over death. One sees "in the art of the catacombs how prominent a place the cult of the dead held in the primitive Church, and how every device of symbolism and imagery was

---

[43] Ibid., 36.

[44] Ibid., 33.

[45] "The Martyrdom of Perpetua," in *A Lost Tradition: Women Writers of the Early Church,* Patricia Wilson-Kastner, G. Ronald Kastner, Ann Millin, Rosemary Rader, and Jeremiah Reedy, eds. (Washington, D.C.: University Press of America, 1981), 30.

employed to bring home to the spectator the great fact of the triumph of life over death, a triumph which proceeds without interruption from its beginning in the sacramental mystery of the Resurrection," Dawson wrote in 1933. "For the keynote of the Christian doctrine of future life is not Immortality, but Resurrection; not the survival of an immaterial principle, but the vital restitution of human nature in its integrity" for the next world.[46] Though it has become somewhat cliché, the "blood of the martyrs" truly did lay the foundation of the Church, in a variety of different ways.

After the vast and often unrestrained persecutions, the Roman Empire accepted Christianity in the fourth century. "From being the religion of a persecuted minority," Dawson wrote, "Christianity now became the established religion of the greatest power that existed, an empire which was regarded by the peoples of the Mediterranean as embracing the whole of the civilized world."[47] At the moment that persecutions became most severe, Greek, Roman, Judaic, and Christian culture finally fused under the leadership of Emperor Constantine. Hellenism had a long and painful search for the full Truth, Dawson argued. Christianity arrived at the culmination of the interaction of the many cultures, but it also answered their questions and fulfilled their longings. The Church, then, gave meaning to an adrift population, pursued eternal truths, and opened its doors to men and women of all social classes. Ultimately, Dawson argued, Christianity made the empire "spiritually tolerable." It especially protected the weak—"the poor, the orphan, and the [rights of the] criminal"—in an otherwise exploitative society.[48]

Yet tensions existed. Which would become dominant, asked many, the Catholic Church or the Roman Empire? In an uneasy truce, the Christian Empire existed only briefly in the West. As best represented in the writings of Eusebius, the emperor stood as the most powerful figure within the new Christian society. Yet the Church still attempted, through such powerful figures as St. Ambrose, to challenge the violence within political rule and the arbitrary authority of an emperor. This tension over possible Caesaropapism decreased dramatically with the barbarian invasions of the West in the fifth century, but it continued in the East until the collapse of the Byzantine empire in 1453. The western tradition followed Augustine rather than Eusebius. The former argued that since a state is nothing but a gang of thieves, the Church must not tie its fortunes to it. It is permissible, in St. Augustine's thinking, for the Church to be superior to the state. It is never permissible for the Church to be subject to the state. States rise and fall, but the Church traverses this earth on its pilgrimage to the next.

---

[46]Christopher Dawson, "The Future Life: A Roman Catholic View," *The Spectator*, vol. 151 (1933), 889.

[47]Christopher Dawson, *The Formation of Christendom* (New York: Sheed and Ward, 1967), 118.

[48]Ibid., 124–25.

The Birth of European Christendom

Despite the world shattering events of 410, Dawson was not willing to assign any single year to the end of the patristic era and the beginning of the middle ages. In his famous Gifford Lectures, Dawson argued that one could find no break—especially on an intellectual level—between the classical and the medieval period.[49] Instead, there existed a continuity in the West simultaneously with a number of "dark ages" and transitions which slowly occurred throughout and across Europe, beginning in Italy and Africa. Dawson cautioned, though, that much of Europe and the Middle East still enjoyed the civilization protected and energized by the Byzantine world. Dawson labeled the years 200–1000, the "phase of regression" in which the "traditions of Greece and Rome . . . had become no more than an island surrounded on every side by the advancing tide of Islamic conquest and barbarian invasion."[50] Still, the earlier Germanic barbarian invasion had laid the foundation for an even greater society, medieval Christendom. Two factors helped create the new Christian Europe: the fortitude of the Celtic and Anglo-Saxon monasteries, and the heroism of the missionary saints, such as St. Boniface, coming out of those monasteries.[51]

The monasteries originated in the Egyptian desert as a "protest against any compromise between the Christian ideal of perfection and the worldliness of life in the cities."[52] Led by the Egyptian Fathers such as St. Antony, the first monks attempted to "fly" from the secular and Hellenistic world and preserve Christian culture in relative isolation. The mission of this Coptic tradition, Dawson argued, was "entirely oriental in spirit."[53] It was antithetical to the communitarian and social notions of Aristotle. Like the Jews who fled Egypt into the desert, so the Coptic monks fled civilization "to meet God alone in the desert and to find a new way of life according to the Spirit."[54] Soon, those who fled in isolation came together in community and the monastery was born.

Many prominent Christians visited the monasteries to study and learn, and their writings were translated into numerous languages. Athanasius's *Life*

---

[49]Christopher Dawson, *Religion and the Rise of Western Culture* (1950; New York: Image Books, 1991), 18.

[50]Christopher Dawson, *Medieval Essays* (London: Sheed and Ward, 1953), 12.

[51]On the Anglo-Saxon world, see volume one of the series Dawson edited, *The Makers of Christendom*, entitled, *The Anglo-Saxon Missionaries in Germany: Being the Lives of Ss. Willibrord, Boniface, Sturm, Leoba and Lebuin, Together With the Hodoeporicon of St. Willibald and a Selection from the Correspondence of St. Boniface,* ed. and trans. C. H. Talbot (New York: Sheed and Ward, 1954).

[52]Dawson, *Formation of Christendom,* 132. See also *Mediæval Christianity*, Rev. E. C. Messenger, ed. (London: Catholic Truth Society, 1935), 25; and *Christianity in East and West* (La Salle, IL: Sherwood Sugden, 1981), 23.

[53]Dawson, *Medieval Essays,* 19.

[54]Ibid.

of Antony, filled with miracles, exorcisms, and spiritual warfare, especially inspired followers, including St. Augustine.[55] Coptic thought spread quickly into Syria, which Dawson argued served as a vital nexus between the East and the West. Neither Greek nor Latin, the great Syriac saints and the Aramaic culture left some of the most important and inspired writings and teachings of the era. Especially rich in its emphasis on artistry as an essential part of creation and its enjoyment, Syriac culture produced some of the finest and most imaginative poetry ever written.[56] Dawson considered the Syriac culture a vital, third center of Christianity, the "oriental Christian culture," spreading its beliefs from the Christian city of Edessa to the Nestorians, the Armenians, and the Georgians. Byzantium, according to Dawson, allowed the Muslims to destroy this third center through an ill-chosen and selfish foreign policy. Indeed, with Byzantium's neglect, the destruction of the Syriac culture prevented any real alliance in the middle ages between Europe and China.[57]

Ironically, considering that the monks were rejecting Hellenism as best expressed in Aristotle's *Politics*, the monasteries of the medieval period became the new *Poleis*. Irishmen even referred to the monasteries as "civitas."[58] Like the *poleis* of Hellas, the individual citizens of each *polis* might not be free, but each *polis* was autonomous, independent politically and ecclesiastically, one from every other. They shared a common language, common culture, and a common theology. But they remained diverse as well as decentralized politically. Each member of the community believed himself to be a citizen of the City of God, already possessing eternal membership.[59] Each member also became what the early church considered a "living martyr." Each vow against the secular world—in favor of chastity, poverty, and obedience—was taken as proof of God's grace, grace given to leave the materialism and sexuality of the world, to give oneself completely to a Christian life. The monk's "heroic feats of asceticism were, like the suffering of the martyrs," Dawson explained, "signs of the completeness" of Christ's power.[60]

During the fourth century, the monasteries took the institutional shape they would possess during the medieval period. They became communities "living in obedience under a common rule and a common superior, and devoting their time not only to solitary prayers and meditation but to organized common work and common worship."[61] St. Augustine (c. 397) also wrote a monastic rule, but the most commonly used rule in non-Celtic monaster-

---

[55] David Brakke, "Antony," in *Late Antiquity: A Guide to the Postclassical World*, G. W. Bowerstock, Peter Brown, and Oleg Grabar, eds. (Cambridge, MA: Belknap Press, 1999), 304.

[56] Franz Rosenthal, "Syriac," in Bowerstock, *Late Antiquity*, 712.

[57] Dawson, *Medieval Essays*, 22–26.

[58] Dawson, *Formation of Christendom*, 168.

[59] Dawson, *Religion and the Rise of Western Culture*, 47, 49.

[60] Dawson, *Formation of Christendom*, 134.

[61] Ibid., 133.

ies was that of St. Benedict (c. 530) which focused on obedience and love. The monasteries also symbolized the universality of Catholicism, as each monastery recruited and accepted new members without regard to class or ethnic distinctions.

Though the monasteries had rejected the predominant culture of the second through fourth centuries, they served the vital function of preserving and transmitting both classical and Christian culture, philosophy, and theology after the fall of the western Roman Empire. Dawson never tempered his language regarding the overwhelming importance of the institution. "The great social institution by which the Church carried out the work of Christian acculturation and which dominated the whole development of early medieval culture was the *monastic community*," Dawson told his Harvard students.[62] Each monastery "provided an oasis of peace in a land of war, a cell of Christian culture in a barbarous and semi-pagan world."[63] Indeed, though the barbarians may have destroyed every city and every village of Rome, had even one monastery survived, western culture could survive. "Ninety-nine out of a hundred monasteries could be burnt and the monks killed or driven out," Dawson wrote, "and yet the whole tradition could be reconstituted from the one survivor, and the desolate sites could be repeopled by fresh supplies of monks who would take up again the broken tradition, following the same rule, singing the same liturgy, reading the same books and thinking the same thoughts as their predecessors."[64] While the Dark Ages never witnessed such vast and apocalyptic devastation as might have been possible, the monks of Ireland, Wales, and England did play exactly such a role in preserving western culture. Protected by the Channel, the English, Welsh, and Irish monasteries were geographically situated to preserve western culture while avoiding the larger barbarian land invasions.[65]

The Celtic peoples of these areas adopted Christianity quickly because of the bardic and druidic traditions, both of which anticipated much of Christian theology and spiritual thought. The Christian monks "entered in a sense into the inheritance of this native tradition," replacing "the old druidic and bardic schools as the intellectual organs of Irish society."[66] More than any other peoples of Europe, the Irish blended comfortably their native and literary traditions with Christian culture. Each monastery, for example, represented individual clans in Ireland. Overall, the Irish monastic tradition bore greater resemblance to that of the Desert Fathers than to that of the Benedictines. The Irish tradition also stressed the importance of journeys and voyages. Men such as St. Brendan best represented this impulse, which gave way to "mission ac-

---

[62] Ibid., 165.

[63] Ibid., 171.

[64] Dawson, *Religion and the Rise of Western Culture,* 66.

[65] Ibid., 51.

[66] Dawson, *Making of Europe,* 178.

tivity," sending Irish monasticism into what is now Scotland, France, Flanders, and parts of Germany. Raised in rural settings with keen understandings of nature—in an almost Franciscan understanding, Dawson believed—the Irish monastic tradition mixed well with the peasants of Europe. "The presence of these colonies of black-robed ascetics must have impressed the peasant mind with the sense of a new power that was stronger than the nature spirit" of the barbarian mind. Because of the Irish love of the natural, "the sacred wells, the sacred trees and the sacred stones retained the devotion of the people, but they were consecrated to new powers, and acquired new associations," Dawson wrote.[67] The pagan remained in form, Dawson pointedly argued, but Christianity changed its essence.

The Vikings launched their first attack on the British Isles in 789, and the safety of the Irish, Welsh, and English monasteries firmly collapsed on June 8, 793.[68] "In this year [793] dire portents appeared over Northumbria and sorely frightened the people. They consisted of immense whirlwinds and flashes of lightning, and fiery dragons were seen flying in the air," the *Anglo-Saxon Chronicle* for that year recorded. "A great famine immediately followed those signs, and a little after that in the same year, on 8 June, the ravages of heathen men miserably destroyed God's church in Lindisfarne, with plunder and slaughter."[69] Alcuin of York's description was even more brutal. "The church of St. Cuthbert is splattered with the blood of the priests of God, stripped of all its furnishings, exposed to the plundering of pagans," he lamented.[70]

Despite the new insecurities caused by the heathen Scandinavians, the monks of Ireland and England had already secured much of the continent in favor of Christendom. Indeed, the synthesis of classical and Christian cultures in England, especially, had witnessed the rise of one of the most important figures in the history of Christendom, St. Boniface, who evangelized the pagan tribes of what is now northern Germany.[71] Dawson believed that understanding Boniface was the key to understanding the origins of Europe. When encountering a Hessian tribe worshipping an oak tree dedicated to the Norse god Thor, St. Boniface promptly grabbed an axe and cut down the tree. According to legend, the tree exploded into four parts at the first touch of the axe's blade. And, much to the surprise of the chagrined Hessians, Thor remained aloof and the intruder went unpunished.[72] "But when he had made a

---

[67] Ibid., 179–182.

[68] John Haywood, *The Penguin Historical Atlas of the Vikings* (London: Penguin, 1995), 54.

[69] *The Anglo-Saxon Chronicle: An Anthology,* ed. and trans. Kevin Crossley-Holland (Oxford: Oxford University Press, 1999), 39.

[70] Haywood, *Historical Atlas of the Vikings,* 54.

[71] Dawson believed that Christian missionary expansion after 1800 followed the Anglo-Saxon pattern. See his "The Expansion of Christianity," *Commonweal*, vol. 69 (January 9, 1959), 379.

[72] Warren H. Carroll, *The Building of Christendom* (Front Royal, VA: Christendom College Press, 1987), 276.

superficial cut, suddenly the oak's vast bulk, shaken by a mighty blast of wind from above, crashed to the ground shivering its topmost branches into fragments in its fall," a posthumous account recorded. "As if by the express will of God (for the brethren present had done nothing to cause it) the oak burst asunder into four parts, each part having a trunk of equal length."[73] Awed, the barbarians were ready to listen. Legend tells that in the spot of the felled oak, an evergreen instantly sprang forth from the ground, and Boniface's followers placed candles on it so that Boniface could preach the Gospel late into the night, thus creating the tradition of the Christmas tree.

Closely studying the exploits of the intrepid saint, Dawson proclaimed St. Boniface "a man who had a deeper influence on the history of Europe than any Englishman who has ever lived."[74] In his *Medieval Essays*, Dawson took this even further. His many accomplishments almost give Boniface "the right to be called the founder of medieval Christendom."[75] Perhaps providentially, every significant moment in Boniface's life coincided with a further Islamic incursion into Christian Europe. "During the generation before the birth of St. Boniface the whole of the Christian East had been conquered," and Byzantium almost fell. When Boniface was a "monk at Nursling in 711–713[,] Spain was being conquered by the Saracens, and while he was beginning his mission to Germany the Saracens were beginning their invasions of France."[76] Boniface's genius came from his realization that Christian Europe would need a Christianianized German people to serve as a barrier to the growing Islamic threat in the South. He also needed the protection of the powerful Martel family in the Frankish regions. Each, then, would allow the classical documents, classical tradition, and Christian scriptures to remain protected in the relative safety of the British Isles. Boniface was a diplomat as well as a spiritual figure, who attempted to infuse Christianity into barbarian culture.

> The work of St. Boniface did more than any other fact to lay the foundations of medieval Christendom. His mission to Germany was not an isolated spiritual adventure like the achievements of his Celtic predecessors; it was part of a farsighted programme of construction and reform planned with all the method and statesmanship of the Roman tradition. It involved a triple alliance between the Anglo-Saxon missionaries, the papacy, and the family of Charles Martel, the de facto rulers of the Frankish kingdom, out of which the Carolingian Empire and the Carolingian culture ultimately emerged.[77]

---

[73] Willibald, "The Life of St. Boniface," in *Soldiers of Christ: Saints and Saints' Lives from Late Antiquity and the Early Middle Ages,* Thomas F. X. Noble and Thomas Head, eds. (University Park: Pennsylvania State University Press, 1995), 126–27.

[74] Dawson, *Making of Europe,* 189.

[75] Dawson, *Medieval Essays,* 63.

[76] Christopher Dawson, "St. Boniface," in *Saints and Ourselves,* Philip Caraman, S.J., ed. (London: Hollis and Carter, 1955), 3.

[77] Dawson, *Religion and the Rise of Western Culture,* 62.

Like all good Christians, Dawson argued, Boniface surrendered his own will and became "a servant rather than a master of his age ... accepting every charge and never attempting to impress his personality on the course of history."[78] Though eventually martyred for his selfless and grace-filled efforts, St. Boniface succeeded in creating what we would now recognize as the beginnings of Europe, a synthesis of the classical, Christian, and Germanic.[79] His contributions in the formation of Christian Europe are equaled only by St. Gregory the Great and St. Benedict. Fulda, established by St. Sturmius, a disciple of Boniface, in the year 744 as a center for evangelizing the Saxons, remained a center of European evangelization long after Boniface's martyrdom.[80] St. Boniface had also carried with him the Benedictine rule into central Europe.[81] As the Archbishop of Canterbury eulogized in the year of Boniface's death, 754, "We recall the wondrous—nay, the ineffable—grace of God and render thanks that the English people were found worthy, foreigners as they are, to send this gifted student of heavenly learning, this noble soldier of Christ, with many pupils well taught and trained, to far-off spiritual conflicts and for the salvation of many souls through the grace of Almighty God."[82]

When he discussed the contributions of the monasteries and the heroic monks, Dawson resembled, at least in tone and enthusiasm, the Archbishop of Canterbury of the eighth century. "As Christians we cherish—or ought to cherish—a genuine *pietas* towards the institutions and the men who laid the foundations of Christianity in the West."[83] Unlike the "deceived men" of the so-called eighteenth-century Enlightenment and of nineteenth-century liberalism, Dawson stated in his Harvard lectures, the twentieth-century Christian can see through haze and identify a thriving and dynamic culture, far from the darkness decried by its opponents.[84] The early middle ages, then, "which have not unjustly been called *dark*, are most interesting of all, since they contain the germ of a thousand years of cultural development." The same time period witnessed the mass conversions of Europeans—western and eastern—to the faith.[85] Few eras could rival such missionary activity.

---

[78] Dawson, "St. Boniface," 1.

[79] On Boniface, see especially *The Letters of St. Boniface,* trans. Ephraim Emerton (New York: Columbia University Press, 2000).

[80] Carroll, *Building of Christendom,* 307, n. 83.

[81] Dawson, *Formation of Christendom,* 171.

[82] Boniface, *The Letters of St. Boniface,* 162.

[83] Dawson, *Formation of Christendom,* 173.

[84] Christopher Dawson, *Medieval Religion and Other Essays* (London: Sheed and Ward, 1934), 3.

[85] Dawson, *Formation of Christendom,* 173.

The Achievements of the Medieval Period

The age also witnessed the development of brilliant chroniclers, such as St. Gregory of Tours, Adamnan, and, preeminently, St. Bede, "a man whose immediate ancestors were illiterate barbarians," but who wrote as well as any educated Roman had ever written, with the exception of Marcus T. Cicero. What better proof could there be, Dawson asked, of the achievements of a "genuinely and profoundly Christian" culture?[86] The chroniclers, according to Dawson, more than proved that Christendom could succeed beyond the intellectual and educational achievements of the Roman empire. Culture and religion could trump politics. Christendom could take the best of the best, a past it gratefully inherited, and rework timeless truths in a new fashion. In short, the medievals possessed the moral imagination, and their creativity and imagination allowed the West to flourish in a time of troubles.

The barbarians also contributed significantly to the formation of Christian Europe; they were not merely acted upon. While the Catholic church took its notions of politics and ecclesiastical control from Scripture, Augustine, and the Romans, the barbarians brought with them the idea of kingship. For the barbarian, the king embodied the land, and the land embodied the king. The same was true of the people, as the king represented the people, almost completely, though his will could often be tempered through some tribal mechanisms such as a council, which eventually evolved into the Icelandic Allthing and the English Parliament. But aside from this, each barbarian tribe had its own specific traditions of kingship and political theory. The Anglo-Saxon kings and political beliefs promoted decentralization of the tribe and familial and personal liberties, whereas the Visigothic kings centralized power and ruled their people jealously. But just as the king represented the people and the land, Dawson argued, he also was God's chosen. As Dawson explained:

> [A]ll the elaborate ritual and symbolism which make up the ceremony have their origin in the ancient conception of the king as a sacred representative figure, the head of the Christian society, standing between God and the people, bound by reciprocal bonds of loyalty and fidelity to one and the other, since the royal charisma, the grace conferred by unction, was manifested and justified only in so far as the king was the servant of God, the guardian of justice and the protector of the rights of his people. For if the people are bound to obey the king, the king himself is no less bound to keep his oath, which makes him a minister of God, as well as a sovereign.[87]

Unlike the absolutist sovereigns of the early modern period or the Persian or Byzantine emperors, no Latin medieval king could rule arbitrarily or counter to the culture and traditions of a people for long, for medieval king-

---

[86]Ibid., 174.
[87]Dawson, *Religion and the Rise of Western Culture,* 82.

ship was ultimately revocable.[88] In theory, and quite often in practice, the medieval king was as much a servant as he was a leader.

The English Magna Carta best represented this tradition of checking the king through tradition, the natural law, and the common law. Discontent with the behavior of King John, the nobles of England forced him to sign this "Great Charter" in 1215. The document begins by invoking the name of God "for the health of our soul and those of our ancestors and heirs," to honor God, the Church, the kingdom, and the ancestors. The document listed the rights of Englishmen for the generation writing it and all future generations. One can trace the tradition found here from the Angles and Saxons to the founding of America.[89]

St. Thomas Aquinas best explained the role of the medieval king in his "On Kingship." The king is not the man who oppresses, but the one who is the most virtuous, the one who acts as Christ would. In this grand work, Aquinas was not innovating, but stating what the medievals already believed. Injustice results when the king "pays no heed to the common good" and instead "seeks his own private good."[90] In other words, avarice replaces sacrifice in the unjust state. As with much of the medieval period, Aquinas was attempting to sanctify the pagan notions of kingship. Dawson considered this one of the most important aspects of the development of medieval natural-law theory. "It was also due to the revolutionary change of thought by which medieval philosophy had assimilated the Aristotelian ethical and sociological principles and integrated them into the structure of Christian thought, so that the Law of Nature—the moral law revealed by the light of reason—was confirmed and developed by the spiritual law revealed by faith," Dawson claimed. "This does not of course abolish the fundamental Christian distinction between nature and grace, reason and faith, the World and the Church, but it puts the emphasis on the concordance and harmonization of the two orders rather than on their opposition and conflict."[91] Because of this sanctification, the medieval period was far from oppressive, but instead was theocratically constitutional.[92] Those who lived in it, referred to it as the *Christiana Res Publica*, the Christian Republic, or Christendom. Erasmus, living after the division of the medieval republic, stated it in these somewhat nostalgic terms: "I saw monarchy without tyranny, aristocracy without factions, democracy with-

---

[88] Ibid., 83.

[89] For a brilliant analysis of local rights in the English tradition, see Bruce Frohnen, "Revolutions, Not Made, But Prevented: 1776, 1688, and the Triumph of the Old Whigs," in Gary Gregg II, ed., *Vital Remnants: America's Founding and the Western Tradition* (Wilmington, DE: ISI Books, 1999), 275–303.

[90] St. Thomas Aquinas, "On Kingship," Book I, Chapter III.

[91] Dawson, *Religion and the Rise of Western Culture,* 176.

[92] Ibid., 82.

out tumult, wealth without luxury. . . . Would that it had been your lot, divine Plato, to come upon such a republic."[93]

The diversity and paradoxical unity of the medieval republic fascinated Dawson. The papacy, the universities, a love of ancient philosophy, and Latin all served to unify the medieval world at a high cultural level. But even within the Church, there existed diverse political and theological thought. It is possible to argue, for example, that the Benedictines were the first Protestants. Unlike the Protestants of the sixteenth century, however, the Benedictines remained firmly within the larger Church, loyal to Rome. Indeed, the orders represent vast diversity within Catholic tradition and theology. At a lower-cultural level, every ethnic group possessed its own traditions. And every local area had its own rulers: kings, dukes, bishops, etc. A Magyar scholar, for example, could travel from Hungary to Oxford and encounter a plethora of polycentric polities. Dawson laid out this diversity clearly in his Harvard lectures:

> There were a vast number of political and social units—feudal fiefs, duchies, counties and baronies, loosely held together by their allegiance to king or Emperor. There were Free Cities and Leagues of Cities, like the Lombard Commune or the Hanseatic League. There were ecclesiastical principalities like the German prince-bishoprics, and the great independent abbeys. Finally there were the religious and military Orders—international organizations which lived their own lives and obeyed their own authorities in whatever country in Europe they might happen to be situated.[94]

Upon arriving in Oxford, the Magyar could study with the greatest minds of his day, speaking Latin and agreeing to the same apostolic tradition. The English, in our example, would absorb some of his culture, he much of theirs. "The heavenly city, then, while it sojourns on earth, calls citizens out of all nations, and gathers together a society of pilgrims of all languages, not scrupling about diversities in the manners, laws, and institutions," St. Augustine explained in the *City of God*. The Church "therefore is so far from rescinding and abolishing these diversities, that it even preserves and adapts them, so long only as no hindrance to the worship of the one supreme and true God is thus introduced."[95]

The rule of the Frankish emperor, Charles the Great, or Charlemagne, provides the one important exception to the rule of political diversity. Filling the void left by the Byzantine withdrawal of support for western Europe in the early eighth century, the three generations prior to Charles the Great had carefully laid the groundwork for the Carolingian Age. The alliance between the Franks and the papacy, devised and enacted by St. Boniface, especially

---

[93] Ibid., 173–74.

[94] Christopher Dawson, *The Dividing of Christendom* (New York: Sheed and Ward, 1965), 20.

[95] St. Augustine, *The City of God,* trans. Marcus Dods (New York: Modern Library, 1993), Book 19, Section 17.

played a vital role. The Franks took their promise to protect the pope very seriously, whatever their motives for doing so. The great medieval scholar and chronicler Alcuin wrote to Charlemagne in the summer of 799, delineating the hierarchy within creation: "First the Vicar of St. Peter, Prince of the Apostles; second the holder of the imperial dignity who exercises the secular government of the Second Rome [Byzantium]; finally, in the third place, the royal dignity that Our Lord Christ has reserved for you who govern the Christian People. It raises you above the other two." Therefore, he continued, "It is now on you alone that the Churches of Christ depend, to you alone that they look for safety—to you avenger of crime, guide of those who err, comforter of the afflicted and support of the good."[96] To unify his realm, Charles militarily expanded his frontiers; created 300 counties, each with a ruling Count loyal to him; sent legates—both secular and clerical—to inspect the realm and prevent corruption and abuse; and promoted the liberal arts for clerics. "No doubt these reforms did not always go very deep," Dawson concluded, but "they were by no means superficial. To the diverse peoples of the Empire they brought home the reality of Christendom as a living society of Christian peoples united by a common religious faith and common political allegiance."[97] Ultimately, though, Charles's reign was but a "premature attempt to realize the unity of Western Christendom," and Charles drifted close to an eastern, theocratic tyranny. Simplifying Augustine's "ideal of the City of God" into "something dangerously similar to a Christian version of Islam with Charles as the Commander of the Faithful," the ruler turned the faith into "a religion of the sword, and [Charles's] private life, in spite of his sincere piety, resembled that of a Moslem ruler."[98] Like many effective rulers, though, Charles failed to pass his considerable skills on to his sons, and his empire collapsed during the reign of his son, Louis.[99]

No matter what the political results or failures of Charles's reign, his most effective accomplishments resulted from his patronage of the arts and education, Dawson argued. Led by a brilliant teacher and Anglo-Saxon monk, Alcuin of York (735–804), the Carolingian Renaissance encouraged more accurate Latin, better and more artistic liturgies, better translations of Scripture, and a re-incorporation of classical Greek and Roman texts into the curriculum for clerics. Scholars from England, Ireland, Lombardy, and the various states of Germany came together to learn a common classical and Catholic culture while bringing together the contributions of their own ethnic groups into larger Christendom and medieval scholarship. As Dawson noted, though, the Anglo-Saxon and Celtic scholars contributed the most to the new Renaissance. The vast years of labor of the monks of the British Isles to preserve the

---

[96] Alcuin quoted in Dawson, *Formation of Christendom*, 181.
[97] Dawson, *Formation of Christendom*, 185.
[98] Dawson, *Making of Europe*, 196.
[99] Dawson, *Formation of Christendom*, 186.

best of classical and patristic culture had proven essential to the formation of modern Europe. While Louis may have lost all that his father had built politically, the influence of the Carolingian Renaissance continued long afterwards, especially in the greatest of medieval institutions, the monastery.[100]

The great sagas and tales—*Beowulf*, *Njal's Saga*, and the *Song of Roland*, to name a few—of the medieval period also greatly impressed Dawson as important successes.[101] They too were originally barbarian, and their Christianized forms represented sanctifications of the pagan. One can see this best in *Beowulf*. Though the *Beowulf* poet remains anonymous to history, he was most likely a first generation religious who recognized the value of the pagan poem. Rather than throw it out with the arrival of the new Christian culture, he kept the form of the traditional story while changing its essence.

The story revolves around a great and powerful warrior, Beowulf. During the epic, Beowulf successfully challenges and defeats the monster Grendel and the mother of Grendel. Later, as an old man, King Beowulf faces the entrance of a dragon in his realm. Beowulf and his companions hunt the dragon. Upon encountering it, Beowulf and the dragon fight to a mutual death. All of Beowulf's companions but one—the ever faithful Wiglaf—flee. Beowulf, the great pagan hero, sacrifices himself through sheer will power. The dragon is a Satan figure, Beowulf is a Christ figure, and Wiglaf is a St. John figure. The most important difference between Beowulf and the true Christ is that Beowulf, like all northern pagans, relied on will rather than grace. As Dawson's contemporary and fellow parishioner at St. Aloysius in Oxford, J. R. R. Tolkien, wrote, "One of the most potent elements in that fusion [of Christianity and old traditions] is the Northern courage: the theory of courage, which is the great contribution of early Northern literature." It is this essential difference that separates the pagan from the Christian hero. "For the monsters do not depart, whether the gods go or come," Tolkien continued. "A Christian was (and is) still like his forefathers a mortal hemmed in a hostile world. The monsters remained the enemies of mankind, the infantry of the old war, and became inevitably the enemies of the one God."[102]

A great tension also existed between the Latin Christian church and the barbarians, for at heart, the two cultures were radically different, and the former could not easily sanctify the latter, Dawson argued. This should not surprise the modern reader, Dawson continued, for Christianity inherited and

---

[100]Dawson, *Making of Europe*, 199–208.

[101]Dawson once said in an interview that his reading of Icelandic sagas first attracted him to the study of history and culture. See Frank Sheed, "Frank Sheed Talks with Christopher Dawson," *The Sign*, vol. 38 (December 1958), 35.

[102]J. R. R. Tolkien, "*Beowulf*: The Monsters and the Critics," in *An Anthology of Beowulf Criticism*, Lewis E. Nicholson, ed. (Notre Dame, IN: University of Notre Dame Press, 1963), 70, 72. Dawson was quite taken with the Magyar incorporation of their pagan traditions and their new Christian religion. See his excellent article, "Hungarian Middle Ages," *Hungarian Quarterly*, vol. 5 (1939), 585–590.

possessed long, time-proven traditions when it met the Germanic barbarian. "[T]o the Northern barbarians Christianity was the religion of the Roman Empire and to them it stood for the Latin order with all its heritage of law and civilization."[103] In other words, the barbarians desired the prestige and power of Rome without necessarily embracing all of its most fundamental beliefs.

Dawson saw this tension most clearly in the medieval development of the "cult of the saints." The practice of asking the saints to pray for an individual or a community began in the first century of Christian history, and it has been theologically acceptable outside of the Protestant world for nearly two thousand years. Such a tradition reinforced the Christian notion of the Church as timeless and eternal, connecting the living, the dead, and the yet to be born as the "Community of Saints." But during the early middle ages, the practice—if not the theology—regarding saints changed dramatically. The saints became "not merely patterns of moral perfection, whose prayers were invoked by the Church," Dawson wrote. Instead, the Germanic culture transformed them into "supernatural powers who inhabited sanctuaries and continued to watch over the welfare of their land and their people."[104] The Germans merely replaced the local god and the local places of worship with worship of the saints. Still, Dawson seems to lament, without this compromise on doctrine, the barbarians would never have converted, for, they were ruthless and ignorant, and they sought primarily power.[105]

Dawson viewed the tension between Latin and barbarian in the rise of chivalry as well. Most likely developing in Islamic Spain, chivalry fit comfortably with the old warrior ethics of the Germanic barbarians. This code of ethics and manners had little if anything to do originally with Christianity, or German or Latin culture, appearing immediately after the first crusade.[106] Pagan in origin, it often attacked Christian ideals and theology, focusing instead on the material, "the glorification of life, the assertion of the individual personality and the cultivation of the pleasures of the senses," Dawson argued.[107] Chivalry argued, for example, that it was better to spend eternity in hell with one's friends, rather than eternity in Heaven, populated by "old priests and the old cripples and the maimed who all day and all night crouch in front of the altars and the old crypts and those who are clad in old worn-out coats and tattered rags, who go naked and barefoot and full of sores, who die of hunger and hardship and cold and wretchedness."[108] Dawson believed that the Arthurian legends best represent this tension in the characters of Lancelot

---

[103] Dawson, *Medieval Essays,* 55.

[104] Dawson, *Religion and the Rise of Western Culture,* 33.

[105] Ibid., 35.

[106] Ibid., 152ff.

[107] Christopher Dawson, "The Origins of the Romantic Tradition," *The Criterion,* vol. 11 (1932), 224–225.

[108] Quoted in Ibid., 225.

and Galahad. The question for the medieval Christian became: does one seek the worldly beauty of Guinevere or the eternal beauty of the Holy Grail, the cup of Christ at the Last Supper?[109] Lancelot chose poorly.

In spite of the tensions—or perhaps because of them—the medieval period also witnessed the development of a profoundly deep and successful Christian culture. One sees this in its literature, politics, painting, and architecture. Some of its most important contributions, Dawson believed, came in its philosophical and theological attainments. While St. Augustine was the founder of medieval thought in his *City of God*, St. Thomas Aquinas represented the highest—that is, the culminating—point of the middle ages for Dawson. "It is clear that the intellectual synthesis of the thirteenth century was not a contradiction but the crown and completion of continuous effort to achieve an integration of the religious doctrine of the Christian Church with the intellectual tradition of ancient culture," Dawson argued in the Gifford lectures.[110] According to Dawson, St. Thomas completed the work of St. Augustine, the other Latin church fathers, and the neo-Platonists on grace by sanctifying Aristotelian thought as well as incorporating Eastern Orthodox notions of Christification and the sacraments as means for deification. Dawson believed that Thomas's reconciliation of Aristotle's *Nichomachean Ethics*— which "embody the essential principles of humanist ethics and have an incomparable importance in the history of humanist education"—was his greatest achievement.[111] By combining Eastern Orthodox thought with Augustinian thought, Dawson contended, Thomas dramatically changed the western notion of grace. St. Thomas viewed grace as a "new spiritual principle which transforms and renews human nature by the communication of the Divine Life," remarkably similar to the Orthodox notion of Christification. "It is not merely a power that moves the will but a *light* that illuminates the mind and transfigures the whole spirit." It was this new East-West synthesis that the Protestant Reformers fought in the sixteenth century, while the Catholics of the Counter-Reformation defended it vehemently.[112]

If Dawson held St. Thomas in high regard, he seemed to have felt nothing but contempt for many of the post-Thomas Scholastics. Drawing significantly on Gilson's work on medieval philosophy, Dawson believed that the Thomist emphasis on logic destroyed the medieval liberal arts, because it attempted to render the imagination impotent, and led directly to the "anti-theological reaction of the Renaissance."[113] Even worse, the Scholastic "theological-philosophical monopoly in the universities killed medieval cul-

---

[109]Dawson, *Religion and the Rise of Western Culture,* 157.

[110]Ibid., 194.

[111]Christopher Dawson, "Christianity and the Humanist Tradition," *Dublin Review*, vol. 226 (1952), 5.

[112]Dawson, *Medieval Essays,* 101–02.

[113]Dawson to Mulloy, August 4, 1954, in Box 1, Folder 16, ND/CDAW.

ture" and led directly to the Reformation.[114]   Once the Scholastics turned Thomism into a rigid pseudo-ideology, as Dawson believed they had, the opponents of Scholasticism responded with their own rigidity. This new rigidity, however, attacked the Church and its traditions rather than defending them. While Dawson had a profound respect for St. Thomas Aquinas, Dawson's criticism of the Thomists continued into his own day.

Even if Aquinas represented the high point of medieval thinking, he needed to be balanced with his contemporary, St. Bonaventure. John Hellman, then a student of the medieval period at Marquette University, remembered having tea with the Dawsons in 1961. "The most memorable part of the conversation," Hellman wrote, "was when Dawson, frowning at discovering what I was being taught by the Thomist legion at Marquette, went over to his bookshelves and took down a volume of Bonaventure (in Latin) which he passed on for me to leaf through, a practical antidote to the tunnel vision of those Gilson-formed scholastics."[115] St. Bonaventure, if not as brilliant as Thomas, still allowed for the flexibility of the Spirit and the imagination.

Dante the poet, rather than the Scholastic adherents of Aquinas, offered the best expression of Thomism, Dawson argued. "There is none who has incorporated in his work," Dawson explained, "so much of the science and philosophy and theology of his age." Rather than the grand finale of the middle ages, as some scholars have called it, Dawson argued that the *Divine Comedy* was "in reality a kind of mystical humanism which had a formative influence on the new Italian culture." In other words, Dante provided the continuity between medieval and Renaissance cultures. For Dante, an objective reality existed. "There is no subjectivism or idealism in his world," Dawson claimed; "everything has its profound ontological basis in an objective spiritual order."[116] Unfortunately, Dawson lamented, no one of Dante's caliber followed him. Both Chaucer and Petrarch came close, but neither succeeded completely. This was unfortunate, Dawson wrote; "otherwise we might have been saved alike from the narrow rationalism of eighteenth-century Classicism and from the emotional debauches of nineteenth-century Romanticism."[117]

If St. Thomas offers the intellectual high point and Dante the poetic high point, St. Francis offers the most beautiful illustration of medieval Christianity found in the human person. Francis, through word and action, attempted to become a "picture of Christ," with Franciscan teachings focusing on the humanity of Christ, his death and suffering.[118] This pietist tradition spoke to

---

[114]Dawson to Mulloy, undated, in Box 1, Folder 16, ND/CDAW.

[115]John Hellman, "Christopher Dawson, The New Theology, and Harvard in the 1960s," *The Christopher Dawson Centre of Christian Culture Newsletter*, vol. 2 (July 1999).

[116]Christopher Dawson, review of *Mediæval Culture* and *New Light on the Youth of Dante* in *The Criterion*, vol. 9 (July 1930), 721.

[117]Dawson, *Medieval Essays*, 237.

[118]Dawson, *Mediæval Christianity*, 11–12.

the medieval world as much as it speaks to ours, Dawson believed. St. Francis wanted each person to follow Christ radically, to "shake off the encumbrances of tradition and organization and property and learning and recover an immediate personal contact with the divine source of eternal life."[119] Though his theology reflected the theology of many of the heretics of his day, St. Francis maintained his desire to live as primitively as possible within the larger Catholic community and order.[120] Like the Benedictines, and unlike the heretics of his day, St. Francis remained faithful to the ecclesiastical structures of the Church, respecting its authority and universality. Such an argument in defense of St. Francis reveals Dawson's overriding desire for Christian unity. A sheer genius, according to Dawson, St. Francis perfectly brought together culture and religion. "The whole man is Christian, and the Christian spirit is united with the Western nature as intimately and inseparably as the union of soul and body," Dawson argued.[121] His successes, through grace, should be the successes of all Christians; all should live as St. Francis, combining the worldly and the spiritual in such a complete manner.

As should be obvious from this chapter, though, many problems existed in medieval society. These problems proved so large that the medieval world of universals crumbled into the particulars and nationalisms of the Reformers. The West, divided, became a poor vehicle for Christendom. Like Camelot after Lancelot pursued Guinevere and Galahad pursued the Holy Grail, the West too suffered and then crumbled. The Lady of the Lake came to reclaim the sword and its chosen wielder was removed and sent to rest in Avalon.

The Protestant Reformation

The rise of the early modern nation states, beginning in 1302, destroyed the medieval synthesis, leading to the growth of an unrestrained nationalism. One finds the results of the immediate cause of disunity with the collapse of the Christian kingdom of Acre in Palestine, Dawson argued. The lackadaisical response to its fall indicated to Dawson that the universality of Christendom had been replaced by particular nationalist longings. Perhaps even more important, with the call of the Estates of the Realm in 1302, France began to think of herself as a nation-state, in some critical ways separate from the larger understanding of western and Latin Christendom. As the nation-state developed, it found its most significant opposition in the only bureaucracy extant during the medieval period, that of the papacy. The rising nation-states discovered theological support in their rivalry with the papacy from the more radical Franciscans as well as from profound thinkers such as William

---

[119]Dawson, *Religion and the Rise of Western Culture,* 212; and *Progress and Religion,* 135.
[120]Dawson, *Religion and the Rise of Western Culture,* 210–212.
[121]Dawson, *Medieval Essays,* 111.

of Occam, who were fighting the corruption within the papacy.[122] While the nation-state could rise and grow for its own selfish reasons and its insatiable desire for power, it could appear to be doing so for reasons of virtue, especially in its attack on the corruption of the papacy.

Several important figures, all fighting against the authority of the Church, gave the rising nation-states a theological basis to survive and remain cohesive. Indeed, Dawson argued, there are very few men who are first heretics and then schismatics. "Heresy is as a rule not the cause of schism but an excuse for it," Dawson claimed.[123] Instead, most schismatics in Church history were closed-minded, or one-sided thinkers, who failed to see beyond their own culture, national aspirations, or temporal surroundings.[124] The Church, following the teaching of St. Augustine, had always allowed specific cultural and ethnic manifestations within church liturgies and celebrations of faith. Therefore, a safety valve existed, allowing each ethnic or linguistic group its own form of worship. As long as each local church followed certain universal rules and theological principles, its liturgy and expression of the sacraments could remain local.

Dawson never blamed the Protestants for the tension between universalism and nationalism, even though nationalism exploded with the Lutheran movement. Such tension, Dawson believed in Augustinian fashion, existed as a natural part of the inherent dualism between this world and the next. In his unpublished "Notes on Secularism," dated 1953, Dawson wrote that "The conception of the sacred and the secular manifests itself at every stage of culture from the primitive to the most highly civilized and in every form of religion." He specifically noted "the influence of Nationalism" as one of the obvious outbreaks of this tension.[125]

The western manifestation of the tension between the two forces that came to a head in the Reformation, though, had its beginnings as early as when the Church moved into Europe, spreading the faith among the Germanic barbarians.[126] Each barbarian tribe—the Angles, the Saxons, the Goths, the Franks, etc.—had viewed itself as separate and superior to every other barbarian tribe. The Church, as best represented by St. Boniface, promoted universalism and the unity of all peoples in the body of Christ. Dawson described the entire one-thousand years of medieval unity as one of extreme tension, a balancing act between these two great forces. The rise of the nation, by necessity, then, must witness the corresponding decline of objective religious influence

---

[122]Dawson, *Dividing of Christendom,* 21, 23, 24.

[123]Christopher Dawson, "The Social Factor in the Problem of Christian Unity," *Colosseum,* vol. 4 (1938), 7.

[124]Ibid.

[125]Dawson, "Notes on Secularism," 1953, in Box 1, Folder 15, ND/CDAW.

[126]Christopher Dawson, "On Nationalism," *Tablet* (April 13, 1940), 349; and *Religion and the Rise of Western Culture,* 24.

and thought. While Christianity embraces a traditional, objective truth, each nation-state ultimately demands a unity of thought, culture, and politics for its particular people. It rejects, by necessity, dissent of individuals and groups of individuals. National unity, then, comes from a specific understanding of truth, different from every other national understanding of truth. Sometimes religious, ideological, or the predominant ethnic belief serves as the glue for the unity, Dawson argued. Sometimes the unity comes from a combination of all three elements, and sometimes—though very rarely—it arrives out of whole cloth. "And in each case what we find is a substitute religion or counter religion which transcends the juridical limits of the political State and creates a kind of secular Church," Dawson explained.[127] Nationalism unifies its disparate peoples, ethnic groups, cultures, and religions through an ideology which takes "the place of theology as the creator of social ideals and the guide of public opinion."[128]

Such competing nationalist visions and truths ultimately result in Occam's theological and philosophical nominalism applied to an international level. Indeed, William of Occam, according to Dawson, played one of the most important roles in the breakup of Christendom and in the growth of nationalism. As "the leading mind of his age," Occam "was the initiator—the 'venerabilis inceptor'—of the *via moderna* [nominalism] which took the place of the classical scholasticism of the 13th century—the *via antiqua*—as the accepted doctrine of the universities for nearly two centuries, down to the time of Luther."[129] In between the development of the nominalism of Occam and the revolt of the Protestant Reformers stood such nationalists as the Englishman John Wycliffe (ca. 1330–84) and the Bohemian Jan Hus (ca. 1370–1415). Their nationalisms were so strong that Dawson labeled each a heretic. Wycliffe, for example, not only attacked the papacy and Transubstantiation, but he also argued in favor of absolute predestination and the right of the state to confiscate church property and punish the clergy. Through extreme, swift, and brutal oppression, the English suppressed Wycliffe's influence and following, but it spread quickly in Bohemia, where the Czechs were experiencing a proto-nationalist awakening. When the leader of the Czech nationalist movement, Jan Hus, met a church council—itself formed to challenge the power of the papacy—the council found him too extreme. It ordered his execution in 1415.[130]

---

[127] Christopher Dawson, "Education and the State," *Commonweal*, vol. 65 (January 25, 1957), 425.

[128] Christopher Dawson, "Christianity and Ideologies," *Commonweal*, vol. 64 (May 11, 1956), 139.

[129] Dawson, *Dividing of Christendom,* 24. On Occam, see Frederick Copleston, S.J., *A History of Philosophy* (Westminster, MD: Newman Press, 1953), vol. 3, 43–152.

[130] Dawson, *Dividing of Christendom,* 34–36.

In addition to the intellectual convulsions and influences of Occam, Wycliffe, and Hus, medieval Christendom experienced a number of specific events that helped shatter it. "Monasticism decayed, the Crusade was abandoned, the scholastic synthesis disintegrated under the influence of Nominalism, and the alliance between the papacy and the movement of ecclesiastical reform was dissolved," Dawson wrote. "And at the same time the focal area of medieval culture was divided and ruined by the destructive conflict of the Hundred Years War and the internecine feud between France and Burgundy."[131] Additionally, the rise and influence of the Italian city-states in the fifteenth century brought to the southern parts of Europe considerable wealth and power, as they developed stronger cultural and economic ties with the Byzantine Empire and the Orient.[132] The North resented the inordinate power of the Mediterranean. The growth of pre-Reformation nationalism and the challenges to the power of the papacy came, ironically, just as the ties between the Italian city-states and the Byzantine Empire were developing real fruit, attempting to bridge the differences between Latin Christendom and Greek Christendom. Throughout the late 1430s, the papacy and the patriarch at Constantinople were attempting to reunify the churches. In 1439, most importantly, the Latin pope and Byzantine patriarch and emperor "succeeded in ending the ancient schism between East and West." At that exact moment, "the West as represented by the Council of Basel was deposing the Pope."[133] Because of the unfortunate events of 1453—the Turkish destruction of Constantinople and the end of the second Rome—the Council of Florence's 1439 rulings meant little, if anything. Christendom remained not only divided between East and West, but the West remained vulnerable to further internal division and susceptible to invasion from Islam.

In terms of the growth of the nation-state, Dawson viewed the Reformation as disastrous. The other nationalist movements and proto-nationalist movements may never have flowered had the Reformation not precipitated the still mostly latent barbarian nationalisms of Europe. One should not be surprised, Dawson argued, that Martin Luther came from northern Germany where the "spirit of the old gods was imperfectly exorcised by the sword and ... has continued to haunt the background of the German mind."[134] Indeed, Luther, unwittingly or not, looked back to Germany's pagan roots. "But when Luther spoke of 'the people' he was not thinking in the medieval Catholic sense," Dawson believed, "but of his own people, 'the glorious Teutonic people' who had lost their birthright of freedom by admitting the claims of the clergy and the universal domination of a foreign ecclesiasti-

---

[131] Christopher Dawson, *The Movement of World Revolution* (New York: Sheed and Ward, 1959), 31.

[132] Ibid.

[133] Ibid., 33. Also his *Dividing of Christendom,* 32–33.

[134] Christopher Dawson, *The Judgment of the Nations* (New York: Sheed and Ward, 1942), 30.

cal power."[135] Following other nationalists of the previous centuries such as Wycliffe and Hus, Luther "embodies the revolt of the awakening German national spirit" against the rising power of Mediterranean Europe, the papacy, and Christian unity.[136] "The European situation was ripe for an explosion," Dawson wrote, and Luther "was simply the revolutionary leader whose passionate genius fired the train."[137] To prove the point, Dawson noted that numerous knights rebelled against the princes in 1522, peasants rebelled against the nobles two years later, and the Turks stood at Viennese gates five years after that.[138]

Like all nationalisms, Dawson believed, Luther's rejected the complexity of Christendom—its nuanced but unitary high culture and polycentric political system—and attempted to de-intellectualize the Catholic continuity with the classical. "He took St. Paul without his Hellenism, and St. Augustine without his Platonism," Dawson wrote.[139] By attacking the natural law and creating the Manichean dualism of Law and Gospel, Luther attempted to destroy the human need for mystery and "prepared the way for the secularization of the world and the abolition of objective standards." The real dualism, Dawson had argued time and again, came from the fight between the secular and the other worldly, not between the Law and the Gospel or the Old and New Testaments. The New Testament followed the Old in a continuum, in no less of a fashion than did the Christian and the classical. With Luther's false dualism, though, the former Augustinian monk was forced to argue that man is fallen to such an extent that he can know nothing outside of the truth of scripture. "The profound pessimism of Luther saw in Nature nothing but the kingdom of death and the law of Nature as a law of wrath and punishment," Dawson believed.[140] If the world tells us nothing of value, the past, equally, sheds no new light on the situation of humanity and becomes worthless.[141]

Further, Dawson argued, the Lutheran Reformation habituated the populations of Europe to think in ideological rather than organic and communitarian terms, thus preparing them for the world of the so-called Enlightened despotisms of Early Modern Europe. Lutheranism also allowed the Rousseauvian idea of national democratic communities, in which the state democratically

---

[135]Christopher Dawson, "The Christian Church and the Democratic State," *Triumph*, vol. 1 (1966), 21.

[136]Dawson, *Progress and Religion,* 142; and "Christian Church and the Democratic State," 22.

[137]Dawson, *Movement of World Revolution,* 33.

[138]Dawson, *Dividing of Christendom,* 84.

[139]Dawson, *Progress and Religion,* 142. In his analysis, Dawson places too much blame on the single figure of Martin Luther. Equally important, Dawson ignores the critical intellect of the author of the Augsburg Confession, Phillip Melancthon.

[140]Dawson, *Judgment of the Nations,* 138.

[141]Christopher Dawson, *The Crisis of Western Education* (1961; Steubenville, OH: Franciscan University Press, 1989), 35.

subsumes the individual human person, to take hold.[142] Almost alone among Protestants and certainly alien to the western tradition, Luther sought an alliance between Church and State. The West, after all, followed Augustine, not Eusebius, keeping the state from controlling the Church. The people, however, have no right to oppose either church or state, Luther asserted.

> In this revolution Luther himself led the way. It was his idea that Church and people should be one in a very literal sense. There should be no distinction between the two orders of the temporal and spiritual estates, for all the states of a Christian lord were spiritual, and as the prince was the natural head of his people, so he should be their spiritual head also.[143]

When the German peasants revolted in the name of Luther in 1524–25, threatening the new nationalisms, Luther sought nothing more than to oppress them. "One cannot argue reasonably with a rebel but one must answer him with the fist so that his nose bleeds," Luther forcibly argued. "It is better that all the peasants should be killed than that the princes and magistrates should perish, for the rustics took the sword without divine authority."[144] From the beginning, Dawson argued, Luther's movement was as much political as it was theological. What "drove a great religious leader like Martin Luther into schism and heresy was not purely religious in origin, but was the outcome of a spiritual conflict in which religious motives were hopelessly confused," Dawson claimed, "so that if Luther had not been such a 'psychic' person, to use the word in Saint Paul's sense as well as the modern one, he would have been able to judge the deep things of God as a spiritual man: he would still have been a reformer without becoming an heresiarch."[145] Luther, in sum, was a medieval man possessing numerous internal, psychological conflicts but who was equally unable to reconcile these contradictions. In the end, though, all of Luther's views were simply personal, as he had already destroyed the principle of authority and tradition.[146]

If Dawson considered Luther a simple-minded nationalist (though he also regarded him as a genius in terms of energy and charisma), he held John Calvin in great respect, at least on an intellectual level. Perhaps most important for Dawson, Calvin and his followers took St. Augustine and the theology of the Church Fathers very seriously. Additionally, Dawson noted, Calvinists and Catholics held a common view of the natural law and church-state relations.[147] Unfortunately, Dawson lamented, Calvin believed in a de-centralized

---

[142]Dawson, "Christianity and Ideologies," 140.

[143]Dawson, "Christian Church and the Democratic State," 21.

[144]Quoted in Dawson, *Judgment of the Nations,* 42.

[145]Christopher Dawson, *Dynamics of World History*, John J. Mulloy, ed. (1957; Wilmington, DE: ISI Books, 2002), 92.

[146]Dawson, *Dividing of Christendom,* 76–77.

[147]Dawson, *Judgment of the Nations,* 45, 53.

Christendom, rather than a unified Christendom.[148] Dawson labeled him "the great organizing genius," arguing that Calvin prepared his new Christendom to defend itself against both Catholic and non-Calvinist Protestant thought through a strong, local, and hierarchical network of community watchmen. These watchmen—pastors, elders, and deacons—preserved the traditional Christian morals and discipline of Christendom without duplicating the impersonal bureaucracy and formulaic sacramental life of the Roman Catholics. "This domestic inquisition was far more effective and practical than the papal Inquisition," Dawson wrote, as "it was not hampered by the forms and procedures of ecclesiastical bureaucracy."[149] Though Calvin abhorred war, anarchy, and violence, he recognized the need for self-defense. He, therefore, turned his Protestant-elect saints into well-armed soldiers, following a tradition that reached back to the ancient Greeks and their notion of citizenship and manhood. And, unlike Luther, Calvin also recognized the necessity of the classics and the liberal arts.[150] If unity were to come again, Dawson hoped, it would most likely come through an alliance of Catholics and Calvinists, rather than between Catholics and Lutherans. The essence of Calvinism and Roman Catholicism are similar, even though Catholicism and Lutherans appear in form—that is, only on the surface—to have a greater connection.

The issue of sanctifying grace and imputation, however, would always separate Catholics from Protestants. To Luther's thinking, for example, "sin is passion, for Catholicism sin is in the will—the act of choice." And, for the Catholic, justification continues as a process after the act of faith. For the Protestant, faith, salvation, and justification occur at a single moment.[151] In his Harvard lectures, Dawson defended the Catholic position on good works. Luther, he said,

> is convinced of the worthlessness of pious practices—that it is no use fasting or saying long prayers or making a pilgrimage or a vow. Good works, however, are not merely pious practices, they are simply what the words denote—doing good—and it is a fallacy to argue that such action has no value from a religious point of view. Luther himself argues that whatever is done in faith is good, even if it is just the course of the day's business, but if the assurance of faith is absent, the work is bad however good it may be objectively.[152]

Such a view, Dawson warned, tended to antinomianism, to which Luther objected, but veered towards in spite of himself.

Whatever its virtues and whatever the necessity to root out corruption, the Reformation tasked Dawson, as he considered it one of the greatest—if

---

[148]Dawson, "Christian Church and the Democratic State," 22.

[149]Dawson, *Dividing of Christendom,* 125, 129–30.

[150]Dawson to Mulloy, January 6, 1955, in Box 1, Folder 16, ND/CDAW; and Dawson, *The Crisis of Western Education*, 37.

[151]Dawson, *Dividing of Christendom*, 78.

[152]Ibid., 79.

not the greatest—scandals in the history of humanity. How could the world give up the Church, the unified body of Christ, for particular nationalisms? As Dawson pointedly argued, the "Reformation that they brought about was not a reformation of the Church but rather a reformation of the medieval state at the expense of the Church."[153] Toward the end of his life, Dawson wrote that "the great religious revolution which destroyed the unity of Christendom was not merely a theological movement; it was also a revolutionary attempt to abolish the complexities and confusions of medieval Christendom (the universal Christian society embracing both Church and state) and to establish a new simplified pattern of church-state relations."[154] No level of political or ecclesiastical corruption, Dawson argued, justified the division of Christendom, now for nearly 500 years. Corruption had existed from the first century of the Christian Church, and its 1,500 year history up to the Reformation was a history of corruption, decline, and reform. The division in the body of Christ serves as a great scandal to non-Christians, who witness only the division and infighting within the Christian body.[155] Equally important and related, the Reformation attenuated the virtue of hope by destroying the idea of beauty and the power of imagination in the world.

> In Protestant Europe it was not only the religious drama that was outlawed but Christian art as well, and with it disappeared all the other expressions of Christian culture which united the Church with the life of the people. Religion became a specialized activity which was confined to Church and Chapel and limited to one day in the week. Thus the destruction of Christian culture was the work of Christians themselves who allowed the new Babylon of modern materialist civilization to be built on the soil of Christendom.[156]

Totally depraved men, after all, can see no beautiful things and can never trust their imagination as being anything other than delusional.

But for the Catholic, the imagination and the ability to create is a gift of the Holy Spirit. Indeed, the imagination bridges both the appetites and the higher reason as well as the material and the spiritual. Without the imagination, man cannot sanctify the world. Further, without the imagination, man cannot envision unity. Instead, trapped in his own subjective understandings of the world, the man drowns in his own appetites and reasons, never seeing the beauty of all other things in the Created Order. The Protestant Reformation, therefore, did great damage not only to the unified Body of Christ— ravenously ripping it apart—but it also fundamentally changed the meaning of man, at least as man understands himself. Equally important, the Reformation, by denying the imagination as a holy function and mistrusting it as if

---

[153]Ibid., 73–74.

[154]Dawson, "Christian Church and the Democratic State," 21.

[155]Dawson, *Dividing of Christendom,* 5.

[156]Christopher Dawson, "Hope and Culture: Christian Culture as a Culture of Hope," *Lumen Vitae,* vol. 9 (1954), 430.

it were from the devil, ultimately distorted and perverted man's relationship to the Holy Spirit. It is no wonder then, Dawson believed, that this breakdown in society and this disordering of the human soul and its relationship to God led to secularism, liberalism, and, ultimately, to totalitarianism. Once the imagination is destroyed, man becomes the measure of all things, and whoever wields the most power becomes "right." With the imagination mocked, distorted, and ignored, man sees another only as a collection of parts, to be used and manipulated. Hence, the loss of imagination leads to the gulags, the holocaust camps, and the killing fields.

Even on a more basic level, Dawson firmly believed that the propaganda of the Reformation paved the way for the politicization of society, the rise of ideologies, and the centralization of the state.

> The ideological diversity and tension of modern Europe is comparable to, and to some extent caused by, the religious diversity and tension of post-Reformation Europe. The theological disputes of the Reformation familiarized the masses with ideological issues, and the religious wars of the sixteenth and seventeenth centuries involved the same confusion of convictions, propaganda, and power politics with which are we so familiar today. Moreover, the eighteenth century Enlightenment, the source of the modern ideological development, may be regarded historically as a kind of Second Reformation which in certain respects, as, for instance, in the destruction of the temporal power of the Church and the secularization of church property, carried out the work of the earlier Reformation in those parts of Europe which had previously been immune.[157]

Division and propaganda led to more division and propaganda, Dawson argued. The only way in which society can function is to bypass religion, to relegate it to private life or to do away with it forever. Thus, the Reformation resulted first in liberalism, or private judgment, and then in the secularization of society. "This progressive extrusion of Christianity from culture is the price that Christendom has had to pay for its loss of unity" due to the Reformation, Dawson explained in his Harvard lectures. "The tragedy of schism is that it is a progressive evil. Schism breeds schism, until every social antagonism is reflected in some new religious division." The Protestant countries, because of their divisive nature, were the first to secularize.[158] Still, Dawson conceded, had not Luther begun the Reformation, someone—perhaps Zwingli—would have.[159] There were simply too many tensions and grievances in the sixteenth century, and a revolution was most likely waiting to explode.

But no matter how much theologians or historians temper, rationalize, or justify the significance of the Reformation, Dawson claimed, the Catholic cannot but fail to see almost absolute ruin to the body of Christ. For the Catholic Church, "the common mother of the whole Christian people, lay prostrate and

---

[157]Dawson, "Christianity and Ideologies," 140.
[158]Dawson, *Dividing of Christendom,* 8–9.
[159]Ibid., 81.

helpless," while various elements calling themselves every conceivable name, "fought over her body. Christendom was divided not merely by the war of words and the conflict of opinions, but by rivers of blood, countless executions and exiles, and a spirit of vendetta which dwelt on the atrocities of the past."[160] In these views, as in many others, Dawson echoed the organic communitarianism and conservatism of Edmund Burke. What takes centuries to build, Burke had argued, can be destroyed in a matter of days. Civilization is fragile, precious, and rare. Individual men and individual generations tinker with it only at civilization's peril.

---

[160]Ibid., 139.

Chapter 5

The *Dublin Review*, The Sword of the Spirit, and a Post-War Catholic Order

1940–1946

THE FIRST HALF OF THE 1940S PROVED TO BE SOME OF THE MOST DIFFICULT years in Dawson's life. Though he produced his greatest book in these years, *The Judgment of the Nations*, he suffered from serious depression, bouts of anxiety, and continued insomnia. As a result of these difficulties, he almost lost his friendship and alliance with Frank Sheed. Two movements in which he was significantly involved—as editor of the *Dublin Review* and as vice president of the Sword of the Spirit—failed miserably and resulted in the loss of some of Dawson's considerable prestige. The unfortunate events also led to the breakup of some of his most important friendships. To make matters even worse, a Roman Catholic reviewer of *The Judgment of the Nations* believed Dawson to have been in serious theological error and began an informal process of censoring Dawson's past and future works. Further, he simply carried too little weight outside of Roman Catholic circles. Perhaps worst of all, despite all of Dawson's best efforts, the victorious allied powers embraced a secularized, liberal post-war international order, thus repeating the mistakes of the World War I settlement and the League of Nations. The world had changed too dramatically, as Dawson had been recording and analyzing for his entire adult life.

The *Dublin Review*

Though *Essays in Order* had fizzled, Wall's *Colosseum* had collapsed, and *Europe* had never gotten off the ground, Dawson remained desirous of editing

187

a journal. As chance or providence would have it, such an opportunity arose for Dawson in 1940 when the editorship of the venerable *Dublin Review* became available. The journal was owned by the Roman Catholic Church but privately managed by Douglas Jerrold's publishing enterprises, and Cardinal Hinsley wanted Dawson to serve as editor when Arnold Lunn retired from the position. Father David Mathew and Thomas Gilby, two of Dawson's oldest friends, not only supported the decision but quietly approached Dawson on the cardinal's behalf regarding the matter. After being assured of full editorial control over the journal, Dawson quickly accepted.[1] One of the most prominent religious papers in England, the *Church Times*, immediately approved. "The readers and proprietors of the *Dublin Review* are to be congratulated on the appointment of Mr. Christopher Dawson, as its editor," the paper wrote. "Christopher Dawson, a bearded, fragile-looking and gentle-mannered man, is a writer and thinker of great distinction, with Jacques Maritain, one of the two most considerable lay Roman Catholic writers."[2] The *Church Times* also happily noted that the *Dublin* under Dawson would be more open to non-Roman Catholics, and would most likely publish such distinguished men as T. S. Eliot and Nicholas Berdyaev.

Dawson's first edited issue appeared in July 1940. The issue contained two of his most important pieces, the "Editorial Note," which served as a Catholic call to arms, and his famous piece, "Democracy and Total War," which inspired Cardinal Hinsley to found the ecumenical Sword of the Spirit movement.[3] In the former, Dawson argued that Catholics "have an historical mission to maintain and strengthen the unity of Western culture which had its roots in Christendom against the destructive forces which are attempting its total subversion." Equally important, twentieth-century Catholics "are the heirs and successors of the makers of Europe—the men who saved civilization from perishing in the storm of barbarian invasion and who built the bridge between the ancient and modern worlds."[4] In this, Dawson must have been thinking of such figures as St. Augustine of Hippo, St. Augustine of Canterbury, the Venerable Bede, and St. Boniface, all of whom advanced Catholic civilization in the face of significant Germanic and Islamic adversity. "Behind the war of arms," Dawson continued, "there is a spiritual conflict which is described as psychological or ideological and which extends far beyond the province of propaganda in the old sense of the word." To protect the order of the culture and the polity, he argued, one must first protect the order of the soul. Without

---

[1]Christina Scott, *A Historian and His World: A Life of Christopher Dawson* (New Brunswick, NJ: Transaction, 1992), 135; Dawson to Robert Speaight, August 27, 1942, in Box 15, Folder 137, UST/CDC.

[2]Laicus Ignotus, "The Dublin Review," *Church Times*, July 26, 1940.

[3]Lt. Col. C. E. G. Hope, "Christopher Dawson's Warning," *Sword of the Spirit*, no. 106 (June 1947), 3.

[4]Christopher Dawson, "Editorial Note," *Dublin Review*, vol. 207 (1940), 1.

the order of the soul, all will fall. "All the Western powers, whether they are involved in the war or not, must face the consequences of the totalitarian challenge," Dawson wrote. "A first necessity is to make public opinion alive to the issues that are at stake and to develop the consciousness of Western culture and the spirit of loyalty to the Western tradition." For Dawson, the West included America too. With the crisis of the West at hand, Dawson wrote the following in a private letter to Allen Tate, an American literary critic and general man of letters: "I am particularly anxious to secure the collaboration of American writers," as "America, too, is vitally concerned with the survival of the cultural tradition of the West."[5] The *Dublin*, under Dawson's direction, promised to work for spiritual clarification, proclaiming Western Civilization to be the bearer of the Christian spirit and tradition.[6] And just as Dawson had built significant relations between English and continental thinkers, so he would now, he hoped, make similar ties to like-minded scholars in America. "The line of the new DUBLIN is somewhat similar to that of the CRITERION or the AMERICAN REVIEW," Dawson wrote to Tate. "But we have been hit hard by the impossibility of getting continental contributors under existing circumstances, so we are all the more in need of American co-operation."[7]

The makeup of the first few issues proved a sign of things to come under Dawson's leadership. In essence, Dawson wanted a journal that reflected the best of Christendom, that is, a Christian—not simply a Catholic—Republic of Letters, transcending the denominational squabbles that plagued and divided the larger Christian Church. In addition to Dawson's own fiery pieces, articles appeared from such important non-Catholics as Charles Williams, a hetero-dox Anglican and one of the members of the Inklings from 1939 until his death in 1945. Indeed, Williams contributed at least six significant pieces of work—poetry or social or literary criticism—during Dawson's tenure, in ad-dition to his several book reviews. Only Dawson wrote and published more articles in the *Dublin* than did Williams during his own tenure.[8] The second issue was equally telling in Dawson's desire to publish the best, regardless of the thinker's personal or subjective Christian views, as it had articles penned by novelist and social critic George Bernanos, who had not supported Franco, a crucial and controversial issue of the day among English Roman Catholics;

---

[5]Dawson to Alan Tait [Allen Tate], via his publisher in New York, G. P. Putnams' Sons, April 26, 1940, in Box 14, Folder 45, UST/CDC.

[6]Dawson, "Editorial Note," 2–3.

[7]Dawson to Allen Tate, August 27, 1940, in Box 14, Folder 45, UST/CDC.

[8]See *To Michal from Serge: Letters from Charles Williams to His Wife, Florence, 1939–1945*, Roma A. King, ed. (Kent, OH: Kent State University, 2002), 61–62, 69, 73, 78. Williams does not seem to have thought very highly of Dawson, but he did appreciate the *Dublin*. Further, even within the Inklings, Williams was a controversial figure. J. R. R. Tolkien, for example, thought little of his theological views, referring to him as the "witch doctor." See Bradley J. Birzer, *J. R. R. Tolkien's Sanctifying Myth: Understanding Middle-Earth* (Wilmington, DE: ISI Books, 2002), 52–53.

Jacques Maritain, who had already declared himself a man of the Left and a person of whom Dawson had intellectual apprehensions; E. I. Watkin, a blatant and outspoken Pacifist; and Barbara Ward, a friend of Dawson's, associate editor of the journal, and a woman suspected of leftist leanings.

From his first issue, though, Dawson encountered considerable difficulties, not only from his associates, but also from the publisher, Douglas Jerrold, who seemingly considered Dawson too soft on the political and cultural left and too sympathetic to Protestants and Protestantism. On the former, Speaight explained in his autobiography that Jerrold "was still fighting the Spanish Civil War," and articles by well-known critics of Spanish General Franco, such as those by George Bernanos and Jacques Maritain, greatly angered him.[9] Barbara Ward wrote to Dawson regarding this problem in the spring of 1942. "I think Jerrold is being wretchedly tiresome and probably wants to squeeze us out one way, having failed the other," she complained. "It is all very well for him to say that there are all these good Catholic writers—a) I don't think they are awfully good, and b) they don't always write."[10] To alleviate the problem, Cardinal Hinsley intervened by asking Father Martin D'Arcy, one of Dawson's oldest friends, to serve as an informal censor over non-Catholic submissions.[11] Dawson was assured, though, that he would still maintain "control over editorial policy," having agreed, voluntarily, to "submit non-Catholic articles to D'Arcy for approval."[12] Another friend of Dawson's, Manya Harari, talked with Bishop David Mathew and Cardinal Hinsley on Dawson's behalf in the summer of 1942. "David is, of course, extremely keen on your full editorial independence," she assured Dawson, and "so is the Cardinal." Still, she admitted, the arrangement would most certainly prove itself unsatisfactory and would be, at best, a short-term solution. Dawson's and Jerrold's views of the world differed too greatly for any long-term relationship.[13]

Things became increasingly problematic for Dawson when Barbara Ward took an extended trip to America in late 1942. Ward asked Robert Speaight to take her place until she returned.[14] In what can only be called an attempt at a nasty editorial coup, Jerrold wanted to manipulate the situation to get rid of Ward, whom he considered too left in her cultural and political views. As soon as Ward left, he tried to appoint the temporary replacement Speaight as the permanent assistant editor. Jerrold's machinations shocked Dawson, and he quickly came to Ward's defense. "It seems to me out of the question to sack Barbara when she is out of the country and it is impossible to ascer-

---

[9]Robert Speaight, *The Property Basket: Recollections of a Divided Life* (London: Collins and Harvill, 1970), 220–21.

[10]Barbara Ward, London, to Dawson, May 14, 1942, in Box 15, Folder 175, UST/CDC.

[11]Ward, London, to Dawson, July 1, 1942, in Box 15, Folder 175, UST/CDC.

[12]Ward, London, to Dawson, July 8, 1942, in Box 15, Folder 175, UST/CDC.

[13]Manya Harari, London, July 28, 1942, in Box 14, Folder 86, UST/CDC.

[14]Ward, London, to Dawson, July 1, 1942, in Box 15, Folder 175, UST/CDC.

tain her view," Dawson wrote Speaight. "I understood that the arrangement was a purely temporary one to cover her time of absence and that she had discussed it with you before she left."[15] Speaight replied to Dawson a month later. "I have had long conversations with Hollis and Gerrold [Jerrold] and the basis of their worry about the 'Dublin' can be summed up in one sentence; that Barbara edits it and you don't."[16] Simply put, Barbara Ward was too left wing for the publishers, and Dawson gave her too much authority in editorial decisions, thus allowing her supposed leftism to seep into the journal. Jerrold must have assumed that Ward's influence accounted for the publishing of articles by the anti-Franco Jacques Maritain and George Bernanos. Dawson, however, continued to fight for Ward and for his own autonomy as the editor. "I don't think you quite recognize the divergence between myself and Jerrold on the question of policy," Dawson replied to Speaight a week later. "I have just had a further letter from him and it seems to me quite clear that he is determined that the Dublin should be the organ of his own rather die-hard type of conservatism."[17]

Arnold Lunn, the former editor of *The Dublin*, confided his views to Dawson. Jerrold, he assured Dawson, respected Dawson's intellectual integrity. Indeed, Jerrold "got quite lyrical about this subject at a cocktail party the other day, but he has a profound distrust of poor Barbara and thinks she is trying to turn the Dublin which should be a monument to Catholic scholarship into an" arm of the Labour Party. Further, Lunn admitted, Jerrold believed Ward's scholarship and intellectual abilities were trite and insignificant, and she "gives the DR an amateurish flavour." Then Lunn may have come to the exact problem. As much as Jerrold liked Dawson, he resented Dawson for not coming to see him and discuss editorial issues with him directly. Dawson, of course, was painfully shy. Jerrold, most likely, took this as an insult, assuming that Dawson did not think Jerrold's views worth considering.[18] As it turned out, though, Dawson held his ground on the Ward matter, and she was able to keep her position as long as Dawson did, until 1944.

The general problem of publishing works by non-Catholics or giving preference to Catholic authors became specific when an article on the famous distributist Eric Gill, once a good friend of Dawson's, landed on Dawson's desk in 1943. Dawson rejected it. Speaight was furious, threatening to resign his position. "For the last two or three years the Dublin Review has been full of articles and book reviews by contributors like Charles Williams and Gerard Hopkins and Peter Mayer, who are not Catholics at all." When,

[15]Dawson to Speaight, August 27, 1942, in Box 15, Folder 137, UST/CDC.

[16]Speaight to Dawson, August 30, 1942, in Box 15, Folder 137, UST/CDC.

[17]Dawson, Oxford, to Robert Speaight, September 5, 1942, in Box 15, Folder 137, UST/CDC. Dawson was complaining of his problems to other friends too. See, for example, Dawson, Oxford, to Dom Romanus, OSB, Kent, September 5, 1942, in Box 15, Folder 112, UST/CDC.

[18]Arnold Lunn, London, to Dawson, n.d., in Box 14, Folder 14, UST/CDC.

however, an article by a Catholic regarding a profoundly important Catholic arrived, Speaight claimed, Dawson rejected it. "If, however, you have decided to reject the article under any condition, I really don't feel that I can be of much more use to you on the editorial side," threatened Speaight.[19] Dawson expressed shock at Speaight's letter and threat. "I am not *standing* for editorial infallibility," Dawson explained, "but I think that the editor has a right to express an opinion on any article submitted and not have his opinions overridden without discussion."[20] Still, Dawson relented, accepting the article for the late 1944 issue of the *Dublin*.

Problems seemed to plague Dawson's editorial position almost from the beginning of his tenure. As early as the summer of 1942, Dawson was already regretting his decision to take over the *Dublin*, but he felt driven to promote the ideas of Western Civilization and Christian culture, and the *Dublin* provided the best venue.[21] In late 1943, he wrote a letter to Ward, describing his situation, wretched as he saw it. "Either you don't realise how bad it is or you have not grasped the effect it is bound to have on the ideas in the name of which both [the *Dublin* and the Sword of the Spirit] were launched. I am quite ready to give up either or both of them, if it is necessary (and it seems it will be necessary)," Dawson lamented, "but only if I can work for the same cause in some other way."[22] As Dawson saw it, despite his good will and best intentions, both Ward and Speaight had abandoned him. As proof of this, he had recently made two trips to London to see either of them, but neither had been available.[23]

To make matters even worse, Cardinal Hinsley died in the spring of 1943, and Dawson lost his most important protector. He seemed to be biding time, waiting for Jerrold to fire him, and Jerrold obliged him in late 1944. As Speaight put it in his memoirs, Jerrold "ousted Dawson from the editorial chair in a manoeuver that was anything but pretty."[24] Jerrold never officially consulted Dawson before firing him. Instead, Jerrold told Dawson simply that he wanted an editor who resided in London, not Oxford.[25] Dawson believed it had to do with what Speaight had told him earlier, that he had allowed Barbara Ward too much control over editorial policy. When Ward refused to defend Dawson against Jerrold in 1944, Dawson expressed feelings of betrayal.

---

[19]Speaight, London, to Dawson, Oxford, July 22, 1943, in Box 15, Folder 137, in UST/CDC. Speaight admitted in his memoirs, published in 1970, that the *Dublin Review* "had never, since Wilfrid Ward was in charge of it, been so good, and was never to be so again, as under" Dawson's leadership. See Speaight, *Property Basket*, 220.

[20]Dawson to Speaight, July 24, 1943, in Box 15, Folder 137, UST/CDC.

[21]Dawson to Speaight, August 27, 1942, in Box 15, Folder 137, UST/CDC.

[22]Dawson to Barbara Ward, December 5, 1943, in Box 15, Folder 174, UST/CDC.

[23]Ibid.

[24]Speaight, *Property Basket*, 221

[25]Dawson, Oxford, to Alexander Farquharson, February 6, 1945, in Box 14, Folder 127, UST/CDC.

"I refused to let him shove you out when he tried to do so in the previous year," Dawson complained to Ward. "But when he proceeded to do the same thing with me, I got no support from you and you simply broke off all communications."[26] Jerrold's reason may have had some merit. Certainly, he disliked the fact that Dawson refused to consult with him on editorial issues.

When Dawson explained the situation to Sheed, his friend offered little in the way of sympathy. Sheed later told his wife that Dawson first explained how Jerrold "had fired him from the Dublin: without notice . . . then he added bitterly, 'he expected me to go on editing it for six months.' I observed that this *was* notice." Upon which observation, Dawson "only fell into gloomy silence."[27]

Sheed, though, soon had his own run-in with Jerrold. "I think Jerrold is more than a little mad," he admitted to Maisie only a week later. "He told Connor quite casually at lunch that if I did not accept his proposal to hand over the London branch, he would be forced to start up in New York and smash us."[28]

Others were far more sympathetic to Dawson. Dawson's old friend and collaborator from the LePlay House, Alexander Farquharson, wrote a letter of considerable concern. "I deeply and sincerely regret the change," Farquharson wrote after noticing Dawson's name missing in the first issue of 1945. "I have read the Review regularly and with care during your editorship and cannot easily find words to say how much I have admired your conduct of the periodical and how greatly I have gained by studying it."[29] Calming though they were, Farquharson's words failed to alleviate Dawson's discomfort at being fired. Jerrold's action and the reactions of Sheed and Barbara Ward only confirmed for Dawson that he was doing little for the cause of Christendom, and that he, indeed, had little to give.

The Sword of the Spirit

"The extremes of Right and Left among Catholics are disastrous to the essential cause. Because we are Catholics we must be loyal and reasonable patriots. If the Latin Catholic Bloc is against our country we are against that Bloc because it is setting up a false principle—i.e. exaggerated nationalism—against true loyalty to Fatherland," Roman Catholic Cardinal Hinsley, Dawson's ally in the *Dublin* fiasco, had written to him in 1940. "We must insist on the one thing necessary—to resist the philosophy of racialism, of class hatred, [or anything that desires] to dominate and enslave." Therefore, the Cardinal continued, "I

---

[26]Dawson, Oxford, to Barbara Ward, November 3, 1945, in Box 15, Folder 174, UST/CDC.

[27]Frank Sheed to Maisie Sheed, November 17, 1944, in Box 1, Folder 6, ND/CSWD.

[28]Sheed to Maisie, November 24, 1944, in Box 1, Folder 6, ND/CSWD.

[29]Alexander Farquharson, London, to Dawson, February 5, 1945, in Box 14, Folder 127, UST/CDC.

rely on your help in the crusade of 'The Sword of the Spirit.'"[30] Thus began one of the most important movements of Dawson's life. To wage war against the Axis powers better and for the right reasons, the organization known as the Sword of the Spirit attempted to unify Catholic and Protestant Christians in England, America, and continental Europe. Two things had inspired Cardinal Hinsley to form the movement. The first inspiration came from the Christmas 1939 papal call for a new Crusade, "to bring men back from the broken cisterns of national interest to the fountain of Divine Justice" and to promote a new and international understanding of the natural law.[31] "Every great civilization has upheld the Natural Law—Tao, the way of heaven; Rita, the law; Dike, the norm," the secretary of the organization, Barbara Ward, explained in 1942. "These are different ways in different civilizations of expressing the fundamental belief that unless men and institutions follow the pattern which exists for them outside space and time in the mind of God, then tragedy not only will but must result, for to violate the law of one's nature is to wound that nature, perhaps unto death."[32] The new nationalisms focused on particulars, rather than universals. Some nationalisms are based on class, some on conquest, some on race, but none on the universality of human nature. Ward's arguments strongly reflected those developed by Dawson in his 1929 *Progress and Religion*. They also anticipated C. S. Lewis's arguments in *The Abolition of Man* and the thought of Pope Benedict XVI throughout much of his career as Cardinal.[33]

In addition to being inspired by the Pope's call for a new crusade in 1939, Dawson had also inspired the Cardinal to create the movement through his first article as editor of the *Dublin Review*, entitled "Democracy and Total War."[34] Published nine months after the invasion of Poland, the article discussed the possibility of the fall of the West, especially if Britain and France, the "two eastern pillars of Atlantis," were broken.[35] What Dawson meant by "Atlantis" is unclear, though he was clearly viewing the West in mythical terms. Further, Dawson explained, the totalitarian powers—Russia and Germany—were fighting not just against men, but against the very basis of western culture, the Christian religion. "Total war respects none of these things and leaves no spiritual value intact," Dawson wrote. "It treats religion itself as

---

[30] Archbishop Hinsley, London, to Dawson, July 20, 1940, in Box 14, Folder 169, UST/CDC.

[31] Barbara Ward, "'Sword of the Spirit' Crusade Is a Clear Call out of Chaos," *America*, vol. 67 (1942), 567.

[32] Ibid., 566.

[33] On Pope Benedict XVI's views on the natural law, see, for example, "Cardinal Ratzinger in Cambridge," *Canadian C. S. Lewis Journal*, Summer 1988, 4–5.

[34] Hope, "Christopher Dawson's Warning," 3.

[35] Christopher Dawson, "Democracy and Total War," *Dublin Review*, vol. 207 (July 1940), 4. It is fascinating to note Dawson's use of mythology here. At roughly the same time, Tolkien was writing his own version of Atlantis in his Númenórean tales, and C. S. Lewis was busy incorporating Tolkien's version in his own Space Trilogy.

another weapon in its armoury." Further, the war itself reveals the darkest of powers, for "Hitler and his colleagues" are "its creatures, not its creators."[36] Here, Dawson reflected on the scriptural passages of St. Paul that Christians fight against "powers and principalities." Further, Dawson anticipated his arguments of the late 1940s in the Gifford Lectures. The Catholic Church, as Dawson believed it, had failed in its mission to sanctify fully the barbarianism it encountered and converted. It had become too lax, content with outward conversions rather than wrestling for the essences of things, cultures, and persons. "The spirit of the old gods was imperfectly exorcized by the sword," Dawson wrote, "and it has continued to haunt the background of the German mind." With such forces contending with one another, Dawson cautioned, the very essence of the West and its current democratic powers was threatened. The democracies needed to learn to "reconcile the needs of mass organization and mechanized power," Dawson believed.[37] Otherwise, the West, too, would succumb to the forces of the machine.

Taking its name from St. Paul's letter to the Ephesians (chapter 6, verse 17), the Sword of the Spirit launched officially on August 1, 1940, with Dawson as its vice president and intellectual touchstone.[38] The movement had four stated goals:

1. to fight for the natural and revealed law, "common to all mankind"

2. to fight until victory

3. to reconstruct Europe on Christian principles, after the war

4. to unite all Catholics in Great Britain in the common cause[39]

Dawson issued a profound statement of principles in the first issue of its bulletin.

> England and the whole world are passing through a terrible crisis. We are fighting not merely against external enemies but against powerful forces that threaten the very existence of our culture. And therefore it is vital that all the positive intellectual and spiritual forces of Western culture should come together in defence of their common values and traditions against their common enemies. It is here that Catholics have a special responsibility. They are not involved in the immediate issues of the conflict in the same way as are the political parties, for they belong to a supranational spiritual society, which is more organically united than any political body and which possesses an autonomous body of principles and doctrines on which to base their judgments. Moreover, they have an historical mission to

---

[36]Dawson, "Democracy and Total War," 5–6.

[37]Ibid., 12, 15.

[38]Frank Sheed, "The Sword of the Spirit," *Ecclesiastical Review*, vol. 107 (1942), 81–82.

[39]Reprinted in John C. Heenan, *Cardinal Hinsley* (London: Burns, Oates and Washbourne, 1944), 183.

> maintain and strengthen the unity of Western culture which had its roots in Chris-
> tendom against the destructive forces which are attempting its total subversion.[40]

Britain would serve its old and traditional function, the preservation of what is true, good, and beautiful in the classical and Christian tradition, and then re-convert Europe. Catholics in Great Britain would stand like Kings Arthur or Alfred, protecting the Church from the barbarian invasions. Once they had resisted the barbarian onslaught, they would then move like the great Anglo-Saxon monk, St. Boniface of Crediton, evangelizing the Germans. "Now we have come to the time of testing," Dawson wrote in September 1940. "We are all united in a common peril, and if we are to survive the test, we must be united in spirit also."[41] The true war, Dawson reminded his reading audience, is not for mere material. Instead, the Second World War was, for Dawson, a "battle for the possession of the human soul."[42] British Roman Catholics would provide the example of how to wage a true war. Through "prayer, study, and action," they would wield their weapons for a true Christian Culture, based on the virtue of love.[43] "A nation without religion is a nation without a soul; and England has not lost her soul," Dawson assured his readers. "We may not be a Christian nation in the full sense of the word, but this does not mean that we are not a people with a Christian inheritance which every Englishman has a right to share and a duty to defend."[44] Should Englishmen presume this mission an arrogant one? Of course not, Dawson answered. Instead, British and western history, as demonstrated by such figures as St. Boniface, had already shown the way. England's position was to hold firm and protect the culture of the West, awaiting the current tide of barbarism, and then proceed forth to convert the world yet again. "We are not forbidden to hope great things," Dawson answered. "What is condemned in the gospel is the short sighted cautious policy of the man who buries his money in the ground and refuses to take risks because God is such a strict master. But our God is a generous master who pays the late comer for a full day's work, who scatters His seed broadcast and takes His harvest where He finds it."[45] Therefore, the members of the Sword of the Spirit would "study the social teaching of the Church," Barbara Ward wrote, and use "every opportunity—through writing, meetings, discussion groups, pressure on local and national governments—to secure the recognition of the natural law and to dispel the darkness in men's minds."[46] Dawson's vision was the vision of

---

[40]Reprinted in Ibid., 183–84.

[41]Christopher Dawson, "The Mission of England," *The Sword of the Spirit*, no. 4 (September 21, 1940).

[42]Reprinted in Heenan, *Cardinal Hinsley,* 184.

[43]Reprinted in Ibid., and Sheed, "The Sword of the Spirit," 82.

[44]Dawson, "The Mission of England."

[45]Ibid.

[46]Ward, " 'Sword of the Spirit,' " 567; and Speaight, *Property Basket,* 219.

St. Augustine and Edmund Burke. The barbarians may be different, but the mission remained the same.

As a means to bolster the Sword of the Spirit movement, Sheed and Ward published Dawson's greatest work, *The Judgment of the Nations*, in 1942 in the United States and in 1943 in Great Britain. As Sheed assured his most famous author, "it will be the bible of the movement."[47] Sheed believed the book was timeless.[48] Writing to his wife, the publisher proved equally enthusiastic. It "contains the only possible principles that should be in the minds of post-war settlement-makers."[49] Certainly, it was the culmination and conclusion to Dawson's previous four anti-totalitarian books. According to E. I. Watkin, Dawson never again changed his views—on politics or culture—after writing *The Judgment of the Nations*.[50]

Dawson also found it one of his most difficult books to write, and it took all of his intellectual power as well as the editorial skill of Frank Sheed to complete it. Sheed had first suggested the book to Dawson, almost immediately after the invasion of Poland. "I am more convinced than ever that the book which only you can do is the one I suggested—on the arrangement of peoples that should follow victory supposing the victory comes our way," Sheed had originally told Dawson. Without it, Sheed continued, the post-World War II world would greatly resemble the post-World War I world, with a "new un-equilibrium leading to a new war."[51] Without Christian direction, Sheed believed, the world would continue to sink into a soft and meaningless liberalism, ruled by secular nation-states, concerned only with power and Machiavellian politics, and giving lip-service to humanitarianism.

Judgment proved an immense struggle for Dawson as well as for Sheed. Sheed described the process to his wife in a somewhat brutal fashion. "Dawson has presented me with some fifteen articles he has written since the war, all of them superb." Dawson, however, had no idea how to combine them, and, therefore, simply wanted to publish them as a collection of disparate essays. "I knew that this would damn them from the start," Sheed feared.

> The problem was to find a plan which would make them chapters in a book. It meant making a full written analysis of each of them trying a sort of jig-saw puzzle to fit them into one picture. Finally it worked: a few bits transferred from one essay to another, a few bits cuts out, a few gaps where linking paragraphs must be written, and a preface which I outlined for him.

When Sheed handed Dawson the edited product, "he said 'Ah!'; no, on second thoughts he said 'Ah'—without the exclamation mark." And, then, in

---

[47] Sheed, London, to Dawson, August 22, 1941, in Box 11, Folder 7, UST/CDC.

[48] Sheed, London, to Dawson, October 10, 1941, in Box 11, Folder 7, UST/CDC.

[49] Sheed to Maisie, February 7, 1942, in Box 1, Folder 5, ND/CSWD.

[50] E. I. Watkin, "Reflections on the Work of Christopher Dawson," *Downside Review*, vol. 89 (1971), 9.

[51] Sheed, London, to Dawson, September 29, 1939, in Box 11, Folder 5, UST/CDC.

total exasperation to his wife, Sheed concluded, "What a man."[52]   Though
the ideas were Dawson's, one should certainly credit the organization and the
presentation of the ideas to Sheed. The process of producing the book jointly
continued for several days. Towards the conclusion of the project, Dawson
suddenly expressed paranoid fears to Sheed about those he believed resented
him and did everything in their power to attenuate his own influence. "He is
profounder, brillianter [sic], and battier than ever," Sheed wrote to his wife,
Maisie. "He's convinced that Pressure Groups are working secretly against
him—this emerged on the last morning while I was snatching an early breakfast before getting an early train. To hear all this from a bearded man smiling
sombrely [sic] and without his teeth (for in the excitement of my going he
had forgotten to insert them) was macabre in the extreme." Still, Sheed admitted, Dawson may have been at his greatest point, intellectually, as the two
worked out the final form of *Judgment*. "Fortunately, his battiness never affects his writing," Sheed concluded to his wife, "which convinces me that it is
to a large extent an act he's putting on."[53] While it might certainly have been
an act, as Sheed suspected, it might also have been legitimate psychological
depression. Dawson, after all, has been battling it most of his adult life. And
while a divinely-oriented mission—such as the writing of *Judgment*, which
might very well become a guide for the post-war world—often gave Dawson
a sense of purpose, the sheer weight of the project and its goals might have
also depressed him. He may very well have thought himself inadequate for
such a task as re-forming the post-war world.

Indeed, given the tumultuous times and the labor that went into it, the
book also profoundly shaped Dawson's beliefs about the world—seemingly
for the last time, according to Watkin. Dawson's dedication in the English
edition reveals his own hopes and fears. "Four years have gone to the making
of this book—years more disastrous than any that Europe has known since the
fourteenth century. Small as it is, it has cost me greater labour and thought
than any book that I have written," Dawson admitted in a rare moment of
public openness. He then, tellingly, dedicated the book to those who still
believed in the possibilities and morality of Christendom, "to all those who
have not despaired of the republic, the commonwealth of Christian peoples,
in these dark times."[54] The western world, Dawson warned, slinks ever closer
to the abyss. An unholy combination of science on an inhumane scale, individualism, liberalism, corporate-capitalistic materialism, Soviet materialism,
and urbanization pushed and pulled the world increasingly closer to the creation of the mass, mechanized man. Once man is mechanized, he is one step
away from annihilation, Dawson feared. With mechanization, the soul is destroyed, but the body remains. But a body without a soul is a dead body. Such

---

[52] Sheed to Maisie, August 7, 1941, in Box 1, Folder 5, ND/CSWD.
[53] Sheed to Maisie, August 14, 1941, in Box 1, Folder 5, ND/CSWD.
[54] Dawson, "Foreword," in *The Judgment of the Nations* (New York: Sheed and Ward, 1942).

language may seem strange to twenty-first century ears, but Dawson's language grew increasingly apocalyptic throughout the book precisely because he feared that westerners of the near future would believe such language awkward if not outright embarrassing or idiotic. "The time is approaching when the cities become one city," Dawson wrote in the introduction to *The Judgment of the Nations*. It will be "a Babylon which sets its mark on the mind of every man and woman and imposes the same pattern of behaviour on every human activity."[55] This new conformity will disrupt and attenuate the natural and divine order of grace, in which each thing uniquely has its place, gifts, and purpose. One can effectively label all of these creeping, adulterating forces "progressivism," Dawson continued. They result from "the unloosing of the powers of the abyss—the dark forces that have been chained by a thousand years of Christian civilization and which have been set free to conquer the world." Together, these dark forces have "the will to power." The darkest forces first emerged in the French Revolution, and then re-emerged in the Soviet Union, spreading "westward, into the very heart of Europe." Many turn their hopes to democracy, Dawson noted. But it too often practices the "new black arts of mass suggestion and propaganda," Dawson feared.[56]

As in all times, Dawson claimed in true Pauline and Augustinian fashion, humanity wars with unseen powers, powers that surround, manipulate, and often dominate us.[57] Such powers and principalities use ideologies and totalitarian states as both their witting and unwitting tools. Certainly, Dawson believed, the Catholic should never expect an easy life. Such a thing has never been promised to him, and the true receiver of grace will almost necessarily suffer from spiritual attacks. One must wonder if Dawson was, at least in part, writing autobiographically here. After all, Dawson argued, "to the Christian the world is always ending, and every historical crisis is, as it were, a rehearsal for the real thing."[58] Some of the greatest men in western civilization have died at the hands of corrupt persons who have used the power of the state for their own disingenuous ends. "The Athenians killed Socrates and the Romans killed Cicero and the English killed Thomas More," Dawson wrote in 1946.[59] Such is the nature of government in a fallen world, the Augustinian Dawson concluded.

The only solution to the follies of the modern and ideological world of the twentieth-century, according to Dawson, is to re-consecrate the state as an arm of the Church, to sanctify the secular once again.[60] "Even the modern

---

[55] Dawson, *Judgment of the Nations*, 3.

[56] Ibid., 5, 8, 13, 16.

[57] Christopher Dawson, *Beyond Politics* (New York: Sheed and Ward, 1939), 122.

[58] Ibid., 129, 136.

[59] Christopher Dawson, "The Omnicompetent State," *Tablet* (1946), 98.

[60] Christopher Dawson, "Church, State, and Community: Concordats or Catacombs?" *Tablet* (1937), 910.

State, the new Leviathan, that 'King over all the children of pride,' is not irrelevant to the work of grace nor impenetrable to its influence," Dawson wrote. After all, Christianity is a historical religion, and God, through His Church, acts in history.[61] Guided by the Holy Spirit, the Church must take its role as the continuation of the Incarnation of the Body of Christ seriously and become militant. A militant Church and its worthy ally, a consecrated state, just might win the battle against the powers and principalities behind the dark forces of fascism. With the world rapidly collapsing into camps of ideologues and nationalists, with the average person mechanized, ignored, or destroyed, Dawson argued, western civilization could choose no other course. The defeat of totalitarianism, Dawson wrote, "depends in the last resort, not on the force of arms but on the power of the Spirit, the mysterious influence which alone can change human nature and renew the face of the earth."[62] Therefore, the fight will not be one of guns, but of all things spiritual, Dawson concluded, quoting St. Paul's discussion of "powers and principalities."

Still, just as legitimate democracy could easily transmute into corrupt mass democracy, the Church militant must avoid becoming the Church tyrannical. The ideological forces had already demonstrated the effectiveness of propaganda and mass control in various types of states, both democratic and non-democratic. The Church, tempted with such power to do good, must not succumb to the temptation and delusion of creating a religious mass man in its own image. In such a case, the Church would be directed by deluded and fallen will rather than by grace. "This is an impossible solution for the Christian, since it would be a sin against the Holy Ghost in the most absolute sense," Dawson wrote. "Therefore the Church must once more take up her prophetic office and bear witness to the Word even if it means the judgment of nations and an open war with the powers of the world."[63]

Citing the profound Anglo-Irish statesman and fellow Augustinian Edmund Burke as his authority, Dawson contended that some wars are necessary, especially if they are waged for kin, country, and God.[64] The best solution for the true Christian is to deny almost all human power over other persons, trusting to the Spirit to guide and animate life and culture. The real purpose of society and community is to allow the individual human person, made in the image of God, to use the gifts that the Spirit has distributed to each person uniquely and according to God's own will. Being singular in time and space, each person has a God-given and God-willed purpose. In the mystery of the gift of freedom, human will accepts God's grace, using the gift for the better-

---

[61] Dawson, *Beyond Politics,* 115, 127.

[62] Dawson, *Judgment of the Nations,* 147.

[63] Ibid., 155. See also his "What Is the Alternative to Totalitarianism?" *Christian News-Letter,* no. 107 (November 12, 1941).

[64] Dawson, *Judgment of the Nations,* 155–6. For Burke's influence on Dawson, see Mulloy, "Record of Conversation with Dawson, August 24, 1953," in Box 1, Folder 2, ND/CDAW.

ment of the community, and, ultimately, for the entire Communion of Saints, Christ's Army. To succumb to the temptation of power, to embrace the tools of the enemy, would mean the willful desecration and adulteration of God's economy of grace.[65] To make us equal and homogenous, is to make us less than what God intends us to be. Only through the acceptance of the grace of the Holy Spirit can the world witness "the birth of a true community which is neither an inorganic mass of individuals nor a mechanized organization of power, but a living spiritual order."[66] Western civilization must again accept the mystery of grace rather than nominal security and the supposed surety of the human will.

A return to Christendom along spiritual lines did not mean that religious and ethnic differences would somehow disappear or simply be erased. Instead, a Protestant would remain a Protestant, and an Irish Catholic would not become a German Catholic.[67] Indeed, through the organic nature of history and culture, such theological and ethnic differences should be celebrated rather than condemned and destroyed. Past differences should be forgotten and forgiven, recognizing that they merely served as wounds in the Body of Christ as well as exceedingly poor witnesses and examples to non-Christians and marginal Christians.[68] In this, as in many things, Dawson echoed the words of St. Augustine. "This heavenly city, then, while it sojourns on earth, calls citizens out of all nations, and gathers together a society of pilgrims of all languages, not scrupling about diversities in the manners, laws, and institutions whereby earthly peace is secured and maintained, but recognising that, however various these are, they all tend to one and the same end of earthly peace," St. Augustine wrote in Book 19 of the *City of God*. Additionally, the Church "is so far from rescinding and abolishing these diversities, that it even preserves and adapts them, so long only as no hindrance to the worship of the one supreme and true God is thus introduced."[69] Protestants, Catholics, and Orthodox alike should be allied in the basics of Christianity: the three Christian virtues as presented in St. Paul's first letter to the Christian peoples of Corinth; a belief in the natural law; and a reliance on the Holy Spirit to take such ecumenism further than human effort can. In an unpublished part of *The Judgment of the Nations*, Dawson wrote: "The more our religion rises above the level of human idea and human behaviour into the sphere of the supernatural and the divine, the nearer we come to the attainment of unity." The real loss of unity comes not from the divisions within Christendom of

---

[65]Dawson, *Judgment of the Nations,* 158–9; and his "The Threat to the West," *Commonweal,* vol. 21 (February 2, 1940), 318.

[66]Dawson, *Judgment of the Nations,* 160.

[67]Ibid., 170–78.

[68]Ibid., 162–3.

[69]St. Augustine, *The City of God,* trans. Marcus Dods (New York: Modern Library, 1993), Book 19, Chapter 17.

Roman Catholic, Protestant, and Eastern Orthodox, but from the secularization and humanization, improperly understood, of society itself. "The more we make our religion a human thing," Dawson argued, "the more deeply it is involved in the temporal, this worldly sphere, the more we lose the spirit of unity." Real schism, then, comes not from Protestants protesting Catholics or Catholics protesting the Orthodox, but "is the breach which results from the collision between the spirit of the age and the spirit of God."[70]

Still, Dawson noted, the West as a whole had several advantages in the war against the dark forces, and Catholics must recognize and use these. First, western society is at least twenty-five hundred years old and organic. The opposition had failed to destroy all traditions, Dawson believed, but instead merely perverted them and corrupted them. The present generation must uncover and employ the truth, as handed down for many, many generations. Second, the most evil of ideologues is not a creator, but merely a creature, originally made good but tainted by evil choices and overbearing human will. Hence, the tyrannical ideologue can be neither creative nor imaginative. He is merely derivative, a shadow of the true Enemy, himself just a creature, albeit a very powerful one within time. The greatest tool of the remnants of Christendom, then, is the Sword of the Spirit. Through the Holy Spirit, all things are possible, Dawson reminded his readers. "For the powers of the world, formidable as they appear, are blind powers which are working in the dark, and which derive their strength from negative and destructive forces," Dawson wrote. "They are powerless against that Spirit who is the Lord and Giver of Life."[71] All evil powers, themselves negations of the Good, are powerless against the most powerful force in the universe, the love of the Holy Spirit. The Holy Spirit, however, will never force Himself on any person. One must, therefore, ask for and accept the Holy Spirit's guidance. "I have been thinking continuously of the notion you threw out the last time we met of a book on the Holy Ghost—theology, spirituality, sociology, history," Sheed wrote to Dawson in 1944. "It seems pretty clear that only the Holy Ghost can renew the face of the earth, and it also seems that He tends to operate more intensively the more He is solicited; and [the] more we solicit Him, the more that we know of Him."[72] The relationship between humanity and the Spirit increases with prayer and trust.

Since the good relationship between the Spirit and humanity is not forced and automatic, the relationship, rather than progressing, can just as easily regress. This results when humanity ignores the grace and love of the Holy Spirit, or when it acts according to its own will. Consequently, according to Dawson's argumentation, the Sword of the Spirit movement failed for one simple reason (and many complex ones): what Dawson called the greatest

---

[70]Quoted in Scott, *A Historian and His World,* 150.

[71]Dawson, *Judgment of the Nations,* 222.

[72]Sheed, New York, to Dawson, Oxford, February 3, 1944, in Box 11, Folder 10, UST/CDC.

scandal in history, the scandal of the division of the Body of Christ. Both Sheed and Dawson knew that Catholics would need help from Protestants for the movement to be successful. "I've seen a good deal of Chris and have had hours of discussion about the Sword of the Spirit—the principal problem, of course, being the mode of collaboration with Protestants," Sheed wrote to his wife. "It seems to me inescapable that neither in England nor America can Catholics *alone* form the Social Order: therefore if we want a Christian social order we must persuade others to work with us, no matter what the difficulties."[73] Sheed did not need to worry about non-Catholics joining, for as the success of the movement soared in the first year, numerous Protestant denominations demanded to join. But soon after joining, jealousies and rivalries arose, with non-Catholic groups fearing that the Catholics were trying to co-opt them. To solve the problem, the Sword divided into several denominational groups, each having its own agenda. The Anglicans and Free Churches of Britain formed their own version of the Sword of the Spirit, known as the "Religion and Life Movement."[74] The two groups, it was decided, would meet once a year as a national committee. Energies that could have been used for fighting a common front flowed into the opposite, however: protecting one's turf. As early as the fall of 1941, Christian apologist and detective novelist Dorothy Sayers commented that "Dawson seems quite hopeless."[75] Half a year later, Dawson was blunt in his own correspondence about the issue of division. "I am very worried over the way things are going with the Sword of the Spirit, as shown, e.g., in the minutes of the last meeting," Dawson wrote in March 1942. "There seems to be a deadlock with everybody pulling in different directions, and I fear things will be worse now that the Cardinal is withdrawing from active leadership of the movement."[76] The tension between the Protestant and Catholic versions reached an irreparable breaking point at the June 1943 meeting, when a Protestant member needlessly endorsed the use of birth control and divorce, two exceedingly unnecessary points, since the object of the movement was to fight the Axis powers on Christian principles.[77]

There were other, more complex reasons as well. In his letters to his wife Maisie, Frank Sheed mentioned numerous problems. "The Sword of the Spirit fascinates me," he wrote in August 1941. "If only there were some first-rate people in it, or indeed some first-rate people anywhere. It's a mediocre moment."[78] Additionally, though Dawson could and did write the "bible of the

---

[73] Sheed to Maisie, July 24, 1941, in Box 1, Folder 5, ND/CSWD.

[74] Ward, " 'Sword of the Spirit,' " 567.

[75] *The Letters of Dorothy Sayers, Vol II: 1937–1943, From Novelist to Playwright*, Barbara Reynolds, ed. (New York: St. Martin's, 1997), 334.

[76] Dawson, Oxford, to Robert Speaight, March 17, 1942, in Box 15, Folder 137, UST/CDC.

[77] Michael J. Walsh, "Ecumenism in War Time Britain: the Sword of the Spirit and Religion and Life, 1940–1945, Part II," *Heythrop Journal*, vol. 24 (1982), 383.

[78] Sheed to Maisie, August 14, 1941, in Box 1, Folder 5, ND/CSWD.

movement," Sheed rightly understood that he was certainly the wrong man for any organizational, recruitment, or fund-raising activities. At one such recruitment meeting, Sheed complained that Dawson had said nothing. "I don't see how the Sword is to progress under a man who can't meet anybody," Sheed wrote. "Yet it needs his mind," the publisher conceded.[79]

There were also difficulties in getting America and Great Britain to cooperate. The American Christians feared looking as though they were riding the coattails of Englishmen. Catholics and Episcopalians in America "are prepared for some degree of collaboration (though only behind-scenes) and I have put them in touch," Sheed informed Dawson after an exploratory trip to the United States. "But they remain firmly of the opinion that America *cannot* adopt a movement, or at any rate the title of a movement, from England."[80] This seemed the final straw for Sheed. "I doubt if there's a lot of life left in the Sword of the Spirit movement," the publisher lamented.[81] Events proved Sheed right. It remained an organization in name only, having lost its vitality and its purpose only two years after the movement's genesis. With the death of its founder, Cardinal Hinsley, in the spring of 1943, the Sword of the Spirit died as well.

The Increasing Strain

As should be obvious from Sheed's letters to Maisie quoted above, he and Dawson were experiencing a very difficult time in their relationship. Reading their various letters from the late 1930s until the end of World War II, one gets the impression of nothing short of a roller-coaster relationship. Dawson's insomnia and health began to decline around 1936 for a variety of reasons. Certainly he was anxious to continue writing, and he seems to have had trouble doing so after 1935. Additionally, he had invested a considerable sum of money in the *Tablet* after Burns, being one of several owners, took it over in 1936. Bernard Wall "tells me that the situation of the Tablet is worrying Dawson horribly (he suspects that Dawson has put money into it)," Sheed wrote in 1937. "They all find it impossible to work with Burns. Wall thinks Burns is getting a little queer. He can't get him to talk: neither can others who used to be his intimate friends."[82] Then, there were the misunderstandings with Sheed and Ward over its role with *Colosseum*, *Essays in Order*, and *Europe*. Dawson also began to suspect that Sheed and Ward were not advertising his works effectively. In 1938, Dawson had complained that Sheed and Ward were treating his work as though "the book [*Religion and the Modern State*] has just been thrown on the market to take its own chance and that

---

[79]Sheed to Maisie, July 30, 1941, in Box 1, Folder 5, ND/CSWD.

[80]Sheed, New York, to Dawson, Oxford, February 18, 1942, in Box 11, Folder 8, UST/CDC.

[81]Sheed to Maisie, October 23, 1942, in Box 1, Folder 5, ND/CSWD.

[82]Sheed to Maisie, February 3, 1937, in Box 1, Folder 5, ND/CSWD.

the firm has not taken any life interest in it." Even worse, "They have treated it rather in the way that books published at the authors [sic] expense are often said to be treated."[83] Sheed, the man who did more than anyone to promote his friend's work, was furious with Dawson. "You will find it hard to convince anyone really in the publishing game that you could have got better sales through some other publisher," Sheed replied to Dawson. "It is because of the sheer figures that we go on publishing for Noyes, Ronald Knox, Lunn, Martindale, Belloc, Chesterton—most of whom deal with us through pretty hard-boiled agents who have told me that our figures are better than other people's: we have never lost an author we wanted to keep."[84] Though Sheed seemed to have resolved the matter with Dawson, it arose again with the publication of *Beyond Politics*. "Hasn't something gone wrong with the advertising of it?" Bernard Wall asked Dawson, aghast. "No advert. in the T.L.S., none in the Observer, Sunday Times, Spectator: far too little even in the Cath. Herald and the Tablet! It is murder to a book, isn't it?" Murder? Perhaps, Dawson must have thought. Further, Wall continued, "I am certain lots of people don't even know you have published a book."[85] Wall's comments convinced him, and Dawson never fully trusted Sheed and Ward after the 1930s.

Dawson, however, was happy with Sheed and Ward's efforts for *The Judgment of the Nations*. "It has begun 1944 at a great pace," Sheed wrote happily to Dawson. "No previous book of yours ever sold as this one."[86] Indeed, the book did exceedingly well in sales as well as in influence of important persons. A person no less eminent than Clare Boothe Luce, for example, had declared that *The Judgment of the Nations* served as "her bible while she was in Congress."[87] Her husband, *Time* publisher Henry Luce, was also taken with it, and he demanded that his staff at *Time* magazine read it.[88] In response to all of the good praise, Sheed reported that Dawson was pleased with Sheed and Ward. Indeed, Sheed reported after a visit at Dawson's home that for once Dawson "was in excellent form, no complaints, brilliant comments on things."[89] The success of *Judgment* so pleased Dawson that he immediately wanted to begin a sequel, *The Twentieth Century: Cause and Cure*. Sheed could not remember a more joyous time he had ever spent with Dawson. Despite all of this, there was a dark side. Dawson "is very pleased with us, but with no other Catholic at all: or anybody else for that matter."[90] Sheed tried to ignore Dawson's vitriolic comments, and, instead, encouraged him to write

---

[83] Dawson to Sheed, April 4, 1938, in Box 11, Folder 4, UST/CDC.
[84] Sheed, London, to Dawson, Kilburn, 14 July 1938, in Box 11, Folder 4, UST/CDC.
[85] Wall, Paris, to Dawson, [February or March 1939], in Box 15, Folder 174, UST/CDC.
[86] Sheed, New York, to Dawson, February 3, 1944, in Box 11, Folder 10, UST/CDC.
[87] Sheed, London, to Dawson, Oxford, June 4, 1952, in Box 11, Folder 45, UST/CDC.
[88] Sheed, New York, to Dawson, Oxford [1942], in Box 11, Folder 8, UST/CDC.
[89] Sheed to Maisie Ward, July 14, 1943, in Box 1, Folder 6, ND/CSWD.
[90] Ibid.

a sequel to *Judgment*, basing it on strictly religious principles, rather than political ones.[91]

The good will between these two Catholic allies faltered quickly. When Sheed left England for several months, Dawson grew increasingly bitter with Sheed and Ward. When Dawson wrote to E. H. Connor, the director of the publishing firm in Sheed's absence, asking about sales and advertising figures, Connor replied tersely: "The real trouble is that owing to the fact that you have been unable to keep yourself before the Catholic public by writings, lectures and broadcasts they tend to forget you and the present demand for your books is very slight indeed." Further, Connor chided Dawson, he could only redeem himself by writing new books, keeping himself in the eyes and mind of the public.[92] Frustrated, Dawson then asked for a sales count on his books. Again, Connor lashed out at Dawson. "As for your not being aware of the position of your books, I should like to point out that this is revealed by the royalty statements rendered to you and does not call for any special comment on my part," he bitingly wrote to Dawson. "Quite apart from the fact that I have neither the staff nor the time to make detailed reports to authors at present."[93]

Even more frustrated, Dawson took on an agent, Mr. Kilham-Roberts of the London agency, The Society of Authors, to represent him. Dawson explained to Kilham-Roberts that Connor seemed to be "in complete control" of Sheed and Ward. "But it is a very disturbing one from my point of view as hitherto I have relied implicitly on Sheed and Ward and they have had my entire published work."[94] Further, Dawson contacted his friend and ally T. S. Eliot, asking for acceptance as a permanent author with his firm, Faber and Faber.[95] When Kilham-Roberts approached Sheed and Ward on behalf of Dawson, Connor rebuffed him. "I wrote two perfectly civil letters to Sheed & Ward enquiring tentatively about Mr. Sheed's future plans, and merely received a somewhat brusque note telling me in effect to mind my own business!" Kilham-Roberts reported to Dawson. "If Messrs. Sheed and Ward are under the impression they can treat the Society of Authors to rudeness of this kind, it is a poor look out for their authors, and it would seem to be high time that Mr. Sheed came back and put his house in order."[96]

---

[91]Sheed, New York, to Dawson, February 3, 1944, in Box 11, Folder 10, UST/CDC.

[92]E. Connor, London SHEED AND WARD offices, to Dawson, August 8, 1944, in Box 11, Folder 40, UST/CDC.

[93]E. Connor, London SHEED AND WARD offices, to Dawson, August 10, 1944, in Box 11, Folder 40, UST/CDC.

[94]Dawson, Oxford, to Mr. Kilham-Roberts, London, August 11, 1944, in Box 11, Folder 40, UST/CDC.

[95]Dawson, Oxford, to Mr. Kilham-Roberts, London, August 17, 1944, in Box 11, Folder 40, UST/CDC.

[96]Mr. Kilham-Roberts, Society of Authors, London, to Dawson, Oxford, September 28, 1944, in Box 11, Folder 40, UST/CDC.

When Sheed returned from Australia in the late fall, the reports from Connor disturbed him. "Talking of which, Chris sounds pretty hopeless. He obviously hasn't lifted a finger in a year and doesn't mean to," he wrote to Maisie. "I half feel that there are no more books coming from him. The aimlessness of his correspondence with Connor is unbelievable. The letters got nowhere and could get nowhere, yet I'm certain that after each he felt he had done a day's work."[97] Dawson, however, wrote to Sheed, immediately upon his return from Australia, hoping to clear up matters between himself and the firm.[98] Sheed, though, had just received terrible news himself upon his return to England. His son, Wilfrid, had become very ill, and it was soon discovered that he had polio.[99] Though in a terrible frame of mind, Sheed hoped to resolve quickly things with Dawson and decided to visit him in Oxford. He found a disgruntled Dawson when the two met. "Bad as today has been it is as nothing to yesterday; for yesterday I visited Christopher and it was rather worse than usual. When I left he was all smiling and I could barely crawl into the taxi," Sheed reported to Maisie. Dawson had drained Sheed of any good cheer he might have possessed. "But he began with complaints and I suggested instantly that he should get another publisher," Sheed admitted to his wife. "After a long pause he said this was impossible because of a wartime agreement among publishers not to bag each other's authors without each other's consent. But, said I, you have my consent. He then began to talk of his next book and made no more complaints against us, but only against everybody else."[100] Sheed's reverse psychology seems to have worked on Dawson, and the publisher traveled to Oxford again as soon as possible to meet with Dawson, still hoping to clear up matters between them.

> Christopher has quite a useful collection of essays. They are worth publishing as they stand, but they would not make a book, without the writing of some extra essays to fill in gaps in the outline. He has a thousand reasons why he should not write any extra essays. Again, the essays he has got would be universally more illuminating if he would develop and expand certain points in them. He won't do that either. I'd say he was now incurably lazy if I did not think there is a strong element of impotence. I feel sure he could not write a book now. I'm going down to Oxford again tomorrow to see what I can do. I sometimes think there is a streak of tenacity in me that no one suspects.[101]

Sheed tried to encourage him to take on a new project as quickly as possible. A "book on St. Paul would delight your admirers everywhere and, if I may venture an opinion, would give a better chance to your own special genius than any other subject I can think of," Sheed wrote hopefully. "We shall

---

[97] Sheed to Maisie, November 8, 1944, in Box 1, Folder 6, ND/CSWD.

[98] Dawson, Oxford, to Sheed, London, November 8, 1944, in Box 11, Folder 10, UST/CDC.

[99] Sheed, London, to Dawson, Oxford, November 9, 1944, in Box 11, Folder 10, UST/CDC.

[100] Sheed to Maisie, November 17, 1944, in Box 1, Folder 6, ND/CSWD.

[101] Sheed to Maisie, December 5, 1944, in Box 1, Folder 6, ND/CSWD.

be glad to pay an advance of 400 [pounds] for such a book."[102] To Maisie, Frank wrote that a biography of St. Paul would be, at present, the best use of Dawson's skills. "It's the sort of work that anyone who can do it should be doing it. The political and social orders are in a mess so irretrievable by any direct action upon them that the only thing is to double or quadruple or centuple work on the spiritual roots."[103]

To complicate matters, all of Dawson's paranoid suspicions seemed true when he received news that several members of the Roman Catholic hierarchy wanted to begin censoring his scholarship as heterodox. This was not the first time Dawson had encountered the censors of the Church. In 1930, the censor had almost stopped *A Monument to St. Augustine*. Again, when Sheed and Ward wanted to republish the 1920 edited work, *God and the Supernatural*, Dawson's essay "The Nature and Destiny of Man" caused a delay in the republication. " 'This higher life was of course not entirely absent . . . [It] dominate[d] the whole nature of man.' The meaning of this would appear to be that humanity before Christ was not *actually* endowed with sanctifying grace (the higher life), but only potentially," the censor had determined. "Nor is there anything in the context which allowed the reader to interpret the passage otherwise. The statement is untrue."[104] Dawson's closest friend, E. I. Watkin, had had numerous problems with the censors as well, and it had served as a bit of a tragic joke to the two of them.[105]

Now, in 1944, Dawson was attacked for his theological views as expressed in *The Judgment of the Nations*, and it drove him even further into depression. In late November 1944, Dawson's wife Valery secretly let it be known through friends that Sheed needed to visit Dawson as soon as possible. "Apparently he has been cast further into the doldrums by an article in the Clergy Review criticising some of the theology of his Judgment of the Nations followed by a demand from Archbp Griffin that such books in future be submitted for censorship," Sheed wrote.[106] The problem began the previous March, when Father Andrew Beck, although praising Dawson's ability to write and think, expressed serious reservations about Dawson's theology or, at the very least, Dawson's ability to explain his theology. The very fact that Dawson was brilliant worked against him, as it meant that he must be kept in check by the Church. "The whole of this part of Mr. Dawson's book is instinct with prophetic force, is so burningly sincere, and has so obviously been wrung from the author at the cost of intense effort, as a result of an overmastering sense

---

[102]Sheed, London, to Dawson, Oxford, December 15, 1944, in Box 11, Folder 10, UST/CDC.

[103]Sheed to Maisie, December 15, 1944, in Box 1, Folder 6, ND/CSWD.

[104]Enclosure to T. F. Burns' letter to Dawson, April 16, 1936, in Box 14, Folder 61, UST/CDC.

[105]On Watkin, see Magdalen Goffin, "Fighting under the Lash," *Downside Review*, vol. 113 (1995), 203–18; Frank Sheed to E. I. Watkin, Torquay, December 5, 1947, in Box 1, Folder 7, ND/CSWD; and E. I. Watkin to Frank Sheed, June 14, 1964, in Box 4, Folder 1, ND/CSWD.

[106]Sheed to Maisie, November 24, 1944, in Box 1, Folder 6, ND/CSWD.

of the doom of our time, that it must seem an impertinence to suggest doubts or to voice criticism," Beck wrote. However, "precisely because this is such a moving book, because its author's name carries so much weight, because there is so much in it which is true and fine and inspiring, there is a duty to underline expressions and suggestions which cause a certain uneasiness in the mind of a Catholic reader."[107]

First, Beck believed that Dawson never fully explained the difference between political and spiritual freedom, and, ultimately, was too soft on liberalism. Dawson had argued that liberalism, taken collectively, was a political philosophy that had inherited its ethics and morality from Christianity, but that it had disregarded the supernatural elements of Christianity. Beck thought otherwise. "One would rather say that the old Liberalism by-passed centuries of Catholic thought and went back to the Pelagian heresy and to the self-sufficiency of man to work out his own salvation," Beck argued.[108] Second, Dawson seemed extremely Protestant—especially Calvinist—in his understanding of Dispensationalism, that is, in his embracing too much of the Old Testament and the role of the prophets. Dawson "seems to think in terms of the former dispensation, where the vehicle of God's revelation and the work of the Spirit was a chosen people under a theocracy," Beck noted. "This theocratic sense was strong among the Puritans of the seventeenth century, and in the Wesleyan revival, and Mr. Dawson seems to have caught something of the same atmosphere with its deep moral earnestness."[109] Finally, in a footnote, Beck criticized Dawson for calling into question mistakes made by the Church. "He seems to suggest elsewhere (p. 125) that the Church may be unfaithful to its mission," Beck wrote. "Is it wrong to read into such expressions the possibility of a defectible [sic] Church?"[110]

While Dawson grew upset with Beck's review and privately wrote him a multiple page, six-point response, he was more upset with the results of the review.[111] Archbishop Griffin contacted Sheed and Ward, and "enquired whether the Nihil Obstat had been applied for as he was most concerned lest some mischief making person might place the whole matter before the authorities at Rome with a view to provoking a condemnation."[112] Dawson, already reeling from failures with the *Dublin*, the Sword of the Spirit, and his own depression, understandably sank even deeper into a mental morass. Dawson consulted Father D'Arcy about the matter. One of his oldest friends,

---

[107] Andrew Beck, "The Judgment of the Nations," *The Clergy Review*, vol. 24 (1944), 102.

[108] Ibid., 100.

[109] Ibid., 103.

[110] Ibid., 104.

[111] Dawson to Father Andrew Beck, April 10, 1944, in Box 14, Folder 39, UST/CDC.

[112] E. H. Connor, London, to Dawson, Oxford, March 22, 1944, in Box 11, Folder 40, UST/CDC.

D'Arcy encouraged him to ignore the Archbishop's letter and let the issue die quietly.[113]

In the meantime, Sheed's second in command, E. H. Connor, met with the Archbishop. The two reached an agreement, as Sheed and Ward promised the archbishop to be more careful in the future and to submit any questionable works to the censor.[114] Though the matter had been cleared up in April 1944, it still weighed heavily on Dawson at the end of that same year, especially as he contemplated writing a sequel to *The Judgment of the Nations*.[115]

Soon, on May 14, 1945, life would change dramatically, and Dawson would slowly begin to leave behind his decade-long depression. But in 1944, of course, he could foresee no such thing. He still felt himself a dinosaur. After all, where did a man such as himself fit into the world? In a letter to Wall, he explained: "There are (1) the dons (2) the scientists (3) the journalists (4) the Brain Trusts of various parties and groups (5) the men of letters," Dawson explained in a letter to Wall. "All these groups spill over into one another and the one which we always think about, the fifth, the men of letters is the weakest and the most disintegrated of the lot. In fact the man of letters only exists in so far as he gets a footing in one of the other categories."[116] He had no real place in the politicized, post-war world, he feared, a world that distrusted imagination and spirit, and embraced only mere fact and tangible reality. As early as 1939, he had already lamented in a personal letter that politics and political thought were dominating Catholic writing. "It seems to me that the humanities are getting edged out and I think it is a pity," Dawson wrote in a personal letter. "What I liked about Sheed & Ward in the old days was that one felt that one was cooperating in a genuine attempt to raise the level of English Catholic culture, even if it was not always successful or far seeing or adequately financed."[117] Even Sheed and Ward seemed to be embracing a less intelligent community of readers and authors, Dawson complained.[118] Sheed seems to have acknowledged this as well. In a speech given in 1959, Sheed explained that even during the height of the Catholic Literary Revival of the 1920s and 1930s, "we were not producing our own writers in sufficient numbers even in that pleasant time. The revival, in England anyhow, was strictly literary—there was no comparable outpouring of notable work by Catholics in painting or architecture." Instead, the revival was "mainly the work of the word-bearing intellect—not very much poetry or drama: the dominant poet of the period was the Catholic Gerard Manley Hopkins, but he was long dead."

---

[113]E. H. Connor, London, to Dawson, Oxford, March 21, 1944, in Box 11, Folder 40, UST/CDC.

[114]E. H. Connor, London, to Dawson, Oxford, April 26, 1944, in Box 11, Folder 40, UST/CDC.

[115]Sheed to Maisie, November 24, 1944, in Box 1, Folder 6, ND/CSWD.

[116]Dawson to Bernard Wall, August 30, 1944, in Box 15, Folder 174, UST/CDC.

[117]Dawson to Dom Christopher, July 29, 1939, in Box 14, Folder 65, UST/CDC.

[118]Sheed to Maisie, March 2, 1944, in Box 1, Folder 6, ND/CSWD.

As of 1959, he concluded, "We are at a pause in the production of first-rate Catholic writers."[119]

In a telling conversation with David Jones in 1942, Dawson complained that the Church herself was losing the moral imagination and embracing instead bureaucratic machinery and uniformity. Dawson "said that he found that Catholics, in his experience, since he became a Catholic, were getting far more, not less, 'institutional' (in the bad sense) and mechanical, so to say." Further, Dawson argued, the propaganda of the ideologues—or, at least the idea of propaganda—had infiltrated the Church. There were times in history that called for propaganda from the Catholics, but such times were exceedingly rare, and they should be followed by times that embrace the imagination. The "age of von Hugel, the 'belief' in the Holy Ghost, in the subtlety of where truth resides etc. seemed far away—and a belief in effecting things by organization and formulas etc. etc. (among Catholics) growing rather than lessening."[120] He complained again in 1946, in several letters to his long-time friend, Bernard Wall, who wanted to found a new journal to follow up on the efforts of *Order* and *Colosseum*. Wall had hoped that Dawson would join him again. To Wall's queries, Dawson wrote, "One has to face the fact that there had been a kind of slump in ideas during the past 10 years." Instead of thinking creatively, intelligent men had turned to realism, science, and politics to explain everything. "There is not only a positive lack of new ideas but also a subjective loss of interest in ideas as such."[121] A few weeks later, Dawson wrote on the same topic, lamenting the rise of politics in all areas of thought. "There is a terrible dearth of writers and of ideas at present, and even in France, things are not too good, judging from the little I have seen." The old Catholic Republic of Letters seemed to have collapsed, according to Dawson. "Italy has been unproductive for a long time, and I know nothing of what is happening in other countries," Dawson continued. "Politics seem to be swamping everything and the non-political writer becomes increasingly uprooted and helpless." Nothing in the world can improve if writers focus only on the sterile subject of politics, Dawson argued. The world "won't improve without new blood and new ideas and I don't see at present where these are to be found."[122]

Imagination was vital to Dawson, as it had been to Edmund Burke. It was a gift from—and allowed one to connect to—the Holy Spirit, to see something beyond the physical appearance of a thing. The Church "has always

---

[119]Frank Sheed, "I am a Catholic Publisher," *Westminster Cathedral Chronicle* (September–October 1959), 137.

[120]René Hague, ed., *Dai Greatcoat: A Self-Portrait of David Jones in His Letters*, René Hague, ed. (London: Faber and Faber, 1980), 120.

[121]Dawson, Oxford, to Wall, London, August 26, 1946, in Box 15, Folder 174, UST/CDC.

[122]Dawson, Oxford, to Bernard Wall, London, September 9, 1946, in Box 15, Folder 174, UST/CDC.

used imagination as the normal means of transforming a notional assent into a real one," Dawson explained in 1946.[123] If the Church lost the ability to embrace and encourage the imagination, the venerable institution itself might become a tool of rigidity and oppression, Dawson feared. Should the Church lose its ability to imagine, especially in the art and expressions of the liturgy of the mass, the Catholic laity would suffer and turn to mechanical pleasures. "With the imagination being kicked out of the church," man "is forced to take refuge in the cinema." Ultimately, Dawson argued, the theologian must also be a poet, or his theology "may become nothing more than the application of logic to a series of dogmatic propositions."[124] All great theologians, Dawson argued, had always been endowed with the poetic imagination. Indeed, one of the most important gifts offered by the Holy Spirit is the gift of creativity and imagination. "It is the nature of grace to be gratuitous, prevenient, and creative," Dawson wrote in 1955. "In this, it only carries on the process of natural creation."[125] The human person, made as *Imago Dei*, must also act as a creator, but only to glorify God and creation. Only by allowing the Holy Spirit to work old truths into new forms, what Newman called the "illative sense" and what T. S. Eliot called the "moral imagination," could the world hope to overcome the madmen, their visions and their massacres. Only the Transcendent and a proper understanding of the economy of grace can renew the earth. "It is a creative spiritual force," Dawson wrote, "which has for its end nothing less than the re-creation of humanity. The Church is no sect or human organization, but a new creation—the seed of the new order which is ultimately destined to transform the world."[126] Importantly, imagination "becomes a channel of the life of the spirit like the other powers of the soul."[127] The creativity of the Spirit, alone, will save civilization before it succumbs to self-destruction.[128]

There was only one possible solution, Dawson believed, though it would be exceedingly difficult to implement. "If one could meet this difficulty by producing a group of brilliant new writers who would make an immediate impression on public opinion, that would be the ideal solution."[129] As with imagination, ideas were becoming mere propaganda, mechanized, and, there-

---

[123]Dawson, Oxford, to Frank Sheed, London, July 28, 1946, in Box 11, Folder 12, UST/CDC. See also Christopher Dawson, "The Future of National Government," *Dublin Review* (1935), 250.

[124]Dawson, Oxford, to Frank Sheed, London, July 28, 1946, in Box 11, Folder 12, UST/CDC.

[125]Dawson, "Memorandum," dated August 1, 1955, in Box 1, Folder 15, ND/CDAW; and his *The Historic Reality of Christian Culture: A Way to the Renewal of Human Life* (London: Routledge and Kegan Paul, 1960), 17.

[126]Christopher Dawson, "Christianity and the New Age," in *Essays in Order,* Christopher Dawson and Tom Burns, eds. (New York: Macmillan, 1931), 227.

[127]Dawson, Oxford, to Frank Sheed, July 28, 1946, in Box 11, Folder 12, UST/CDC.

[128]Dawson, *Historic Reality of Christian Culture,* 93.

[129]Dawson, Oxford, to Bernard Wall, London, September 9, 1946, in Box 15, Folder 174, UST/CDC.

fore, no longer really ideas. Politics—with a rigid left and right—was quickly replacing poetry as the language of humanity.

Meanwhile, the imagination failed internationally, or so Dawson thought. As he watched the Sword of the Spirit collapse, he saw that, consequently, World War II ended much as the first world war had, with an attempt to establish a world order based on liberal international order and power. Each post-war solution fatally ignored the higher Christian, spiritual principles. To make matters worse, the so-called liberal international order included as one of its protectors Josef Stalin. For a variety of reasons, though, Dawson wrote, the men creating the United Nations were doing so with more trepidation than had the men who had fashioned the League of Nations. Without a solid foundation of "common principles of international law and common conceptions of justice and truth," based on a universal understanding of the natural law, the international order will become a mere contest of power with a lowering of "ideals to the level of what is called political realism."[130] As it stood then, Dawson feared, the men at Dumbarton Oaks, formulating the United Nations, embraced "entirely positivist and utilitarian" principles and hoped to create a new world with a "sort of international social contract."[131] This, Dawson believed, would only lead to a repetition of the follies of the League of Nations.

In a private letter, Dawson added several other concerns. "History shows that there are two dangers which a concert of this kind has to meet," he claimed. First, there always exist unpredictable "revolutionary movements from outside the system." Nazism arising out of the failures of World War I and liberal nationalism arising out of the Holy Alliance provided two such examples, Dawson contended. What other unforeseen things—possibly even unimaginable to contemporary men—lurked behind the scenes? Additionally, he asked, why should all of the five powers on the Security Council agree with one another? What if the Soviets and the United States, for example, decide they have different goals for the world?[132] If so, would they simply divide the world into two materialist powers—one communist and the other capitalist—vying for control? Dawson had feared such a possibility throughout the 1920s and 1930s. Now, such a Manichean division seemed imminently possible. If so, the U.S. and the U.S.S.R. would focus their own respective strategies on numbers and weapons, geographical troop replacement, and resource control, what was becoming known in the post-World War II world as *realpolitik*. What would happen to the ideals, principles, rights, and duties that made western civilization? What would happen to nobility in a world of numbers? If one worried only about the material aspect of things, how could

---

[130]Christopher Dawson, "Dawson Makes Plea for Common Principles," *Los Angeles Tidings*, May 4, 1945, 1.

[131]Ibid., 15.

[132]Dawson, Oxford, to Richard O'Sullivan, November 8, 1944, in Box 15, Folder 83, UST/CDC.

another 300 warriors ever hold off—even if only for days—100,000 invaders at a new Gates of Fire? What would happen to the diversity once so celebrated by St. Augustine? The answer seemed clear: it would be mechanized and stamped into conformity with one of two materialist powers.

By the late 1940s, Dawson believed two things were necessary if the West was to survive. First, he believed that the world, devoid of imagination, had totally forgotten the principles of Christendom and western civilization. In his personal notes, he wrote:

> What is Europe? Not a geographical expansion, not a racial unity, but a spiritual community. It is a dynamic tradition of thought and life which has been transmitted from people to people from land to land through the ages for nearly 3000 years. It began almost outside geographical Europe on both sides of the Aegean and then it has passed slowly westward and northward, until finally it passed the ocean and became the organizing principle of a new work. Europe has never been a static self sufficient unitary culture like the great civilizations of the ancient east. Multiplicity and change are its essence. The oriental civilizations have been like pyramids standing powerfully and heavily in the same foundations, seemingly built for eternity but slowly eaten by the erosion of time. But the West is always building afresh in new foundations, and changing its form and content in every age, yet for all that preserving spiritual continuity.[133]

Second, Dawson believed that the Christendom could only be rebuilt through education. To these two things—imagination and education—Dawson dedicated the remainder of his professional life.

---

[133]Dawson, ["What is Europe," 1940s], in Box 9, Folder 22, UST/CDC.

Chapter 6

Recovering the West:
Programs in Christian Culture

1945–1962

ON MAY 14, 1945, W. A. FLEMING, THE DEPUTY SECRETARY OF THE UNIVER-
sity of Edinburgh, wrote a letter to Dawson that would change his life, gradually pulling him—perhaps permanently, the records seem to indicate—out
of his ten-year depression. "I have the great pleasure in informing you that
the Senatus Academicus at their meeting on 11ᵗʰ May unanimously approved
the recommendation of their Gifford Lectureship Committee," Fleming wrote,
"that you should be invited to undertake the Lectureship for the two years,
1946–47 and 1947–48, and I now convey that invitation to you."[1] This was
certainly the most prestigious honor Dawson had ever received, for it lent academic credibility to all for which he had worked in his life. And, "then on to
Christopher," Frank wrote to Maisie in 1945. "I'd been there a couple of hours
of heavy silences broken by short gloomy phrases, when he mentioned quite
casually that he had been asked to do the Gifford Lectures for *two* years—
the first English Catholic to get the appointment (Gilson is the only other
Catholic): each year he does 10 lectures (2 a week for five weeks) and for
each year he pouches 900 [pounds]." Sheed was excited, even if Dawson was
not yet. "The whole prospect seemed to weigh his spirits beyond bearing.
Anyhow it settles the question of his next two books, and with no trouble for
me. The Good Lord Gifford and me never before able to find a satisfactory
translation of *deus ex machina*. Two books in two years: whew!"[2]

The realization of the honor, rather than the burden that it offered, came
over Dawson very slowly. "I had a thoroughly agreeable day with the Chrisses

---

[1]W. A. Fleming, Edinburgh, to Dawson, Oxford, May 14, 1945, in Box 15, Folder 168,
UST/CDC.

[2]Sheed to Maisie, July 16, 1945, in Box 1, Folder 6, ND/CSWD.

[the Dawsons] yesterday," Sheed noted two months later. "Chris was in his best mood, we had a long walk in the woods."[3] Dawson told Sheed about his ideas for the proposed Gifford lectures. He would first offer his most thorough examination of culture and its relation to theology, history, and the natural law. While rooted in historical reality, it would be somewhat abstract in its analysis. Second, he would discuss the role of religion in the rise of European culture. While rooted in theory, this set of lectures would be somewhat concrete in its analysis. The honor had begun to sink in, and the burden became a joy, for by the end of August, 1945, Dawson seemed much better. He appeared, at least briefly, to have found purpose again. "My visit to Dawson was agreeable once he got used to my being there (it took a frigid quarter hour) he began to be something like his old self," Sheed wrote. "He talked brilliantly, dropping in on all sorts of odd corners of history."[4] And, two weeks after that, Frank reported that he and Dawson had talked late into the night. Dawson "was in good conversational form: indeed there was an air of cheerfulness in the house." Dawson's wife had even "addressed Chris as 'darling.'" Still, Sheed worried. "The only fly in the ointment was that Christopher 'finds it very hard to work with no one to consult.'" Sheed did not accept Dawson's explanation, considering this a worn excuse. "What he means is that it's so long since he worked on a book that he's all but lost the Knack."[5]

Health problems soon plagued Dawson as he attempted to write his Gifford lectures. This time erysipelas—a bacterial skin infection popularly known as "St. Anthony's Fire"—plagued him. He "had a white bandage on his head covering the outbreak on his forehead," Sheed explained to Maisie, "and his nose was all swollen, broadening his face considerably."[6] By the summer of 1946, insecurities and anxiety plagued Dawson again, to the point of rendering him intellectually impotent. Anxious, he decided to resign the Gifford fellowship, but sent a feeler to his friend, John Baillie, a professor at Edinburgh, first. "I am sorry to say that my work for the Gifford Lectures has not been going well, and I fear that I shall not be able to deliver them," Dawson explained. Still, he offered Baillie some hope. "However I thought that I would write to you confidentially before I take any steps to send my resignation to the committee." Dawson claimed himself inadequate for the task of the two sets of lectures. "The fact is that for many years now I have been out of touch with philosophical studies and with the currents of philosophical thought in the universities and I have found it much harder than I expected to recover contact." Dawson claimed to "see no present hope of completing

---

[3]Sheed to Maisie, August 5, 1945, in Box 1, Folder 6, ND/CSWD.
[4]Sheed to Maisie, August 31, 1945, in Box 1, Folder 6, ND/CSWD.
[5]Sheed to Maisie, September 15, 1945, in Box 1, Folder 6, ND/CSWD.
[6]Sheed to Maisie, January 28, 1946, in Box 1, Folder 7, ND/CSWD.

the course, even the first part of it, in time for the coming university year."[7]
Professor Baillie replied with relative equanimity, noting that should Dawson
fail to give the lectures, they would remain unfilled. He elaborated:

1. I believe the Gifford Committee would agree to your giving all the lectures in
   the second of these years, if necessary, i.e. eighteen months or more hence.

2. Rather than resign the whole lectureship, you might (if you feel you must)
   ask to be allowed to give only one course of the lectures—resigning from
   the other half of the appointment. I believe the Committee would agree to
   this, however sorry they would feel that we were not going to [hear] more
   of you.

3. The outline you sent me some time ago was so largely historical in nature
   that neither Kemp Smith nor I can see that it would be necessary for you
   to come to terms with quite recent developments in philosophical theology,
   especially with such books as Farrer's *Finite and Infinite*. The course you
   suggested was on 'Religion and Culture', Part I being 'Phenomenological' and
   Part II purely historical—'the Religious Development of Western Culture.'[8]

Dawson sent what he had outlined and written thus far on the lectures
to Baillie, and Baillie quickly approved. This assurance, plus the delaying
of the appointments to the 1947–48 and 1948–49 school years, proved the
keys to Dawson's ultimate acquiescence to the project. He spent the next six
months writing the first set of lectures. When Sheed visited Dawson in the
winter of 1947, he wrote: "Saturday's visit to Dawson went admirably: he is
in great form. Has nearly finished his Gifford Lectures: the whole Dawson
family cheerful."[9] Dawson gave the completed lectures, in manuscript form,
to Sheed in January, 1948, and was "getting on well with the second lot."[10]
Dawson delivered the first set of lectures in late spring 1947, and the second
set in the fall of 1948.[11]

The Gifford Lectures represented the culmination of Dawson's work to this
point in his life, and they also revealed his post-war return to the fundamental issues of culture and history rather than politics and ideologies. Dawson
would continue to deal with the latter for the remainder of his writing career,
to be sure, but the question of culture and how to recapture a form of Christendom dominated most of his remaining thoughts, works, and—strangely
for Dawson—even his actions. Tellingly, the first set of lectures dealt with the
question of natural theology and the natural law, explored in detail in Interlude I of this work. Sheed and Ward published the set as *Religion and Culture*
in 1949. The second set of lectures returned to the themes first presented

[7] Christopher Dawson, Oxford, to John Baillie, Edinburgh, June 7, 1946, in Box 14, Folder 36,
UST/CDC.

[8] Baillie, Edinburgh, to Dawson, Oxford, June 11, 1946, in Box 14, Folder 36, UST/CDC.

[9] Sheed to Maisie, February 3, 1947, in Box 1, Folder 7, ND/CSWD.

[10] Sheed to Maisie, January 12, 1946, in Box 1, Folder 8, ND/CSWD.

[11] Christina Scott, *A Historian and His World: A Life of Christopher Dawson* (New Brunswick, NJ:
Transaction, 1992), 154.

in Dawson's 1932 historical book, *The Making of Europe,* and Dawson continued to identify the role of the Christian religion as the basis of European history. While Christianity did not give birth to the West, it did give birth to one of the most important manifestations of the West, Europe. Sheed and Ward published the second set of Gifford Lectures as *Religion and the Rise of Western Culture* in 1950, and an analysis of its significance to Dawson's overall thought can be found in Interludes I and II.

The Makers of Christendom

With the failure of the Sword of the Spirit in the mid-1940s, Dawson believed that the West was collapsing rapidly. Though the Allies were conquering the Axis powers militarily, they were failing to re-energize the true spirit of the West. Having lost the power of imagination, the West would prove itself little better off than a more benign version of the remaining totalitarian ideologues. Liberalism and secularism, rather than Christianity, emerged triumphant. To worsen the situation, the Soviet Union no longer lingered in the background, proclaiming itself the future of democracy. Instead, it was becoming intensely aggressive, finally revealing its true colors to the world. The costs of World War II and the Spanish Civil War, prior to it, had "such a distracting and disintegrating influence on Catholic writing on the continent." In other words, the Catholic writers between the two wars—especially men such as Romano Guardini and Jacques Maritain—were those keeping alive the true spirit of the West. In the era immediately following World War II, the great Catholic thinkers, poets, and scholars were distracted, and the West suffered immeasurably for these sins of omission.[12] "At the present time I do not know where we are to look for the new centres of life and activity," Dawson lamented. "The problem is as much a religious one as a literary one, but it seems to me that the present religious tendency is to look for a solution to intensive organization and specialized activities which are apt to end in a cul de sac."[13] What was needed, Dawson wrote elsewhere, "is not the current contemporary literature which is likely to be ephemeral, but the outstanding achievements of the pre-war period which represent something permanent."[14] The publication of these important texts could bring together the great religious thinkers of all European cultures and nations: Russian, German, Spanish, Italian, and Irish.[15] Though he did not mention them by name, Dawson seemed to have desired to revive the spirit of *Order* and *Colosseum,* bringing together Christians of all stripes and ethnicities into a new Christian Republic of Letters.

---

[12]Dawson, Memorandum to Sheed and Ward, February 1944, in Box 11, Folder 10, UST/CDC.

[13]Dawson, Oxford, to Manya Harari, September 9, 1946, in Box 14, Folder 86, UST/CDC.

[14]Dawson, Memorandum to Sheed and Ward, February 1944, in Box 11, Folder 10, UST/CDC.

[15]Ibid.

In the late 1940s, Dawson proposed several projects to Sheed and Ward. Originally, he had hoped to produce a historical series that would trace, through secondary texts written by prominent Christian Humanists, a comprehensive history of the West and Christendom.[16] The few good Christian scholars, though, as mentioned above, were distracted by politics, and Dawson feared a lack of talent capable of producing such a history. Dawson's second idea was to create a series of biographies of the saints and assorted great figures in Christendom, to be called the "Library of Christian Biography."[17] Eventually, though, Dawson rejected this second idea, as he saw no way in which he could effectively research for it. "Even the writing of historical biographies which you have often proposed is not really possible without opportunities for research which I do not possess," Dawson wrote to Frank Sheed, "so the difficulty is a very real and a very far reaching one."[18] When neither of these ideas took root, Dawson decided to publish a series of the "Greats" of Christendom, equivalent to the "Greats" of the classical world. In the latter, one might read Herodotus, Thucydides, Plato, Aristotle, Livy, and Cicero. In the former, one would read Origen, Justin Martyr, Augustine, Ambrose, Jerome, Bede, and Boniface, to name just a few. But, Dawson cautioned, it could not limit itself to the medieval period; it must encompass all of Christendom from the beginnings of the Church through the present day.[19] To limit Christendom to medieval Catholic culture would not only give a false impression to Catholics and non-Catholics, it would ultimately perpetuate the lie that "Europe was the faith."

In his initial outline and proposal for the series, Dawson explained the need for some kind of a biography and saints series. "This cult of the saints still exists as an essential element of Catholic piety," Dawson explained. "But with the secularization of modern culture it has lost its traditional channels of expression, so that even among Catholics it exerts a far smaller influence on the intellect and imagination that it did in the past."[20] Where the cult remained, it had become trite and superstitious. Whatever shape this new scholarly and pietistic effort might take, he hoped it would serve as the foundational series behind a revival of Christian culture. By 1952, Dawson was calling the series "Makers of Christendom." In a letter to one of his contributors and editors, Dom Gerard Sitwell, Dawson explained the motive for the series. "The idea of the series is a collection of biographical documents illustrating the Christian past (not necessarily lives only, but also letters of travels)," he wrote, "and it is intended to appeal to all who are interested in

---

[16]Sheed to Watkin, Torquay, January 17, 1949, in Box 1, Folder 8, ND/CSWD.

[17]Sheed, London, to Dawson, Oxford, September 14, 1949, in Box 11, Folder 15, ND/CSWD.

[18]Dawson to Frank Sheed, April 26, 1954, in Box 11, Folder 19, UST/CDC.

[19]Dawson to Father Crohan, May 29, 1953, in Box 14, Folder 108, UST/CDC.

[20]Dawson, "Christian Biography and History—Typescript of Series Proposal," in Box 1a, Folder 36, UST/CDC.

that past whether they are students in the technical sense or not." Further, Dawson wanted only authors who could demonstrate enthusiasm for their subjects. After all, he wanted the Catholic reading public to absorb "the religious motive of *pietas* towards these men who are our spiritual ancestors and our fathers in the faith and the religious life, and the historical interest of seeing how the saints saw themselves and each other."[21] Just as the Roman Stoics understood the necessity of tradition, the natural law, and those men and women who had through great sacrifice passed such wisdom down from generation to generation, so too could Catholics understand the wisdom and the heroism of those who reflected in ultimate ways the light of the Logos. From the action of Catholic saints, Dawson believed, one could come to understand the very essence of Christian culture and western civilization.

But the project never gained any serious ground. As editor, Dawson only published six books in the series: his own excellent *Mongol Mission: Narratives and Letters of the Franciscan Missionaries in Mongolia and China in the Thirteenth and Fourteenth Centuries*; C. H. Talbot's *Anglo-Saxon Missionaries in Germany: Being the Lives of SS. Willibrord, Boniface, Sturm, Leoba, and Libuin, together with the Hodoeporicon of St. Willibald and a selection from the Correspondence of St. Boniface*; F. R. Hoare's *Western Fathers: Being the Lives of SS. Martin of Tours, Ambrose, Augustine of Hippo, Honoratus of Arles, and Germanus Auxerre*; Dom Gerard Sitwell's *St. Odo of Cluny, Being the Life of St. Odo of Cluny*; T. A. Birrell's *Lives of Ange de Joyeuse and Benet Canfield*; and John of Joinville's *The Life of St. Louis*.

Several things account for the failure of the series. First, though they provided money and a forum for the venture, the Sheeds adamantly believed Dawson should be using his time in other ways. "But I feel another point *is* worth raising: *should* you continue with" Makers of Christendom, Maisie asked Dawson in the autumn of 1953. "I was dismayed from one important viewpoint when first I heard you had planned it," Maisie admitted to Dawson. "To my mind anything [that] takes you away from writing your own books is a major calamity." Further, she told Dawson, "It is not, a thousand times it is not, worth putting that aside for the sake of this series....To my mind a book like *The Making of Europe* is far more effective than the whole of this series could be."[22] Maisie failed to convince Dawson to end the project. He had invested too much in the series and felt too responsible for its creation to end it. Even worse, he feared nothing else existed for him to do. "Nor should I wish" to end the series, "unless I had some alternative work, and I have nothing of the kind in view at present."[23] Several months later, Frank again—not so subtly—reminded Dawson of Maisie's advice to him.[24] But to

---

[21]Dawson, Devon, to Dom Gerard Sitwell, March 21, 1955, in Box 15, Folder 131, UST/CDC.

[22]Maisie Sheed, London, to Dawson, October 1953, in Box 11, Folder 18, UST/CDC.

[23]Dawson to Maisie Sheed, October 13, 1953, in Box 11, Folder 18, UST/CDC.

[24]Frank Sheed, London, to Dawson, Devon, April 28, 1954, in Box 11, Folder 19, UST/CDC.

his wife, he wrote sarcastically, "Dawson! A new basis for his work. For his what?"[25] Clearly, the Sheeds had little faith in Dawson's ability or will to produce anything of long-term depth or quality in terms of scholarship. But, to him, they offered encouragement.

Only a year earlier, Sheed had privately complained that not only Dawson's will, but his abilities, had faded. "I've put together a selection of the best essays in Enquiries with the best in Religion and the Modern State to make a really magnificent book on Religion and Sociology—Dawson's Bible in fact," Frank wrote to Maisie. "He has agreed to the idea in principle. Dunno [sic] what he'll do about the actual selection. His stuff really *was* better twenty years ago."[26] They also believed that Dawson cared only about himself, despite his many writings promoting sacrifice and the gifts of the Holy Spirit for the good of the Body of Christ. In 1952, Sheed found the absolute proof—as he saw it—of Dawson's selfishness. Sheed asked Dawson to critique a section of his (Frank's) new theology book, but Dawson lost the section. In response, Sheed wrote bitterly to Maisie: "I sometimes think I work harder on his books than he on mine. Control yourself, my dear, this violence is unladylike. Where did you learn those words? Not from Chris, I'll be bound."[27] Only three years later, Sheed stated his views about Dawson as bluntly as possible: "Generosity is not his middle name."[28]

The second reason the project failed, at least as far as Dawson believed, was that Sheed and Ward never seemed interested in getting a priest to help supervise the project with him. "I am more than ever convinced that the key of the problem is this question of clerical cooperation: and without it I fear the series is bound to shipwreck," he complained to Frank in the spring of 1954. "Since the clergy possess complete control both in theory and fact over the whole marketing of Catholic publicity, it is useless to attempt to launch a project of this kind without their cooperation."[29] Without clerical support, perceived or real, Dawson believed himself isolated from the Catholic as well as the academic literary worlds. Most likely, Dawson was painfully remembering his battle with certain clergy and the possibilities of hierarchal censorship in 1944 regarding his understanding of the Trinity in *The Judgment of the Nations*. But his fears went beyond simple censorship. Not atypically, Dawson felt isolated and alienated from the dominant Catholic culture. "It is difficult to exaggerate the extreme difficulty of" the isolated scholar and Catholic writer, Dawson complained to Sheed. It "makes itself felt in all sorts of ways so that one often feels that any serious work is becoming out of the

---

[25] Frank Sheed, London, to Maisie, November 3, 1953, in Box 1, Folder 11, ND/CSWD.

[26] Frank Sheed, London, to Maisie, October 21, 1952, in Box 1, Folder 10, ND/CSWD.

[27] Frank Sheed, New York, to Maisie Sheed, September 3, 1952, in Box 1, Folder 10, ND/CSWD.

[28] Frank Sheed, South Bend, IN, to Maisie Sheed, November 29, 1955, in Box 1, Folder 12, UST/CDC.

[29] Dawson to Frank Sheed, April 24, 1953, in Box 11, Folder 19, UST/CDC.

question. It would be a different matter if I was a translator, but I have no vocation for that kind of work, and I don't know what else there is I can do."[30] Sheed, though, did not believe a priest existed who had any real historical background or the scholarly qualifications to keep up with Dawson's desires. "Apart from Philip Hughes," he wrote to Dawson, "*I can hardly think of one priest who has published anything at all on history.*"[31]

There were also practical realities involved in the failure of the series. First, the series never sold well.[32] Second, Dawson had a difficult time finding any scholars—priestly or otherwise—with the ability to translate the original documents.[33] *The Makers of Christendom* also encountered unexpected competition from American university presses, which were attempting to create similar series, though for academic rather than spiritual purposes. And, as always, health problems plagued Dawson. In 1956, Dawson returned to the hospital, probably for psychosomatic reasons. "I've just had a letter from Christopher D, written from a nursing home. He took a turn for the worse yesterday and has cancelled my visit on Monday next," Sheed wrote to Maisie. "I wish they could find out what's wrong with him."[34] Sheed failed to take Dawson's health problems too seriously, and wrote callously only three days later: "I lunched yesterday with Manya Harari; She told me a friend of Dawson's from Budleigh" telephoned the English Catholic publisher "Collins to ask would they please found a periodical for Dawson to edit. Collins laughed heartily."[35]

Finally, it should be acknowledged—as well as being obvious at this point in the book—that Dawson possessed no administrative skills. The Lord of the universe had clearly made Dawson to think and to write, not to strategize, manage, and organize. First and foremost, ideas and imagination dominated Dawson's mind and soul.

---

[30]Dawson to Frank Sheed, April 26, 1953, in Box 11, Folder 19, UST/CDC. Even without clerical support, Dawson's series earned several accolades. The Thomas More Association, for example, gave it an honorary mention in its prestigious "most distinguished contribution to Catholic publishing" award in 1955. See "Books—Authors," *New York Times* (May 5, 1955), 31.

[31]Frank Sheed, London, to Dawson, April 28, 1954, in Box 11, Folder 19, UST/CDC.

[32]Dawson, Harvard, to Professor T. A. Birrell, Nijmegen, Netherlands, November 5, 1958, in Box 14, Folder 44, UST/CDC.

[33]Dawson, Oxford, to Michael Mason, Sheed and Ward Offices, London, February 2, 1950, in Box 11, Folder 45, UST/CDC.

[34]Frank Sheed, South Bend, IN, to Maisie Sheed, March 20, 1956, in Box 1, Folder 12, ND/CSWD.

[35]Frank Sheed, South Bend, IN, to Maisie Sheed, March 23, 1956, in Box 1, Folder 12, ND/CSWD.

Program for Christian Culture

As a part of his post-war efforts, Dawson also wished to reform the educational policies of the institutions of higher learning. Only by teaching the young the traditions of Christendom, Dawson argued, could a new Christendom be appreciated and achieved. Dawson offered several possibilities for reform. First, the western universities could focus more on the liberal-arts and less on the servile arts. "But the modern university is an intellectual workshop or factory which turns out specialists by the thousands," Dawson argued.[36] A return to the liberal-arts, rightly understood, could serve as a Platonic *anamnesis*, a wake-up call to right reason and first principles. Classical education and the renewal of culture worked in tandem, Dawson thought. "Virgil and Cicero, Ovid and Seneca, Horace and Quintilian were not merely school books, they became the seeds of a new growth of classical humanism in Western soil," Dawson wrote. Studying such men in the educational process reified their ideas in reality. "My original suggestion envisaged something like the School of Litterae Humaniores at Oxford, i.e. an advanced whole time study for a comparatively small number of students," Dawson explained to Father Leo Ward in 1954, "but with a change of subject matter from the culture of Classical Greece and Rome to that of Christian Europe."[37] Historically, Dawson believed this point a proven one. "Again and again—in the eighth century as well as in the twelfth and fifteenth centuries—the higher culture of Western Europe was fertilized by renewed contacts with the literary sources of classical culture."[38] Second, Catholic colleges and universities, more than any other in western civilization, had a duty to take up the challenge and shoulder the burden of reform. Far more than the Protestants, Catholics had inherited the great learning of the Greeks and the Romans. They had preserved it in the monasteries in the middle ages, and ingeniously, if somewhat inadequately, they had baptized the pagan as Christian, sanctifying it for the world. Further, "Catholicism makes its appeal, not to those who demand the latest intellectual novelty nor to those who always want to be on the winning side, but to those who seek spiritual reality," Dawson had written in 1931. "Our advantage lies not in the excellence of our brains, but in the strength of our principles." Additionally, Dawson said, while a Catholic respects scholarly freedom and integrity, he is not "'free' in the sense that [he] is at liberty to create [his] own principles and to make gods in [his] own image." Instead,

---

[36] "'New Apostolate of the Intellect' Is Urged by Christopher Dawson," *Catholic Messenger*, vol. 79 (June 8, 1961), 8.

[37] Dawson, Devonshire, to Father Leo Ward, University of Notre Dame, IN, June 7, 1954, in Box 15, Folder 176, UST/CDC.

[38] Christopher Dawson, "Christianity and Ideologies," *Commonweal*, vol. 64 (May 11, 1956), 141.

the Catholic is free to do what is right, Dawson argued, echoing notions of freedom from the Stoics and from St. Paul in his letter to the Galatians.[39]

Indeed, if the culture comes from the cult, as Dawson repeatedly argued, the culture must be passed down, generation to generation, through the institution of education. To break the continuity of education necessitates a break in and degeneration of the culture. Such a breach results in a discontinuity of and within western civilization itself.[40] One such breach came with the Reformation, Dawson argued, as it destroyed the liturgy, itself essential for the education of the whole person, and instead offered the first universal education in "the Bible, the Bible only and the Bible for all."[41] Focusing almost exclusively on the written word of the Bible, Protestantism nearly destroyed art, the imagination, and creativity. While Protestantism rightly adored the Word of God, it forgot that the Word of God is both the Bible and the Eucharist. It exaggerated the former at the expense of the latter. In a private letter written in 1958, Dawson proved even more forceful in his views:

> Only the Protestants can maintain that Faith is completely unrelated to social institutions and purely individual in operation. In Catholicism there is complete continuity between Faith, sacraments and institutions on the one hand, and Faith, morals and behaviour on the other. In this sense, it is obviously impossible to maintain that Catholicism and culture are completely independent of one another. It is all a question of the continuity of the Incarnational process. It is the mission of the Church to transform human life like a leaven, and to transform all forms of life, i.e. all cultures; but where its influence has worked and social life has been changed, we cannot say that this Christian life or culture is not more Catholic than pagan or Hindu life and culture.[42]

Dawson believed firmly that the grace imparted by the Incarnation offers the Catholic the chance to rebuild the world in the Image of Christ. For, Dawson believed, each man and each culture reveal elements of the power of the Incarnation, "the same process at work in history that may be seen in detail in the lives of men."[43] True education, then, must both reflect and continue the process begun with the Incarnation, and it must cultivate the soul to receive the "light that lighteth up every man."

Far more recently than the Reformation, the ideologues of the twentieth century had grossly simplified what should be and are nuanced issues into black and white matters. The ideologues, Dawson understood, were modern

---

[39] Christopher Dawson, "General Introduction," in *Essays in Order*, Christopher Dawson and Tom Burns, eds. (New York: Macmillan, 1931), xix–xx.

[40] Christopher Dawson, "The Study of Christian Culture as a Means of Education," *Lumen Vitae*, vol. 5 (1950), 171; and "Education and the Study of Christian Culture," *Studies*, vol. 42 (1953), 293.

[41] Christopher Dawson, "Education and the Crisis of Christian Culture," *Lumen Vitae*, vol. 1 (1946), 209.

[42] Dawson to Mulloy, January 15, 1958, in Folder 16, Box 1, ND/CDAW.

[43] Christopher Dawson, *The Crisis of Western Education* (1961; Steubenville, OH: Franciscan University Press, 1989), 165.

Manicheans. The ideologue rejects art and, instead, pursues propaganda, as he attempts to conform the minds of men into a grey, non-distinctive mush that embraces neither imagination nor reason, but instead rejects both outright. Therefore, if Catholics attempt to restore Christendom, they must do so through a proper education and repair the breaches created by the scandal of division within the larger Body of Christ, by the secularism introduced by the Liberals, and by modernity. "I believe that Western civilization can only be saved from going the same way as Russia and Germany did," Dawson stated in a public speech in 1961, "by redirecting the whole system (of education) towards its spiritual end."[44] The "Christian college, therefore, must be the cornerstone of any attempt to rebuild the order of Western civilization."[45]

The Catholic must learn at least three lessons in his endeavor to rebuild Christendom. First, Dawson stressed, one can never restore any kind of effective Christendom through the political, legal, or economic process. It must come first, as noted above, through education. Dawson defined education as "an initiation into the Christian way of life and thought" which introduced the student to divine mystery and what T. S. Eliot called "the moral imagination."[46] The education of the Christian goes beyond mere words, and incorporates "the whole man" into the liturgy of life, making him a citizen of the City of God as it sojourns through the world.[47] In a famous speech delivered at St. Mary's College at Notre Dame, Indiana, on April 29, 1960, Dawson explained the importance not just of culture, but of Christian Culture: "With Christianity a new dynamic principle enters the life of humanity and reorganizes it round a new spiritual center and toward a new supernatural end." This applies to the individual as well as to the community. Properly understood, the Church should reach and influence "every aspect of human life and every form of social activity." Indeed, though many of the most important institutions in society—"family, economic association, city and state—remain the same, but in proportion as they come under the influence of the higher spiritual order, they are directed to new ends."[48] The form remains, but the Church, through grace, has sanctified the essence of these things.

No matter how obscure the past becomes, it remains, as solid as the earth itself. For Dawson, it remains "like a river in the desert, and a genuine religious education can still use it to irrigate the thirsty lands and to change the face of the world with the promise of new life." There exists one great obstacle for the Christian living in modernity. "Christians themselves [fail] to

---

[44] "'New Apostolate of the Intellect,'" 8.

[45] Dawson, *Crisis of Western Education*, 150.

[46] Dawson, "Education and the Crisis of Christian Culture," 206–7. On Eliot and the moral imagination, see his University of Virginia lectures, *After Strange Gods: A Primer on Modern Heresy* (London: Faber and Faber, 1934). See also Russell Kirk, *Eliot and His Age; T. S. Eliot's Moral Imagination in the Twentieth Century* (Peru, IL: Sherwood Sugden, 1988).

[47] Dawson, "Education and the Crisis of Christian Culture," 207.

[48] Christopher Dawson, "The Study of Christian Culture," *Thought*, vol. 35 (1960), 489.

understand the depth of that tradition and the inexhaustible possibilities of new life that it contains," Dawson claimed.[49]

This was especially true of American Catholic higher education. In America, despite the freedom to educate in any way a Catholic sees fit, Catholics had "confined" their own educational system "to the utilitarian task of providing our own people [that is, Catholics] with good safe Catholic education."[50] Despite the possibilities inherent in the American university system, American Catholics had produced neither geniuses nor profound theologians to defend the faith, Dawson lamented. "We are up against the difficulty that, given the condition in which the parents and grandparents of so many American Catholics arrived in the country from Europe, there had, of necessity, to be a long period of building and re-building, with the accent on primary education," Dawson said in an interview with an American reporter. "Thus, when you speak of enduring philosophical traditions, there are none such of an especially American character."[51] Because of historical circumstances and culturally-oppressive conditions, American Catholicism had become fundamentally anti-intellectual.[52]

The second lesson that Catholics must learn is that Christendom can never be restored as any previous incarnation. Many Catholic Romantics—from Chesterton to Russell Kirk—had embraced the thirteenth century as the "perfect example of Christian civilization."[53] The present-day Catholic, however, must accept that "the later Middle Ages was only one of the five or six successive ages of Christian culture, each of which had its own mission and vocation and deserves to be studied for its own sake."[54] God's purpose for the Middle Ages had been fulfilled, and, because God works through history, the Christian of today must understand that today, not yesterday, must be sanctified. A return to Christendom must entail something radically new, something incomprehensible to the finite vision of any one man. Unless there is a sudden and swift infusion of overwhelming grace, Christendom, most likely, will come only after a slow and patient process. It will, according to Dawson, come from human cooperation with grace. It will, though, never come from the historical memory or the futuristic utopian visions of any man or group of men.

---

[49]Dawson, "Education and the Crisis of Christian Culture," 215.

[50]Christopher Dawson, "American Education and Christian Culture," *American Benedictine Review*, vol. 9 (1958), 16.

[51]Frank Sheed, "Frank Sheed Talks with Christopher Dawson," *The Sign*, vol. 38 (December 1958), 36.

[52]"The Catholic at Harvard," *Newsweek*, April 28, 1958, 58; Aubrey Haines, "Catholic Historian at Harvard," *Voice of St. Jude* (1961), 28; and Dawson, Oxford, to Sheed, London, February 21, 1950, in Folder 16, Box 11, UST/CDC. On a brilliant and comprehensive history of American attitudes regarding Catholicism, see John McGreevy, *Catholicism and American Freedom* (New York: W. W. Norton, 2003).

[53]Dawson, "Study of Christian Culture," 487.

[54]Ibid., 493. Also see his "Ploughing a Lone Furrow," in *Christianity and Culture*, J. Stanley Murphy, ed. (Baltimore, MD: Helicon, 1960), 18.

Third, Catholics must, in some way, compensate for the de-humanization of industry, ideologies, bureaucracies, and even educational systems. Such mechanization had reached into the very groves of academe and transformed it into something quite anti-liberal and quite anti-scholarly. "The modern university," he stated at Grailville Community College in 1961, "is an intellectual workshop or factory which turns out specialists by the thousands. It does not develop as a unique self-sufficient whole like the old universities."[55] The educational system as it now exists creates only intellectual cogs to run the machine, to create a vast network of inter-connected technological components. The machine feeds on the intellect and thrives on it, Dawson feared.[56] No room exists in modern education for the poet or the man of letters who can imagine new possibilities for old truths. Instead, education, wittingly or not, accepts the propaganda of the machine age, and it dehumanizes the human person, making him less than God intended him to be. While the gulags of the East might attempt to destroy the soul by torture and mutilation of the body, the universities of the West tricked the soul into believing the body a mere shell to be trained, organized, and used according to the will of the corporation, state, or whomever might wield power.

Modernity, then, reflects creation poorly. It attempts to reorder the universe according to the measure of men. Hence, modernity merely offers a shadow world, artificial and forced, finite, flawed, and, ultimately, violent. Modern man's "whole life is spent inside highly organized artificial units—factory, trade union, office, civil service, party—and his success or failure depends on the relations with this organization."[57] In reality, Dawson argued, the twentieth-century secular and technological society made men less than human. "The trouble is that our modern secular culture is sub-literary as well as sub-religious," Dawson wrote in 1956. "The forces that affect it are in the West the great commercialized amusement industries and in the East the forces of political propaganda."[58] Such mechanization seemed especially true in the United States. "I think a lot of nonsense is being talked about pluralism and the ideal of a pluralist society, and the United States as a typical pluralist society," Dawson told an American Jesuit in 1961. "Modern American society isn't pluralist, but monist," Dawson said, "in the sense of a uniform, middle-class, liberal secularism as compared with the uniform, working-class, Marxist secularism of the USSR."[59] These would have been harsh words in an America believing itself the land of the free and the home of the brave

---

[55]"'New Apostolate of the Intellect,'" 8; and Christopher Dawson, "Today's Challenge to U.S. Colleges," *America*, vol. 99 (September 4, 1954), 537.

[56]"'New Apostolate of the Intellect,'" 8; and Christopher Dawson, "Mr. Dawson Replies to Father Mursurillo," *Thought*, vol. 31 (1956–57), 159.

[57]Dawson, *Crisis of Western Education*, 173.

[58]Christopher Dawson, "The Challenge of Secularism," *Catholic World*, vol. 182 (1956), 326.

[59]C. J. McNaspy, "Motel Near Walden II," *America*, vol. 104 (January 21, 1961), 510.

during the Manichean struggle of the Cold War. But Dawson continued to expound his views firmly, despite their unpopularity. In America, education and university specialists must attempt to create new education theories to justify the purpose of their universities, or they must simply watch their universities disintegrate into a thousand sub-specialties of vocational training, including that of an "undertaker, a film director, or a nuclear physicist."[60] However it might happen, the particular was quickly replacing the universal.

Though in a much more benign fashion than in the ideological tyrannies of the East, modern educationalists and academics in the modern West see the human person and his intellect merely in utilitarian terms, Dawson feared.[61] This utilitarian vision of education proved deficient in at least two ways. First, the utilitarian quantitative vision presents a materialist anthropological vision. The materialists think only in terms of "statistics" with history as "a chronicle of events." The Christian, though, must see Man as rooted in the great chain of being, lower than the angels, but higher than the animals, seriously fallen, but made in the image of God and endowed with love and free will.[62] The utilitarian opposes "the old hierarchy of Divinity, Humanity, and Natural Science," Dawson wrote.[63] Materialists, therefore, can only create a "pseudo culture which is the real opium of the people, since it is at once a drug and an intoxicant and a poison."[64] Second, the utilitarian vision comes from the democratic desire for universalist education, with governments throwing immense sums of money at the average citizen and the school bureaucracies.[65] For education to be universal at its lower levels, it must descend to the lowest common denominator to meet the needs of all of its students. It will shun excellence in favor of the mean, who, strangely, enough, will view themselves as the highest beings of the universe.[66] "To-day we are witnessing a regular war against culture and the apotheosis of the common man and the little man and the tough guy," Dawson wrote as early as 1946. A "regular pantheon of strange gods," Dawson claimed, are "emerging from some underworld of culture in the half light between the old European day and the dark night of total barbarism."[67] In these arguments, Dawson must have been significantly influenced by Alexis de Tocqueville, especially in his *Democracy in America*. For rather than teaching students the meaning and significance of

---

[60]Christopher Dawson, "Universities Ancient and Modern," *Catholic Educational Review*, vol. 56 (1958), 30; and Dawson, "American Education and Christian Culture," 9.

[61]Dawson, "Education and the Crisis of Christian Culture," 205.

[62]Christopher Dawson, February 15, 1958, to Father Leo Ward, University of Notre Dame, IN, in Box 15, Folder 176, UST/CDC.

[63]See his booklet, *Education and the Crisis of Christian Culture* (Chicago, IL: Henry Regnery Company, 1949), 6.

[64]Dawson, "Education and the Crisis of Christian Culture," 213.

[65]Dawson, "Study of Christian Culture as a Means of Education," 171.

[66]Dawson, "Education and the Crisis of Christian Culture," 204.

[67]Ibid., 205.

the human person in the Divine Economy, modern education, instead, teaches students a plethora of facts, dates, and names, each out of context and without real substance. This data floats in the ether, unattached to that which is essential. Tragically, universal education must also be at its core secular, so as to overcome religious differences among a religiously-diverse population. The divorcing of religion from culture and the shame of discussing religion in public "arose among the half-educated and gradually spread both upwards and downwards."[68]

Paradoxically, Dawson argued, while modern education attempts to deify the common man, universal education must, by necessity, homogenize men, thus molding "the whole mind of the whole community."[69] Politicians rooted in the democratic and totalitarian ethos will use "the mass conditioning of populations for purposes of power politics," and the member of any society unable to think for himself will fall even lower than the animals.[70] One sees this especially in the philosophy of John Dewey, Dawson argued. Indeed, as Dawson saw it, the Columbia University philosopher went "as far as the Communists in their subordination of education to the needs of the political community."[71] Dewey desired that "every individual participate in the formation of social values and contribute to . . . the democratic mind."[72] Dewey was intensely religious, as were his educational theories. But Dewey's god was not the Christian God. Rather, his god was Demos, and he promoted it as a form of an American religion, in which all become initiated into the larger democratic, national community.[73] A "completely secularized civilization is inhuman in the absolute sense—hostile to human life and irreconcilable with human nature itself," Dawson explained.[74] Because it directly attacks the natural law, Deweyite education must end, Dawson feared, in dystopia.[75] Additionally, Dewey never viewed the common man as material "to be transformed" through a proper education into something higher and better, but instead saw him as the ideal, already formed fully.[76] But as Dawson argued, the only real solution for the Christian was an initiation into "a universalist

---

[68]Christopher Dawson, "The Study of Christian Culture," *Commonweal*, vol. 71 (October 30, 1959), 153; and "Education and the State," *Commonweal*, vol. 65 (January 25, 1957), 423.

[69]Dawson, "Education and the Crisis of Christian Culture," 205; and "Education and the Study of Christian Culture," 298.

[70]Dawson, "Education and the Crisis of Christian Culture," 205; "Study of Christian Culture as a Means of Education," 171; and *Education and the Crisis of Christian Culture*, 7.

[71]Dawson, "Education and the Study of Christian Culture," 298; and Dawson, Devon, England, to Father Leo Ward, University of Notre Dame, IN, June 7, 1954, in Folder 176, Box 15, UST/CDC. See also Michael Novak, "Undistracted Philosopher: Historian Christopher Dawson Spurns Publicity for the Quiet Life of the Mind," *Jubilee*, vol. 8 (1961), 27.

[72]Dawson, "Education and the Study of Christian Culture," 298.

[73]Dawson, "Education and the State," 424.

[74]Dawson, "Education and the Crisis of Christian Culture," 214.

[75]Dawson, "Study of Christian Culture as a Means of Education," 173.

[76]Dawson to Mulloy, December 22, 1960, in Box 1, Folder 16, ND/CDAW.

[community] in the fullest sense of the word: it is the community of the *civitas Dei*," that is, of St. Augustine's City of God.[77]

Christian Humanism and the Liberal Arts

By the late 1940s, Dawson became convinced that any future Christendom lay in a return to a true liberal-arts education, rooted in the continuity of the classical and the medieval traditions, a liberal-arts education that promoted heroism, the seven virtues, poetry, art, and music.[78] "Christianity is the religion of humanism, and the first chapter of St. John proclaims the identity of the Hellenic Logos with the Jewish Messiah and the Christian Incarnate God: and this is the cornerstone on which the Catholic Church and the Christian Culture have been built and stand."[79] Further, Dawson argued, the only good humanism has been Christian humanism. Divorced from Christianity, humanism does little for the world or humanity. Historically, one could witness this. The pagan humanists did little in the way of charity. But "the great Christian humanists, men like St. Thomas More, Vives, Erasmus, Castellion and others, were ever so much more humanitarian than the secular humanists."[80]

Immediately, Dawson cautioned, such an understanding of education would suffer the extreme opposition of American liberals, conservatives, and Protestants. The liberals would see it, he argued, as purely reactionary, "too bound up with dogmatic Catholic presuppositions."[81] The liberals also had the power to back up their words and thoughts, as they had built a "modern Leviathan [which is] such a formidable monster that he can swallow religious schools whole without suffering from indigestion."[82] Should the advocate of Christian culture survive the wrath and power of the liberals, he would also have to confront the anger and reaction of the conservatives. This latter group would object to his presentation of the continuity of the classical and medieval as tampering with the classics, seeing his proposal as "a revolutionary threat."[83] The conservative educational theorists unwittingly bought into the Renaissance vision of the Middle Ages as a "a kind of cultural vacuum between two ages of cultural achievement."[84] Still, Dawson forcefully argued, only a Christianized humanism would prove beneficial. As it was, the conser-

---

[77]Dawson, "Memorandum," dated February 17, 1954, in Box 1, Folder 16, ND/CDAW.

[78]Dawson, "Education and the Crisis of Christian Culture," 208.

[79]Dawson to Mulloy, February 21, 1955, in Box 1, Folder 16, ND/CDAW.

[80]C. J. McNaspy, "A Chat with Christopher Dawson," *America*, vol. 106 (October 28, 1961), 121.

[81]Dawson, "Study of Christian Culture," 486.

[82]Dawson, "The Challenge of Secularism," 326. See also his "Civilization in Crisis," *Catholic World*, vol. 182 (1956), 252.

[83]Dawson, "Study of Christian Culture," 486.

[84]Ibid., 487. On a very quick assessment of the medieval period as "dark" in current scholarship and popular memory, see Bradley J. Birzer, "Renewing the West," *Crisis*, vol. 23 (2005), 47.

vatives had failed to grasp the reality of the breakdown of the classics, and therefore failed to offer a solution to save them.[85] American conservatives, Dawson argued privately, were merely nineteenth-century European liberals. They were not conservatives in the true sense of the word. Protestants, *en masse*, would also oppose Dawson's program. "The Reformers did not recognize the concept of Christian culture," he explained. "They believed that in proportion as Christianity entered into and transfused Western culture, it became corrupted and paganized. Catholicism was the result of this process of syncretism, and the history of Catholic culture was a progressive process of corruption and degradation," Dawson continued. "Hence, they attempted to reassert the absolute transcendence of the Gospel and to detach Christianity from its immersion in history."[86] Dawson had no reason to believe that twentieth-century Protestants would feel any differently than had the first followers of Calvin and Luther. Opposition, it seemed to the English historian, would come from every angle.

One such attempt to revive the study of western culture had been made at Columbia University, but Dawson considered it a noble failure. Its western civilization course was centered around the reading of a plethora of primary documents with little or no theme to hold them together. They were abstractions floating in a subjective ether, Dawson thought. First and foremost, Dawson opposed the prestigious university's core because he viewed it as both unwieldy and ultimately Gnostic. Looking over Columbia's first-year curriculum, Dawson responded, "No First Year student can possibly absorb such a pabulum. It needs a lifetime to digest it. And the same difficulty stands in the way of all attempts to find the necessary principle of unity in an encyclopaedic subject like World History."[87] Equally important, the Columbia core program favored politics and economics to the exclusion of literature and religion, Dawson feared.[88] Dawson believed all "Great Books" programs—such as those to be found at the University of Chicago, St. John's, and the University of Notre Dame—to be potential failures. Lacking an overall narrative, such programs would inevitably prove unable to explain the depth of Christian culture. These programs could never effectively understand "how spiritual forces are transmitted and how they change culture, often in unexpected ways." If students only see the high points of a culture or the "final products—the great writers—they won't look beyond. A culture as I see it is essentially a network of relations, and it is only by studying a number of personalities that

---

[85]Christopher Dawson, "The Study of Christian Culture in the American College," *Catholic World*, vol. 182 (1956), 198.

[86]Dawson, "Memorandum," dated August 7, 1955, in Box 1, Folder 16, ND/CDAW.

[87]Dawson, "Education and the Study of Christian Culture," 300; and Dawson to Mulloy, February 6, 1954, in Box 1, Folder 16, ND/CDAW.

[88]Dawson, "Today's Challenge to U.S. Colleges," 537.

you can trace this network."[89] As with Columbia, these programs—by picking and choosing the writings of the elite of the past—also verged on Gnosticism. They seemed to claim that the key to history lay in a few principal works. In reality, the works simply represent living the life of the mind and the spirit at that particular moment in history.

Only a Christian-Humanist vision, Dawson believed, would provide a proper and true liberal-arts education, as it demonstrated the continuity of the Jewish, Greek, and Roman to the Christian. Such an education would be Christian Humanist in the purest sense, as it revealed that the medieval did not thwart, repress, or ignore the classics, but rather fulfilled them and answered the questions raised. Real humanism, Dawson argued, is not the pagan humanism of the ancient world. Instead, humanism, properly understood, has been baptized and sanctified by Christianity. "It is not merely that Erasmus and Vives and Grotius deserve our attention just as much as Quintilian and Cicero," Dawson argued. "It is that behind these men there is a living tradition, reaching back through Petrarch and John of Salisbury to Alcuin and Bede and Boethius and it was this that built the spiritual bridge across the ages by which classical culture passed into the life of Western man."[90]

Despite their initial efforts, the Protestant reformers could not undo this continuity of the classical and Christian. "Even Calvin, in spite of the 'Hebraism' of his theology, was a son of the Renaissance, a man who valued humane letters only second to the Scriptures," Dawson wrote.[91] After all, John Calvin's first book had been on Seneca, and his famous *Institutes* were, in many ways, a re-write of St. Augustine's *City of God*, itself a sanctification of Plato, Aristotle, and Cicero. Philip Melanchthon, author of the modern German school system, is a second example. Though Luther argued for *sola fide* and *sola scriptura*, the Lutherans, led by Melanchthon after Luther's death, quickly re-adopted a *prima scriptura* position—whether overtly recognized or not—and re-incorporated classical learning into the Christian education system.[92]

John Henry Cardinal Newman best understood the continuity of the classical and Christian in the nineteenth century, Dawson believed. Newman had correctly argued that "the inchoate world community of Western Culture provided the natural preparation and foundation for the diffusion of the new spiritual society in which the human race was finally to recover its lost unity."

---

[89]Dawson to Mulloy, July 19, 1957, in Box 1, Folder 16, ND/CDAW.

[90]Dawson, "Study of Christian Culture as a Means of Education," 178.

[91]Dawson to Mulloy, January 6, 1955, in Box 1, Folder 16, ND/CDAW.

[92]Philip Melanchthon, *Orations on Philosophy and Education*, Sachiko Kusukawa, ed. (Cambridge: Cambridge University Press, 1999), especially 1–25.

Or, as Newman put it, "the grace stored in Jerusalem and the gifts which radiate from Athens are made over and concentrated in Rome."[93]

A liberal-arts education—rooted in Christian humanism—also promotes a true universalism. "The primary school taught the children their letters, the grammar school taught them Latin and Greek, so that educated men everywhere possessed a common language and the knowledge of a common literature." Though the modernist considers a classical education as oppressively and impractically narrow, Dawson believed that "we need it more than ever before" to confront the horrors of mechanized and bureaucratized totalitarian modernity.[94] "At first sight it seems highly absurd to take an English farmer's son or the son of a German shopkeeper and thrust him into writing imitation Ciceronian prose or copies of Latin verses," Dawson wrote. "Yet for all that it did set the stamp of a common classical tradition on a dozen vernacular European literatures and gave the educated classes of every European country a common sense of the standard classical values."[95]

As with most things, Dawson found proof for his ideas for the future of Christendom in the past, specifically in the "Republic of Letters" that developed under Erasmus during the Reformation.[96] The liberal-arts vision served a vital purpose during the Reformation, as it provided the only glue that prevented northern Protestant Europe from completely separating from Catholic Central and Southern Europe. Dawson offered a chilling possibility, had not the classical liberal-arts vision prevailed. "There would have been two completely separate cultures in the Protestant North and Catholic South," Dawson predicted counterfactually, "divided by an iron curtain of persecution and repression which would have made the two parts of Europe as alien and incomprehensible from one another as Christendom was from Islam."[97] If the liberal-arts vision could prevent the complete balkanization of Reformation Europe, it could also edify and unify western society in an age of ideologies.

Specifics of Dawson's "Christian Culture" Studies

To the chagrin of his supporters and the glee of his detractors, Dawson rarely detailed the specifics of the education program he called "Christian Culture Studies." In his primary book on education, *The Crisis of Western Education*, for example, Dawson refused to outline anything specific for a curriculum. Instead, he asked an American devotee of his, John J. Mulloy, to outline it. Frank Sheed, Dawson's publisher, grew increasingly frustrated with Dawson

---

[93]Both quotes, Dawson and Newman, are from Dawson, "Education and the Study of Christian Culture," 297.

[94]Dawson, "Study of Christian Culture as a Means of Education," 171, 173.

[95]Ibid., 174–5.

[96]Dawson to Mulloy, February 27, 1960, in Folder 12, Box 1, ND/CDAW.

[97]Dawson, *Crisis of Western Education,* 36.

over his lack of course specifics. In 1958, Sheed told Dawson that his American editor is "wholly of my own mind on the necessity of the blueprint. I may be exaggerating when I say that another book on Christian Culture without a blueprint would go close to killing the idea once for all; but I am certain that it would damage it. Everyone I talk to has the same feeling that they want to know what the Course would include."[98] On the same day, Sheed sent an even more pointed letter to Maisie. "Have fun with Chris," Sheed wrote. "He's trying to shuffle out of a job again. He's supposed to be doing a book on Christian Culture; now suggests publishing the first two parts and leaving the third part—the blue print—for a later book. I've told him that if he writes once more on C. C. without producing a blueprint, he'll kill the whole thing stone dead."[99] Whether out of laziness, as Sheed suspected, or inability, Dawson refused to be pinned down on this issue. The moment he was specific, he assumed, the critics would attack the specifics rather than consider the merit of the broader idea. Dawson must have also feared falling into a "Gnostic" system as he believed the various Great Books programs had already done to the detriment of the participants and the future of the West.

In broad outline, though, Dawson argued that his Christian-Humanist vision would be historically and poetically grounded rather than theologically grounded. The true "centre of the liberal-arts course must always be humanist rather than theological or metaphysical."[100] The student of Christian culture should consult the theologians, but he should not rely upon them. The theologians, especially the neo-Thomists, had abstracted Christianity and Christian culture to too great an extent, Dawson believed.[101] And while Dawson greatly appreciated St. Thomas's approach to culture, he believed that the neo-Thomists had "tended to concentrate on the Aristotelian metaphysics and have devoted too little attention to his study of society."[102] In his private criticism of the neo-Thomists, Dawson offered the examples of "Paradise Lost" and "The Rape of the Lock."

> If you treat them both a la Maritain, you won't get good educational results to my mind, whereas if you study them as culture—products or expressions of different culture—traditions, their study can be very educative and illuminating. Literature is language *in excelsis*, and just as you can't understand words without things, so you can't understand a poem or a novel unless you know the culture that it expresses.... What the contemporary literaturologists (and I think Maritain also) do not recognize is the historical fact that a culture only achieves full literary expression at particular moments, so that we may be living in a dumb epoch without knowing it.[103]

---

[98] Sheed, New York, to Dawson, Devon, February 11, 1958, in Box 11, Folder 23, UST/CDC.
[99] Sheed to Maisie, February 11, 1958, in Box 1, Folder 13, ND/CSWD.
[100] Dawson, "Memorandum," dated February 17, 1954, in Box 1, Folder 16, ND/CDAW.
[101] Ibid.
[102] Dawson to Mulloy, July 30, 1954, in Box 1, Folder 16, ND/CDAW.
[103] Dawson to Mulloy, April 9, 1955, in Box 1, Folder 16, ND/CDAW.

Even worse, Dawson feared, having gained control of many of the Catholic universities, the neo-Thomists had turned the abstract principles of Thomas Aquinas into a rigid ideology, thus identifying Catholic education "with an authoritarian ideology, like Marxism."[104]

Unlike the discipline of philosophy, history, properly understood, reveals much about God and man's relationship to God. In a 1959 speech to the Harvard Divinity School, Dawson stated that one could never understand theology without understanding the sanctified history as presented in the fullness of scripture. "And this Sacred Tradition is concerned with the development through history of a spiritual order which is embodied in a sacred community, or in two consecutive and related sacred communities—that of the Old and the New Law," Dawson explained. Importantly, "the law and institutional and liturgical order of this second community *is* Christian culture in its essential nature and the Christian cultures that are the objects of historical study are the secondary expressions of it on the plane of human history and social development."[105] The student of Christian culture, therefore, must approach his subject grounded "from below in the light of history—*ex parte hominis*."[106] He must understand three vital parts of Christian culture:

1. the Christian way of life, which is the field of study he shares with the theologian;

2. the pre-existing or co-existing forms of human culture, which is the field he shares with the anthropologist and the historian; and

3. the interaction of the two which produces the concrete historical reality of Christendom or Christian culture, which is his own specific field of study.[107]

Using these three fields of study, the student of Christian culture, then, would approach six distinct topics:

1. theological principles

2. literary traditions

3. Christian social institutions

4. Christian philosophy

5. Christian history

---

[104]Dawson, "Study of Christian Culture," 491.
[105]Dawson, Speech to Harvard Divinity School, May 27, 1959, in Box 1, Folder 11, ND/CDAW.
[106]Dawson, "Study of Christian Culture," 490.
[107]Ibid.

6. post-medieval social and economic developments[108]

Dawson's conception of these topics will be briefly sketched out below.

Theological Principles

The Incarnation is the center of all of history, and, therefore, the primary concept for all study. Only through the Logos becoming Flesh can men truly understand themselves. Just as God became Man to understand our pain, the human person understands himself through the Light of the Incarnation as well as through the example of Christ's life and death. The Incarnation, therefore, remains the central moment of man's history. The Author, after all, had entered His story, and the Church is the continuation of the Incarnation after the Ascension of Christ. Additionally, Dawson argued, one must understand a specifically Augustinian concept of history, the communion of saints, the cult of the saints, the shrines of Christendom, Christian art, and, finally, the liturgy as it relates to the above and to culture.

The Literary Traditions

As the Protestants have done very effectively, Catholics must re-learn the Bible in its fullness. Catholics must take very seriously the notion of *prima scriptura*. In Church teaching, tradition serves the Word. The Church, as well, is the only institution to have declared scripture canon. For the Protestant, the Bible, by necessity, must remain an open book, subject to the judgment of each individual person. Additionally, Catholics should study the Latin and Greek Fathers of the Church as well as the various Germanic and Icelandic sagas, histories, and legends, whether Christianized or not. More often than not, these pagan works reflect elements of the Logos, and Christianity must sanctify them. If such myths, such as *Beowulf*, have already been sanctified, the student of Christian culture must learn the manner and the effectiveness of the sanctifying process.

Christian Social Institutions

The Catholic must understand that social institutions are not arbitrary, but rooted in the Laws of Nature, in the very structure of reality and creation. Therefore, the Catholic must study natural-law theory.[109] He must also study the concepts, even if abstracted, of rights—whether inherited in the Burkean sense or natural in the Jeffersonian sense—and of the human person as well as of intermediary institutions. The student of Christian culture must also understand the basic principles of social justice, recognizing the

---

[108]Outlined in Christopher Dawson, "Christian Culture: Its Meaning and Its Value," *Jubilee*, vol. 4 (1956), 38–39.

[109]Dawson, *Crisis of Western Education,* 185.

Church's preference to aid the poor and weak wherever the weak and poor demand aid. Finally, the Christian scholar should study the ways in which the natural law, various institutions of subsidiarity, and social justice are specifically manifested in various cultures.

Christian Thought

As a Christian Humanist, the student of Christian culture must understand the continuity of the Greco-Roman with the Judeo-Christian. He must realize that true humanism is commensurate with true Christianity. He must ably identify the Platonism of the Latin and Greek Fathers and the Aristotelianism of Aquinas and the scholastics. He should understand that modern science comes from the scholastics, not the nominalists. Finally, Dawson believed, the student of Christian Culture must recognize the leaders of the Enlightenment and the technological revolutions, but he must also know the arguments of the opponents, the Romantics as well as the Catholic mystics, saints, and theologians.

Christian History and Post-Medieval Social and Economic Developments

Though Dawson broke down the study of history into two parts in 1956, he had identified six distinct periods in Christian history by 1960, each of which offered its unique contribution to the "successive campaigns in this unending war" between the City of God and the City of Man.[110] The student of Christian culture must also know and understand the uniqueness and contribution of each, but, equally important, he must, with Burke, understand the continuity and unity of Christendom, the eternal contract between the living, the dead, and the yet unborn. "To the Catholic," Dawson argued, "all the successive ages of the Church and all the forms of Christian culture form part of one living whole in which we still participate as a contemporary reality."[111] Each person, born into a unique time and place, has a mission to fulfill, a vocation to discover and to develop. "The greater is our knowledge of nature and man and history," Dawson believed, "the greater is the obligation to use these increased resources for God."[112] What is true for the individual human person is also true for every people on the face of the earth, for "God continually calls new peoples into divine society, multiplying the Church by the vocation of the Gentiles."[113]

The first age ran from roughly Pentecost, the birth and baptism of the Church, to the conversion of the Emperor Constantine. In this phase,

---

[110]Christopher Dawson, *The Historic Reality of Christian Culture: A Way to the Renewal of Human Life* (London: Routledge and Kegan Paul, 1960), 48; and "Christian Culture Symposium," Harvard Divinity School, May 27, 1959, in Box 1, Folder 11, ND/CDAW.

[111]Dawson, *Historic Reality of Christian Culture*, 58.

[112]Dawson, "Education and the Crisis of Christian Culture," 214.

[113]Dawson, *Historic Reality of Christian Culture*, 58; and *Crisis of Western Education*, 138.

the Church sought to define itself and deal with internal disagreement and heresy as well as with external persecution. Despite the power of its many adversaries, the Church ably penetrated "the dominant urban Roman-Hellenistic culture," Dawson argued, and it "became the greatest creative force in the culture of the Roman world in the second and third centuries," re-invigorating literature and art.[114]

The second age was that of the Christian Empire in the West, ca. 325 to the 600s, when the new barbarians, members of Islam, invaded the West. In this age, Christian theology had to attack, incorporate, and, ultimately, replace the Hellenistic culture of the Roman Empire as well as the pagan culture of the German barbarians. Most importantly for Dawson, it was the "Age of the Fathers," who "formed the mind of the Church and determined the norms of theological thought."[115] This phase also witnessed the rise of the quintessential medieval institution, the monastery. The period ended not only with the threat from Islam but also the internal threat of the eastern churches splitting into various national groups, opposed to the leadership of both Rome and Constantinople.

The Islamic invasions of the seventh century and the Viking invasions from the north in the eighth century initiated the third age. Because of the invasions, the Church stood as the "sole representative of the higher culture and possessed a monopoly of all forms of literary education, so that the relation between religion and culture was closer than in any other period." Under siege, Europe found its identity in men of action such as St. Boniface, who painstakingly and patiently built the political, cultural, and economic structures of the continent. Equally important in this time, according to Dawson, was Charlemagne, who laid the permanent foundations of a "Latin ecclesiastical culture" and supported the poets and artists of society as he created a Christian-Humanist culture and educational system.[116]

Two hundred years after Charles the Great, around the year 1000, the fourth age began. It "began with a movement of spiritual reaction against the secularization of the Church and its absorption in the feudal society."[117] The first spiritual revolt occurred in Burgundy and Lorraine, spreading quickly throughout all of Latin Christendom. The papacy formed a deep and meaningful alliance with monastic reformers—St. Hugh, St. Anselm, and St. Bernard—holding the secular and temporal rulers at bay. The alliance also promoted the creation of the universities to promote theology and philosophy. Not for the elites alone, the age also witnessed the rise of men such as St. Francis of Assisi and the popularity of a simple pietism to imitate the life of Christ. Nationalism, in the form of Wycliffe, Hus, and Luther, eventually ended the great successes of the papacy, the universities, the monastic reformers, and the pietists. Nationalists such as Luther

---

[114]Dawson, *Historic Reality of Christian Culture,* 48–9.
[115]Ibid., 49–50.
[116]Ibid., 52–53.
[117]Ibid.

destroyed the successes of the monastic reformers, aligning significant elements of the Church with secular and temporal powers.

The Protestant Reformation inaugurated the fifth age of the Church, according to Dawson. The Church and Christendom had already been divided East from West because of the rise of nationalist movements in the Eastern Church; now the western Church and Christendom would split yet again, into North and South. Rather than three permanent Christendoms, though, the original two remained while the new one split into a myriad of sects, each an authority unto itself. In reaction, the Catholic Baroque and Counter-Reformation re-initiated the Christian-Humanist movement, a fusion of the best of the Renaissance and Catholic theology. The Church, though, traditionally relied too significantly on the Catholic monarchs of this period. Consequently, when the monarchs fell, as they did in the French Revolution, the Church suffered intensely as well.

The sixth age began with the Church at one of its lowest points in 1789, the beginning of the revolutionary fervor in France, but it soon again blossomed in the early to mid-nineteenth-century, led by men such as the Romantics and John Henry Cardinal Newman. Many European Catholics, ironically, found refuge in the very Protestant United States of America. In America, though, former rural peasants of the Old World had to adapt to the urban conditions of the New World. The sixth age remains unfinished, Dawson wrote in 1960. To comment further, he argued, would be to place one in the position of diviner. Still, the Catholic of the sixth age could be sure of one thing: he faced the most serious threat any Christian had ever faced. The machine world of capitalism and communism would do everything possible to mechanize all men, destroying the individual human person as unique.[118]

Finally, any effective Christian Culture Studies program must promote true leisure. Citing the ground-breaking theories of Thomist Josef Pieper, Dawson stressed the necessity of contemplation rather than action. For without true leisure—time to read and reflect, not the leisure of a Coney Island—"the mind cannot grow and the culture cannot flourish."[119] Such leisure allows the poet—that is, the man of letters—to imagine the possibilities of the world, by taking old ideas and re-working them in a new fashion, palatable to his specific time and culture. According to Dawson, the poet is, in his initiation or re-introduction of an idea or a movement, far superior to the politician or the man of action. The politicians may organize, and the man of action may lead, but each does so armed with the ideas of the poet. Therefore, the poet has a particular responsibility to spend his time in thought and contemplation.[120]

[118] Ibid., 57–8.
[119] Dawson, "American Education and Christian Culture," 8.
[120] Christopher Dawson, "The Claims of Politics," *Scrutiny*, vol. 8 (1939), 138–39.

A Lay Apostolate for the Intellect

As is obvious from the above, Dawson never effectively articulated the specifics of his program. He kept his vision in broad outline. The medium for the program's transmission also remained vague. By the time he reached Harvard, as explained in the next chapter, he had decided the best means might be through the creation of a Roman Catholic Lay Order, an apostolate dedicated specifically to the promotion of the study of Christian culture. Dawson toyed with the idea of a trying to get an existing order to promote Christian culture, but feared they were too busy. He also thought that a single monastery or college might be able to get the program started, serving as an example for others to follow.[121] Such an apostolate would gather and form an elite group of thinkers, "a group or groups who are aware of the evils and dangers of mass culture and conscious of Christian culture and its opportunities," Dawson explained in 1960. "It is for the creation of such an elite that I am working, and anything we can do for the Christian culture curriculum is subordinate to that" or to any thing, including the writing of new books.[122] Again, in conversation with John Mulloy, Dawson admitted that the formation of an institution of some form to promote Christian culture would, in the long run, prove far more influential than any book he could write.[123] Dawson was most likely inspired by his own study of the Oxford Movement of the early to mid-nineteenth century, of which he was an expert. Just as Newman had leavened the study of the liberal-arts and traditional theology in very Protestant and secularizing nineteenth-century England, so might a group arise in relatively Protestant and secularizing twentieth-century America. Other groups inspired him as well, Mulloy reported. The Quakers and the Fabians, especially, seemed worthy models. Each, through the power of ideas and the actions of their respective members, had changed various aspects of society.[124] When asked about his ideal group of elites, Dawson responded:

> I think the elite we have to reach is best represented by the teachers in the non-Catholic American universities. I judge this first by the poets, who are a very important group and who can be influential, as we see in the case of T. S. Eliot; secondly, the medievalists, of whom there were in the past men like Laistner and Rand and (in Canada) Cochrane and Gilson. Thirdly, the anthropologists of whom Redfield is a good example. There are also the literary historians like A. O. Lovejoy and many others.[125]

---

[121] Mulloy, "Recollection of Conversations with Christopher Dawson on the formation of an Institute for Christian Culture," dated August 28–September 2, 1953, in Box 1, Folder 1, ND/CDAW.

[122] Dawson to Mulloy, December 22, 1960, in Box 1, Folder 16, ND/CDAW.

[123] Mulloy, "Recollection of Conversations with Christopher Dawson on the formation of an Institute for Christian Culture," dated August 28–September 2, 1953, in Box 1, Folder 1, ND/CDAW.

[124] Ibid.

[125] Dawson to Mulloy, January 6, 1955, in Box 1, Folder 16, ND/CDAW.

Dawson's elite were not specifically Roman Catholic, and he chose them according to their willingness to be open-minded scholars. "There is of course a danger that the narrower and more dogmatic minds will take up the idea and then the more cultured and liberal ones will be antagonized," Dawson feared.[126] Should the study become "too apologetic and sectarian," potential allies would balk at promoting it.[127] He assumed that his ideas, as he conceived them, might become rigid and ideological rather than open, tolerant, fluid, and scholarly. To keep the scholars honest, though, Dawson believed the lay apostolate should have a number of priests to serve as guides. The priests would, Dawson believed, prevent the program from following the practices of the world and secularizing. They would, importantly, keep the essence of the program Christian.[128]

Dawson announced his intentions and desires to form such an institute at a public lecture at Grailville Community College, a two-year college that educated nuns for mission work overseas, in June 1961.[129] His health prevented him from following up on his ideas, and such an apostolate has yet to be formed.

Prospects for Reform

Throughout the 1950s and 1960s, Dawson remained highly skeptical that Catholic universities would adopt his program. More than anything else, Dawson conceded, it did not seem practical in an already specialized, politicized, and mechanized world.[130] In addition to the opposition from both liberals and conservatives, mentioned above, Dawson specifically feared that his Christian-Humanist vision would encounter three significant problems. First, he wrote to John Mulloy, "one must do all one can to bring the study of Christian culture into modern education. So long as that is neglected, as it is, at present, especially in the English speaking world—no progress is possible. One has the whole weight of the secularist against one."[131] Second, the liberalism of America has rendered Catholicism just one denomination among many competing ones. "Now the problem is that while culture and society are unitary, *religion* is pluralistic, most of all perhaps in the U.S.A., and this makes it exceedingly difficult for any particular religion like Catholicism to stand out against the pervasion and overwhelming pressure of the 'common way of life.' This is why the problem of the study of Christian culture is of such paramount

---

[126]Dawson to Mulloy, March 9, 1955, in Box 1, Folder 16, ND/CDAW.

[127]Dawson to Mulloy, February 21, 1955, in Box 1, Folder 16, ND/CDAW.

[128]Mulloy, "Recollection of Conversations with Christopher Dawson on the formation of an Institute for Christian Culture," dated August 28-September 2, 1953, in Box 1, Folder 1, ND/CDAW.

[129]"'New Apostolate of the Intellect,'" 8.

[130]Dawson, "Education and the Study of Christian Culture," 302.

[131]Dawson to Mulloy, March 5, 1952, in Box 1, Folder 1, ND/CDAW.

importance."[132] Third, any educational reform must confront the impressive power and desires of the nation-state, itself highly protective and possessive of its power and control. Nationalism "takes all it can from the common treasure of European culture and rejects with hostility and contempt all that it cannot claim as its own." Rather than promoting the liberal-arts and the community of scholars, "it divides the republic of letters by a civil war of rival propaganda which is as ruthless and unscrupulous as civil wars have always been." Dangerously, the new nation states have armed themselves "with the new weapons of psychological warfare, mass suggestion and disintegration which threaten mankind with a spiritual tyranny more formidable than anything the world has hitherto known."[133] Since the Protestant Reformation, Christendom has faced this threat, and Dawson knew it would be a difficult problem for any reformer to overcome.[134]

There was always, Dawson hoped, the prospect of a new Catholic Literary Revival in the United States or England. Roman Catholicism was the "only power in America which stands for these deeper spiritual realities and traditions which secular civilization has lost and for lack of which is dying," Dawson told the graduating class of St. John's University in New York in 1959.[135] Still, it would have to identify its advocates and exemplars. "Of course the obvious remedy for this situation is to find a Catholic writer of the calibre of Tolstoy who will reassert the validity of Christian values in such a way that the world is forced to take notice," Dawson wrote to Father Leo Ward of Notre Dame. "Unfortunately such writers are not immediately available."[136] Allen Tate, John Crowe Ransom, and T. S. Eliot seemed to be at the forefront of a new revival, Dawson thought. "But no great figure yet. The reason is, I think, that it is much harder to react against the secularization of culture in America, where it is triumphant, than in Europe where the traditions of the presecularist culture are so much more prominent and visible," Dawson wrote to Mulloy. "But one can use Henry Adams and Santayana as good examples of the failure of a secularist society to satisfy the whole man, so that men of culture show a nostalgia for the Christian past, even though they have lost spiritual contact with it."[137] One must wonder what Dawson would have thought of the success of his fellow parishioner at St. Aloysius's, J. R. R. Tolkien, whose intensely Catholic *Lord of the Rings* has become one of the best-selling books of all time.

---

[132]Dawson to Leo Ward, March 4, 1954, Box 1, Folder 16, ND/CDAW; and Novak, "Undistracted Philosopher," 27.

[133]Dawson, "Today's Challenge to U.S. Colleges," 540; and *Crisis of Western Education,* 145.

[134]Dawson, "Study of Christian Culture as a Means of Education," 176.

[135]"1,247 Graduated from St. John's," *New York Times* (June 15, 1959).

[136]Dawson, Devon, England, to Father Ward, Notre Dame, IN, January 10, 1956, in Box 1, Folder 8, ND/CDAW.

[137]Dawson to Mulloy, June 3, 1960, in Box 1, Folder 12, ND/CDAW.

Still, Dawson contended, the effort to create a program in Christian Culture Studies was worth it, no matter what the opposition. Just as the liberal-arts created a Republic of Letters preventing a permanent balkanization between Protestants and Catholics during the Reformation, education can heal the division today in the Body of Christ. Perhaps the greatest scandal in Christian history, the schism among Christians, "must be solved if Christian culture is to survive." Not just the fate of Christians, but "the fate of humanity" depends upon it.[138] Only through a proper education can the moral imagination be reawakened, and only then can one understand the shadow world of modernity that has distracted and fooled him into believing the real is artificial and the artificial is real.[139] "The imagination becomes a channel of the life of the spirit like the other powers of the soul," Dawson assured his publisher.[140] If nothing else, Dawson thought, those who advocated a return to Christendom would shake up the convictions and confidence of the mechanics and world tinkerers of modernity.[141]

> We may not be able to build cathedrals like the Catholics of the thirteenth century, or write epics like Dante, but we can all do something to make man conscious of the existence of religious truth and the relevance of Catholic thought, and to let the light into the dark world of a closed secularist culture.[142]

---

[138]Dawson, "Education and the Study of Christian Culture," 302.

[139]Dawson, *Crisis of Western Education,* 175.

[140]Dawson, Oxford, to Frank Sheed, July 28, 1946, in Box 11, Folder 12, UST/CDC.

[141]Dawson, *Crisis of Western Education*, 176.

[142]Ibid., 180.

Chapter 7

The Legacy of Christopher Dawson

DAWSON'S SEVERAL ARTICLES ON A RETURN TO A CHRISTIAN LIBERAL ARTS ED-ucation appeared in numerous American journals of opinion, most promi-nently in *Commonweal*. His ideas were taken very seriously, and they helped account for the number of invitations to speak, teach, or lead faculty semi-nars from American universities, detailed at the beginning of this book. One of the most tempting invitations must have been one from Father Theodore Hesburgh, President of the University of Notre Dame. President Hesburgh assured Dawson that many faculty and administrators at the northern Indi-ana Catholic university were reading Dawson's articles and books with great enthusiasm. Hesburgh further declared in the letter that his "chief goal" as the new president was to "re-center the emphasis at Notre Dame...on those studies which belong to the Catholic university as Catholic." Dawson's job at Notre Dame would be to lecture and lead "seminars and discussions with the faculty on the objectives and means of a concentration in Christian culture." Hesburgh offered Dawson $1,000 per month "for as long a period as you may be able to spare" and also promised that he would have the library order any books or materials that Dawson might need. Notre Dame also planned to invite C. S. Lewis, historian Arnold Toynbee, and theologian Father John Courtney Murray to aid Dawson in his efforts.[1]

Dawson turned down the vast majority of the invitations, including Notre Dame's, but he finally accepted two invitations in 1958. The first was to lead a summer seminar for North American scholars at Gonzaga University in Spokane, Washington. The response to the seminar was immense. "You have no idea as to how broad and rich your reputation is in this country,"

---

[1] Father Theodore Hesburgh, President of the University of Notre Dame du Lac, Notre Dame, IN, to Dawson, Oxford, January 30, 1954, in Box 14, Folder 15, UST/CDC.

Father John Leary, the vice president of Gonzaga University, wrote. "We have people coming from Boston, Toronto, New Orleans, New York City, Chicago, Los Angeles."[2] Unfortunately, the first invitation conflicted with the second, and, also because of bureaucratic holdups, Dawson was not able to make it to the Jesuit college.

A Catholic Scholar at Harvard

The second invitation came from Harvard University. Dean Douglas Horton of the Divinity School of Harvard handed Dawson the invitation personally in late February, 1958. Harvard wanted Dawson to accept a five-year appointment as the first Charles Chauncey Stillman Chair in Roman Catholic Studies. Horton, Dawson, and Valery were all shocked by Dawson's immediate answer: Yes. Dawson believed it to be a divine call.[3] The call for a Catholic scholar in a formerly Puritan university was unprecedented. "It offers such a remarkable and unlooked for opportunity of advancing Catholic studies that I felt that it was my bounden duty to accept the chair, whatever practical difficulties and inconveniences it involved," Dawson admitted.[4] Harvard offered Dawson $12,000 a year, plus moving expenses, which were high due to Dawson's extensive library. When Dawson confidentially wrote Sheed, telling him of the university offer, but not mentioning the school, his friend and publisher responded immediately: "Your letter about the confidential offer has just come in. Please, Please, PLEASE accept it."[5] Harvard announced his appointment on April 14, 1958.[6] Two weeks later, the *New York Times* reported: Dawson "will be the first Charles Chauncey Stillman Guest Professor of Roman Catholic Theological Studies at the Harvard Divinity School. He will lecture to future Protestant ministers on the history and dogma of the Roman Catholic Church."[7]

Dawson had never ventured to North America, and many Catholics—even some of Dawson's friends—were worried about his presence in the United States. Americans knew Dawson only from his books, and he was an excellent writer. But his speaking and teaching abilities could never live up to his writing, and Dawson would never fulfill the expectations his writing created. His old friend, Father Martin D'Arcy, for example, expressed shock at

---

[2]John Leary, S.J., Spokane, WA, to Dawson, Devonshire, May 7, 1958, in Box 14, Folder 145, UST/CDC.

[3]Christina Scott, *A Historian and His World: A Life of Christopher Dawson* (New Brunswick, NJ: Transaction, 1992), 181.

[4]Dawson, Devonshire, to Father Leary, Spokane, WA, April 15, 1958, in Box 14, Folder 145, UST/CDC.

[5]Sheed, London, to Dawson, Devonshire, February 26, 1958, in Box 11, Folder 23, UST/CDC.

[6]"2 Theologians Named: Dawson and Slater Get New Posts at Harvard Divinity," *New York Times* (April 15, 1958), 31.

[7]"Education News," *New York Times* (April 27, 1958), E9.

the news. He told Sheed that Harvard "was foolish to give the job to Dawson anyway since he couldn't lecture."[8] Indeed, the Catholic press built up Dawson's move to the United States in what might only be described as a minor frenzy.

The bureaucracy of the United States also descended upon Dawson. The U. S. Department of Immigration and Naturalization held up Dawson's arrival in the U. S. because of a very small possibility that Dawson had tuberculosis. The pressure on the U. S. government from Gonzaga and Harvard was immense. In addition to Senator Magnuson of Washington State, both of Massachusetts's senators were attempting to expedite the process, as were prominent Catholic groups and donor Chauncey Stillman.[9] U. S. officials finally got their acts together, and issued Dawson his visa on September 9, 1958. Dawson and Valery arrived in New York on September 30, 1958. Like many coming to America for the first time, the New York skyline awed Dawson. "No one from the Old World can land at New York without being immediately impressed by this spectacle of gigantic material power."[10]

This was, for Dawson, not just a meeting of the old and new worlds: it was a meeting of the Catholic and Protestant worlds. Catholics had much to learn from the Protestants, Dawson believed. In an interview with an orthodox Catholic periodical, Dawson gave his thoughts on this in great detail. They are worth reprinting:

> I think Catholics can learn a number of things from Protestants. For instance, a greater familiarity with the Bible—especially the Old Testament—which we have neglected. We can learn to value the regular performance of the daily office, even though this may involve more use of the vernacular. We can learn greater appreciation of the English religious tradition, especially the Catholic elements in that tradition which the Anglicans have retained. We can learn a greater sense of social responsibility. Cardinal Manning used to insist that all the great social and humanitarian reforms of the nineteenth century were initiated by the Protestants.[11]

But Protestants had much to learn from Catholics too.

> Protestants can learn from us that the true Church must necessarily be universal and international. They can learn from us the objectivity and authority of theological truth, which has become lost by Protestant relativism and private judgment. They can learn from us the sense of the supernatural as a living reality manifested in the Sacraments and in the lives of the Saints.[12]

His appointment at Harvard would also prove to be a meeting of the Christian and the secular worlds. Though originally founded by several groups of

---

[8]Sheed to Maisie, July 11, 1958, in Box 1, Folder 13, ND/CSWD.

[9]Father Leary, Spokane, WA, to Dawson, Devonshire, June 6, 1958, in Box 14, Folder 145, UST/CDC.

[10]Quoted in Scott, *A Historian and His World*, 187. On the visa being issued, see "Dawson Gets U.S. Visa," *New York Times* (September 10, 1958), 11.

[11]Aubrey Haines, "Catholic Historian at Harvard," *Voice of St. Jude* (1961), 28.

[12]Ibid.

Protestants all desiring to create a Protestant-based Christendom, America had instead become the fountainhead of a technological, mechanized culture. All of this combined—the Catholic and Protestant interaction as well as the Christian and secular interaction—convinced Dawson that he had been divinely called to teach at Harvard. This was more than the purpose Dawson had sought all of his life; this was confirmation—to him—of the worth of all that he had done, and this was his reward near the end of his career. While he was to learn, he was especially supposed to instruct. Sheed agreed with Dawson on this. "But it scares me all the same," he wrote his old ally. "You clearly have so important a mission here in America," Sheed wrote, when Dawson's health began to decline seriously in the summer and autumn of 1961. "I am urging the good God to see that you accomplish it."[13]   In many ways, the Harvard appointment for Dawson was a culmination of Sheed's work as well.

As part of his own continuing learning process, Dawson hoped to explore American Catholicism while residing in the United States. He was especially interested in discovering why American Catholicism had traditionally been anti-intellectual. In an interview with a *Newsweek* reporter, Dawson said he wanted to explore why most American Catholics remained suspicious of scholarship and academia. Though American Catholics have much energy, they produce little in terms of scholarship and culture. This was especially true of Catholic higher education which "in America bears no fruit."[14] In a letter to the London editor of *Newsweek*, Dawson complained that the American magazine had misunderstood him. "Surely I did not say that Catholic education in American bears *no* fruit, only that the *theological* fruits were not comparable with those of the French Church."[15] Still, no matter how tempered, the point remained: Why was American Catholicism less intellectual than its counterparts in Europe? It was a question with which Dawson would wrestle during his four years in the Commonwealth of Massachusetts.

As Father D'Arcy had feared, the power of Dawson's teaching never equaled his writing ability. Dawson's first research assistant, Daniel Callahan, wrote, "Mr. Dawson came to American with a number of illusions about American students: that they knew, as a matter of course, French, German, and Latin, world history, the classics." This, of course, was a compliment on Dawson's part. He assumed everyone as well-read and as intelligent as himself, American students included. Dawson also expected his students "to read three or four books a week for one course; and that their term papers would be models of scholarly research." As Dawson's liaison to the students, Callahan informed the students that they need only read part of Dawson's assigned five-thousand pages per week. "Eventually these problems worked

---

[13]Sheed, New York, to Dawson, Harvard, September 18, 1961, in Box 11, Folder 25, UST/CDC.

[14]"The Catholic at Harvard," *Newsweek*, April 28, 1958, 58.

[15]Dawson, Devonshire, to Sheward Hagerty, April 30, 1958, in Box 15, Folder 72, UST/CDC.

themselves out: the students read two hundred pages, I read two hundred and one, and Professor Dawson of course read all five thousand."[16]

At first, due to the novelty of a Catholic professor at Harvard, numerous students signed up for his courses, and Dawson found the atmosphere very inviting.[17] Dawson, though, had had little teaching or lecturing experience, and his voice would not carry in a lecture hall.[18] "His classes dwindled after an initial burst of enthusiasm," the *Harvard Theological Review* reported posthumously.[19] Dawson was also unsure how to handle his non-Catholic students. He asked Callahan to grade them easier than the Catholics, as the non-Catholics "do not have the elementary background which can be assumed with the Catholic ones."[20] Dawson was also frustrated with the changing culture of the post-war world and the diminishing respect for authority. He could especially sense this among his own students. In a letter to John Mulloy, he worried: "Things aren't going too well with my lectures here at Harvard as it seems impossible to interest the non Catholics in Catholic culture while the Catholics at the moment are reacting so strongly against the tradition of Catholic teaching in the Catholic colleges that they too are not very sympathetic to the tradition of Catholic culture and its European background."[21] Still, the *Harvard Theological Review* admitted after Dawson's death, those students who were willing to work with Dawson and meet his demands, benefited greatly from his instruction.[22] "There was universal sadness that your illness cut short your work at Harvard: it is my hope that by now you have made a strong and full recovery. Can we ever hope for your return?" one of his students asked, two years after he left. "Please give my sincere regards to Mrs. Dawson and thank her for her many kindnesses to me. I often recall the tea and cake on Saturday afternoons: it was such a relief to drink tea again after all the coffee of Harkness Commons."[23] And, touchingly, the same student remembered: "I want to thank you again from my heart for the interest which you took in me when you were at Harvard: in later years when I look back upon my time here I think that the hours I spent with you will be among the happiest of my memories. When, years ago, I read 'The Making of Europe' I little thought that I would one day be privileged to know its au-

---

[16]Daniel Callahan, "Christopher Dawson at Harvard," *Commonweal*, June 15, 1962, 294.

[17]Dawson, Harvard, to Father John Lafarge, S.J., October 15, 1958, in Box 15, Folder 23, UST/CDC.

[18]Chauncey Stillman, "Christopher Dawson: Recollections from America," in *The Dynamic of Christian Character: Essays on Dawsonian Themes,* Peter J. Cataldo, ed. (Lanham, MD: University Press of America, 1983), 217.

[19]Daniel Callahan et al., "Christopher Dawson: 12 October 1889–25 May 1970," *Harvard Theological Review,* vol. 66 (April 1973), 173.

[20]Dawson to Callahan, both Harvard, May 29, 1959, in Box 14, Folder 68, UST/CDC.

[21]Dawson, Harvard, to Mulloy, November 10, 1960, in Box 1, Folder 12, ND/CDAW.

[22]Callahan et al., "Christopher Dawson: 12 October 1889–25 May 1970," 174.

[23]Valentine Rice, Harvard, to Dawson, January 26, 1964, Box 15, Folder 111, UST/CDC.

thor," he admitted. "You taught me above all to be open-minded and liberal in my thinking: you gave me courage to see that the Irish way is not the only Catholic way."[24] It is the letter that any professor would wish to receive from a student.

Students at a neighboring college also found Dawson impressive. In a student article, entitled "Christopher Dawson at Harvard," the author reported:

> Not only an effective ambassador of Catholicism, Dawson is a refreshing antithesis to the American conception of 'stuffy' Englishmen and ivory towerish Intellectuals. He is a genuinely charming gentleman who converses with the vigor of a collegian, but with the true mark of an intellectual—humility. His range of topics and perception of people are as amazing as his sense of humor is constant.[25]

Dawson also enjoyed a certain vogue with young conservatives such as William F. Buckley, though Dawson considered him too liberal in his economic views.[26] Had Dawson fulfilled his five-year contract at Harvard, Boston College might have hired him. Certainly Sheed had been working for Dawson with the Jesuits, and Dawson and his wife had already formed several good friendships with many on the Boston faculty. Sheed considered Luce and Stillman as possible financial donors for a position for Dawson at Boston College, but ultimately he dismissed this. Further, Dawson's health would prevent any additional teaching after 1962.[27]

Though he was friends with several of the faculty at Boston College, Dawson had a difficult time identifying with his own colleagues at Harvard. When his department chair asked him why he had missed the latest department meeting, Dawson revealed his own confusion as to his place at Harvard. "I am sorry I have been so remiss in my attendance at the Department's meetings, but the fact is that I have never been very clear about my relations to the Department." Was he, he asked, to be a church historian? Or a historian of culture? "My point of departure has always been historical in the broad sense—that is to say I come from the study of Western history (as understood by the secular historians, like J. B. Bary [sic]) and then attempt to see how this stream of temporal change has affected and has been affected by religion whether considered as a way of life or as a vision of reality," Dawson explained.[28] As it turned out, the Harvard faculty believed Dawson "was earnestly—a bit too energetically—trying to establish a reputation for academic rigour in the eyes of the rest of the university." Additionally, many

---

[24]Ibid.

[25]"Christopher Dawson at Harvard," [1958], no author listed, but most likely a student from Boston University. In Box 2a, Folder 11, UST/CDC.

[26]On Buckley being too liberal, see Dawson, Cambridge, MA, to Kevin Corrigan, Riverside, CT, January 23, 1961, in Box 14, Folder 102, UST/CDC.

[27]Sheed to John J. Mulloy, August 18, 1961, in Box 1, Folder 13, ND/CSWD.

[28]Dawson, Harvard, to George Williams, Department of Church History, Harvard, October 17, 1961, in Box 14, Folder 164, UST/CDC.

academics at Harvard viewed him as nothing more than a "mere apologist" for the Catholic Church.[29]

Dawson also created a brief national sensation when he suggested in an interview with Michael Novak that America's rejection of religion within public education derived from John Dewey. "No doubt his influence is a thing of the past, but the principle for which he stood has become victorious and has become an almost universally accepted dogma—it has become hypostatically united with the First Amendment, as an article of faith which no loyal American can question."[30] The press reported this as Dawson attacking the First Amendment as "a bulwark of secularist dogma."[31] Dawson's "attack" came just as many Protestants feared that the newly-elected John F. Kennedy would take his orders from the Vatican. Further, Dawson argued, "To deny government support to parochial schools is an obvious injustice and a denial of religious freedom, and any attempt to remedy it is invariably blocked by an appeal to the first amendment to the constitution."[32] Most of the American Catholic hierarchy had argued the same for years, but many evangelicals and fundamentalists were not happy with Dawson or with Harvard. "If the minions of the Vatican who hold citizenship in some other country want to live here for a season and enjoy American freedom we should suggest that they attend their own business and let Americans take care of their own," E. S. James, editor of the Dallas *Baptist Standard*, complained in an open editorial. Further, James demanded, how did it come that "a Protestant divinity school happened to have a chair of Catholic studies"?[33]

Dawson responded quickly to James's accusations. "I believe that every Christian, whether he is a Baptist or one of those whom you so picturesquely term, 'minions of the Vatican', has a natural right to" religious education.[34] In a following letter, Dawson again stressed the importance of American republican liberty, noting that "it is a matter of vital concern for all Christians everywhere that this country should not lapse into the state of neo-paganism which is becoming so widespread in this modern world."[35] By 1961, Dawson had clearly embraced the Puritan notion that America is the City Upon a Hill, with a mission to re-evangelize the world. Additionally, his language is reveal-

---

[29]John Hellman, "Christopher Dawson, The New Theology, and Harvard in the 1960s," *The Christopher Dawson Centre of Christian Culture Newsletter*, vol. 2 (July 1999), 2.

[30]Christopher Dawson and Michael Novak, "Undistracted Philosopher: Historian Christopher Dawson Spurns Publicity for the Quiet Life of the Mind," *Jubilee*, vol. 8 (1961), 27.

[31]"Christopher Dawson Dies at 80," *Christian Century*, vol. 87 (June 10, 1970), 719.

[32]E. S. James, "Englishman's Interpretation Not Needed," *Baptist Standard*, in Box 15, Folder 7, UST/CDC.

[33]Ibid.

[34]Christopher Dawson, Cambridge, MA, to E. S. James, Dallas, TX, July 13, 1961, in Box 15, Folder 7, UST/CDC.

[35]Dawson, Cambridge, MA, to E. S. James, Dallas, TX, August 23, 1961, in Box 15, Folder 7, UST/CDC.

ing, for Dawson rarely wrote or spoke of natural rights. He more often wrote of duties, and, when he wrote about rights, he did so in a Burkean sense rather than in a Jeffersonian sense. Clearly, American culture and thought was influencing him.

Protestants were not the only ones who found Dawson a threat. When Dawson argued in his graduation address to St. John's University that Catholicism stood as the single most important power to combat secularism, Rabbi Jacob Sodden of the New York Van Cortlandt Jewish Center responded in anger, "I wish that people like you, in positions of respect and influence, would refrain from throwing such innuendos at impressionable minds." Further, the rabbi asked, "Don't you think that irreparable damage can be done to youthful and pliable minds at a graduation exercise, which can provincialize them mentally and blind them psychologically to the contributions to the higher values of our civilization which other religious groups and cultures make?"[36] In a return letter, Dawson apologized, but also stressed that the *New York Times* had quoted him out of context. However, Dawson stressed, he believed Catholicism held a "unique providential mission," and he had every right to speak his mind. To do otherwise would be to sacrifice "religious truth to social convention."[37] There can be little doubt, though, that Dawson was not anti-Semitic in the least. While he was very pro-Catholic, he held Jewish culture, heroes, and wisdom in great esteem.

All negatives aside, Dawson enjoyed a richly productive four years at Harvard. Indeed, he had not been so productive since 1935. While at Harvard, he published *The Movement of World Revolution*, a study of nationalisms and ideologies in Europe and Asia, as well as his two-part study of Christian Culture, *The Historic Reality of Christian Culture* and *The Crisis of Western Education*.[38] He also wrote three straight historical works, *The Formation of Christendom*, *The Dividing of Christendom*, and *The Return to Christian Unity*. The latter remains unpublished and *The Dividing of Christendom* and *The Formation of Christendom* were published only after substantial editing by E. I. Watkin.[39] These latter works, especially, offered some of Dawson's most profound thoughts on history and culture. In addition to his many writings, Dawson also gave numerous talks, commencement addresses, and even appeared on radio and television shows. Nothing that Dawson presented in any of these media was simply a rehash of his older arguments. Instead, Dawson continued to build on his already considerable body of thought. Teaching—

---

[36]Rabbi Jacob Sodden, New York, to Dawson, Cambridge, MA, June 16, 1959, in Box 15, Folder 170, UST/CDC.

[37]Dawson, Cambridge, MA, to Rabbi Sodden, New York, [1959], in Box 15, Folder 170, UST/CDC.

[38]On the two books being two parts of one study, see Dawson to Mulloy, January 7, 1958, in Box 1, Folder 14, ND/CDAW.

[39]Louise H. Wijnhausen, New York, to Anne Munro-Kerr, London, November 14, 1966, in Box 11, Folder 65, UST/CDC.

though it did not always go well—and American culture provided strong stimuli to Dawson's thought. Hence, one should regard these final works not only as a culmination of a lifetime of study and thought, but also as some of Dawson's finest intellectual achievements. Happily for the Dawsons, they even enjoyed "a considerable social life."[40]

Retirement

Illness, a recurring plague on Christopher, forced Dawson to retire from Harvard and return to England. "I've just had Valery on the telephone," Sheed wrote to Maisie. "She told me that in the hospital he [Dawson] had had a stroke—so I was right in my instinct: the doctor had not told her. He's back at home, but I gather he's through: there's no question of his going on at Harvard or anywhere else."[41] Harvard accepted his resignation on June 4, 1962.[42] Dawson was age 73. In response to his retirement, Boston's Richard Cardinal Cushing offered the Dawsons three very important gifts. First, in April, Cardinal Cushing had Regis College award Valery, Dawson's devoted wife, an honorary LL.D. for her contributions to scholarship, that is, keeping Dawson from becoming too distracted by the world.[43] Certainly, Dawson's friends had always regarded her as a "delightful companion and skilful hostess in the hardest of war or peacetime circumstances."[44] At Dawson's retirement dinner, Cardinal Cushing offered the English Roman Catholic his second gift, declaring Dawson "one of the great scholars of the world and one of the intellectual leaders of the universal Church."[45] His third gift was a personal note from Pope John XXIII, providing an apostolic blessing for Dawson's retirement. The telegram read:

> Holy Father cordially imparts Christopher Dawson occasion retirement as Professor Catholic Culture Harvard University Paternal Apostolic benediction implore pledge abiding divine assistance praise worthy endeavors Catholic intellectual and educational fields.[46]

It would, of course, have been impossible to receive a higher recognition for his contributions to the Catholic Church and to his efforts to rebuild Christendom. The Holy Father himself had blessed Dawson's career.

---

[40] Marietta Bisson, Harvard Divinity School, to Bruno Schlesinger, Notre Dame, IN, November 18, 1959, in Box 15, Folder 125, UST/CDC.

[41] Sheed to Maisie, March 20, 1962, in Box 1, Folder 13, ND/CSWD.

[42] Unattached notice, in Box 14, Folder 164, UST/CDC.

[43] Stillman, "Recollections from America," 220.

[44] Maisie Ward, "Dawson the Philosopher," *Duckett's Register*, vol. 4 (1949), 37.

[45] "Christopher Dawson Dies at 80," 719.

[46] Telegram, dated May 30, 1962, from Cardinal Cocognani, Vatican City, to Cardinal Cushing, Commonwealth of Massachusetts, in Box 2a, Folder 6, UST/CDC.

The final eight years were not easy ones for Dawson. His health declined rapidly, and he had a difficult time speaking and writing because of the effect of the various strokes he suffered in the 1960s. This greatly worried Dawson, as he wanted to complete the manuscripts derived from his Harvard lectures. Sheed was stunned by Dawson's condition in January 1964. "I found Christopher happy but as tired as last time," Sheed wrote to Watkin, who had volunteered to edit and finish Dawson's final trilogy, "Christendom." "He passed the galleys with one reading and no questions! He also said that he hoped you would not raise any problems. One can almost feel his fatigue."[47] Still, Dawson did care. In very shaky handwriting, he wrote to Sheed in April 1964, "Has the typist got my MSS down yet?" Dawson was especially concerned about the legibility of his handwriting. "I hope he [Watkin] was able to cope with my hand writing, which is a serious obstacle to my work now," Dawson confessed to Sheed. "I have not been very well lately, but I hope I shall get better."[48] Two months later, Watkin reported on his condition. "I wrote to Dawson a short time ago to inquire what was happening to the book [*Dividing of Christendom*]. I helped him last January to put [it] into shape. But he is too ill even to reply. My daughter has been to visit them and brings back a very bad report of his and Valery's health."[49] In the spring of 1965, Dawson made Watkin his literary executor. Sheed had assumed that Dawson would make his American friend, John Mulloy, executor, but Watkin believed it important that an Englishman accept the job.[50] By late 1966, Christopher was in such bad health that Valery had to take over all of his correspondence.[51] A little over a year before Dawson's death, Watkin wrote that "Christopher is continually falling asleep and I fear slowly but—thank God—painlessly sinking down to the end."[52]

After Dawson suffered a serious heart attack in May 1970, Watkin visited him in the nursing home. As Watkin left, Dawson told the nurse, "You know he made me a Catholic."[53] Chauncey Stillman, his great American patron, also saw Dawson right before his death, remembering:

> At least three times, on my subsequent visits to England, I would go to see them at Budleigh Salterton in Devonshire. I recall my daughter, Elizabeth, going from London to Budleigh by train on her own to lunch with them. After a time, Christopher, although still frail and weak, put on a bit of weight and had better colour. He would be sitting in a wheelchair, smoking cigarettes incessantly. The last time I

[47] Sheed to E. I. Watkin, January 4, 1964, in Box 1, Folder 14, ND/CSWD.

[48] Dawson, Devon, to Sheed, April 23, 1964, in Box 4, Folder 1, ND/CSWD.

[49] E. I. Watkin to Sheed, June 14, 1964, in Box 4, Folder 1, ND/CSWD.

[50] E. I. Watkin to Sheed, April 6, 1965, in Box 4, Folder 1, ND/CSWD.

[51] Anne Munro-Kerr, Society of Authors, London, to Louise H. Wijnhausen, Sheed and Ward, New York, November 28, 1966, in Box 11, Folder 65, UST/CDC.

[52] E. I Watkin, Torquay, to Bernard Wall, February 28, 1969, in Box 1, Folder 24, Bernard Wall Collection, Georgetown University Archives (hereafter, Wall/GU).

[53] Quoted in Scott, *A Historian and His World,* 207.

called, his son, Philip, met me at the door saying that his father was dying. I tried to drive away, but Philip said, "You must come in; my father wants to see you." Christopher opened his eyes and smiled warmly, pressing my hand silently. The next day, in London, I heard that he died that night.[54]

Stillman wrote a condolence note to Valery on June 5, 1970, the feast of St. Boniface: "It is a source of satisfaction to me that I arrived at your house in time to see Christopher, and the smile of recognition that he gave me is a farewell glimpse of his beautiful nature that I shall always prize."[55]

Dawson's death, on the Feast of St. Bede, 1970, was a joyous one. For after several strokes in the mid- to late-1960s, which left him mostly dumb, Dawson suddenly spoke on Trinity Sunday. "All of a sudden he opened his eyes and staring at the painting of the crucifixion, which was on the wall at the foot of his bed, he had a beautiful smile and his eyes were wide open," Dawson's daughter reported. "He then said: 'This is Trinity Sunday. I see it all and it is beautiful.' He then returned to the coma never to regain consciousness."[56] This moment of grace served as a fitting end to his many ventures in the service of God and Church.

The Legacy of Christopher Dawson

That Dawson had his share of critics during and after his lifetime would not have surprised Dawson or anyone else, allies or opponents. After all, in almost every way, Dawson was an oddity in the twentieth-century. This scholar of culture and history was one of the most counter-cultural of all intellectuals. As the world rejected God, Dawson embraced God. As the world rejected myth, Dawson embraced myth. As the world rejected the significance of prophets, Dawson attempted to speak as one. As the world mocked the saints as superstition, Dawson regarded them as the only lights—reflecting the true light of the Logos—in history.

Prior to the 1950s, however, a number of non-Catholic scholars had praised Dawson's work. They recognized it as importantly innovative, especially its willingness to transcend nationalist trends in historiography. Not atypical in this part of his career, Dawson received this compliment from an anthropologist on his first book, *The Age of the Gods*: "Only occasionally has a fresh writer the courage, and the command of his materials, to reconstruct any considerable part of the general setting, and, as some painters have done, sit down before a familiar scene and sketch it, from a fresh point of view."[57] A

---

[54]Stillman, "Recollections from America," 221–22.

[55]Chauncey Stillman to Valery Dawson, June 5, 1970, in Box 2a, Folder 5, UST/CDC.

[56]Quoted in Scott, *A Historian and His World,* 207.

[57]J. L. Myres, "Review of *Age of the Gods,*" *Man*, vol. 28 (1928), 180.

reviewer for the *New York Times Book Review*, while not uncritical, judged that *The Age of the Gods* "was well worth writing. It is well worth being read."[58]

Most scholars offered Dawson high praise for being impartial, especially as a Catholic historian.[59] The *Nation* wrote: "Mr. Dawson writes with an impartiality very unusual in a Catholic historian, and appears to have studied all the available authorities."[60] A reviewer for *Time* stated, "Although a Roman Catholic himself, Dawson does not take the tack of the conventional Catholic medieval apologist, who regards the period as a happy but vanished Golden Age when there were no Protestants around." Instead, the reviewer claimed, Dawson "writes with the smooth mixture of clarity, scholarship and happy metaphor that characterizes good British historians."[61] One of the original signers of the atheist 1933 Humanist Manifesto, historian Harry Elmer Barnes, concluded that "not even the most militant Protestant or skeptical historian, if he is fair and honest can read [*Dynamics*] without being impressed by Dawson's learning, comprehension, and perspective or stimulated by his remarkable ability to go to the heart of an issue, to state his points and conclusions with great cogency and brilliant precision."[62]

While some Catholics were quick to note that Dawson "is singularly free from insularity or prejudice," a significant number of non-Catholics simply "dismissed [Dawson's scholarship] as a shallow Eurocentric and papist apologetic."[63] John Mecklin of Dartmouth College, for example, claimed that Dawson was good until he discussed Catholicism. "But when we ask how the totalitarian Catholic church is to be reconciled with the totalitarian state this clear and stimulating writer becomes singularly vague and unconvincing," Mecklin complained.[64] The usually fair *Times Literary Supplement* rated Dawson as generally an excellent researcher and writer, but one who all-too-often railed against Protestants. "Like the priest in the Irish joke," the paper wrote, Dawson "can take historical prostitutes (metaphorically speaking) in his stride, but seems to draw the line at Protestant historians."[65] A fellow member of T. S. Eliot's Moot, Reinhold Niebuhr, dismissed Dawson as "strictly controlled by dogmatic Catholic presuppositions." Niebuhr continued: "A tight

---

[58] Gregory Mason, "Origins of Culture," *New York Times Book Review*, November 18, 1928, 16.

[59] Patrick Allitt, *Catholic Converts: British and American Intellectuals Turn to Rome* (Ithaca, NY: Cornell University Press, 1997), 254.

[60] "Review of *The Making of Europe*," *Nation*, vol. 135 (December 1932), 575.

[61] "The Case for Christendom," *Time*, February 15, 1954, 104.

[62] Harry Elmer Barnes, "Review of *The Dynamics of World History*," *American Historical Review*, vol. 63 (October 1957), 78.

[63] Patrick Healy, "Constructive Dark Ages," *Commonweal*, vol. 17 (January 4, 1933), 274; Michael Novak, *A Time to Build* (New York: Macmillan, 1967), 24; and Paul Costello, *World Historians and Their Goals: Twentieth-Century Answers to Modernism* (DeKalb, IL: Northern Illinois University Press, 1993), 128.

[64] John M. Mecklin, "Catholicism, Protestantism, and Capitalism: Religion and the Modern State," *American Sociological Review*, vol. 1 (1936), 310.

[65] "God and History," *Times Literary Supplement*, December 27, 1957.

dogmatism does not make for good historiography. And it may be questioned whether its lack of modesty makes for good apologetics." As a contrast, Niebuhr praised Father Martin D'Arcy's recent book on history which "proves that a good Catholic can view the mystery and meaning of history from a wider perspective and with less restrictive dogmatism than Mr. Dawson."[66] Those who gave Dawson a chance, however, including some Marxist historians, were also impressed with Dawson's emphasis on culture rather than economics, geography, environmental factors, or politics, as the prime mover in history, even if they disagreed with his personal faith.[67]

Even fellow Catholics sometimes resented Dawson's supposedly ghetto-Catholic view. Justus George Lawler, a prominent professor at Xavier University, argued in a number of publications that Dawson's understanding of Christian Culture was nothing more than a glorification and idealization of the thirteenth-century. Dawson, Lawler claimed, only pointed out the good of medieval society, by conveniently focusing on medieval philosophy and theology in the abstract. In so doing, though, Lawler believed, Dawson had to discount all of the human rights abuses and denial of fundamental human rights during the 1000 years of medieval Europe. "Again we are faced with one of those judgments, based on a romantic view of the past, which, though one would have thought it untenable even in the New Jerusalem or Ruskin or Morris, is nevertheless irrefutable—unless one can devise some valid method of determining the cultural dynamics, i.e. the peace of mind of helots, freedmen, and serfs."[68] By propagating such an abstraction, Lawler continued, Dawson must fundamentally deny original sin. "If culture is to be made a study of human nature, you cannot have a Christian Culture. It is a contradiction in terms to attempt a sinless culture of sinful man." For Lawler, Dawson was not writing history and promoting a true Christian Culture, as much as just writing "rather mundanely, [what] is called Church History." Further, by emphasizing the importance of the medieval period, Dawson undermined the importance of classical culture, at a time in which academia was already dismissing it as irrelevant.[69] "There is, I suggest, a parallel between the efforts of Mr. Dawson in favor of 'Christian Culture' and the efforts of medieval thinkers to subordinate the liberal arts to the new disciplines of Scholastic thought."[70] This is nothing more, at best, than a glossed-up utilitarianism, Lawler claimed. At its worst, it serves as mere propaganda in the vein of Belloc or the "Action Française." Lawler's criticism of Dawson applied even

---

[66]Reinhold Niebuhr, "What's a Mote to One Is a Beam to Another," *New York Times Book Review*, March 13, 1960, 17.

[67]Allitt, *Catholic Converts*, 254–56.

[68]Justus George Lawler, "The Crisis of Western Education," *Harvard Education Review*, vol. 32 (Spring 1962), 217.

[69]Ibid., 215, 218–219.

[70]Ibid., 220.

more to Dawson's "American defenders and disciples" who espoused "historicism and neo-medievalism" to the "uncommitted observer."[71] A similar attack came from Sister Marie Corde McNichols. When Dawson wrote about Christian culture, she feared, he was "almost exclusively concerned with the Middle Ages and Western Europe."[72]

Many scholars, especially after 1950, simply rejected Dawson's ideas outright. They did so for a variety of reasons. A professor of religion, Gabriel Vahanian, claimed that Dawson's arguments in *The Historical Reality of Christian Culture* were simply "disturbing."[73] William Barrett, an editor of the Marxist *Partisan Review* dismissed Dawson as an elitist snob. "One feels something is lacking, all the more so in relation to the seriousness of the theme," he wrote in a review of Dawson's 1952 *Understanding Europe*. "The prelude to a rebirth of the spirit ought to be some deeper and more abysmal experience than anything Mr. Dawson appears to have been touched by." Barrett imagined Dawson as the stereotypical "imperturbable Englishman facing Armageddon with bowler hat, umbrella and morning coat."[74] Martin Wight, a reviewer for *International Affairs*, reached a similar conclusion. "There is an aloofness about Mr Dawson's writing, as if it were done in a recluse's study."[75]

Perhaps the most surprising and entertaining critique came from Oxford historian Christopher Hill in the *Spectator*. In 1957, he wrote definitively, "the late Mr. Dawson was not a great historian; he was a diligent Roman Catholic publicist with a considerable and genuine interest in history." Dawson, who would not end his earthly pilgrimage for another thirteen years, was rightfully alarmed. In a letter entitled "Manalive" Dawson replied, "I do not wish to assert I am 'great,' but I do most emphatically deny that I am 'late.'"[76] Nothing, of course, could reveal just how distanced Dawson was from the Oxford dons. Dawson, though, got a jab in. "It seems to me that there is no more sense in asking, like Mr. Hill, 'What *is* the use of history' than in asking what is the use of memory. An individual who has lost his memory is a lost individual, and a society that has no history and no historical consciousness is a barbarous society. It is as simple as that."[77] Frank Sheed wrote a private letter to the editor of the *Spectator* as well: "Mr. Dawson is not dead. I take it that the

---

[71]Ibid., 10.

[72]Sr. Marie Corde McNichols, R.S.M, "Western Culture and the Mystical Body," *Catholic World*, vol. 186 (1957), 170.

[73]Gabriel Vahanian, "How to Say 'God," *Nation*, vol. 192 (1961), 286.

[74]William Barrett, "The Europe That Was, and Might Be," *New York Times Book Review*, December 28, 1952, 9.

[75]Martin Wight, "Review of *Understanding Europe*," *International Affairs*, vol. 29 (July 1953), 341.

[76]Dawson to the editor of the *Spectator*, September 24, 1957, in Folder 22, Box 11, UST/CDC; Christopher Dawson, "Manalive," *Spectator*, September 27, 1957, 398; and "Dangers of Journalism," *Commonweal*, November 29, 1957, 221.

[77]Dawson to the editor of the *Spectator*, September 24, 1957, in Folder 22, Box 11, UST/CDC.

belief that he is emboldened your reviewer to make the contemptuous remarks he did." Further, "what is written in your paper is a direct and totally
unwarranted attack upon his professional standing."[78] Hill wrote a personal
apology to Dawson "for my unintended assassination of you."[79] The Oxford
historian also wrote a letter of apology, published in the October 11, 1957
issue of the *Spectator*. "I much regret the pain and embarrassment which my
mistake may have caused Mr. Dawson and his friends," Hill wrote.[80] True to
character, Dawson graciously accepted Hill's apology and even offered Hill his
own apology for his defensiveness.[81]

If Hill wrote the most awkward review, the *Times Literary Supplement's*
anonymous reviewers wrote the most objective reviews of Dawson's works.
In its review of *The Dynamics of World History*, entitled "God and History,"
the *TLS* offered Dawson a high compliment. Readers, the newspaper argued,
should recognize Dawson as the "most distinguished" of those many "amateur
scholars" who were attempting to mix history and metaphysics, something
the professional historians were often unwilling to do. Dawson "manages to
square his religious views, in the most ingenious way, with a stanch advocacy
of anthropology and sociology as ancillary techniques in historical method."[82]
Additionally, the reviewer continued, Dawson treats his opponents in an unfair manner. Rather than dealing with criticism directly, the *TLS* claimed that
what Dawson "appears to have done, through the guidance of some unconscious instinct, is to neutralize his most dangerous opponents by apparently
assimilating them into this system." Though Dawson often arrived at brilliant insights, the *TLS* reviewer complained, he never effectively married the
scholarly pursuits with his personal faith and, thus, achieved only a "subtly
schizoid quality" in "some of his best work."[83] Therefore, Dawson's stronger
work will always be his first, *The Age of the Gods*, which dealt only with the
scholarly side of Dawson's brain. Two years after Dawson's death, in an article
dedicated to a review of his work, the *TLS* continued this line of thought.

> The range of his reading had always been remarkable, but when he comes again
> to still more recent periods his knowledge is more limited, he suffers from defec-

---

[78]Frank Sheed to the editor of the *Spectator*, September 23, 1957, in Folder 22, Box 11,
UST/CDC.

[79]Christopher Hill, Balliol College, Oxford, to Dawson, September 27, 1957, in Folder 22, Box
11, UST/CDC.

[80]Dawson, "Manalive."

[81]Dawson to Hill, October 1, 1957, in Folder 22, Box 11, UST/CDC. Strangely, other historians
have wrongly accepted Hill's assertion that Dawson died in 1957. See, for example, Caroline Marshall, "Protestantism and Cultural Fragmentation in the Thought of Christopher Dawson," *Fides
et Historia*, vol. 31 (1999), 27. In an earlier piece on Dawson, though, Marshall got his death date
correct. See her "Christopher Dawson," in *Historians of the Christian Tradition: Their Methodology
and Influence on Western Thought*, Michael Bauman and Martin I. Klauber, eds. (Nashville, TN:
Broadman and Holman, 1995), 431–48.

[82]"God and History."

[83]Ibid.

tive sympathies, and at times he falls into ordinary recapitulation . . . [and] uncon-
sciously transposes to the modern field the kind of patterns that he had found in
remoter ages.[84]

Dawson's reputation declined rapidly in the 1960s. On the surface, this dramatic shift in reputation makes little sense. After all, in 1958, Dawson was regarded as one of the top scholars in the world, and, as tentatively argued at the beginning of this book, one of the greatest Catholic minds of his generation. Amazingly, by 1967, Dawson was almost entirely forgotten by both Catholics and non-Catholics. "Dawson's grand synthesizing technique, widely admired in the 1940s and just right for the post-war religious revival, seemed archaic by the early 1960s," historian of Catholicism Patrick Allitt has argued.[85] "The sudden change in American Catholicism" has resulted in a belief that "Christopher is completely outmoded," Watkin wrote in the spring of 1969.[86]

Indeed, the cultural changes accompanying Vatican II swept away Dawson's reputation, as they had done to the other great European Christian humanists of the twentieth century: Maritain, Gilson, and Guardini.[87] Each found that American and European Catholics regarded them as no longer relevant to the post-Conciliar church. A professor at the University of Notre Dame stated it bluntly in 1967: "English Catholic writers of a generation now almost gone have, it is regretfully conceded, an oddly dated quality which make them, already, little more than objects of antiquarian interest." The greats of the previous generation such as Knox, Belloc, and Chesterton "have bit the dust!" The reviewer ended with a small amount of hope. "Perhaps Christopher Dawson alone will be saved from that debilitating fate by the quality of his historical research, the craft of his writing and the durability of his central thesis as to the make-up of European history and culture."[88] These thinkers—with Maritain and Guardini included—represented, the standard story ran, the outdated and oppressive, the Church of Hierarchy and Censorship, the Church of the Past. These thinkers—no matter how bright—were a part of the Catholic ghetto, and Catholics must now reach beyond their own faith and institutions. Instead, they must build the future,

Not in the dark of buildings confining
Not in some heaven light years away

---

[84]"Religion's Part in History," *Times Literary Supplement*, July 28, 1972.

[85]Allitt, *Catholic Converts,* 240.

[86]E. I. Watkin, Torquay, to Bernard Wall, March 4, 1969, in Box 1, Folder 2a, Wall/GU.

[87]See James Hitchcock, "Postmortem on a Rebirth: The Catholic Intellectual Renaissance," *American Scholar*, vol. 49 (1980), 211–225.

[88]William C. Storey, "The Formation of Christendom," *Commonweal*, vol. 86 (September 8, 1967).

But here in this place, the new light is shining.[89]

So ran the thought of many prominent Roman Catholics in the decade (and decades) following Vatican II.[90] By the end of the 1960s, any historian or scholar who had ever embraced any part of the medieval world "made even moderately progressive Catholics cringe to be reminded that such things had ever been said or done."[91] Vatican II instead, it had seemed, opened up the Church to whole new modern and democratic vistas of freedom, the past to be forgotten as embarrassing.

From what Dawson saw of the changes wrought by the second Vatican Council, the imagination was being driven from the Church, and ideas were becoming mechanized. "I hate the changes in the Liturgy and even the translations are so bad," he wrote to E. I. Watkin. Dawson saw the loss of the common use of Latin as detrimental to the unity of the Church. "I think the 'Latinism' of the medieval culture was essential to its existence," wrote Dawson, again to Watkin. "It was essentially a hierarchical culture, and in theory the people received 'illumination' from the clergy who themselves acquired illumination from the contemplation of truth in the liturgy. Modern democratic culture is essentially unhierarchical and unliturgical."[92] Consequently, the argument runs, the vernacular would destroy the teaching function of the liturgy, thus diminishing the participation and understanding of the clergy and the laity. Perhaps more shocking to Dawson, the Protestants seemed to have won, as the Catholics were finally accepting the arguments of their sixteenth-century opponents. "It is extraordinary to read the pro-Lutheran utterances in the Catholic press," wrote Dawson, who, it must be remembered, spent his adult life fighting for the reunification of Christendom and possessed a strong ecumenical streak. "I can't understand how they reconcile this with their liturgical principles."[93] Such a stance also seemed to negate that which came immediately after Trent, the great Counter-Reformation and Baroque art, culture, and philosophy, which Dawson dearly admired. He expressed to Watkin his hope that enough sympathy for the Counter-Reformation and the Baroque existed for a tempering of the cultural and liturgical changes accompanying Vatican II. Still, Watkin admitted in retrospect, long after Dawson

---

[89]Marty Haugen, "Gather Us In," (GIA Publications). The song is poorly written, sappy, and heterodox at best, heretical at worst. But many Catholic parishes have embraced it without trepidation.

[90]Arnold Sparr, *To Promote, Defend, and Redeem: The Catholic Literary Revival and the Cultural Transformation of American Catholicism, 1920–1960* (New York: Greenwood Press, 1990), 165.

[91]Philip Gleason, *Keeping the Faith: American Catholicism Past and Present* (Notre Dame, IN: University of Notre Dame Press, 1987), 13.

[92]Quoted in E. I. Watkin, "Reflections on the Work of Christopher Dawson," *Downside Review*, vol. 89 (1971), 11. See also Adam Schwartz, " 'I Thought the Church and I Wanted the Same Thing': Opposition to Twentieth-Century Liturgical Change in the Thought of Graham Greene, Christopher Dawson, and David Jones," *Logos*, vol. 1 (1998), 36–65.

[93]Watkin, "Reflections," 11.

had been able to write, his friend would have remained fully loyal to Rome. "And here I am well aware that I differ from the attitude Christopher adopted and would I am certain have contrived to adopt such as I described it in my article, obedient [and loyal] to the Pope whatever his actions," Watkin admitted. "I on the contrary am quite unable to accept the man who had ruined the Church and demolished the liturgy."[94] Though Dawson would have "deplored his [Pope Paul's] destructive work," he would have yet remained loyal.[95]

But the decline of Dawson's reputation had nothing to do with his personal views on Vatican II, which remained private until Watkin discussed them in a 1971 article, long after the decline of his reputation and a full year after Dawson's death. The decline had occurred almost immediately after Dawson had left Harvard. When, for example, Sheed and Ward published Dawson's last work prior to the author's death, *The Formation of Christendom*, the American editor for the Catholic press lamented: "There is, however, as you are aware, a lack of interest in his work which I find regrettable in the extreme. At the same time, I can only point out that there seems to be an overall lack of interest in Church history in general; at least some of our other publications in this area have had a reception as disappointing as that which met Dawson's *Dividing of Christendom* and, seemingly, will meet *The Formation of Christendom*."[96] Dawson and Sheed had originally envisioned Dawson's lectures to be published as a three-volume set, or perhaps as a trilogy, to be called "Christendom." Hence, they would have become:

Christendom: The Formation of Christendom

Christendom: The Division of Christendom

Christendom: The Return to Christian Unity[97]

Dawson came up with the idea for the trilogy in late 1963, and Sheed quickly agreed. "The three parts must be seen as parts of one book," Sheed admitted. Because of Dawson's stature at the beginning of Vatican II, Sheed had assumed that the three volumes would significantly influence the conference proceedings.[98]

Dawson's reputation plummeted, rather than climbed, with the church council. Because of the cultural changes accompanying Vatican II and because of changes in leadership at Sheed and Ward, no press ever published volume III, and it remains in manuscript form in the Harvard theological library. Significantly, Dawson's literary agent, E. I. Watkin, who had been appointed in the early 1960s, failed to find an English publisher for the two

---

[94] Watkin, Torquay, to Bernard Wall, March 24, 1971, in Box 1, Folder 2a, Wall/GU.

[95] Watkin, Torquay, to Bernard Wall, May 14, 1971, in Box 1, Folder 2a, Wall/GU.

[96] Philip Scharper to John Mulloy, November 29, 1967, in Box 13, Folder 44, ND/CSAW.

[97] Sheed to Dawson, December 16, 1963, in Box 1, Folder 13, ND/CSWD.

[98] Sheed to Dawson, December 10, 1963, in Box 1, Folder 13, ND/CSWD.

Harvard books. Furious, Watkin, who callously referred to Vatican II as the "Deformation," tried to explain the situation to Valery, after the Catholic publisher, Collins, refused to print the books. "I replied at length, trying to get her to see that since Christopher was at Harvard abroad and praised by the Catholic intelligentsia there had been nothing less than a revolution in the Church—and Christopher's religion-culture can have no appeal to these" new "barbarians."[99] To make matters worse for Dawson, his greatest advocate, Frank Sheed, retired from the publishing business in 1963, leaving no one at Sheed and Ward to push and defend the English historian who had for nearly forty years been the intellectual cornerstone of the firm.[100]

Dawson was not alone in witnessing his reputation decline. Numerous interwar Catholic intellectuals and scholars found themselves ignored, maligned, or forgotten in the first decade after Vatican II. "It is as though all those powerful writings of Dawson, Maritain, Guardini and so many others had never really taken root," lamented Michael Novak in a ten-year retrospective.[101] Novak had known Dawson personally and interviewed him when they were both at Harvard. Unfortunately, some of the decline in Dawson's reputation was long coming. John Hellman, a historian at McGill University in Canada, remembers arriving at Harvard immediately after Dawson's days there, only to find that most of his fellow graduate students considered Dawson little more than "an apologist" for the faith in the history department, and most theology departments were far more interested in what was then called "the new theology."[102] In a tribute to Dawson in 1969, celebrating his eightieth birthday, E. I. Watkin noted that American Catholics especially had "discarded as outdated" Dawson and all of his books, considering him and them "without value or even significance for the contemporary Catholic."[103] Most people had forgotten him. His moment of *anamnesis* was over.

But Watkin asserted that despite his sudden unpopularity in the massive cultural, social, and political upheaval in the years following Vatican II, Dawson "has not been refuted. He cannot be. For his interpretations are anchored securely to historical fact. He is simply discarded."[104] And, as the London *Times* claimed, he will not remain discarded forever. "It is unlikely that, whatever the temporary eclipse that he may suffer, he will not in the long run be the loser for that."[105] Russell Kirk, not atypically, put his sentiments succinctly: "A

---

[99] E. I. Watkin, Torquay, to Bernard Wall, February 28, 1969, in Box 1, Folder 24, Wall/GU; and Sheed to E. I. Watkin, December 31, 1973, in Box 1, Folder 15, ND/CSWD.

[100] Sheed to "Read of our books," October 27, 1971, in Box 1, Folder 14, ND/CSWD.

[101] Michael Novak, "The Political Identity of Catholics," *Commonweal*, vol. 97 (February 16, 1973), 441.

[102] Hellman, "Harvard in the 1960s."

[103] E. I. Watkin, "Tribute to Christopher Dawson," *Tablet* (1969), 974.

[104] Ibid.

[105] *London Times* obituary quoted in C. J. McNaspy, "Christopher Dawson: In Memoriam," *America*, vol. 122 (June 13, 1970), 634.

renewed historical consciousness of the past may redeem us from many horrors of the present. If this renewal of the historical consciousness does come to pass, Christopher Dawson may yet be chief among its authors."[106] Perhaps Father McNaspy put it best. Dawson, the Louisiana Jesuit argued, could never seem elderly, "for he had always seemed part of our mental furniture, never old, ageless. This, I believe, is true of his writing."[107]

Despite events of the 1960s, Dawson had supreme faith in the Church, and he expressed it in public writings as well as in private correspondence.

> As long as the Church is alive, Christian culture is alive and continues to bear some fruit. After all the saint is a manifestation of Christian culture. He is alive; he acts on the world and is acted on by it. He is the microcosm of Christian culture. Of course I agree with Tavard that eventually the Church will produce a universal ecumenical cosmic culture. But when? If we say 'tomorrow' we shall only be fostering the illusion of the millennarists which have proved so dangerous alike in theology and in politics. If we say 'perhaps a thousand years,' we shall still have plenty of time for a systematic study of Christian culture.[108]

---

[106]Russell Kirk, "The High Achievement of Christopher Dawson," *Chesterton Review*, vol. 10 (1984), 438.

[107]McNaspy, "In Memoriam," 634.

[108]Dawson, Harvard, to Bruno Schlesinger, Notre Dame, IN, January 18, 1962, in Box 15, Folder 124, UST/CDC.

Conclusion

The Human Person and the City of God

AFTER READING CHRISTOPHER DAWSON'S MANY WORKS—AND, PERHAPS, THIS book as well—one must wonder what the role of the human person is in the larger order of the universe. After all, Dawson more often than not wrote in sweeping terms. After reading any of his varied works, one comes away overwhelmed by his many profound, deep, and sometimes bewildering thoughts regarding the various forces at work within creation: God, nature, time, eternity, the Church, culture, and language, to name just a few. Where does the individual human person fit in? Does he have agency at all, or is he merely a player in a larger drama in which he never chooses to participate or in what manner to act? Is the human person merely a part of the vast, uncontrollable machinery of the universe, even if that universe was created by a benevolent Being?

For Dawson, history was certainly a story—the Gospel (literally: "God's spell" or story)—a myth in the best sense of the word. In true Aristotelian and Pauline fashion, Dawson believed, this grand story "has a beginning, a centre, and an end."[109] It is through history, then, that God works. The Author even entered His work. Indeed, He redeemed the world by entering the story with the Incarnation, Death, and Resurrection of the Son. As Dawson viewed it, one can never understand Christianity without understanding God's vehicle of history. From the Christian perspective, Dawson explained, history is more than just a record of revelation. For "an attempt to create a theory of history from the data of revealed truth alone will give us not a history but a theodicy" like those written by St. Augustine or Eusebius.[110] And yet, man can be overwhelmed by Providence at any—or indeed, in every—moment. "The Kingdom of God is not the work of man and does not emerge by a natural law of progress from the course of human history. It makes a violent irruption

---

[109] Christopher Dawson, *Dynamics of World History*, John J. Mulloy, ed. (1957; Wilmington, DE: ISI Books, 2002), 248.

[110] Ibid., 285.

into history and confounds the work of man," Dawson explained.[111] Man, as a member of the story, confronts God at many levels: through the prophets, the saints, the revealed word, the Incarnate Word, the Church, the sacraments, and through the uniqueness of each new individual human person, himself *imago Dei*, a singular, finite reflection of the infinite Creator.

And, yet, man is not merely acted upon. Instead, he has a significant role in the City of Man and in the City of God. Certainly, according to Dawson, he can only find himself in relation to God, the pure Being. "Just as behind all religion and all spiritual philosophy there is a metaphysical assent—the affirmation of Being—so behind materialism and the materialist explaining away of history there is a metaphysical negation—the denial of Being—which is the ultimate and quasi-mystical ground of the materialistic position," Dawson wrote in volume three of *Essays in Order*.[112] Further, he wrote in the same work, "The one ultimate reality is the Being of God, and the world of man and nature itself are only real in so far as they have their ground and principle of being in that supreme reality."[113] The universe itself is a shadow of ultimate Being, fallen, and redeemable only through the Light of the Logos. Jesus is "the Divine Intelligence, the Principle of the order and intelligibility of the created world."[114] Therefore, when the Church acts as it was created to do, "it becomes the visible embodiment of this positive divine principle standing over against the eternal negative of evil."[115] Goodness is reality, and evil is un-reality, Dawson argued, following the thought of St. Augustine and Boethius. When a man behaves in a proper fashion, he becomes increasingly ordered to the proper order of God's economy of grace. When a man behaves contrary to the established rules of right and first principles, he becomes progressively less of a man and moves toward annihilation.

The human person, though, created *imago Dei*, is unique in time and space. God places each person in His order for His purposes. Born in a certain time and a certain place, each person offers a unique reflection of the Infinite, as well as offering gifts to be added to the universal mission of the Church, the Body of Christ. He finds himself in the order of creation through his own being. "Every Christian mind is a seed of change so long as it is a living mind," Dawson wrote. "A Christian has only *to be* in order to change the world, for in that act of being there is contained all the mystery of supernatural life."[116] Further, "Christianity may be denied and persecuted, or forgotten and ignored, but it still lives on deep in our social and individual

---

[111] Ibid., 290.

[112] Christopher Dawson, "Christianity and the New Age," in *Essays in Order,* Christopher Dawson and Tom Burns, eds. (New York: Macmillan, 1931), 165–66.

[113] Ibid., 174.

[114] Ibid., 176, 222.

[115] Christopher Dawson, "The Social Factor in the Problem of Christian Unity," *Colosseum*, vol. 4 (1938), 14.

[116] Dawson, "Christianity and the New Age," 242–43.

consciousness," he wrote in 1953.[117] Through the creativity of the Holy Spirit as manifested through the vitality and sacraments of the Church, men turn from the animal and the material to the spiritual and become, contra Nietzsche, real "supermen."[118] Man, in the words of G. K. Chesterton, is a little word, a reflection of the Incarnate Word, but important and glorious for that very reason and reflection.

Always, the individual human person must resist the drift of the world, generation after generation, for the conflict of the world with God "is inescapable," Dawson argued.[119] "The whole tendency of modern life is toward scientific planning and organization, central control, standardization and specialization."[120] In other words, the modern world attempts to de-humanize the individual person by making him less than he is meant to be. The West, especially, Dawson feared, tempted the weaker side of man, as "it is the sign of the dollar rather than the cross that now marshals the forces of Western civilization."[121] But, Dawson warned time and time again, we are not merely economic men. Like Jeremiah, Dawson condemned modern man as a whore, willing to prostitute himself and his gifts to the highest bidder. Like a saint, Dawson attempted to get people to see that God has given them the ability to see behind and beyond the material.

Indeed, to live up to His promise, Dawson argued, God gave man the gift of creativity and imagination, that is, the ability to see things as more than what they simply appear to be. The gift of true imagination comes with the Incarnation, and it allows man to see the essence of a thing. Prior to Jesus' first coming, God seems to have claimed a near monopoly on imagination and creativity in the sense that Dawson meant it. For example, when God speaks to the prophet Samuel, He says: "Man looks at the outward appearance, but the Lord looks at the heart."[122] With the Light of the Logos entering the world, though, St. Paul wrote that "everything exposed by the light becomes visible."[123] In other words, the imagination provided by the Word Becoming Flesh allows one to see beyond the physical, the accidental, and directly to the essence of something. Once the essence is found, it can and must be sanctified for use for the City of God. "As man needs God and nature requires grace for its own perfecting, so humane culture is the natural foundation and preparation for spiritual culture," Dawson wrote in 1952. "Humanism and

---

[117]Christopher Dawson, "Religion," in *The Unity of European Culture*, BBC, ed. (London: B.B.C., 1953), 7.

[118]Dawson, "Christianity and the New Age," 242–43.

[119]Christopher Dawson, "The Problem of Christ and Culture," *Dublin Review*, vol. 226 (1952), 67.

[120]Christopher Dawson, *The Historic Reality of Christian Culture: A Way to the Renewal of Human Life* (London: Routledge and Kegan Paul, 1960), 26.

[121]Ibid., 39.

[122]1 Samuel 16:7 (NIV)

[123]Ephesians 5:13 (NIV)

Divinity are as complementary to one another in the order of culture, as are Nature and Grace in the order of being."[124]

Armed with creativity, the citizen of the City of God must also take on specific roles, Dawson believed. Sometimes, the human person must be a mystic, capable of breaking down the barriers of time to see into eternity, getting past the shadow to see the beauty of Pure Being.[125] Sometimes, the human person must be a prophet, decrying the ravages of the world. Always, though, the human person must be a saint, redeemed by the intersection of eternity and time, remade as a new being. He must, according to Dawson, allow the light of the Logos to reflect within him, in his being and in his works, thus serving as a witness to the power of the Spirit. "The victory that overcomes the world is not success," Dawson cautioned, "but faith and it is only the eye of faith that understands the true value of history."[126] Sometimes the Holocaust camps and Gulags will overwhelm the fortitude of man, and he must accept martyrdom. The Church "wins not by majorities but by martyrs and the cross is her victory," Dawson asserted.[127] One sees this in the catacombs of the early Church, Dawson wrote in 1933. "For the keynote of the Christian doctrine of future life is not Immortality, but Resurrection; not the survival of an immaterial principle, but the vital restitution of human nature in its integrity."[128]

Even at the worst moments of history—whether the Vandals' sacking of Rome or the ideological atrocities of the mid-twentieth century—the human person can call on divine help, Dawson believed. With Soviet tyranny and oppression in Poland, Dawson wrote in the middle of the Cold War, the spiritual element allowed the Poles and other Eastern Europeans "to survive," for they were living in "a situation which tests the spiritual quality of a community more than most people realize."[129] Dawson died nineteen years prior to the collapse of the Berlin Wall, but he already understood that the force of arms would not crack the wall. Instead, words and acts of love brought down the heinous symbol of tyranny. John Paul II told the Poles to "be not afraid" in 1979. Further, he told them to fight with prayer, fasting, and sacrifice, following the examples of Sts. Stanislaw and Maximilian Kolbe, as the Church had always taught resistance.

---

[124]Christopher Dawson, "Christianity and the Humanist Tradition," *Dublin Review*, vol. 226 (1952), 11; and *Progress and Religion: An Historical Inquiry* (1929; Washington, D.C.: Catholic University of America Press, 2001), 62.

[125]Dawson, "Christianity and the New Age," 176.

[126]Dawson, *Dynamics of World History,* 299.

[127]Ibid.

[128]Christopher Dawson, "The Future Life: A Roman Catholic View," *The Spectator*, vol. 151 (1933), 889.

[129]Christopher Dawson, "Christian Culture in Eastern Europe," *Dublin Review*, vol. 224 (1950), 30–31.

Writing about Pius XII, Dawson concluded that "the pontificates of the twentieth-century have been a catastrophic period, full of wars and rumours of wars and the distress of nations, but they have also seen the dawn of a new hope for humanity." After all, Dawson argued, the pontificates "foreshadow the birth of a new Christendom—a Society which is not confined as in the past to a single group of nations and a single civilization but which is common to every people and language and unites all the members of the human family in the divine community of the Mystical Body of Christ."[130] What better pope than John Paul II, who started the Velvet Revolution through words of hope and peace, but who spent his papacy apologizing to Jews, Orthodox, and Protestants for the past crimes of the Church, to fulfill Dawson's predictions. None of Dawson's hope was mere wishful thinking on his part or misplaced romantic longings. Love not only created the universe, as Dawson always believed, it also renews and sustains it. As Barbara Elliott has demonstrated conclusively in her brilliant book on the Velvet Revolution, *Candles Behind the Wall*, Christian peace groups throughout Eastern Europe, rallied by John Paul's visionary and stirring rhetoric, brought communism down from within.[131] When the false spiritual vision of communism failed, the people returned to their first principles and right reason. Importantly, they embraced the Word, not the gun. As John Paul II wrote after the collapse of communism: "The fall of this kind of 'bloc' or empire was accomplished almost everywhere by means of peaceful protest, using only the weapons of truth and justice" and sought "to reawaken" in the ideologue "a sense of shared human dignity."[132] Truth is truth—it can be obscured, hidden, or misplaced, but it cannot be destroyed. It only awaits to be called upon and recovered.

Though Dawson did not live to witness the events that destroyed communism, 1979 through 1989, he had hope. As early as 1933, he had written, "While the City of God is stronger than it appears to be, the city of man is weaker." The world of man only appears strong. "The forces that appear to make human civilization so irresistible—its wealth, its economic organization, and its military power—are essentially hollow, and crumble to dust as soon as the human purpose that animates them loses its strength." The world had no soul, no center, and, therefore, no purpose. "The real forces that rule the world are spiritual ones, and every empire and civilization waits for the hour when the sentence of the watchers goes forth and its kingdom is numbered and finished."[133] Dawson's hope is the same hope that inspired

---

[130]Christopher Dawson, *Christianity in East and West* (La Salle, IL: Sherwood Sugden, 1981), 221.

[131]Barbara [von der Heydt] Elliott, *Candles Behind the Wall: Heroes of the Peaceful Revolution That Shattered Communism* (Grand Rapids, MI: William B. Eerdmans, 1993).

[132] John Paul II, *On the Hundredth Anniversary of* Rerum Novarum, (Paulist Press, 1991), 35.

[133]Christopher Dawson, "Man and Civilization," in *God and the World: Through Christian Eyes (Second Series)*, Leonard Hodgson, ed. (London: Student Christian Movement Press, 1934), 45.

such anti-communist figures as John Paul II, Ronald Reagan, and Alexandr Solzhenitsyn. Dawson knew that hope, the second highest virtue, remains, no matter what transpires in this world.[134] It comes not from humanity, but from outside of humanity. It is a Divine Gift.

The Church, then, serves as the beacon of hope: protected by its Spiritual Host, it rallies the faithful around the sacraments. Indeed, rather than having built or destroyed western civilization, the Church sanctified what it inherited and gave the West new life. As St. Augustine explained in the *City of God*, the Church took the best of what it found—from the Jews, Greeks, and the Romans, and later from the Germans—and gave this inheritance a new and vital essence, the light of the Logos through the sacraments of the Church. Each mass, each martyr, and each saint has offered and will continue to offer a renewal of the West. Indeed, the Incarnation—and the consequent death and resurrection—is the most important moment in the history of this world, an irruption by Eternity into Time itself. This, of course, is why Catholics bow during the recitation of the creed when the Holy Spirit and the Virgin Mary are spoken of. Each mass, each martyr, and each saint is a reflection of the power of the Logos. With the life and death of Christ, the West, for all intents and purposes, was "born again." The power of the Logos, of course, is not limited to the West. It is truth itself, and, through grace, all peoples and all cultures may embrace it.

Through prose, Dawson attempted to put the current situation of the West and the Church in a larger perspective in 1950. "Today the babel of tongues is becoming silent and Western man has lost faith in himself and in his future," Dawson wrote. "But the Church still stands as she stood fifteen hundred years ago, as the only earthly representative of an eternal order which survives the fall of empires and civilizations; and the darker become the prospects of secular culture, the more clearly does the Church stand out as a city of refuge for humanity."[135] During much of Dawson's life, that hope came from an unlikely place: the dead. Certainly, the vast dead of the twentieth century, most of whom disappeared into the shadow worlds of the KGB and the Gestapo, should be testament enough to the power of ideologies and the power of the martyrs, the City of Man versus the City of God. The blood of the martyrs, after all, built the early Church. Perhaps the twentieth-century martyrs will serve as the foundation of a renewed, vigorous twenty-first century Church, ready to challenge the world with all of the fierceness and love necessary.

Perhaps.

Though armed with the sacraments and the Spirit, Dawson knew, the Church was also composed of individual human persons, each unique, each glorious, each armed with gifts. But they were one and all weighed down

---

[134]Dawson, "Christian Culture in Eastern Europe," 30.

[135]Christopher Dawson, "The Victorian Background," *Tablet* (1950), 246. See also Dawson to Mulloy, August 9, 1954, in Box 1, Folder 15, ND/CDAW.

with various and burdensome crosses. The poet, the visionary, the prophet, and the saint—each arise in every generation, carry on the traditions of the past, present them in a fashion acceptable to the current generation, and prepare the truth for future generations. When such men and women arise and willingly sacrifice their very selves for the promotion of the greater good, for God's Church, the world remains ordered. When men and women choose to use their gifts for self-gratification and avarice, the world becomes disordered, mechanized, and violent. For fallen men often behave in fallen ways.

Endowed with free will, men can become like Lancelot, choosing to pursue the earthly beauty of a Guinevere, or they can become like Galahad, pursuing the true, otherworldly beauty of the Holy Grail, the cup of the last supper. Galahad chose wisely, using his gifts to sanctify the world in the name of Christ. But, even he, as wise and brave as he was, could not prevent Arthur's kingdom from crumbling. Indeed, even Excalibur, the sword bequeathed by the Lady of the Lake to a young Romano-Celt with the unlikely name of Arthur, could not undo the mischief of Lancelot. Divided, the kingdom fell. Still, the myth survives, as does its power to move future generations, bestowing upon them the imagination that allows one to envision possibilities. Though Camelot may have fallen, future generations may learn from Lancelot's mistakes and attempt to rebuild the kingdom.

Dawson the prophet and the saint, armed with penetrating intelligence and ceaseless imagination, wielded hope and love creatively. He was a man who recognized his many gifts and his many faults. He was a man who cherished the good in the world, and he was an anxious man, who suffered much from psychological and physical infirmities. Still, he knew he was *imago Dei*, a little word, glorious and unique. "The word," Dawson wrote in the 1960s, "not the sword or the spade, is the power that has created human culture."[136] Dawson spent almost every moment of his adult life attempting to rebuild the kingdom—especially through the power of the written word—to undo the errors of the Lancelots. He offered an Augustinian vision of culture and history to the twentieth century; he encouraged men and women to act like men and women in the best of the western tradition—through the virtue of love; he attacked the ideologues of the left and right as nothing more than false prophets promoting false religions and false gods; and, to revive the world through the imagination, he promoted a new and vigorous understanding of the liberal arts. Despite his personal insecurities, his poor health, and his failure to appreciate all that he offered to the world, Christopher Dawson attempted to live like a Galahad. He desired to sanctify the world, through grace, to embrace truth, beauty, and goodness. Certainly, whatever one might think of Dawson's vision, it must be recognized that in all that he did, whatever his successes and failures, he understood he was a reflection of the One—the One

---

[136]Christopher Dawson, *The Formation of Christendom* (New York: Sheed and Ward, 1967), 33.

Who is pure Being, the creator of all things; the One Who entered His story to redeem His fallen creation; and the One Who, in His own time, will bring all things back to right order. As a creature within the economy of grace, Dawson believed he was born in a certain time, a certain place, and with an immense purpose. Driven by an energy that he believed to be of the Holy Spirit, and armed with a sword sharper than Excalibur, Dawson fought the good fight with all the force imaginable.

A Note on Archival Materials

The publisher and author would like to thank the following for permission to reproduce archival material:

Georgetown University Library for permission to publish materials from the Bernard Wall Papers and the Harmon Grisewood Papers.

Princeton University Library for permission to publish materials from the Paul Elmer More Collection and the Allen Tate Papers.

The University of Notre Dame Archives for permission to reprint materials from the Christopher Dawson Collection, the Leo Ward Papers, the Sheed and Ward Family Papers, and the Sheed and Ward Business Papers.

The Department of Special Collections, University of Saint Thomas, St. Paul, Minnesota, for permission to publish materials from the Christopher Dawson Papers.

Bibliography

As this is an intellectual and historical biography, the bibliography of works by Christopher Dawson is arranged in this book chronologically, while the scholarship about Dawson is arranged alphabetically.

I. Archival Material

Georgetown University Archives, District of Columbia
    Harman Grisewood Papers (Grisewood/GU)
    Bernard Wall Papers (Wall/GU)

Manuscript Division, Department of Rare Books and Special Collections,
Princeton University Library, Princeton, New Jersey
    Paul Elmer More Collection (PFM/Princeton)
    Allen Tate Papers

University of Notre Dame, Notre Dame, Indiana
    Christopher Dawson Collection (ND/CDAW)
    Leo Ward Papers (ND/CLRW)
    Sheed and Ward Family Papers (ND/CSWD)
    Sheed and Ward Business Papers (ND/CSAW)

Department of Special Collections,
University of St. Thomas, St. Paul, Minnesota
    Christopher Dawson Papers (UST/CDC)

Wheaton College, Wheaton, Illinois
    Various Inklings Papers

II. Books/Articles/Chapters by Dawson

1916–1929

Dawson, Christopher. "Catholic Tradition and the Modern State." *Catholic Review* (1916): 24–35.

_____. "Socialism, Capitalism, and the Catholic Tradition." *Universe*, April 11 1919.

_____. "The Land." *Blackfriars* 2 (1921): 137–45.

_____. "On the Development in Relation to the Theory of Progress." *Sociological Review* 13 (1921): 75–83.

_____. "Catholicism and Economics." *Blackfriars* 5 (1924): 89–102, 154–73, 210–19.

_____. "A Scheme of British Culture Periods, and of Their Relationship to European Cultural Developments." *Sociological Review* 16 (1924): 117–25.

_____. "Religion and Primitive Culture." *Sociological Review* 17 (1925): 105–19.

_____. "Religion and the Life of Civilization." In *Religions of the Empire: A Conference on Some Living Religions within the Empire*, ed. William Loftus Hare, 455–69. London, ENG: Duckworth, 1925.

_____. "The Hymn of Casia the Poetess, and the Byzantine Liturgical Tradition." *Chimes* 6 (1926): 277–81.

_____. "Why I Am a Catholic." *Catholic Times*, May 21 1926, 10–11.

_____. "Christianity and the Idea of Progress." *Dublin Review* 180 (1927): 19–39.

_____. "The Mystery of China." *Sociological Review* 19 (1927): 297–303.

_____. "Civilization and Order." *Order: An Occasional Catholic Review* 1 (1928): 42–45.

_____. *The Age of the Gods*. London, ENG: John Murray, 1928.

_____. "The Psychology of Sex and the Catholic Order." *Order: An Occasional Catholic Review* 1 (1929): 79–82.

_____. "The Idea of a Catholic Order." *Order: An Occasional Catholic Review* 1 (1929): 111–115.

_____. "The Revolt of the East and the Catholic Tradition." *Dublin Review* 183 (1928): 1–14.

1930–1939

_____. *Christianity and Sex*. London, ENG: Faber and Faber, 1930.

_____. "The Dark Mirror." *Dublin Review* 187 (1930): 177–200.

_____. "The End of an Age." *Criterion* 9 (1930): 386–401.

_____. "European Democracy and the New Economic Forces." *Sociological Review* 22 (1930): 32–42.

_____. "Islamic Mysticism." *Dublin Review* 186 (1930): 34–61.

_____. Review of *Medieval Culture* and *New Light on the Youth of Dante*. *Criterion* 9 (July 1930): 718–22.

_____. "The Classical Tradition and the Origins of Mediaeval Culture." *Studies* 20 (1931): 209–24.

_____. "Introduction." In Carl Schmitt, *The Necessity of Politics*, 9–28. London, ENG: Sheed and Ward, 1931.

_____. "The Origins of the European Scientific Tradition: St. Thomas and Roger Bacon." *Clergy Review* 2 (1931): 193–205.

_____. "The Problem of Wealth." *Spectator* 147 (1931): 485–6.

_____. "Scholasticism and the Origins of the European Scientific Tradition." *Clergy Review* 2 (1931): 108–21.

_____. "The 'Dark Ages' and Ireland." *Studies* 21 (1932): 259–68.

_____. " 'He Gave . . . His Whole Self'." *Sociological Review* 24 (1932): 24.

_____. "The New Decline and Fall." *Commonweal* 15 (1932): 320–22.

_____. "The Origins of the Romantic Tradition." *Criterion* 11 (1932): 222–48.

_____. "The Significance of Bolshevism." *English Review* 55 (1932): 239–50.

_____. *Enquiries into Religion and Culture*. New York: Sheed and Ward, 1933.

_____. "The Future Life: A Roman Catholic View." *Spectator* 151 (1933): 889–90.

_____. "Introduction." In David Mathew, *The Celtic Peoples and Renaissance Europe: A Study of the Celtic and Spanish Influences on Elizabethan History*, xiii-xv. London and New York: Sheed and Ward, 1933.

_____. "The Modern Dilemma." *Cambridge Review* (1933).

_____. *The Modern Dilemma: The Problem of European Unity*. Vol. 8. 14 vols. *Essays in Order*, ed. Christopher Dawson and Tom Burns. London, ENG: Sheed and Ward, 1933.

_____. "Philosophy of Freedom." *North West Review*, July 20 1933.

_____. "William Langland." In *The English Way: Studies in English Sanctity from St. Bede to Newman*, ed. Maisie Ward, 159–94. London, ENG: Sheed and Ward, 1933.

_____. "The World Crisis and the English Tradition." *English Review* 56 (1933): 248–60.

_____. "Civilization and the Faith." *Theology* 28 (1934): 67–77.

_____. "Edward Gibbon." *Proceedings of the British Academy* 20 (1934): 159–80.

_____. "Last Words on Mr. De Blacam." *G. K.'s Weekly* 20 (1934): 178–79.

_____. *The Making of Europe: An Introduction to the History of European Unity*. New York: Sheed and Ward, 1934.

_____. "Man and Civilization." In *God and the World: Through Christian Eyes (Second Series)*, ed. Leonard Hodgson, 34–45. London, ENG: Student Christian Movement Press, 1934.

_____. "Marx." *Church Times*, May 18 1934.

_____. "Marx's Materialism." *Church Times*, June 1 1934.

_____. *Mediaeval Religion and Other Essays*. London, ENG: Sheed and Ward, 1934.

_____. "Prevision in Religion." *Sociological Review* 26 (1934): 41–54.

_____. "The Real Issue." *Colosseum* 1 (1934): 17–31.

_____. "Rome, Ireland, and the European Tradition." *G. K.'s Weekly* 20 (1934): 89–90.

_____. "Sociology as a Science." In *Science for a New World: The Scientific Outlook on World Problems Explained by Leading Exponents of Modern Scientific Thought*, ed. J. G. Crowther, 151–72. New York: Harper and Brothers, 1934.

_____. "To the Editor." *Catholic Times*, May 11 1934.

_____. "To the Editor." *Catholic Herald*, May 12 1934.

_____. "The Totalitarian State." *Catholic Herald*, October 27 1934.

_____. "Catholicism and the Bourgeois Mind." *Colosseum* 2 (1935): 246–56.

_____. "Fascism and the Corporative State." *Catholic Herald*, August 3 1935.

_____. "The Future of National Government." *Dublin Review* vol. 196 (1935): 236–51.

_____. *Mediæval Christianity*. Rev. E. C. Messenger, ed. Studies in Comparative Religion. London, ENG: Catholic Truth Society, 1935.

_____. "The Making of Britain." *Tablet* (1936): 781–82.

_____. "The Nature and Destiny of Man." In *God and the Supernatural: A Catholic Statement of the Christian Faith*, 57–84. London, ENG: Catholic Book Club, 1936.

_____. "Religion and Romanticism: A Study in the Origin of the Religious Revival in Europe in the Nineteenth Century." *Christendom* 1 (1936): 577–92.

_____. *Religion and the Modern State*. New York: Sheed and Ward, 1936.

_____. "Religion in the Age of Revolution." *Tablet* (1936): 549–50.

_____. "Religion in the Age of Revolution: Joseph De Maistre and the Counter Revolution." *Tablet* (1936): 301–2.

_____. "Religion in the Age of Revolution: The Church and the Revolution." *Tablet* (1936): 265–66.

_____. "Religion in the Age of Revolution: The Triumph of Liberalism." *Tablet* (1936): 477–78.

_____. "Religion in the Age of Revolution: The Turn of the Tide." *Tablet* (1936): 516–17.

_____. "Religion in the Age of Revolution: William Blake and the Religion of Romanticism." *Tablet* (1936): 336–38.

_____. "The Re-Making of Europe." *Tablet* (1936): 428–29.

_____. "The Catholic Attitude to War." *Tablet* (1937): 365–68.

_____. "Church, State, and Community: Concordats or Catacombs?" *Tablet* (1937): 909–10.

_____. "Church, State, and Community: The Significance of the Coronation." *Tablet* (1937): 873–75.

_____. "Industrialism and Social Order." *Tablet* (1937): 625–26.

_____. "The Frontiers of Necessity: The Social Factor in Religious Belief." *Tablet* (1938): 697.

_____. "The Moral of Austria." *Tablet* (1938): 358.

_____. "The Social Factor in the Problem of Christian Unity." *Colosseum* 4 (1938): 7–15.

_____. "Social Fractors in Christian Reunion." *Tablet* (1938): 529–31.

_____. "The Tragedy of Christian Politics." *Sign* 18 (1938): 7–10.

_____. *Beyond Politics*. New York: Sheed and Ward, 1939.

_____. "The Claims of Politics." *Scrutiny* 8 (1939): 136–141.

_____. "European Unity and the League of Nations: European Unity and International Order." *Tablet* (1939): 741–42.

_____. "European Unity and the League of Nations: The Breakdown of the League." *Tablet* (1939): 665–66.

_____. "European Unity and the League of Nations: The Nation-State and European Unity." *Tablet* (1939): 717–18.

_____. "Hitler's 'Mein Kampf'." *Tablet* (1939): 373–74.

_____. "The Hour of Darkness." *Tablet* (1939): 625–626.

_____. "Hungarian Middle Ages." *Hungarian Quarterly* 5 (1939): 585–90.

_____. "The New Community: Fascism, Democracy, and the English Tradition." *Tablet* (1939): 5–7.

_____. "The New Community: The Restoration of Spiritual Order." *Tablet* (1939): 37–39.

_____. "To the Editor." *Tablet* (1939).

_____. "Toward Christian Unity." *Sign* 18 (1939): 407–09.

1940–1949

_____. "A Century of Change, 1840–1940." *Tablet* (1940): 470–71.

_____. "Editorial Note." *Dublin Review* 207 (1940): 1–3.

_____. "On Nationalism." *Tablet* (1940): 348–49.

_____. "Propaganda." *Tablet* (1940): 265–66.

_____. "The Sword of the Spirit." *Tablet* (1940): 172.

_____. "The Threat to the West." *Commonweal* 21 (February 2, 1940): 317–18.

_____. "Christian Unity and the New Order." *Sword of the Spirit*, no. 13 (1941): 2.

_____. "Christianity and Culture." *Dublin Review* 208 (1941): 137–149.

_____. "Europe and Christendom." *Dublin Review* 209 (1941): 109–119.

_____. "What Is the Alternative to Totalitarianism?" *Christian News-Letter*, no. 107 (1941).

_____. "Christian Freedom." *Dublin Review* 211 (1942): 1–8.

_____. "Europe: Its Tradition and Its Future, Cultural and Religious." *Christendom* 12 (1942): 144–56.

_____. "The Foundations of Unity." *Dublin Review* 211 (1942): 97–104.

_____. "Freedom and Vocation." *Dublin Review* 210 (1942): 1–11.

_____. *The Judgment of the Nations*. New York: Sheed and Ward, 1942.

_____. "The Papacy and the New Order." *Dublin Review* 211 (1942): 109–15.

_____. "Spiritual Reconstruction: The Roman Catholic View." In *The Future of Faith: A Diversity of Views*, ed. Percy Colson, 70–77. London, ENG: Hurst and Blackett, 1942.

_____. "What About Heretics." *Commonweal* 36 (September 18, 1942): 513–17.

_____. "Democracy and the British Tradition." *Dublin Review* 212 (1943): 97–103.

_____. "Europe and the Smaller Peoples." *Dublin Review* 212 (1943): 1–10.

_____. "Introduction." In *The Catholic Church and Education*, ed. M. O'Leary, vii-x. London, ENG: Burns, Oates, and Washbourne, 1943.

_____. "The Politics of Hegel." *Dublin Review* 212 (1943): 97–107.

_____. "Foundations of European Order." *Catholic Mind* 42 (1944): 313–16.

_____. "Peace Aims and Power Politics." *Dublin Review* 213 (1944): 97–108.

_____. "Religion and Mass Civilization—the Problem of the Future." *Dublin Review* 213 (1944): 1–8.

_____. "Dawson Makes Plea for Common Principles." *Los Angeles Tidings*, May 4 1945.

_____. "Democracy and the Party System." *Catholic Mind* 43 (1945): 513–20.

_____. "Europe—a Society of Peoples." *Month* 181 (1945): 309–16.

_____. "Parties, Politics, and Peace." *Catholic Mind* 43 (1945): 370–72.

_____. "Religion." In *The Unity of European Culture*, ed. B.B.C., 6–8. London, ENG: B.B.C., 1945.

_____. "The Yogi and the Commissar." *Blackfriars* 26 (1945): 366–71.

_____. "Education and the Crisis of Christian Culture." *Lumen Vitae* 1 (1946): 204–15.

_____. "Italy and the Peace of Europe." *Month* 182 (1946): 267–72.

_____. "The Left-Right Fallacy." *Catholic Mind* 44 (1946): 251–53.

_____. "The Omnicompetent State." *Tablet* (1946): 98.

_____. "To the Editor." *Tablet* (1946).

_____. "Religious Liberty and the New Political Forces." *Month* 183 (1947): 40–7.

_____. "Christianity and the Western Tradition." *Listener* 39 (1948): 742–43.

_____. *Education and the Crisis of Christian Culture*. Chicago, Ill.: Henry Regnery Company, 1949.

_____. "Mr. T. S. Eliot on the Meaning of Culture." *Month* 1 (1949): 151–57.

_____. "The Name of Britain." *London Times*, January 1 1949, 5

_____. "The Relationship between Religion and Culture." *Commonweal* 49 (February 25, 1949): 488–90.

_____. *Religion and Culture*. London, ENG: Sheed and Ward, 1949.

1950–1959

_____. "Catholics in the Modern World: A Survey at Pentecost." *Tablet* (1950): 419–20.

_____. "Christian Culture in Eastern Europe." *Dublin Review* 224 (1950): 17–35.

_____. "The English Catholics, 1850–1950." *Dublin Review* 224 (1950): 1–12.

_____. "European Literature and the Latin Middle Ages." *Dublin Review* 224 (1950): 31–36.

_____. "The Study of Christian Culture as a Means of Education." *Lumen Vitae* 5 (1950): 171–86.

_____. "The Victorian Background." *Tablet* (1950): 245–46.

_____. "Byzantium and the Christian East." *Dublin Review* 225 (1951): 23–30.

_____. "Religious Enthusiasm." *Month* 5 (1951): 7–14.

_____. "The Sanctions of Mass Democracy: Mr. Carr on the New Society." *Tablet* (1951): 285–86.

_____. "Christianity and the Humanist Tradition." *Dublin Review* 226 (1952): 1–11.

_____. "The Problem of Christ and Culture." *Dublin Review* 226 (1952): 64–68.

_____. *Understanding Europe*. New York: Sheed and Ward, 1952.

_____. "Education and Christian Culture." *Commonweal* 59 (December 4, 1953): 216–20.

_____. "Education and the Study of Christian Culture." *Studies* 42 (1953): 293–302.

_____. *Medieval Essays*. London, ENG: Sheed and Ward, 1953.

_____. "The Significance of Roger Bacon." *Month* 9 (1953): 47–52.

_____. "The Tradition of Christian Monarchy." *Month* 9 (1953): 261–66.

_____. "Ages of Change: A Study of the European Inheritance." *Tablet* (1954): 489–90.

_____. "Christian Culture in the Patristic Age." *Folia* 2 (1954): 59–77.

_____. "Education and Christian Culture." *Commonweal* 59 (February 26, 1954): 526–27.

_____. "Dealing with the Enlightenment and the Liberal Ideology." *Commonweal* 60 (May 14, 1954): 138–39.

_____. "The European Revolution." *Catholic World* 179 (1954): 86–95.

_____. "Future of Christian Culture." *Commonweal* 59 (March 19, 1954): 595–98.

_____. "Historic Origins of Liberalism." *Review of Politics* 16 (1954): 267–82.

_____. "Hope and Culture: Christian Culture as a Culture of Hope." *Lumen Vitae* 9 (1954): 425–30.

_____. "Today's Challenge to U. S. College." *America* 99 (September 4, 1954): 357–38.

_____. "Toynbee's Odyssey of the West." *Commonweal* 61 (October 22, 1954): 62–67.

_____. "Communications: Christian Culture." *Commonweal* 61 (April 1, 1955): 678.

_____. "The Institutional Forms of Christian Culture." *Religion in Life* 24 (1955): 373–80.

_____. "The Outlook for Christian Culture Today." *Cross Currents* 5 (1955): 127–36.

_____. "Problems of Christian Culture." *Commonweal* 62 (April 15, 1955): 34–36.

_____. "St. Boniface." In *Saints and Ourselves*, ed. Philip Caraman, 1–8. London, ENG: Hollis and Carter, 1955.

_____. "Toynbee's Study of History: The Place of Civilizations in History." *International Affairs* 31 (1955): 149–58.

_____. "The Challenge of Secularism." *Catholic World* 182 (1956): 326–30.

_____. "Christian Culture: Its Meaning and Its Value." *Jubilee* 4 (1956): 37–40.

_____. "Christianity and Ideologies." *Commonweal* 64 (May 11, 1956): 139–43.

_____. "Christianity and the Orient: The Problem of Oriental Nationalism." *Tablet* (1956): 172–73.

_____. "Christianity and the Orient: The Problem of Oriental Nationalism II." *Tablet* (1956): 196–98.

_____. "Christianity and the Oriental Cultures: The Thirst for Something New." *Tablet* (1956): 222–24.

_____. "Christianity and the Oriental Cultures: The Christian Perspective." *Tablet* (1956): 245–47.

_____. "Civilization in Crisis." *Catholic World* 182 (1956): 246–52.

_____. "The Study of Christian Culture in the American College." *Catholic World* 182 (1956): 197–201.

_____. "Correspondence." *Thought* 31 (1956–57): 159–60.

_____. "Birth of Democracy." *Review of Politics* 19 (1957): 48–61.

_____. "Dr. Toynbee's Turning Away." *Tablet* (1957): 268–69.

_____. "Education and the State." *Commonweal* 65 (January 25, 1957): 423–27.

_____. "The Impact of Religion and the Modern World." *Commonweal* 65 (January 18, 1957): 412–13.

_____. "Manalive." *Spectator* 91 (September 27, 1957): 398.

_____. "Review of an Historian's Approach to Religion." *International Affairs* 33 (1957): 79–80.

_____. "Review of Ellis, Documents of American Church History." *America* 97 (April 27, 1957): 126, 132–136.

_____. "The Tradition and Destiny of American Literature." *Critic* 16 (1957): 7–8, 70–71.

_____. "American Education and Christian Culture." *American Benedictine Review* 9 (1958): 7–16.

_____. "Is the Church Too Western to Satisfy the Aspirations of the Modern World?" In *World Crisis and the Catholic: Studies Published on the Occasion of The Second World Congress for the Lay Apostolate (Rome)*, 163–68. New York: Sheed and Ward, 1958.

_____. "Universities Ancient and Modern." *Catholic Educational Review* 56 (1958): 27–31.

_____. "Western Culture and the Mystical Body: A Postscript." *Catholic World* 187 (1958): 134–35.

_____. "Catholic Culture in America." *Critic* 17 (1959): 7–9, 58–59.

_____. "The Expansion of Christianity." *Commonweal* 69 (January 9, 1959): 378–80.

_____. *The Movement of World Revolution*. New York: Sheed and Ward, 1959.

_____. "The Study of Christian Culture." *Commonweal* 71 (October 30, 1959): 153–54.

1960–1969

_____. *America and the Secularization of Modern Culture*. Houston, Tex.: University of Saint Thomas, 1960.

_____. *The Historic Reality of Christian Culture: A Way to the Renewal of Human Life*. London, ENG: Routledge and Kegan Paul, 1960.

_____. "Review of Historical Atlas and Gazetteer." *International Affairs* 36 (1960): 217–18.

_____. "The Study of Christian Culture." *Thought* 35 (1960): 485–93.

_____. "Catholicism, Secularism and the Modern World." *Catholic Mind* 59 (1961): 261–68.

_____. "Review of Carthy, English Influence on Early American Catholicism." *Catholic Historical Review* 46 (1961): 461–63.

_____. "Joseph De Maistre." *New Statesman and Nation* 62 (August 18, 1961): 213.

———. "On the Place of Religious Study in Education." *Christian Scholar* 45 (1962): 37–43.

———. "Preface." In *The Limits and Divisions of European History*, ed. Oscar Halecki, vii–xi. Notre Dame, Ind.: University of Notre Dame Press, 1962.

———. "Catholic Culture in America." In *Through Other Eyes: Some Impressions of American Catholicism by Foreign Visitors from 1777 to the Present*, ed. Dan Herr and Joel Wells, 229–41. Westminster, Maryland: Newman Press, 1965.

———. *The Dividing of Christendom*. New York: Sheed and Ward, 1965.

———. "The Christian Church and the Democratic State." *Triumph* 1 (1966): 21–24.

———. "Fifty Years of Liberal-Ultramontane Conflict." *Triumph* 2 (1967): 21–26.

———. *The Formation of Christendom*. New York: Sheed and Ward, 1967.

———. "On Jewish History." *Orbis* 30 (1967): 1247–1256.

———. "The 'Renewal' That Failed." *Triumph* 4 (1969): 25–40.

After 1970

———. *The Gods of Revolution*. New York: New York University, 1972.

———. "Newman and the Modern World." *Tablet* (1972): 733–734.

———. *Religion and World History: A Selection from the Works of Christopher Dawson*, ed. Christina Scott and James Oliver. Garden City, New York: Image, 1975.

———. *Christianity in East and West*. La Salle, Ill.: Sherwood Sugden, 1981.

———. "Letter to G. K. Chesterton, June 1, 1932." *Chesterton Review* 9 (1983): 136.

———. *The Crisis of Western Education*. 1961; Steubenville, Ohio: Franciscan University Press, 1989.

———. "The Restoration of Natural Law." *The Sword* (May 1946), reprinted in *Dawson Newsletter* (Fall 1990): 14–15.

———. "Newman and the Sword of the Spirit." *Dawson Newsletter* (Spring/Summer 1991): 12–13.

———. "The Power of Prayer." *Dawson Newsletter* (Spring/Summer 1991), back cover.

———. *Religion and the Rise of Western Culture*. 1950; New York: Image, 1991.

———. "Dawson's Letter to the Cambridge Review 1933." *Chesterton Review* 23 (1997): 529–31.

———. *Christianity and European Culture: Selections from the Work of Christopher Dawson*, ed. Gerald J. Russello. Washington, D.C.: Catholic University of America, 1998.

———. "What Had Grown Old Will Be Made New." *Inside the Vatican* (1999): 53–57.

———. *Progress and Religion: An Historical Inquiry*. 1929; Washington, D.C.: Catholic University of America Press, 2001.

———. *The Spirit of the Oxford Movement*. 1933; London, ENG: Saint Austin Press, 2001.

———. *Dynamics of World History*, ed. John J. Mulloy. 1957; Wilmington, Delaware: ISI Books, 2002.

———. *The Making of Europe: An Introduction to the History of European Unity*. 1932; Washington, D.C.: Catholic University of America Press, 2002.

Dawson, Christopher, and Alexander Farquharson. "Rome: A Historical Survey." *Sociological Review* 15 (1923): 132–47, 296–311.

Dawson, Christopher, Jacques Maritain, and Peter Wust. *Essays in Order*. Vols. 1–3. 14 vols. *Essays in Order*, ed. Christopher Dawson and T. F. Burns. New York: Macmillan, 1931.

Dawson, Christopher, Robert Speaight, E. J. Oliver, Bryan Houghton, Desmond Fitzgerald, and Francis Burdett. "To the Editor of Colosseum." *Colosseum* 3 (1937): 80–81.

Dawson, Christopher, E. I. Watkin, Gerald Vann, Eric Gill, Maurice Reckitt, and Douglas Jerrold. "Christianity and War: A Symposium." *Colosseum* 4 (1937): 7–35.

III. Interviews, Memoirs, etc.

———. "Backgrounds and Beginnings." *A. D.* 1 (1951): 85–111.

———. "Frank Sheed Talks with Christopher Dawson." *Sign* 38 (December 1958): 33–36.

———. "Interview with Christopher Dawson." *World Student* 2 (1959): 3–8.

———. "Ploughing a Lone Furrow." In *Christianity and Culture*, ed. J. Stanley Murphy. Baltimore: Helicon, 1960.

———. *Tradition and Inheritance: Reflections on the Formative Years*. St. Paul, Minn.: Wanderer Press, 1970.

Dawson, Christopher, and C. J. McNaspy. "A View from Abroad." In *The Moral Curve*, 26–30: No place listed; America Press, 1961.

Dawson, Christopher, and Michael Novak. "Undistracted Philosopher: Historian Christopher Dawson Spurns Publicity for the Quiet Life of the Mind." *Jubilee* 8 (1961): 24–27.

McNaspy, C. J., and Christopher Dawson. "Motel Near Walden II." *America* 104 (January 21, 1961): 508–511.

———. "A Chat with Christopher Dawson." *America* 106 (October 28, 1961): 120–22.

Soper, David Wesley. *Exploring the Christian World Minds: Personal Interviews—the United Nations Community*. New York: Philosophical Library, 1964.

IV. Articles dealing with Dawson and/or Christian Humanism

"1,247 Graduated from St. John's." *New York Times*, June 15 1959.

[Burns, Tom]. "An Introductory." *Order: An Occasional Catholic Review* 1 (1928): 39–41.

———. "Observations." *Order: An Occasional Catholic Review* 1 (1928): 50–52.

———. "An Introductory." *Order: An Occasional Catholic Review* 1 (1929): 106–109.

———. "An Introductory: The Position, Plan and Prospects of 'Order'." *Order: An Occasional Catholic Review* 1 (1929): 74–78.

———. "Our Contemporaries: II: The World the Public Lives In." *Order: An Occasional Catholic Review* 1 (1929): 83–86.

———. "Post Scriptum." *Order: An Occasional Catholic Review* 1 (1929): 109–110.

———. "A Present Condition of Catholics." *Order: An Occasional Catholic Review* 1 (1929): 86–82.

[Gill, Eric]. "Repository Art." *Order: An Occasional Catholic Review* 1 (1928): 14–16.

———. "Tuppence Plain, Penny Coloured." *Order: An Occasional Catholic Review* 1 (1928): 58–61.

———. "The Right-Mindedness of Modern Art." *Order: An Occasional Catholic Review* 1 (1929): 116–119.

[Green, Julian]. "A Present Condition of Catholics." *Order: An Occasional Catholic Review* 1 (1929): 86–92.

———. "A Present Condition of Catholics (Continued)." *Order: An Occasional Catholic Review* 1 (1929): 133–36.

[Hamson, Jack]. "The Catholic Public Schools and Religious Education." *Order: An Occasional Catholic Review* 1 (1928): 22–24.

[Watkin, E. I.]. "Ecclesiastical Materialism." *Order: An Occasional Catholic Review* 1 (1928): 9–13.

"Again the Idea of 'Order'." *Order: An Occasional Catholic Review* 1 (1928): 38.

Albright, W. F. *History, Archaeology, and Christian Humanism*. New York: McGraw Hill, 1964.

Allers, Rudolf. *The New Psychologies*. Vol. 9. 14 vols. *Essays in Order*, ed. Christopher Dawson and Tom Burns. London, ENG: Sheed and Ward, 1933.

Allitt, Patrick. *Catholic Converts: British and American Intellectuals Turn to Rome*. Ithaca, N.Y.: Cornell University Press, 1997.

Anthony, Clement. "The Unpublished Second Volume." *Dawson Newsletter* (Spring 1990): 14–16.

"Apologetics at School: Two Views." *Order: An Occasional Catholic Review* 1 (1929): 125–28.

Aquinas, Saint Thomas. *On Kingship to the King of Cyprus*. Trans. by Gerald B. Phelan. Toronto, ONT, Canada: Pontifical Institute of Medieval Studies, 1949.

"Archbishop Downey to Broadcast." *London Universe*, November 25 1932.

Attwater, Donald. "Eric Gill." In *Modern Christian Revolutionaries: An Introduction to the Lives and Thought of Kierkegaard, Eric Gill, G. K. Chesterton, C. F. Andrews, and Berdyaev*, ed. Donald Attwater, 159–228. Freeport, NY: Books for Libraries Press, 1971.

St. Augustine, *Confessions*. Ed. and trans. by Frank Sheed. Hackett: Indianapolis, Ind., 1993.

_____. *The City of God*. Trans. by Marcus Dods. New York: Modern Library, 1993.

"B.B.C. New Series of Talks: 'God and the World through Christian Eyes." *Church of England Newspaper*, December 16 1932.

Babbitt, Irving. *Rousseau and Romanticism*. Boston: Houghton Mifflin, 1947.

Barfield, Owen. *Poetic Diction: A Study in Meaning*. Hanover, Conn.: Wesleyan University Press, 1984.

Barrett, William. "The Europe That Was, and Might Be." *New York Times Book Review*, December 28 1952.

Beck, A. A. "The Judgement of the Nations." *Clergy Review* 24 (1944): 97–108.

Belgrave, Philip. "Reply: The Vision of Christopher Dawson." *Commonweal* 67 (January 24, 1958): 433.

Berdyaev, Nicholas. "The Destiny of Culture." *Colosseum* 1 (1934): 11–17, 61–67.

_____. *Slavery and Freedom*. Translated by R. M. French. New York: Charles Scribner's Sons, 1944.

_____. *The Russian Idea*. New York: MacMillan, 1948.

_____. *Dream and Reality: An Essay in Autobiography*. New York: MacMillan, 1951.

_____. *The Fate of Man in the Modern World*. Translated by Donald A. Lowrie. Ann Arbor: University of Michigan Press, 1961.

_____. *The Meaning of History*. Translated by George Reavey. Cleveland, OH: World Publishing Company, 1969.

Birzer, Bradley J. "The Christian Gifts of J. R. R. Tolkien." *New Oxford Review* 68 (November 2001): 25–29.

_____. "Bradley J. Birzer Talks to Jeffrey O. Nelson." *Saint Austin Review* 2 (2002): 4–8.

_____. *J. R. R. Tolkien's Sanctifying Myth: Understanding Middle-Earth*. Wilmington, Del.: ISI Books, 2002.

_____. "Grace and Will in Tolkien's Legendarium." *Saint Austin Review* 3 (2003): 14–19.

_____. "Tolkien: The Man Behind the Myth." *Christian History* 22 (2003): 10–17.

_____. "The New Men and Women of Letters." In *More People's Guide to J. R. R. Tolkien*, ed. Cynthia L. McNew, 16–19. Cold Springs Harbor, NY: Cold Springs Harbor, 2004.

_____. "Finding the Human Person," *Crisis* 22 (2004), 53–54

———. "Face to Face: Interview with Annette Kirk." *St. Austin Review* 5 (2005): 17–18.

———. "Christopher Dawson: *The* Historian of the Twentieth Century." *St. Austin Review* 5 (2005): 6–8.

———. "Renewing the West," *Crisis* 23 (2005): 47–48.

———. "Redeemer Nation," *Crisis* 24 (2006): 54–56.

Bliese, John R. E. "Christopher Dawson: His Interpretation of History." *Modern Age* 23 (1979): 259–65.

Blissett, William. *The Long Conversation: A Memoir of David Jones.* Oxford: Oxford University Press, 1981.

Blum, Christopher, ed. *Critics of the Enlightenment: Readings in the French Counter-Revolutionary Tradition.* Wilmington, Del.: ISI Books, 2004.

St. Boniface. *The Letters of St. Boniface.* Trans. Ephraim Emerton. New York: Columbia University Press, 2000.

Boorstin, Daniel. *The Creators.* New York: Random House, 1992.

Bosher, Robert S. "Seeds of Christian Society." *New York Times Book Review*, December 24 1950.

Bowersock, G. W., Peter Brown, and Oleg Grabar, eds. *Late Antiquity: A Guide to the Postclassical World.* Cambridge, Mass.: Belknap Press, 1999.

"Bradford Visit of Eminent Lecturer." *Bradford Daily Telegraph*, April 25 1934.

Brinton, Crane. "The Dynamics of World History." *Speculum* 33 (1958): 272–73.

"Briton Here to Lecture at Harvard: Dawson in First Catholic Chair." *New York Herald Tribune*, October 1 1958.

Brusher, Joesph S. "The Gods of Revolution." *America* 126 (May 27, 1972): 579–80.

Brinton, Geoffrey. "Why Civilizations Rise and Decline." *New York Times Book Review*, January 25 1959.

Burke, Edmund. *Reflections on the Revolution in France.* Indianapolis: Liberty Fund, 1999.

Burnham, Philip. "Religion and the Rise of Western Culture." *Commonweal* 52 (June 23, 1950): 273–74.

Burns, T. F., ed. *A Monument to Saint Augustine: Essays on Some Aspects of His Thought Written in Commemoration of His 15th Centenary.* London, ENG: Sheed and Ward, 1945.

———. "Public Schools and Religious Education: II." *Order: An Occasional Catholic Review* 1 (1928): 63–65.

———. *The Use of Memory: Publishing and Further Pursuits.* London, ENG: Sheed and Ward, 1993.

C. C. "Fair Treatment of the Modern Dilemma." *Catholic Times*, November 13 1931.

C. E. "What Is Wrong with the Modern World? The Decay of Culture in Europe." *Belfast Irish Weekly*, December 10 1932.

Caldecott, Stratford. "Conclusion: Eternity in Time." In *Eternity in Time: Christopher Dawson and the Catholic Idea of History*, ed. Stratford Caldecott and John Morrill. Edinburgh, Scotland: T&T Clark, 1997.

Caldecott, Stratford, and John Morrill, eds. *Eternity in Time: Christopher Dawson and the Catholic Idea of History.* Edinburgh, Scotland: T&T Clark, 1997.

Callahan, Daniel. "Christopher Dawson at Harvard." *Commonweal* (June 15, 1962): 294.

———. "Christopher Dawson." *Commonweal* 92 (June 12, 1970): 284.

———. "Europe's Problem—or Ours?" *First Things* (May 2004).

Callahan, Daniel, Mildred Horton, Francis Rogers, Bernard Swain, and George H. Williams. "Christopher Dawson: 12 October 1889–25 May 1970." *Harvard Theological Review* 66 (1973): 161–76.

Callam, Daniel. "Catholics and Fascists." *Chesterton Review* 25 (1999): 53–58.

"Cambridge Summer School: Church and State." *Catholic Herald*, August 3 1935.

"Cambridge Summer School: Church and State." *Tablet* (1935).

Cantor, Norman. *Inventing the Middle Ages: The Lives, Works, and Ideas of the Great Medievalists of the Twentieth Century*. New York: William Morrow, 1991.

"Cardinal Ratzinger in Cambridge." *Briefing 88* 18 (February 5, 1988).

Carlson, Leland H. "Review of the Movement of World Revolution." *Journal of Modern History* 33 (1961): 307.

Carroll, Warren H. *The Building of Christendom*. Front Royal, Virg.: Christendom College Press, 1987.

"The Case for Christendom." *Time*, February 15, 1954, 104–6.

"The Catholic at Harvard." *Newsweek*, April 28, 1958, 58.

"The Catholic Press and Non-Catholic England." *Order: An Occasional Catholic Review* 1 (1928): 25–28.

"Catholicism and Americanism." *Order: An Occasional Catholic Review* 1 (1929): 92–94.

Cervantes, Fernando. "A Vision to Regain? Reconsidering Christopher Dawson (1889–1970)." *New Blackfriars* 70 (1989): 437–49.

———. "Christopher Dawson and Europe." In *Eternity in Time: Christopher Dawson and the Catholic Idea of History*, ed. Stratford Caldecott and John Morrill. Edinburgh, Scotland: T&T Clark, 1997.

———. "Progress and Tradition: Christopher Dawson and Contemporary Thought." *Logos* 2 (1999): 84–108.

"The Christian and the World." *Times Literary Supplement* (1935).

"Christianity in Modern Society." *Catholic Times*, July 3 1931.

"Christopher Dawson." *Arena* 1 (1937): 45–51.

"Christopher Dawson Dies at 80." *Christian Century* 87 (1970): 719.

"Christopher Dawson in an Article in the London Catholic Times." *Ave Maria* 39 (1934): 695.

"Christopher Dawson: Catholic Colleges Held 'Vital' to U. S. Culture." *Los Angeles Tidings*, July 10, 1959.

"Church History: Christopher Dawson." *Life*, March 9 1959, 81.

Clement of Alexandria. *Writings of Clement of Alexandria*. Trans. by William Wilson. In *The Library of the Ante-Nicene Fathers*, Vol. 4.

Collins, James. "Marxist and Secular Humanism." *Social Order* 3 (1953): 207–32.

Collins, James D. "Mr. Dawson after Munich." *Commonweal* 30 (July 28, 1939): 336–37.

"Colosseum." *Church Times*, 1934.

Commentator. "The Church and the World: *Essays in Order*." *Liverpool Post*, 1931.

———. "The Church and the World: Roman Catholic Philosophy." *Liverpool Post*, September 2 1933.

———. "Turn of the Tide." *Liverpool Post*, March 13 1937.

"Common Prayer—an Introductory." *Order: An Occasional Catholic Review* 1 (1928): 65–67.

"Common Prayer, II—The Disease of Ritualism." *Order: An Occasional Catholic Review* 1 (1929): 96–98.

Como, James T., ed. *C. S. Lewis at the Breakfast Table and Other Reminiscences*. New York: Collier, 1979.

Connor, John. "Europe: The Historical Continent." *Commonweal* 57 (November 7, 1952): 126.

Copleston, Frederick. *A History of Philosophy*. Westminster, Maryland: Newman Press, 1953.

Corbishley, Thomas. "Our Present Discontents." *Month* 173 (1939): 434–41.

———. "Christopher Dawson: Prophet of Europe." *Month* 6 (1973): 46–8.

Corrin, Jay P. *Catholic Intellectuals and the Challenge of Democracy*. Notre Dame, Ind.: University of Notre Dame Press, 2001.

Costello, Paul. *World Historians and Their Goals: Twentieth-Century Answers to Modernism*. DeKalb: Northern Illinois University Press, 1993.

Coulborn, Rushton. "Review of the Judgment of Nations." *Journal of Modern History* 15 (1943): 67–68.

Coulton, G. G. "The Modern Dilemma." *Cambridge Review* (1933).

Crosby, John F. *Personalist Papers*. Washington, D.C.: Catholic University of America Press, 2004.

Crossley-Holland, Kevin, ed. and trans. *The Anglo-Saxon Chronicle: An Anthology*. Oxford, ENG: Oxford University Press, 1999.

Cunningham, W. F. "Christian Culture in General Education." *America* 93 (April 16, 1955): 63–64.

Dalberg-Acton, John Emerich Edward. *Essays in the History of Liberty*. Indianapolis, Ind.: Liberty Fund, 1986.

D'Arcy, Martin C. "Science and Theology." In *Science for a New World: The Scientific Outlook on World Problems Explained by Leading Exponents of Modern Scientific Thought*, ed. J. G. Crowther, 173–198. New York: Harper and Brothers, 1934.

———. *Humanism and Christianity*. New York: NAL, 1969.

———. *Laughter and the Love of Friends: Reminiscences of the Distinguished English Priest and Philosopher*. Westminster, Maryland: Christian Classics, 1991.

"Dangers of Journalism." *Commonweal* 67 (November 29, 1957), 221.

Davenport, Guy. "In Love with All Things Made." *New York Times Book Review*, October 17 1982, 9.

de Blacam, Hugh. "Last Words on Caesarism." *G. K.'s Weekly* 20 (November 1, 1934): 144–45.

"De Propaganda Fide." *Order: An Occasional Catholic Review* 1 (1929): 95–96.

Demant, V. A. "The Importance of Christopher Dawson." *Nineteenth Century* 129 (January 1941): 66–75.

"Democracy Versus Freedom? A Plea for Aristocratic Liberalism." *Times Literary Supplement* (1939).

Dilworth, Thomas. *The Shape and Meaning in the Poetry of David Jones*. Toronto: University of Toronto Press, 1988.

Doenecke, Justus D. "Conservatism: The Impassioned Sentiment." *American Quarterly* 28 (1976): 601–09.

Donahue, Charles. "Christopher Dawson: A Note on Experience." *Thought* 25 (1950): 115–19.

"Drastic Brutal Methods: Mr Christopher Dawson's View." *Catholic Herald*, August 12 1933.

"Dublin Review." *Church Times*, July 26 1940.

Duff, Edward. "Social Christian Humanism." *Social Order* 3 (1953): 245–59.

Dupree, Robert S. *Allen Tate and the Augustinian Imagination: A Story of the Poetry*. Baton Rouge: Louisiana State University Press, 1983.

Editor. "Results of Voting on Catholic Authors." *America* 56 (October 10, 1936): 18–19.

Eliot, T. S. "Second Thoughts About Humanism." *Hound and Horn* 2 (June 1929): 339–350.

———. *After Strange Gods: A Primer on Modern Heresy*. London, ENG: Faber and Faber, 1934.

———. "Tradition and Orthodoxy." *American Review* 2 (1934): 513–528.

_____. *Essays Ancient and Modern*. London, ENG: Faber and Faber, 1936.

_____. "The Literature of Politics." *Time and Tide* 36 (April 23, 1955): 523–4.

_____. *To Criticize the Critic and Other Writings*. London, ENG: Faber and Faber, 1965.

_____. *The Complete Poems and Plays, 1909–1950*. New York: Harcourt Brace, 1967.

_____. *Christianity and Culture*. San Diego: Harvest Book, 1976.

Elliott, Barbara [von der Heydt]. *Candles Behind the Wall: Heroes of the Peaceful Revolution That Shattered Communism*. Grand Rapids, Mich.: Eerdmans, 1993.

"Elucidations." *Order: An Occasional Catholic Review* 1 (1928): 7–8.

"English Historian Praises Catholic Education in U. S." *Boston Pilot*, November 29 1958.

"The English Way." *London Mercury* (1934).

"Essay in Order: No. 8." *Examiner*, November 1932.

"Essays in Order." *Catholic Times*, December 1 1931.

"Essays in Order." *Yorkshire Post,* 1932.

"Essays in Order." *Everyman*, December 31 1932.

"Essays in Order." *Baptist Times*, January 19 1933.

"Essays in Order." *Evening Telegraph*, January 14 1933.

F. G. J. "The Editor's Bookshelf." *Saturday Review* 44 (1961): 59.

Fairchild, Hoxie N. "Review of Religion and Culture." *Journal of Modern History* 22 (1950): 267.

Ferrari, Dino. "New Essays on the Humanities." *New York Times*, February 5, 1939, BR10.

Fitzgibbon, George F. "The Cyclical Theory of Christopher Dawson." *American Catholic Sociological Review* 2 (1941): 34–40.

Foerster, Norman, ed. *Humanism and America: Essays on the Outlook of Modern Civilisation*. New York: Farrar and Rinehart, 1930.

Fortin, Ernest L. "A Note on Dawson and St. Augustine." In *The Birth of Philosophic Christianity: Studies in Early Christian and Medieval Thought*, ed. Brian Benestad, 115–22. Lanham, Maryland: Rowman and Littlefield, 1996.

Foster, Kenelm. "Mr. Dawson and Christendom." *Blackfriars* 31 (1950): 421–27.

Foster, Paul. "The Making of Europe." *Chesterton Review* 9 (1983): 137–42.

Franklin, R. William, and Joseph M. Shaw. *The Case for Christian Humanism*. Grand Rapids, Mich.: William B. Eerdmans, 1991.

Fremantle, Anne. "Christopher Dawson Comes to Harvard." *Catholic Digest* 23 (1959): 51–53.

Friedrich, Carl Joachim. "The Central Problem of Today." *Commonweal* 23 (March 27, 1936): 612.

"From Bede to Newman." *Tablet* (1933).

Gilby, Thomas. *Poetic Experience: An Introduction to Thomist Aesthetic*. Vol. 13. 14 vols. Essays in Order, ed. Christopher Dawson and Tom Burns. New York: Sheed and Ward, 1934.

_____. "Religion and Culture." *Changing World* 1, no. 7 (1949): 94–96.

Gilson, Etienne. "Medieval Universalism and Its Present Value." In *The Wisdom of Catholicism*, ed. Anton C. Pegis, 966–83. New York: Modern Library, 1955.

Gleason, John P. "The Study of Christian Culture: A New Approach to General Education." *Educational Record* 40 (1959): 155–58.

Gleason, Philip. "A Practical Experiment in Education: The Study of Christian Culture as the Core of the College Curriculum: Christopher Dawson and the Study of Christian Culture." *Chesterton Review* 9 (1983): 167–71.

_____. *Keeping the Faith: American Catholicism Past and Present*. Notre Dame, Ind.: University of Notre Dame Press, 1987.

_____. *Contending with Modernity: Catholic Higher Education in the Twentieth Century.* New York: Oxford University Press, 1995.

"God and History." *Times Literary Supplement* (1957).

Goffin, Magdalen. "'My Volume, Your Volume, Our Volume'." *Downside Review* 103 (1985): 256–75.

_____. "Fighting under the Lash." *Downside Review* 113 (1995): 202–18.

Gregg II, Gary, ed. *Vital Remnants: America's Founding and the Western Tradition.* Wilmington, Del.: ISI Books, 1999.

Gress, David. *From Plato to Nato: The Idea of the West and Its Opponents.* New York: Free Press, 1998.

Grew, Raymond. "World Historians and Their Goals: Twentieth-Century Answers to Modernism." *History and Theory* 34 (1995): 371–94.

Griffiths, Bede. *The Golden String.* London, ENG: Harvill Press, 1954.

Grisewood, Harman. "Face to Faith: The Ideas of a Catholic Tiger." *Guardian*, October 16 1989.

_____. *One Thing at a Time: An Autobiography.* London, ENG: Hutchinson, 1968.

Guardini, Romano. *The Conversion of Augustine.* Westminster, Maryland: Newman, 1960.

_____. *Letters from Lake Como: Explorations in Technology and the Human Race.* Trans. by George Bromiley. Grand Rapids, Mich.: Eerdmans, 1994.

Gurian, Waldemar. "Dawson's Leitmotif." *Commonweal* 50 (June 3, 1949): 202–3.

Haecker, Theodor. *Virgil, Father of the West.* Translated by A. W. Wheen. New York: Sheed and Ward, 1934.

Hague, Rene, ed. *Dai Greatcoat: A Self-Portrait of David Jones in His Letters.* London, ENG: Faber and Faber, 1980.

Haines, Aubrey. "Catholic Historian at Harvard." *Voice of St. Jude* (1961): 28–30.

Hales, E. E. Y. "The Dawson Legacy." *Tablet* (1972): 299–300.

Hallack, Cecily. "Christopher Dawson's Search Light." *Catholic Times*, January 13 1933.

Hardwick, J. C. "The Intellectuals in Retreat." *Modern Churchman* 24 (1935): 631–37.

Harries, B. A. "The Rare Contact: A Correspondence between T. S. Eliot and P. E. More." *Theology* 75 (1972): 136–144.

Haywood, John. *The Penguin Historical Atlas of the Vikings.* London: ENG: Penguin, 1995.

Healy, Patrick. "Constructive Dark Ages." *Commonweal* 17 (January 4, 1933): 274.

Heenan, John C. *Cardinal Hinsley.* London, ENG: Burns Oates and Washbourne, 1944.

Hellman, John. "The Humanism of Jacques Maritain." In *Understanding Maritain: Philosopher and Friend*, ed. Deal W. Hudson and Matthew J. Mancini, 117–131. Atlanta: Mercer University Press, 1987.

_____. "Christopher Dawson, The New Theology, and Harvard in the 1960s." *The Christopher Dawson Centre of Christian Culture Newsletter* 2 (July 1999): 3–7.

Hendel, Charles W. "Restoration of a Moral Order." *Yale Review* 32 (1943): 818–21.

Henssler, Frederick. "Review of the Dynamics of World History." *American Journal of Sociology* 64 (1958): 203–4.

Hitchcock, James. "Postmortem on a Rebirth: The Catholic Intellectual Renaissance." *American Scholar* 49 (1980): 211–225.

_____. "Christopher Dawson." *American Scholar* 62 (1993): 111–118.

_____. "The Rise and Decline of Christendom in the West." *Touchstone* 14 (2001): 32–43.

_____. "Things Hidden since the Beginning of the World: The Shape of Divine Providence and Human History." *Touchstone* 15 (2002): 31–39.

_____. "Christopher Dawson and the Demise of Christendom." *Historically Speaking* 5 (2003): 23–25.

Hittinger, Russell. "The Metahistorical Vision of Christopher Dawson." In *The Dynamic Character of Christian Culture*, ed. Peter J. Cataldo, 1–56. Lanham, Md.: University Press of America, 1983.

_____. "The Two Cities and the Modern World: A Dawsonian Assessment." *Modern Age* 28 (1984): 193–202.

Hoffman, Ross J. S. *The Spirit of Politics and the Future of Freedom*. Milwaukee: Bruce Publishing Company, 1950.

Hope, C. E. G. "Christopher Dawson's Warning." *Sword of the Spirit*, no. 106 (1947): 3.

Hudson, Deal W., and Matthew J. Mancini, eds. *Understanding Maritain: Philosopher and Friend*. Atlanta, Georgia: Mercer University Press, 1987.

Hughes, Everett. "Review of the Spirit of the Oxford Movement." *American Journal of Sociology* 41 (1935): 261.

Hulme, T. E. *Speculations: Essays on Humanism and the Philosophy of Art*. Ed. by Herbert Read. London, ENG: Kegan Paul, Trench, Trubner, and Co., 1936.

"A Humanist Manifesto: Twenty Years Later." *The Humanist*, no. 2 (1953): 58–71.

Hunt, Peter. "Who Dared Attack My Chesterton." *Chesterton Review* 25 (1999): 58–63.

Huxley, Aldous. *The Olive Tree and Other Essays*. London, ENG: Chatto and Windus, 1936.

Ignotus, Laicus. "The Dublin Review." *The Church Times*, July 26, 1940.

Inge, W. R. "Gentlemen Vs. Players." *London Evening Standard*, November 25 1936.

"An Introductory Restraining Panic." *Order: An Occasional Catholic Review* 1 (1928): 3–7.

" 'It's an Adventure.' Christopher Dawson, Guest Professor of Catholic Studies Comes to H.D.S." *Harvard Divinity School Alumni Bulletin* 24 (1958): 4.

Jenkins, Philip. "The Last Floodgates of the World: Catholic Responses to Fascism." *Chesterton Review* 25 (1999): 65–69.

_____. *The New Faces of Christianity: Believing the Bible in the Global South*. Oxford University Press, 2006.

Joad, C. E. M. "Forward to Christendom." *New Statesman and Nation* 26 (1943): 141–42.

John Navone, S.J. "The Greatest Christian Hero, Philosopher, and Poet: Christopher Dawson's Italian Trinity." *New Blackfriars* 72 (1991): 260–68.

Jones, David. "The Myth of Arthur." In *For Hilaire Belloc: Essays in Honor of His 71st Birthday*, ed. Douglas Woodruff, 175–218. New York: Sheed and Ward, 1942.

_____. "Art and Democracy." *Changing World* vol. 1, no. 1 (1947): 8–20.

_____. "Round About a Burning Tree." *Tablet* (1957): 10–12.

_____. *Epoch and Artist: Selected Writings by David Jones*, ed. Harman Grisewood. London, ENG: Faber and Faber, 1959.

_____. *Anathemata: Fragments of an Attempted Writing*. New York: Viking Press, 1965.

"The Judgment of Nations." *New Republic* 107 (1942): 690.

Kalthoff, Mark. "Contra Ideology." *Faith and Reason* 30 (2005): 221–241.

Kansteiner, Wulf. "Hayden White's Critique of the Writing of History." *History and Theory* 32 (1993): 273–95.

Kelly, Joseph F. "Christianity and European Culture." *The Historian* 62 (2000): 939–40.

Ker, Ian. *The Catholic Revival in English Literature, 1845–1961: Newman, Hopkins, Belloc, Chesterton, Greene, Waugh*. Notre Dame, Ind.: University of Notre Dame, 2003.

Kevane, Eugene. "Christopher Dawson and Study of Christian Culture." *Catholic Educational Review* 57 (1959): 447–462.

King, Roma A., ed. *To Michal from Serge: Letters from Charles Williams to His Wife, Florence, 1939–1945*. Kent, Ohio: Kent State University, 2002.

Kirk, Russell. *The Conservative Mind*. Chicago, Ill.: Regnery, 1953.

_____. *Program for Conservatives*. Chicago, Ill.: Regnery, 1954.

_____. *Academic Freedom: An Essay in Definition*. Chicago, Ill.: Regnery, 1955.

_____. *Beyond the Dreams of Avarice; Essays of a Social Critic*. Chicago, Ill.: Regnery, 1956.

_____. "Behind the Veil of History." *Yale Review* 46 (1957): 466–476.

_____. "The Inhumane Businessman." *Fortune* 55 (1957): 160–161, 248.

_____. "Conservatism: The Shield of Liberty." *Catholic World* 189 (1959): 381–86.

_____. *Confessions of a Bohemian Tory: Episodes and Reflections of a Vagrant Career*. New York: Fleet Publishing Corp., 1963.

_____. "The Struggle for Power with Communism." In *Christianity and World Revolution*, ed. Edwin H. Rian, 3–12. New York: Harper and Row, 1963.

_____. *The Intemperate Professor, and Other Cultural Splenetics*. Baton Rouge: Louisiana State University Press, 1965.

_____. "Beginning in Doubt." *National Review* 19 (March 21, 1967): 306.

_____. *Edmund Burke: A Genius Reconsidered*. New Rochelle, N.Y.: Arlington House, 1967.

_____. "The Myth of Objectivity." *Triumph* 3 (1968): 35–37.

_____. *Enemies of the Permanent Things; Observations of Abnormality in Literature and Politics*. New Rochelle, N.Y.: Arlington House, 1969.

_____. *Eliot and His Age; T. S. Eliot's Moral Imagination in the Twentieth Century*. New York: Random House, 1971.

_____. "The Waste Land Lies Unredeemed." *The Sewanee Review* 80 (1972): 470–78.

_____. *Decadence and Renewal in the Higher Learning: An Episodic History of American University and College since 1953*. South Bend, Ind.: Gateway Editions, 1978.

_____. "An Interview with Russell Kirk." *Christianity and Literature* 29 (1980): 8–17.

_____. *The Portable Conservative Reader*. New York: Viking Press, 1982.

_____. "The High Achievement of Christopher Dawson." *Chesterton Review* 10 (1984): 435–38.

_____. "Babbitt and the Ethical Purpose of Literary Studies." In *Literature and the American College*, 1–68. Washington, D.C.: National Humanities Institute, 1986.

_____. *The Wise Men Know What Wicked Things Are Written on the Sky*. Washington, D.C.: Regnery Gateway, 1987.

_____. *The Conservative Constitution*. Washington, D.C.: Regnery Gateway, 1990.

_____. *The Roots of American Order*. 3rd ed. 1974; Washington, D.C.: Regnery, 1991.

_____. *America's British Culture*. New Brunswick, N.J.: Transaction Publishers, 1993.

_____. "Church Establishments and American Catholics." In *When Conscience and Politics Meet: A Catholic View*, 13–25. San Francisco: Ignatius, 1993.

_____. "Cultivating Educational Wastelands." In *Politics of Prudence*, 239–252. Wilmington, Del.: ISI Books, 1993.

_____. *Politics of Prudence*. Bryn Mawr, Penn.: ISI Books, 1993.

_____. "The Great Mysterious Incorporation of the Human Race." In *Permanent Things: Toward the Recovery of a More Human Scale at the End of the Twentieth Century*, ed. Andrew A. Tadie and Michael H. Macdonald, 1–13. Grand Rapids, Mich.: Eerdmans, 1995.

_____. *The Sword of Imagination: Memoirs of a Half-Century of Literary Conflict*. Grand Rapids, Mich.: William B. Eerdmans Pub., 1995.

_____. "The Conservative Purpose of a Liberal Education." In *Redeeming the Time*, 41–52. Wilmington, Del.: ISI Books, 1996.

_____. *Redeeming the Time*, ed. Jeffrey O. Nelson. Wilmington, Del.: Intercollegiate Studies Institute, 1996.

_____. *Rights and Duties: Reflections on Our Conservative Constitution*. Dallas, Tex.: Spence, 1997.

_____. *The American Cause*. 3rd ed. Ed. by Gleaves Whitney. Wilmington, Del.: ISI Books, 2002.

_____, ed. *The Assault on Religion: Commentaries on the Decline of Religious Liberty*. Lanham, MD/Cumberland, Va.: University Press of America; Center for Judicial Studies, 1986.

Knowles, M.D, E. I. Watkin, John J. Mulloy, and Christina Scott. "Christopher Dawson, 1889–1970." *Proceedings of the British Academy* 57 (1971): 439–52.

Kojecky, Roger. *T. S. Eliot's Social Criticism*. New York: Farrar, Straus, and Giroux, 1971.

Kuklick, Bruce. "Catholic Converts: British and American Intellectuals Turn to Rome." *American Historical Review* 103 (1998): 1558–59.

Labrie, Ross. *The Catholic Imagination in American Literature*. Columbia: University of Missouri Press, 1997.

LaFarge, John. "American Humanist Culture." *Social Order* 3 (1953): 260–68.

Lawler, Justus George. *The Catholic Dimension in Higher Education*. Westminster, Maryland: Newman Press, 1959.

_____. "The Crisis of Western Education." *Harvard Education Review* 32 (Spring 1962): 214–220, 225–26.

Leonard, George B. "What Chance Christian Unity?" *Look* 23 (1959): 21.

Lewis, C. S. *The Abolition of Man: Or Reflections on Education with Special Reference to the Teaching of English in the Upper Forms of Schools*. New York: Touchstone, 1996.

_____. "De Descriptione Temporum," *Essays in Criticism* 6 (1956): 247.

_____. "De Descriptione Temporum." In *Selected Literary Essays*, ed. Walter Hooper. Cambridge, ENG: Cambridge University Press, 1969.

Lewis, W. H., ed., *Letters of C. S. Lewis*. New York: Harcourt, Brace, 1982.

Liddell, Helen. "Planning for Freedom." *International Affairs Review Supplement* 19 (1943): 619–21.

Locas, Claude. "Christopher Dawson: A Bibliography." *Harvard Theological Review* 66 (1973): 177–206.

Lowrie, Donald A. *Rebellious Prophet: A Life of Nicholai Berdyaev*. Westport, Conn.: Greenwood Press, 1974.

MacDonald, Gregory. "St. Augustine." *G. K.'s Weekly* 12 (1930): 27–28.

_____. "Unity in Diversity." *G. K.'s Weekly* 15 (1932): 11–12.

Madeleva, Sister M. *My First Seventy Years*. New York: Macmillan, 1959.

"The Making of Europe." *Nation* 135 (1932): 575.

Malachowski, Alan R., ed. *Reading Rorty: Critical Responses to Philosophy and the Mirror of Nature (and Beyond)*. Oxford: Basil Blackwell, 2002.

Mariet, Philip. "Patriots of Europe." *New English Weekly* (1932): 210.

Maritain, Jacques. "A Note on Revolution." *Colosseum* 1 (1934): 37–38.

_____. "The Possibility of a New Christian Order." *Colosseum* 2 (1935): 85–94.

_____. "The Question of a Holy War." *Colosseum* 3 (1937): 118–130.

_____. "The End of Machiavellianism." *Review of Politics* 4 (1942): 1–33.

———. *Integral Humanism: Temporal and Spiritual Problems of a New Christendom*. New York: Charles Scribner's Sons, 1968.

Marshall, Caroline. "Christopher Dawson." In *Historians of the Christian Tradition: Their Methodology and Influence on Western Thought*, ed. Michael Bauman and Martin I. Klauber, 431–48. Nashville, Tenn.: Broadman and Holman, 1995.

———. "Protestantism and Cultural Fragmentation in the Thought of Christopher Dawson." *Fides et Historia* 31 (1999): 19–29.

"The Martyrdom of Perpetua." In Patricia Wilson-Kastner, G. Ronald Kastner, Ann Millin, Rosemary Rader, and Jeremiah Reedy, eds., *A Lost Tradition: Women Writers of the Early Church*. Washington, D.C.: University Press of America, 1981.

Mason, Gregory. "Origin of Culture." *New York Times Book Review*, November 18 1928, 16.

Mathew, David. "The European Crisis." *History Today* 2 (1952): 575–76.

Matson, Norman. "The Threat to the West." *Commonweal* 31 (February 23, 1940): 385.

Mauriac, Francois. *God and Mammon*. New York: Sheed and Ward, 1936.

McGreevy, John. *Catholicism and American Freedom*. New York: W. W. Norton, 2003.

McInerny, Ralph. *The Very Rich Hours of Jacques Maritain: A Spiritual Life*. Notre Dame, Ind.: University of Notre Dame, 2003.

McMahon, Francis S. "Mankind and the March Toward Unity." *Commonweal* 70 (1959): 108–9.

McNaspy, C. J. "Dawson's New Contribution to Dialogue." *America* 112 (March 27, 1965): 432.

———. "Dawson at 80." *America* 121 (October 11, 1969): 302.

———. "Christopher Dawson: In Memoriam." *America* 122 (June 13, 1970): 634.

———. "Snippets from an Oxford Diary." *New Orleans Review* 6 (1979); 141–42.

McNeill, John T. "Review of *The Dividing of Christendom*." *Journal of Modern History* 38 (1966): 425–26.

McNichols, Marie Corde. "Western Culture and the Mystical Body." *Catholic World* 186 (1957): 166–72.

Mecklin, John M. "Catholicism, Protestantism, and Capitalism: Religion and the Modern State." *American Sociological Review* 1 (1936): 309–10.

Meconi, David Vincent. "Eternity in Time." *Review of Metaphysics* 53 (1999): 148–9.

"The Medieval Synthesis." *Times Literary Supplement* (1932).

Melanchthon, Philip. *Orations on Philosophy and Education*. Ed. by Sachiko Kusukawa. Cambridge: Cambridge University Press, 1999.

Merton, Thomas. *Conjectures of a Guilty Bystander*. New York: Image, 1966.

———. *Turning toward the World: The Pivotal Years*, ed. Victor A. Kramer. San Francisco: Harper, 1995.

———. *The Intimate Merton: His Life from His Journals*, ed. Patrick Hart and Jonathan Montaldo. San Francisco: Harper, 1999.

Milward, Peter. "Memories of Christopher Dawson." *Dawson Newsletter* (Fall 1985): 4–5.

"Modern Dictatorships." *Tablet* (1935): 509.

"The Modern Dilemma." *Catholic Times*, November 6 1931.

"The Modern Dilemma." *Radio Times*, November 20 1931.

Molnar, Thomas. "Toward a Radical Reorientation in Learning." *Commonweal* 74 (June 30, 1961): 356–57.

Montgomery, Marion. *The Truth of Things: Liberal Arts and the Recovery of Reality*. Dallas, Tex.: Spence Publishing, 1999.

————. *Romancing Reality: Homo Viator and the Scandal Called Beauty*. South Bend, Ind.: St. Augustine's Press, 2002.

More, Paul Elmer. *The Christ of the New Testament*. Princeton, N.J.: Princeton University Press, 1924.

————. *The Skeptical Approach to Religion*. Princeton, N.J.: Princeton University Press, 1934.

————. "Marginalia, Part I." *American Review* 8 (1936): 1–30.

————. *On Being Human*. Princeton, N.J.: Princeton University Press, 1936.

————. *Pages from an Oxford Diary*. Princeton, N.J.: Princeton University Press, 1937.

————. *The Essential Paul Elmer More*, ed. Byron C. Lambert. New Rochelle, N.Y.: Arlington House, 1972.

Moreno, Lisa. "The National Catholic Welfare Conference and Catholic Americanism, 1919–1966." Dissertation, University of Maryland, 1999.

Morris, Kevin L. "Fascism and British Catholic Writers, 1924–1939." *Chesterton Review* 25 (1999): 21–51.

"Mr Christopher Dawson." *Catholic Herald,* 1934.

Mulloy, John J. "Specific Programs for the Study of Christian Culture." In *The Crisis of Western Education*, ed. Christopher Dawson, 205–46. New York: Sheed and Ward, 1961.

————. "The Church in History." *Triumph* 2 (1967): 31–33.

————. "Christopher Dawson's America Campaign." *Dawson Newsletter* (Spring 1984): 9–15.

————. "Conversations with Christopher Dawson." *Dawson Newsletter* (Fall 1984): 14–15.

————. "Christopher Dawson and the American Anthropologists: Part I." *Dawson Newsletter* (Summer 1985): 10–12.

————. "Christopher Dawson and the American Anthropologists, Part II." *Dawson Newsletter* (Fall 1985): 7–11.

————. "Conversations with Christopher Dawson." *Dawson Newsletter* (Summer 1985): 13–14.

————. "Who Is Hijacking Christopher Dawson?" *The Wanderer*, March 1 1990, 6.

————. "Christopher Dawson's Vision of World History." *Dawson Newsletter* (Summer 1992): 11.

————. "Exchange of Correspondence by Gerhart Niemeyer and John J. Mulloy." *Dawson Newsletter* (Summer 1992): 10.

————. *Christianity and the Challenge of History*. Front Royal, Virg.: Christendom Press, 1995.

Murphy, Francesca. "Can There Be a Catholic History Today?" In *Eternity in Time: Christopher Dawson and the Catholic Idea of History*, ed. Stratford Caldecott and John Morrill. Edinburgh, Scotland: T&T Clark, 1997.

Murray, J. "The Thought of Mr. Christopher Dawson." *Gregorianum* 34 (1953): 664–68.

Murray, John Courtney. "Christian Humanism in America." *Social Order* 3 (1953): 233–44.

Musurillo, Herbert. "Dawson's Program: A Criticism." *Thought* 30 (1955): 174–87.

————. "Christopher Dawson: Prophet at Harvard." *Homiletic and Pastoral Review* 59 (1958): 231–39.

Myres, J. L. "Review of Age of the Gods." *Man* 28 (1928): 180–83.

"The Necessity of Criticism." *Order: An Occasional Catholic Review* 1 (1929): 124, 131.

Neuhaus, Richard John. "The Much Exaggerated Death of Europe." *First Things* 173 (May 2007): 32–38.

"'New Apostolate of the Intellect' Is Urged by Christopher Dawson." *Catholic Messenger*, June 8 1961, 8.

Newman, John Henry Cardinal Newman. *An Essay on the Development of Christian Doctrine*. Garden City, N.Y.: Image Books, 1960.

_____. *Apologia Pro Vita Sua*. London, ENG: Penguin, 1994.

"New Medal for Prof. Dawson." *Oxford Mail*, September 16 1960, 11.

Nichols, Aidan. "Christopher Dawson's Catholic Setting." In *Eternity in Time: Christopher Dawson and the Catholic Idea of History*, ed. Stratford Caldecott and John Morrill. Edinburgh, Scotland: T&T Clark, 1997.

_____. *Catholic Thought since the Enlightenment: A Survey*. Pretoria: University of South Africa, 1998.

Niebuhr, Reinhold. "What's a Mote to One Is a Beam to Another." *New York Times Book Review*, March 13 1960, 18.

Njal's Saga. Translated by Carl F. Bayerschmidt and Lee M. Hollander. New York: Twayne/The American-Scandinavian Foundation, 1955.

Noble, Thomas F. X. and Thomas Head, eds. *Soldiers of Christ: Saints and Saints' Lives from Late Antiquity and the Early Middle Ages*. University Park: Pennsylvania State University Press, 1995.

Novak, Michael. *A Time to Build*. New York: Macmillan, 1967.

_____. "The Political Identity of Catholics." *Commonweal* 97 (February 16, 1973): 440–43.

_____. "Where Will All the Catholics Go?" *Commonweal* 97 (February 9, 1973): 414, 431.

O'Brien, Michael. "Historical Imagination and the Renewal of Culture." In *Eternity in Time: Christopher Dawson and the Catholic Idea of History*, ed. Stratford Caldecott and John Morrill. Edinburgh, Scotland: T&T Clark, 1997.

O'Connell, Marvin. "Dawson and the Oxford Movement." *Chesterton Review* 9 (1983): 149–60.

O'Connor, Daniel A. *The Relation between Religion and Culture According to Christopher Dawson: A Synthesis of Christopher Dawson's Writings*. Montreal: Librairie Saint-Viateur, 1952.

"Observations: The End of a Century of Emancipation." *Order: An Occasional Catholic Review* 1 (1929): 115, 128–131.

Oldham, J. H. "Introduction: Why a Christian News-Letter." *Christian News-Letter*, no. 0 (1939).

_____. "All Life Is Meeting." *Christian News-Letter*, no. 112 (1941).

Oliver, E. J. "The Religion of Christopher Dawson." *Chesterton Review* 9 (1983): 161–65.

Olsen, Glenn. "Inventing the Middle Ages." *Dawson Newsletter* (June 1992): 4–10.

_____. "Christian Philosophy, Christian History: Parallel Ideas?" In *Eternity in Time: Christopher Dawson and the Catholic Idea of History*, ed. Stratford Caldecott and John Morrill. Edinburgh, Scotland: T&T Clark, 1997.

Olsen, Glenn W. "American Culture and Liberal Ideology in the Thought of Christopher Dawson." *Communio* 22 (1995): 702–20.

Ong, Walter J. *Frontiers in American Catholicism: Essays on Ideology and Culture*. New York: Macmillan, 1957.

Opitz, Edmund A. "Behind Civilization. A Vision." *Freeman* 8 (1958): 56–59.

" 'Ordure'." *Order: An Occasional Catholic Review* 1 (1928): 2021.

Otteson, James R. *Actual Ethics*. Cambridge, ENG: Cambridge University Press, 2006.

_____. *Adam Smith's Marketplace of Life*. Cambridge, ENG: Cambridge University Press, 2002.

"Our Contemporaries." *Order: An Occasional Catholic Review* 1 (1928): 17–20.

Painter, Sidney. "Review of Medieval Essays." *Speculum* 29 (1954): 798–99.

Palmer, Vivien M. "Impressions of Sociology in Great Britain." *American Journal of Sociology* 32 (March 1927).

Panichas, George A., and Claes G. Ryn, eds. *Irving Babbitt in Our Time*. Washington, D.C.: Catholic University of America Press, 1986.

Park, Robert E. "Review of Enquiries into Religion and Culture." *American Journal of Sociology* 41 (1935): 109–111.

Parkes, H. B. "Christopher Dawson." *Scrutiny* 5 (1936–1937): 365–375.

_____. "Christopher Dawson and 'Arena.'" *Scrutiny* 6 (1937–1938): 197–199.

Pearce, Joseph. *Wisdom and Innocence: A Life of G. K. Chesterton.* San Francisco, Calif.: Ignatius, 1996.

_____. *Tolkien: Man and Myth.* San Francisco, Calif.: Ignatius Press, 1998.

_____. "Chesterton and Fascism." *Chesterton Review* 25 (1999): 69–79.

_____. "Tolkien and C. S. Lewis: An Interview with Walter Hooper." In *Tolkien: A Celebration,* ed. Joseph Pearce, 190–98. London, ENG: Fount, 1999.

_____. "Tolkien and the Catholic Literary Revival." In *Tolkien: A Celebration,* ed. Joseph Pearce, 102–23. London, ENG: Fount, 1999.

_____. *Literary Converts: Spiritual Inspiration in an Age of Unbelief.* San Francisco, Calif.: Ignatius, 2000.

_____. *Solzhenitsyn: A Soul in Exile.* Grand Rapids, Mich.: Baker House, 2001.

_____. "True Myth: The Catholicism of the Lord of the Rings." *Catholic World Report,* December 2001, 34–38.

_____. *Bloomsbury and Beyond: The Friends and Enemies of Roy Campbell.* London, ENG: HarperCollins, 2002.

_____. "From the Prancing Pony to the Bird and the Baby: Roy 'Strider' Campbell and the Inklings." *Saint Austin Review* 2 (2002): 32–34.

_____. *Old Thunder: A Life of Hilaire Belloc.* San Francisco, Calif.: Ignatius, 2002.

_____. *Small Is Still Beautiful.* London, ENG: HarperCollins, 2002.

_____. *C. S. Lewis and the Catholic Church.* San Francisco, Calif.: Ignatius, 2003.

_____. "The Christian Humanists." *Christian History* 22 (2003): 18–19.

_____. "Spirit of the Times." *Review of Politics* 5 (2003): 292–93.

_____. *Unafraid of Virginia Woolf: The Friends and Enemies of Roy Campbell.* Wilmington, Del.: ISI Books, 2004.

_____, ed. *Tolkien: A Celebration.* London, ENG: Fount, 1999.

Pegram, Robert. "The Key to History." *New York Times Book Review,* June 12 1949.

Peguy, Charles. *The Portal of the Mystery of Hope.* Grand Rapids, Mich.: Eerdmans, 1996.

Pieslak, Annette M. "The Paradox of Happiness." *Catholic World* 178 (1953): 86–91.

"The Problem of Church and State: Practical Papers at Cambridge Summer School." *Catholic Times,* August 9 1935.

Quinn, Dermot. "Christopher Dawson and the Catholic Idea of History." In *Eternity in Time: Christopher Dawson and the Catholic Idea of History,* ed. Stratford Caldecott and John Morrill. Edinburgh, Scotland: T&T Clark, 1997.

_____. "Christopher Dawson and the Challenge of Metahistory." *Historically Speaking* 5 (2003): 25–28.

Raftis, James Ambrose. "The Development of Christopher Dawson's Thought." *Chesterton Review* 9 (1983): 115–35.

Ratte, John. "The Dividing of Christendom." *Commonweal* 82 (August 6, 1965): 570–71.

Ratzinger, Joseph Cardinal. *Christianity and the Crisis of Cultures.* San Francisco, Calif.: Ignatius, 2006.

Read, Herbert. *Form in Modern Poetry.* Vol. 11. 14 vols. *Essays in Order,* ed. Christopher Dawson and Tom Burns. New York: Sheed and Ward, 1933.

_____. "The Modern Dilemma." *Cambridge Review* (1933).

Reinhold, H. A. "Search for the New Man." *Social Order* 3 (1953): 195–206.

"Religion's Part in History." *Times Literary Supplement* (1972).

"Religion and the Rise of Western Culture." *Current History* (1950): 40.

"Return to United Christendom?" *Times Literary Supplement* (1943).

Reynolds, Barbara, ed. *The Letters of Dorothy Sayers, Vol II: 1937–1943, from Novelist to Playwright*. New York: St. Martin's, 1997.

_____, ed. *The Letters of Dorothy Sayers, Vol III: 1944–1950, a Noble Daring*. Cambridge, ENG: Dorothy L. Sayers Society, 1997.

Riggs, T. Lawrason. "A Voice of Power." *Commonweal* 18 (August 4, 1933): 350.

Roberts, Nancy. "Walker Percy: The Last Catholic Novelist." *Journal of American History* 84 (1997): 1142–43.

"A Roman Catholic Offensive." *Church Times*, April 17 1931.

Rowland, Tracey. *Culture and the Thomist Tradition: After Vatican II*. London, ENG: Routledge, 2003.

_____. "Benedict XVI, Vatican II, and Modernity." *Zenit.org* (2005).

Russello, Gerald J. "Christopher Dawson." *Commonweal* 123 (April 5, 1996): 19–21.

_____, ed. *Christianity and European Culture: Selections from the Work of Christopher Dawson*. Washington, D.C.: Catholic University Press of America, 1998.

Ryan, John S. *Tolkien: Cult or Culture?* Armidale, New South Wales, Australia: University of New England, 1969.

_____. *The Shaping of Middle-Earth's Maker: Influences on the Life and Literature of J. R. R. Tolkien*. Highland, Mich.: American Tolkien Society, 1992.

Sayer, George. *Jack: C. S. Lewis and His Times*. San Francisco, Calif.: Harper and Row, 1988.

Schindler, David L. *Heart of the World, Center of the Church: Communio Ecclesiology, Liberalism, and Liberation*. Grand Rapids, Mich.: Eerdmans, 1996.

Schlesinger, Bruno. "A Practical Experiment in Education: The Study of Christian Culture as the Core of the College Curriculum: Responses to Dawson's Ideas in the United States." *Chesterton Review* 9 (1983): 171–76.

_____. "Christopher Dawson and Sister Madeleva." *Courier* (1994): 12–13.

Schlesinger, Bruno P. *Christopher Dawson and the Modern Political Crisis*. Notre Dame, Ind., 1949.

Schmitt, Carl, Nicholas Berdyaev, and Michael de la Bedoyere. *Vital Realities* Vols. 5–7. 14 vols. *Essays in Order*, ed. Christopher Dawson and Tom Burns. New York: Macmillan, 1932.

Schwartz, Adam. " 'I Thought the Church and I Wanted the Same Thing': Opposition to Twentieth-Century Liturgical Change in the Thought of Graham Greene, Christopher Dawson, and David Jones." *Logos* 1 (1998): 36–65.

_____. "Confronting the 'Totalitarian Antichrist': Christopher Dawson and Totalitarianism." *Catholic Historical Review* 89 (2003): 464–88.

_____. "Sitting Still with Christopher Dawson." *Touchstone* 12 (1999): 46–49.

_____. "What They Saw in America: G. K. Chesterton's and Christopher Dawson's View of the United States." *Faith and Reason* 28 (2003): 23–52.

_____. *The Third Spring: G. K. Chesterton, Graham Greene, Christopher Dawson, and David Jones*. Washington, D.C.: Catholic University of America Press, 2005.

Schwartz, Joseph. "The Theology of History in T. S. Eliot's Four Quartets." *Logos* 2 (1999): 31–47.

Scott, Christina. "Introduction." *Chesterton Review* 9 (1983): 95–6.

———. "Hijack of a Historian." *Tablet* (1989): 1148–49.

———. *A Historian and His World: A Life of Christopher Dawson*. New Brunswick, N.J.: Transaction, 1992.

———. "The Vision and Legacy of Christopher Dawson." In *Eternity in Time: Christopher Dawson and the Catholic Idea of History*, ed. Stratford Caldecott and John Morrill. Edinburgh, Scotland: T&T Clark, 1997.

———. "Christopher Dawson's Reaction to Fascism and Marxism." *Chesterton Review* 25 (1999): 405–407.

———. "The Meaning of the Millennium: The Ideas of Christopher Dawson." *Logos* 2 (1999): 65–83.

Sheed, Frank. "Christopher Dawson." *Sign* 17 (June 1938): 661–63.

———. "Dawson and the Present Crisis." *Sign* 17 (July 1938): 719–21.

———. *Sidelights on the Catholic Revival*. New York: Sheed and Ward, 1940.

———. "The Sword of the Spirit." *Ecclesiastical Review* 107 (1942): 81–92.

———. "I am a Catholic Publisher." *Westminster Cathedral Chronicle* (September-October 1959): 137.

———. *The Church and I*. Garden City, NY: Doubleday and Co., 1974.

Sheed, Wilfrid. "Introduction to Dawson." *Books on Trial* (1957): 295–96, 343–44.

———. *Frank and Maisie: A Memoir with Parents*. New York: Simon and Schuster, 1985.

Shinn, Roger L. "History and Eternity." *Saturday Review* 41 (1958): 26–27.

Shuster, George N. "The Course Is Incomplete." *New York Times Book Review*, April 30 1961.

Simons, John W. "Liberal Education as Transmissor of Values: The Proposals of Christopher Dawson." *Thought* 30 (1955): 165–73.

Smith, Warren Thomas. *Augustine: His Life and Thought*. Atlanta, Georgia: John Knox Press, 1980.

Sparkes, Russell. "Dawson and 'Economic Man'." In *Eternity in Time: Christopher Dawson and the Catholic Idea of History*, ed. Stratford Caldecott and John Morrill. Edinburgh, Scotland: T&T Clark, 1997.

Sparr, Arnold. *To Promote, Defend, and Redeem: The Catholic Literary Revival and the Cultural Transformation of American Catholicism, 1920–1960*. New York: Greenwood Press, 1990.

Speaight, Robert. *The Life of Eric Gill*. New York: P. J. Kenedy and Sons, 1966.

———. *The Property Basket: Recollections of a Divided Life*. London, ENG: Collins and Harvill, 1970.

———, ed. *Letters from Hilaire Belloc*. London, ENG: Hollis and Carter, 1958.

Stillman, Chauncey. "Christopher Dawson: Recollections from America." In *The Dynamic of Christian Character: Essays on Dawsonian Themes*, ed. Peter J. Cataldo, 217–222. Lanham, Md.: University Press of America, 1983.

Storck, Thomas. "The Stale Good Guy/Bad Guy Formula." *New Oxford Review* 71 (2004): 45–46.

Storey, William C. "The Formation of Christendom." *Commonweal* 86 (September 8, 1967): 557–8.

Sugerman, Shirley, ed. *Evolution of Consciousness: Studies in Polarity*. Middletown, Conn.: Wesleyan University Press, 1975.

Sullivan, William L. "The Church and the World: Essays in Order." *New York Herald Tribune*, July 19 1931.

Sykes, Gerald. "A Monument to St. Augustine." *Bookman* 73 (1931): 438–39.

Talbot, C. H., ed. *The Anglo-Saxon Missionaries in Germany: Being the Lives of Ss. Willibrord, Boniface, Sturm, Leoba and Lebuin, Together With the Hodoeporicon of St. Willibald and a Selection from the Correspondence of St. Boniface*. Edited by Christopher Dawson, *The Makers of Christendom*. New York: Sheed and Ward, 1954.

Talbot, Francis. "The Sheed and Ward Imprint." *America* 48 (March 4, 1933): 532–3.

———. "Reflections on the Plebiscite." *America* 54 (March 21, 1936): 573–74.

———. "The Roll Call of American Catholic Authors." *America* 54 (January 4, 1936): 303–4.

Tate, Allen. *Essays of Four Decades*. Wilmington, Del.: ISI Books, 1999.

———, ed. *T. S. Eliot: The Man and His Work; a Critical Evaluation by Twenty-Six Distinguished Writers*. New York: Delacorte Press, 1966.

"These Changing Years by Bernard Wall." *The Wind and the Rain* 4 (1948): 192–93.

Tolkien, J. R. R. "Beowulf: The Monsters and the Critics." In *An Anthology of Beowulf Criticism*, ed. Lewis E. Nicholson, 51–103. Notre Dame, Indiana: University of Notre Dame Press, 1963.

———. "On Fairy-Stories." In *The Monsters and the Critics and Other Essays*, ed. Christopher Tolkien, 109–161. London: George Allen and Unwin, 1983.

Torre, Michael D., ed. *Freedom in the Modern World: Jacques Maritain, Yves R. Simon, Mortimer J. Adler*. Notre Dame, Ind.: University of Notre Dame Press/American Maritain Association, 1989.

"Towards Balanced Thinking." *Beda Review* 4 (1939): 37–38.

Toynbee, Arnold J. "Review of Religion and the Rise of Western Culture." *International Affairs* 26 (1950): 374–75.

———. "Review of the Crisis of Western Education." *International Affairs* 38 (1962): 370.

———. "To the Editor of the Colosseum." *Colosseum* 1 (1934): 80–82.

"U. S. Catholics Spearheading 'Cultural Renaissance,' Prof. Christopher Dawson Declares." *NCWC News Service (Domestic)*, August 10 1959.

Underhill, Evelyn. "Essays in Order." *Spectator* 150 (February 24, 1933): 256.

"Understanding Europe." *Current History* 23 (1952): 272.

Vahanian, Gabriel. "How to Say 'God.'" *Nation* 192 (1961): 286–88.

Vann, Gerald. *On Being Human: St. Thomas and Mr. Aldous Huxley*. Vol. 12. 14 vols. Essays in Order, ed. Christopher Dawson and Tom Burns. New York: Sheed and Ward, 1934.

Vaughan, James N. "Mr. Dawson after Munich." *Commonweal* 29 (April 21, 1939): 723.

Vincent, Paul D. "Christopher Dawson Sees Cultural Renaissance among Young U. S. Catholics." *Pittsburgh Catholic*, August 6 1959.

"Voces Catholicae." *Order: An Occasional Catholic Review* 1 (1929): 132.

von Kuehnelt-Leddihn, Erik. "What I Saw in Leningrad." *Colosseum* 1 (1934): 25–31.

———. "Catholicism and the Bourgeois." *Colosseum* 2 (1935): 95–101.

———. "We're All Marxists Now!" *Colosseum* 5 (1939): 91–99.

W. Norris Clarke, S.J. "Christian Humanism for Today: Fulfillment, Not Destruction, Its Goal." *Social Order* 3 (1953): 269–88.

Wade, Mason. "A Catholic Spengler." *Commonweal* 22 (October 18, 1935): 605–7.

Wain, John. *Sprightly Running: Part of an Autobiography*. New York: St. Martin's, 1962.

Wall, Bernard. "Christopher Dawson—a Lion in Fight against Half-Truth." Unknown source. Found as formatted article in UST/CDC.

———. "Business Note." *Colosseum* 1 (1934): 74–75.

———. "The Colosseum and Mr. Middleton Murray." *Colosseum* 1 (1934): 75–79.

_____. "Commentary." *Colosseum* 1 (1934): 49–52.

_____. "Commentary." *Colosseum* 1 (1934): 7–13.

_____. "Commentary." *Colosseum* 1 (1934): 68–72.

_____. "Commentary." *Colosseum* 1 (1934): 60–62.

_____. "Marxism and Man." *Colosseum* 1 (1934): 32–38.

_____. "Marxism and Man (II)." *Colosseum* 1 (1934): 32–39.

_____. "The Modern Sensability." *Colosseum* 1 (1934): 9–11.

_____. "The New Despair." *Colosseum* 1 (1934): 29–36.

_____. "Positions." *Colosseum* 1 (1934): 11–13.

_____. "Positions II." *Colosseum* 1 (1934): 7–9.

_____. "Programme [Introduction to Colosseum]." *Colosseum* 1 (1934): 5–10.

_____. "Water for the Wasteland." *Colosseum* 1 (1934): 7–13.

_____. "About the Conversion of England." *Colosseum* 2 (1935): 165–67.

_____. "Christian Revolt." *Colosseum* 2 (1935): 79–82.

_____. "Christianity and Politics." *Colosseum* 2 (1935): 82–84.

_____. "Editorial." *Colosseum* 2 (1935): 241–45.

_____. "Editorial." *Colosseum* 3 (1935): 3–10.

_____. "Editorial." *Colosseum* 3 (1935): 243–52.

_____. "The English Scene." *Colosseum* 2 (1935): 3–4.

_____. "Glossary." *Colosseum* 2 (1935): 4–7.

_____. "Unam Sanctam." *Colosseum* 2 (1935): 163–64.

_____. "An Augustine Synthesis." *Colosseum* 3 (1936): 64–66.

_____. "The Chances of Humanism." *Colosseum* 3 (1936): 177–83.

_____. "Editorial." *Colosseum* 3 (1936): 83–88.

_____. "Editorial." *Colosseum* 3 (1936): 165–168.

_____. "Problems of Pacifism." *Colosseum* 3 (1936): 264–75.

_____. "Commentary." *Colosseum* 3 (1937): 64–72.

_____. "Editorial." *Colosseum* 3 (1937): 3–6.

_____. "Three Comments." *Colosseum* 3 (1937): 101–107.

_____. "Editorial." *Colosseum* 4 (1938): 75–83.

_____. "Editorial." *Colosseum* 4 (1938): 1–6.

_____. "Editorial." *Colosseum* 4 (1938): 167–71.

_____. "Editorial." *Colosseum* 5 (1939): 3–7.

_____. "More Personal Reflections about Energy and Submarines." *Colosseum* 5 (1939): 155–59.

_____. "Personal Reflections." *Colosseum* 5 (1939): 83–90.

_____. "Editorial." *Changing World* vol. 1, no. 1 (1947): 3–7.

_____. "Editorial." *Changing World* vol. 1, no. 2 (1947): 3–5.

_____. "Comment on Italian Literature." *Changing World* vol. 1, no. 3 (1947–1948): 73–79.

_____. "Editorial: The Intelligentsia and the Revolution." *Changing World* vol. 1, no. 3 (1947–1948): 3–9.

_____. "Recent Work of Albert Camus." *Changing World* vol. 1, no. 3 (1947–1948): 86–92.

_____. "Editorial." *Changing World* vol. 1, no. 4 (1948): 3–5.

_____. "Editorial." *Changing World* vol. 1, no. 5 (1948): 3–5.

_____. "Editorial." *Changing World* vol. 1, no. 6 (1948–1949): 3–5.

_____. "Editorial." *Changing World* 1, no. 7 (1949): 3–4.

_____. "From a European Notebook, 1948." *Changing World* vol. 1, no. 7 (1949): 48–65.

_____. "Giant Individualists and Orthodoxy." *Twentieth Century* 155 (January 1954): 52–60.

_____. *Headlong into Change: An Autobiography and a Memoir of Ideas since the Thirties.* London, ENG: Harvill, 1969.

Walsh, Michael J. "Ecumenism in War Time Britain: the Sword of the Spirit and Religion and Life, 1940–1945, Part I." *Heythrop Journal* 23 (1982): 243–58.

_____. "Ecumenism in War Time Britain: the Sword of the Spirit and Religion and Life, 1940–1945, Part II." *Heythrop Journal* 24 (1982): 377–94.

Ward, Barbara. "Revolution from the Right." *Dublin Review* 205 (1939): 310–26.

_____. " 'Sword of the Spirit' Crusade Is a Clear Call out of Chaos." *America* 67 (1942): 566–67.

_____. "What the West Sorely Needs Is a Vision of Future Greatness." *New York Times Book Review*, March 29 1950.

_____. "Christian Woman of the World," *Our Sunday Visitor* XLVIII (May 17, 1959).

_____. *The Rich Nations and the Poor Nations.* New York: W. W. Norton, 1962.

Ward, Elizabeth. *David Jones: Myth Maker.* Manchester, England: Manchester University Press, 1983.

Ward, Leo. "Dawson on Education in Christian Culture." *Modern Age* 17 (1973): 399–407.

Ward, Maisie. "The Case of Christopher Dawson." *The Catholic World* 169 (1949): 150–51.

_____. "Dawson the Philosopher." *Duckett's Register* 4 (1949): 37–39.

_____. *Unfinished Business.* New York: Sheed and Ward, 1964.

_____. *To and Fro on the Earth: The Sequel to an Autobiography.* New York: Sheed and Ward, 1973.

Watkin, E. I. "The Rights of Created Beauty." *Order* 1 (1928): 46–49.

_____. *The Bow in the Clouds: An Essay Towards the Integration of Experience.* New York: Macmillan, 1932.

_____. "The Modern Dilemma." *Catholic Herald*, December 17 1932.

_____. "Christopher Dawson." *Commonweal* 18 (October 27, 1933): 607–9.

_____. "Energeticism and the Philosophy of the Totalitarian State." *Colosseum* 2 (1935): 106–118.

_____. "War and Peace." *Colosseum* 3 (1936): 184–88.

_____. "The Destiny of Man." *Colosseum* 3 (1937): 283–86.

_____. *A Philosophy of Form.* London, ENG: Sheed and Ward, 1937.

_____. *The Catholic Centre.* London, ENG: Sheed and Ward, 1939.

_____. "A Prophet Philosophises." *Colosseum* 5 (1939): 148–50.

_____. "Christianity and Humanism." *Dublin Review* 207 (1940): 197–213.

_____. "Review of *Descent of the Dove*." *Dublin Review* 206 (1940): 199–200.

_____. *Catholic Art and Culture.* revised ed. London, ENG: Hollis and Carter, 1947.

_____. " 'He Wanted Art': Ben Jonson's Verdict on Shakespeare." *The Wind and the Rain* 3 (1947): 179–94.

_____. *Neglected Saints.* New York: Sheed and Ward, 1955.

_____. *The Church in Council.* New York: Sheed and Ward, 1960.

_____. "Tribute to Christopher Dawson." *Tablet* (1969): 974.

_____. "Reflections on the Work of Christopher Dawson." *Downside Review* 89 (1971): 1–12.

Weigel, George. "John Paul II and the Crisis of Humanism." *First Things* 98 (1999): 31–36.

"Welcome, Son, Who Are You?" *Life*, March 16 1959, 32.

West, Rebecca. "Some Good Books to Give This Christmas." *Daily Telegraph*, December 16 1932.

"Western Values." *Times Literary Supplement* (1952).

White, Hayden. "Religion, Culture and Western Civilization in Christopher Dawson's Idea of History." *English Miscellany* 9 (1958): 247–87.

Whitney, Gleaves. "Can Western Civilization Survive the 21st Century?: Some Dawsonian Considerations." Paper delivered April 24, 1999, Philadelphia Society Annual Meeting, Philadelphia, Penn.

_____. "Seven Things You Should Know About Russell Kirk: The Origins of the Modern Conservative Movement in the U. S." *Vital Speeches of the Day* 63 (1997): 507–11.

_____. *"'Sowing Seeds in the Wasteland': The Perennial Task of Christian Humanists."* Private paper in hands of author. 1997.

_____. "The Sword of Imagination: Russell Kirk's Battle with Modernity." *Modern Age* 43 (2001): 311–20.

Wight, Martin. "Review of Understanding Europe." *International Affairs* 29 (1953): 341.

Wilhelmsen, Frederick D. "Seeking for the Source of a Long-Lost Unity." *Commonweal* 60 (June 18, 1954): 274–75.

_____. "The Vision of Christopher Dawson." *Commonweal* 67 (January 3, 1958): 355–58.

Williams, Michael. "Views and Reviews." *Commonweal* 30 (August 4, 1939): 355.

_____. "Views and Reviews." *Commonweal* 31 (June 26, 1940): 304.

Wust, Peter. "The Necessity of Metaphysics." *Colosseum* 1 (1934): 14–18.

Index